Praise for *Brian McLaren in Focus*

"The beginning of the twenty-first century has been a tumultuous time in American Protestantism, and no one has articulated the tensions therein better than Brian McLaren. Scott Burson has done us all an enormous service by taking a focused look at two decades of McLaren's work. Make no mistake, this is not just a study of McLaren, but of the times in which he's lived—times that will forever shape the Christian faith."

> —**Tony Jones**, author of *Did God Kill Jesus?* and *The New Christians: Dispatches from the Emergent Frontier*

"In this impressively researched volume, Scott Burson critically examines the development and trajectory of McLaren's thought and provides a fresh perspective on its social and theological location as well as its potential significance for the future of Christian witness in North America. An important book for anyone interested in understanding both Brian McLaren and the emerging Christian movement inspired by his work."

> —**John R. Franke**, theologian in residence, Second Presbyterian Church, Indianapolis, IN, and general coordinator for The Gospel and Our Culture Network in North America

"Scott Burson is just the right kind of person with his clear thinking and beautiful style of writing to propose a new way of doing apologetics in the postmodern world. His analysis of Brian McLaren is both sympathetic and critically constructive."

> —**Laurence W. Wood**, Frank Paul Morris Professor of Systematic Theology, Asbury Theological Seminary

"Brian McLaren has evoked some rather extreme reactions, from scathing attacks to gushing accolades. In this engagingly written book, Scott Burson offers a probing analysis of McLaren that is both critical and charitable. He pulls no punches in assessing McLaren's theology from the standpoint of classical orthodoxy, even as he recognizes that there are valuable lessons to be learned from his work."

> —**Jerry L. Walls**, professor of philosophy and scholar in residence, Houston Baptist University

"Without doubt, Brian McLaren expresses more than any other popular theological commentator the contemporary tensions within North American, conservative Christianity. *Brian McLaren in Focus* lifts McLaren into academic and scholarly conversations and serves as a much-needed companion to the ongoing and important conversations taking place within the Evangelical tradition. Burson's eloquent prose and generous but critical Wesleyan hospitality towards McLaren and his thought make for rich and rewarding reading."

> —**Graham W.P. McFarlane**, director of research, senior lecturer in Systematic Theology, London School of Theology

"Scott Burson provides a comprehensive, valuable, and welcomed synthesis of Brian McLaren's thought. Read it with profit. But do not stop there. Read it to place yourself more fully into the movement which McLaren's convictions have helped generate. Find yourself in his story so that you may live your place in The Story."

—**Steve Harper**, author of *Fresh Wind Blowing*

"In our postmodern world, Brian McLaren is a trailblazer for new and relevant theology. His daring new perspectives on time-honored truths must be taken seriously, and Scott Burson does just that. In this well-researched book, we have an excellent overview of McLaren's thinking and the crucial questions that he attempts to answer. These are questions that more fainthearted Christians often try to avoid."

—**Tony Campolo**, a founder of the Red Letter Christians Movement

"Through his analysis, Burson helps readers better understand the strengths and weaknesses in McLaren's theology, highlighting what Evangelicals need to learn from McLaren. Written for scholars, but accessible to laity, *Brian McLaren in Focus* is a vivid snapshot of many of the contemporary debates in the American Church and of one of the most important theologians of the new millennium."

—**Christopher T. Bounds**, scholar in residence, professor of Wesleyan Studies, Asbury University

"Brian McLaren has been my mentor and guide, and because we have shared such a close and personal friendship for nearly twenty years, reading an academic analysis of his work is a bit surreal. This comprehensive account of Brian's teaching, vision, writing, and passion is a gift to anyone who wishes to understand why and how Brian McLaren seeks to bring about a faith that is, as Brian says it, 'Just and Generous.' *Brian McLaren in Focus* is a 'just and generous' treatment of the man and his work."

—**Doug Pagitt**, pastor of Solomon's Porch, Minneapolis, MN, and author of *Flipped*

"Few have impacted the content *and* tone of Christian discourse as substantively and favorably as Brian McLaren. Hope, generosity, and creativity have oozed from McLaren's life, pen, and ministry for many decades. We are now additionally gifted to have Scott Burson's extensive exploration of McLaren's body of work. His research is remarkably thorough, applying strong theological, historical, and cultural lenses of analysis to McLaren's hopeful dialogue with a postmodern society. But, I am most thankful for Burson's care and intentionality regarding the personal element of this project. In his rigorous scholarship, he does not fail in demonstrating McLaren's kindness, curiosity, prophetic imagination, and hopeful invitation to yet another generation of scholars and seekers."

—**Tim Conder**, founding pastor of Emmaus Way, Durham, N.C.

BRIAN McLAREN IN FOCUS

A NEW KIND OF APOLOGETICS

SCOTT R. BURSON

FOREWORD BY BRIAN D. McLAREN

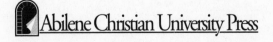
Abilene Christian University Press

BRIAN MCLAREN IN FOCUS
A New Kind of Apologetics

ACU
PRESS

Copyright © 2016 by Scott R. Burson

ISBN 978-0-89112-469-6

Printed in the United States of America

All Scripture quotations, unless otherwise indicated, are taken from the Holy Bible, New International Version®, NIV®. Copyright ©1973, 1978, 1984, 2011 by Biblica, Inc.™ Used by permission of Zondervan. All rights reserved worldwide.

Cover design by Marc Whitaker, MTWdesign
Cover art by Debra Burson
Interior text design by Sandy Armstrong

For information contact:
Abilene Christian University Press
ACU Box 29138
Abilene, Texas 79699
1-877-816-4455
www.acupressbooks.com

16 17 18 19 20 21 22 / 7 6 5 4 3 2 1

CONTENTS

ACKNOWLEDGMENTS

A project of this magnitude is not completed in isolation. I am indebted to many colleagues and family. First, I would like to acknowledge the library staff at Indiana Wesleyan University, especially Sheila Carlblom for extending me permission to check out extra books, and Lynn Crawford, who has processed countless interlibrary loan monographs.

I am particularly grateful to Dave Ward and Melissa Fipps for supporting me during my research and writing. Dave granted me valuable release time, and Melissa provided helpful clerical support. Many colleagues offered sage advice at various stages of this project. I am especially thankful to Laurence Wood, Graham McFarlane, John Franke, Marvin Oxenham, Kevin Corcoran, Chris Bounds, and David Leffler for reading drafts of this manuscript and providing indispensable feedback and encouragement. I am also grateful for the contribution of Jason Fikes, Director of ACU Press. His careful and nuanced editorial guidance greatly improved the readability of this manuscript.

I could not have asked for a more accommodating subject. For the duration of my research, Brian McLaren has corresponded promptly and graciously with me, answering every question that has surfaced. I am deeply indebted to his willingness to cooperate with me as I have sought to faithfully represent his theological and apologetic views.

Finally, my family has offered constant support. My children, Ashley, Lindsey, and Ryan, have provided many hours of relief and pleasant diversion. I am grateful to my stepson, Justin, for tolerating way too many books in the house. Thank you for not turning me in to the *Hoarders* TV program, as you once threatened. Above all, I am most indebted to my wife, Deb, who has supported and encouraged me beyond anyone else. I could not have completed this project without her. She and I have spent countless hours at the kitchen table, side by side—I writing while she worked on her art, including the denim portrait of Brian McLaren that appears on the cover of this book. She has accompanied me to emergent conferences, festivals, and interviews. I have read much of this manuscript to her and she has offered helpful feedback. Her constant presence, love, patience, and support have been indispensable. I love you, Deb. This project ultimately is dedicated to you.

BOOK ABBREVIATIONS

AIFA	A Is for Abductive
AMP	Adventures in Missing the Point
CIEC	The Church in Emerging Culture: Five Perspectives
COOS	The Church on the Other Side (3rd edition) Revised edition of Reinventing Your Church
EMC	Everything Must Change
FF	Finding Faith
FOWA	Finding Our Way Again
GO	A Generous Orthodoxy
GSM	The Great Spiritual Migration
JMBM	Why Did Jesus, Moses, the Buddha, and Mohammed Cross the Road?
JP	The Justice Project
LWWAT	The Last Word and the Word After That
MRTYR	More Ready than You Realize
NKOC	A New Kind of Christian
NKOCY	A New Kind of Christianity
NS	Naked Spirituality
RYC	Reinventing Your Church
SMJ	The Secret Message of Jesus
SWFOI	The Story We Find Ourselves in
VA	The Voice of Acts: The Dust Off Their Feet
VL	The Voice of Luke: Not Even Sandals
WMRBW	We Make the Road by Walking
WP	"Walker Percy: The Point of View for His Work as an Author," unpublished MA thesis, University of Maryland

LIST OF FIGURES

BRIAN MCLAREN (1956-PRESENT) CHRONOLOGY

"EARLY MCLAREN" ERA (1956-1994)

1956 Born in Olean, N.Y., to devoted Plymouth Brethren parents, Ian and Ginnie

1963 Moves to Maryland, where he would live the majority of his life

1971 Introduced to Calvinism by Young Life leader David Miller

Introduced to Jesus Movement

1974 Enrolls at the University of Maryland as a philosophy major

1978 Graduates summa cum laude with B.A. in English from the University of Maryland

Begins teaching college-level English

1981 Writes MA thesis entitled, "Walker Percy: The Point of View for His Work as an Author"

Graduates with MA in English from the University of Maryland

1982 Starts house church with his wife, Grace

1986 Stops teaching English and becomes founding pastor of Cedar Ridge Community Church

1990 Publishes article on John Wesley in *Christian Brethren Review*

1994 In the midst of a spiritual crisis, McLaren writes in his journal: "One year from today, I will not be in the ministry."

"EMERGING MCLAREN" ERA (1995-2005)

1998   Joins the Young Leaders Network

The Church on the Other Side (originally *Reinventing Your Church*) is published

1999   *Finding Faith* is published

2001   *A New Kind of Christian* is published

Phyllis Tickle promotes *A New Kind of Christian* at Christian Booksellers Association Convention

Emergent Village is formed

2002   *A New Kind of Christian* wins *Christianity Today* Award of Merit

More Ready Than You Realize is published

Robert Webber labels McLaren the leader of "The Younger Evangelicals"

2003   *The Story We Find Ourselves in* is published

Co-Authors *A Is for Abductive* (with Leonard Sweet and Jerry Haselmayer)

Co-Authors *Adventures in Missing the Point* (with Tony Campolo)

Contributes to *The Church in Emerging Culture* (general editor, Leonard Sweet)

2004   McLaren awarded honorary Doctor of Divinity degree by Carey Theological College

Justin Taylor describes McLaren as the pastor of Postconservative Evangelicalism

Christianity Today publishes "Emergent Mystique" article

A Generous Orthodoxy is published

2005   *The Last Word and the Word After That* is published

Time magazine selects McLaren as "one of the 25 Most Influential Evangelicals in America"

McLaren appears on "Larry King Live"

D. A. Carson authors *Becoming Conversant with the Emerging Church*

R. Scott Smith authors *Truth and the New Kind of Christian*

McLaren mentor Stanley Grenz dies at the age of 55

McLaren resigns as pastor of Cedar Ridge to become international ambassador for Emergent

Eddie Gibbs and Ryan Bolger co-author *Emerging Churches*

"EMERGENT MCLAREN" ERA (2006-Present)

2006   *The Secret Message of Jesus* is published

McLaren calls for five-year moratorium on making pronouncements on homosexuality and the church

The Voice of Acts is published

2007   *Everything Must Change* is published

The Voice of Luke is published

2008   Twelve-city *Everything Must Change* promotional tour is launched

Finding Our Way Again is published

McLaren campaigns for Barak Obama presidency

Christianity Today publishes "McLaren Emerging" article

Tony Jones authors *The New Christians*

Emergent Village discontinues Jones' National Coordinator position

Phyllis Tickle authors *The Great Emergence,* comparing McLaren's *A Generous Orthodoxy* to Martin Luther's Ninety-Five Theses

2009   *The Justice Project* is published

McLaren observes Ramadan with Muslim friends

2010   *A New Kind of Christianity* is published

McLaren awarded honorary doctorate by Virginia Theological Seminary

"Farewell Emerging Church" article runs in *World* magazine

2011   *Naked Spirituality* is published

McLaren speaks at first Wild Goose Festival—the U.S. analog to England's long-running Greenbelt Festival

2012   *Why Did Jesus, Moses, the Buddha and Mohammed Cross the Road?* is published and wins the Academy Parish Clergy Book of the Year

McLaren leads a commitment ceremony for his gay son Trevor and partner

The Girl with the Dove Tattoo (ebook) is published

The Word of the Lord to Democrats (ebook) is published

The Word of the Lord to Evangelicals (ebook) is published

The Word of the Lord to Republicans (ebook) is published

Phyllis Tickle authors *Emergence Christianity,* comparing McLaren's *New Kind of Christianity* to Luther's *"Here I Stand"* declaration of faith and principles

2014   *We Make the Road by Walking* is published

2015   McLaren helps launch a new organization named "Convergence US"

2016   *The Great Spiritual Migration* is published

Five Questions You Might Be Asking

by Brian D. McLaren

IF I WERE IN YOUR POSITION, READING A FOREWORD LIKE THIS, in which an author introduces a scholarly analysis of his work, I would have five simple questions in my mind:

1. What is your general response to this analysis of your work?
2. Where do you disagree with this analysis?
3. Did you learn anything from the analysis?
4. What does it feel like to read an analysis of your work?
5. What was your favorite part of the book?

Q. What is your general response to this analysis of your work?
First, I feel deeply honored to have my work taken so seriously and engaged with so thoroughly by a scholar of Dr. Scott Burson's intelligence, rigor, and grace.

Second, I'm very impressed. I've written a lot in a relatively short time, and Dr. Burson has not only carefully read my published works, he has also engaged with my blogs and articles and many of my public lectures. No small task just in terms of volume! Not only that, he has read my critics, another major accomplishment. Most impressive of all, I feel that he has fairly engaged even with the dimensions of my work with which he dis-agrees, modeling a level of civility and charity that I often fail to achieve, even though I aspire to it.

Third, as someone who loves good writing and aspires (and often fails) to write well, I'm grateful that Dr. Burson writes so clearly and accessibly. I know you will feel the same way as you read this book.

Q. Where do you disagree with this analysis?

Any disagreements I have with Dr. Burson's analysis are small and light-weight in comparison with my general appreciation for this project. There are a number of small details that I might have put differently. For example, I would probably consider *We Make the Road by Walking* my magnum opus rather than *A New Kind of Christianity* (if I have yet created such a thing at all).

More substantially, in Chapter 4, Dr. Burson focuses on my critique of fundamentalist Calvinism, a point of view that has experienced a resurgence in recent years. As an Arminian himself, Dr. Burson has every reason to pursue this focus, even though I wouldn't describe my work as singling out Calvinism for critique. My deeper concern is finding an alternative to fundamentalism and the broader inflexible, self-protective, and (sadly) racist Christian identity that so often takes refuge in fundamentalism. But again, especially in light of Dr. Burson's own Arminian commitment and his focus on apologetics, I think his analysis is helpful, and it helps explain why some Calvinists have reacted so strongly against my work.

Similarly, in Chapter 8, to the degree that Dr. Burson is seeking to expose tensions between my work and traditional Arminian theology, I thought he made his points fairly and well. However, in some places, I felt that the categories of traditional Arminian theology obscure rather than elucidate some of my thinking. This is not a fault of Dr. Burson's, but an inevitability when a historic framework is applied to a very different context.

For example, Dr. Burson says, "By rejecting the traditional doctrine of total depravity, McLaren is vulnerable to the charge of Pelagianism or at least semi-Pelagianism, and consequently out of step with orthodox Arminianism." I would respond by saying that when one rejects that tra-ditional doctrine of total depravity, I doubt one can be either Pelagian, semi-Pelagian, or Augustinian, since all these schools of thought are based upon shared assumptions about the meaning of salvation, and this shared understanding of salvation is in turn based upon a shared traditional understanding of sin that I believe needs to be re-thought.

Something similar occurs in the section that said I propose a "don't ask, don't tell" policy on the eternal fate of the unevangelized. By failing to answer the question of what happens to the unevangelized, Dr. Burson says, I fail to address a legitimate inquiry regarding the character of God. And within traditional categories, he is right.

But from the vantage point where I now find myself, thinking outside the traditional "six-line narrative," the question of the eternal fate of the unevangelized really doesn't arise. It's not that the question must be suppressed; it's that it simply doesn't come up. To keep bringing it up means returning to the framework or paradigm I think we need to leave behind. (This explains the character Neo's strong reaction to Dan's question on the subject in one of my books.) I understand this will be hard for many readers even to imagine, because I know from personal experience the powerful way the traditional narrative frames thought and boxes in imagination.

This doesn't mean Dr. Burson's critiques are invalid. It may actually mean that the situation is much worse than he suggests! In other words, it's not that when I came to the rough of the ninth hole of the golf course I chose the wrong golf club (to use a metaphor from that chapter). It's that I was birding and so I brought binoculars instead of golf clubs to the course.

And Dr. Burson understands this. He understands that my rejection of what I call "the six-line narrative" puts me out of sync with traditional Arminianism along with Calvinism, not to mention most of Western Christian history, where that narrative has been assumed almost without question. He is right to look for some less radical way of addressing the problems we both see, if that's possible; I suppose only time will tell if he has under-reacted or I have over-reacted. At any rate, I'm glad that he can look beyond those points of concern to find elements of my work that could enhance traditional Arminianism (and Calvinism), and I hope that will be the case–through his influence if not through mine.

Q. Did I learn anything from the analysis?

Yes. Much. For starters, there were a lot of quotes from my work that surprised me, along the lines of, "I said *that* back *then*?" If I ever write an autobiography or memoir, I'll no doubt consult Dr. Burson's timeline and three-part narrative of my theological development to refresh my own memory.

I found Dr. Burson's discussion of my work in relation to Protestant Liberalism fascinating, leaving me to wonder why anyone would not want to be considered at least somewhat liberal.

I was especially interested in his account of resonance between my work and Arminian/Wesleyan values, and I found his discussion on free will and determinism to be instructive. I wish I had studied this subject under his tutelage many years ago! In that section, I thought it was a mark of Dr. Burson's academic impartiality to show how I didn't sufficiently nuance some of my critique of Calvinistic determinism, a position he also is critical of. He is right.

Q. What does it feel like to read an analysis of your work?

In short, humbling. And honoring. As I said earlier, simply to have one's work taken so seriously is a great gift. But my response goes beyond that, tapping into my own story.

When I was in my late teens and early twenties and my faith was passing through many "dangers, toils, and snares" in the form of questions and doubts, I was introduced to two Christian writers whose work meant the world to me: C. S. Lewis and Francis Schaeffer. Though I later came to see a number of things differently from these towering figures in my life, I am eternally grateful to them. They opened up new vistas of theological freedom for me, and modeled a robust Christian life of the mind for me that I had never been exposed to.

Dr. Burson shares my appreciation for these two great Christian thinkers, as evidenced in a book he co-authored in 1998: *C.S. Lewis and Francis Schaeffer: Lessons for a New Century from the Most Influential Apologists of Our Time.* I feel humbled and gratified for Dr. Burson to engage with my work as a contribution to the genre of apologetics along with Lewis and Schaeffer.

Apologetics is often presented as a project to help nonChristians overcome obstacles to faith in Christ, and that certainly is a major concern of mine. But I suspect that most apologetics books are actually bought and read by Christians who are trying to keep their faith during times of questioning and doubt. I am deeply encouraged by the thought that my work could in some small way do for a new generation of Christians what Lewis and Schaeffer did for me.

Scott is also working in the field of apologetics, and because he is working with such an evident reservoir of intelligence, rigor, and grace, I know he will make significant contributions in this great work, I hope far beyond whatever I am able to do with God's help.

Q. What was your favorite part of the book?

Two parts stand out. No offense to Scott, of course, but one was the cover art created by his wife. The other was the book's unforgettable last sentence. But I encourage you not to skip ahead. That would be like reading the punch line before reading the joke. You'll appreciate the ending more if you follow Dr. Burson's line of thought from the cover to the last page.

I love reading theology, especially when the theologian doing the writing has the skill and sensitivity of Dr. Scott Burson. I am confident you'll feel the same way when you get to that last sentence.

Brian D. McLaren

Chapter One

INTRODUCTION

If God has predetermined that the world will get worse and worse until it ends in a cosmic megaconflict between the forces of Light (epitomized most often in the United States) and the forces of Darkness (previously centered in communism, but now, that devil having been vanquished, in Islam), why waste energy on peacemaking, diplomacy, or interreligious dialogue? Aren't those simply endeavors in rearranging deck chairs on the Titanic? And since even Jesus can't set the world right without taking up the sword and shedding swimming pools of his enemies' blood . . . what's so bad about another war, and maybe even a little torture and genocide now and then? If God sanctions it, why can't we?[1]

—Brian McLaren, *A New Kind of Christianity*

THE LAST FEW DECADES HAVE BEEN CHALLENGING FOR THE Christian establishment in the United States.[2] In 1996, the Barna Research Group conducted a study to determine how Americans view Christians and Christianity. The study, entitled "Christianity Has a Strong Positive Image Despite Fewer Active Participants," reported that among non-Christians, "85 percent were favorable toward Christianity's role in society."[3] This largely positive perception was detected across generations.

---

[1] McLaren, *NKOCY*, 193.

[2] Diana Butler Bass calls the decade from 2000 to 2010 the "Horrible Decade" for Christianity in the United States. She lists 9/11, the Roman Catholic sex scandal, the Protestant conflict over LGBT issues, the Religious Right, and "The Great Religious Recession" as a confluence of factors that undermined the credibility of US religious leaders. See Diana Butler Bass, *Christianity After Religion* (New York: HarperOne, 2012), 76–83.

[3] David Kinnaman and Gabe Lyons, *unChristian* (Grand Rapids: Baker, 2007), 24.

By 2007, however, new Barna research suggested a notable shift. In a book entitled *unChristian,* authors Gabe Lyons and David Kinnaman discuss how non-Christian Americans aged sixteen to twenty-nine view Christians. The authors argue that many in this generation describe Christians as "hypocritical," "too focused on converts," "antihomosexual," "sheltered," "overly political," and "judgmental." Moreover, this study reported that many Christians in this age group describe Christianity and their fellow Christians in a similar manner.[4]

In *They Like Jesus but Not the Church,* Dan Kimball offers his own qualitative research that buttresses much of the *unChristian* study. Kimball summarizes how non-Christian Americans in their "late teens to thirties"[5] perceive the Christian church: "1) The church is an organized religion with a political agenda; 2) the church is judgmental and negative; 3) the church is dominated by males and oppressed females; 4) the church is homophobic; 5) the church arrogantly claims all other religions are wrong; and 6) the church is full of fundamentalists who take the Bible literally."[6]

Coinciding with the Barna research and Kimball's observations has been an influx of accessible atheistic literature. Led by retired Oxford University professor Richard Dawkins, author Christopher Hitchens, Tufts University philosopher Daniel Dennett, and neuroscientist Sam Harris, this revitalized atheistic vision of reality started reaching the masses during the past decade through a wave of best-selling books.[7] The apologetic effort

---

[4] Ibid., 17, 29–30, and 18–19. Independent research around the time of *unChristian*'s release appears to support the finding that Christians and Christianity have an image problem not only outside the church but within it as well. In October 2007, *The Christian Century* reported on a study released by the Pew Research Center for the People & the Press. The study claimed that young adult evangelicals, ages eighteen to twenty-nine, are expressing many of the same questions and concerns as others their age. One major issue for younger evangelicals is how the Christian church is dealing with the issue of homosexuality. See "Polls Find Shifts by Young Evangelicals," *Christian Century* 124, no. 22 (October 30, 2007): 14–15. More recently, in a 2015 *Time* article, Elizabeth Dias reported that according to the Public Religion Research Institute, support of gay marriage among younger evangelicals has jumped drastically from 20 percent in 2003 to 42 percent in 2014. See Elizabeth Dias, "A Change of Heart: Inside the Evangelical War over Gay Marriage," *Time* 185, no. 2 (January 26, 2015): 44–48, citing 46. This research lends support to the trajectory that Kinnaman and Lyons began to observe in 2007.

[5] Dan Kimball, *They Like Jesus but Not the Church* (Grand Rapids: Zondervan, 2007), 12. Kimball was a founding member of the Emergent Church Movement.

[6] Ibid., 69.

[7] See Richard Dawkins, *The God Delusion* (New York: Houghton Mifflin, 2006); Christopher Hitchens, *God Isn't Great* (Toronto: McClelland & Stewart, 2007); Daniel C. Dennett, *Breaking the Spell* (New York: Viking Penguin, 2006); and Sam Harris, *The End of Faith* (New York: W.W. Norton & Company, 2004).

of these atheistic writers, self-branded as "The Four Horsemen,"[8] was buttressed by less sophisticated, but no less impassioned, appeals from groups such as the Rational Response Squad, a band of unbelievers who broadcasted an Internet radio show from a basement in Philadelphia.[9] This group gained notoriety when several American news programs, including ABC's *Nightline*, reported on "The Blasphemy Challenge," an initiative that encouraged people to post their personal denials of the Holy Spirit on YouTube.[10] Comedian and talk show host Bill Maher entered the fray in 2009 with a feature film documentary entitled *Religulous*. Maher concluded his film with an appeal to all reasonable people to rise up against the religious fundamentalists whom he claims are hell-bent on destroying the planet.

These are just a few notable recent expressions of neo-atheism.[11] What has motivated this new kind of atheist to take such an aggressive, evangelistic posture? According to Harris, the motivation is not only rational, but also moral. Harris opines, "Imagine the consequences if any significant component of the U.S. government actually believed that the world was about to end and that its ending would be glorious. The fact that nearly half of the American population apparently believes this, purely on the basis of religious dogma, should be considered a moral emergency."[12] This line of reasoning suggests that religion in general and Christianity in particular are not merely a trivial annoyance, but rather a clear and present danger to all rational and morally sensitive people.

The Christian Apologetic Response

So, how have believers responded to this assault upon the Christian faith during the past decade? Some have chosen to fight fire with fire. Several books have been written to combat the rise of neo-atheism, including

---

[8] In 2007, Dawkins, Dennett, Harris, and Hitchens participated in a two-hour roundtable discussion. This recorded conversation is marketed in a video entitled "The Four Horsemen," *YouTube*, July 23, 2012, https://www.youtube.com/watch?v=n7IHU28aR2E.

[9] See www.rationalresponders.com.

[10] See www.blasphemychallenge.com.

[11] It is worth noting that not all contemporary atheists support the tactics and arguments of the Four Horsemen. For example, New York University psychologist Jonathan Haidt, who is a self-proclaimed atheist, believes religion plays a constructive role in society despite the loud objections of the New Atheists. See Jonathan Haidt, *The Righteous Mind* (New York: Pantheon Books, 2012), 246–73. For similar comments, see Andrew Newberg and Mark Robert Waldman, *How God Changes Your Brain* (New York: Ballantine, 2009), 6.

[12] Sam Harris, *Letter to a Christian Nation* (New York: Knopf, 2006), xii.

Alister McGrath and Joanna Collicutt McGrath's *The Dawkins Delusion?*, Dinesh D'Souza's *What's So Great about Christianity*, John Lennox's *God's Undertaker*, Antony Flew's *There Is a God,* and a collection of essays from evangelical scholars that appeared in *God Is Great, God Is Good.*[13]

In July 2008, *Christianity Today (CT)* ran a notable cover story entitled "God Is Not Dead Yet."[14] This cover treatment was a clear homage to the famous 1966 *Time* magazine cover which pondered the demise of the deity.[15] In this *CT* lead article, William Lane Craig explains how many contemporary philosophers are arguing for the existence of God with renewed rigor and passion.[16] Additionally, many formal debates began to spring up across the country. To name a few, Hitchens squared off against D'Souza and Craig,[17] while Dawkins engaged Oxford University colleague Lennox in the God Delusion Debate in Birmingham, Alabama.[18]

While these clashes might make for great theater, not all Christian apologists have responded defensively during the past decade. Brian D. McLaren, a leading voice in the Emerging Church Movement (ECM)[19] and an essay contributor to *unChristian*, is one author who heartily concurs with aspects of both the Barna research and the neo-atheist critique.[20]

---

[13] Alister E. McGrath and Joanna Collicutt McGrath, *The Dawkins Delusion* (Downers Grove: InterVarsity Press, 2007); Dinesh D'Souza, *What's So Great about Christianity* (Washington, DC: Regnery, 2007); John C. Lennox, *God's Undertaker* (Oxford: Lyon, 2007); Antony Flew with Roy Abraham Varghese, *There Is a God* (New York: HarperOne, 2007); and William Lane Craig and Chad Meister, eds., *God Is Great, God Is Good* (Downers Grove: InterVarsity Press, 2009).

[14] William Lane Craig, "God Is Not Dead Yet," *CT* 52, no. 7 (July 2008): 22–27.

[15] *Time* 87, no. 14 (April 8, 1966).

[16] Craig, "God Is Not Dead Yet," 22–27.

[17] These debates have ranged from New York to Los Angeles and several points in between. One memorable encounter between Hitchens and Craig took place on the campus of Biola University in April 2009 in front of a ticketed, sold-out audience of approximately four thousand people. The debate was also webcast to thirty-five other states and four foreign countries.

[18] The God Delusion Debate took place on the campus of the University of Alabama at Birmingham on October 3, 2007.

[19] Social scientists Gerardo Marti and Gladys Ganiel choose the label "Emerging Church Movement," even though many within the ECM are more comfortable characterizing the phenomenon as a "conversation." See Gerardo Marti and Gladys Ganiel, *The Deconstructed Church* (Oxford: Oxford University Press, 2014), 5. For an overview of the development of the US ECM and various ECM classifications, see Appendices A and B.

[20] It is worth noting that McLaren's affinity with the atheist critique is organically correlated to his aversion to Calvinist hubris and arrogance. In response to reading a particular Calvinist periodical during the 1990s, McLaren admits, "Every time I read it, I was pushed not only away from Calvinism, but toward atheism." Brian McLaren, email message to author, July 20, 2009. The fact that McLaren thought in binary Calvinism or atheism terms at that time is telling. McLaren did not explore the full range of historic orthodox Arminian resources when he began questioning his own Calvinistic theology. These points will be explored in greater detail in Chapters Seven and Eight.

Rather than defending the indefensible, McLaren readily agrees that certain articulations of the contemporary Christian narrative contain irrational and immoral plotlines that can lead people to develop and practice a bad form of monotheism.

CLASSIFYING THE ECM

A universally accepted Emerging Church Movement (ECM) taxonomy is illusive. For an overview of several proposed taxonomies, see Appendix A. For the sake of this study, the following terms will be used accordingly: ECM will refer to all segments of the broader emerging church conversation without doctrinal, ecclesial, or methodological discrimination; "emergent" will be used in specific reference to leading voices, most notably Brian McLaren, Tony Jones, and Doug Pagitt, historically associated with Emergent Village; and "emerging" will be applied to those participating in the broader ECM, but who do not align themselves with "emergent." It should be noted that Emergent Village is no longer in existence and the term "ECM" is rarely used to describe contemporary expressions of this movement. Nevertheless, the ethos of "emergent" and "emerging" carries on as separate streams in the broader flow of what Phyllis Tickle calls "Emergence," which also includes the "neo-Monastics," the "House Church," the "Missionals," the "Hyphenated," and the "Cyber Church." Therefore, for the purpose of this study, "emergent" will be used to designate McLaren's position as the progressive stream of the ECM that continues to flow into this broader phenomenon labeled "Emergence."

See also Tickle, *The Great Emergence*; Marti and Ganiel, *The Deconstructed Church*

These distorted expressions of the Christian message, he argues, often do more damage than any attack leveled by disenchanted youth, radical atheists, or adherents to other religions.[21]

---

[21] McLaren, *FF*, 119–22.

Consider the following assessment from McLaren, which serves as a fitting complement to Harris's earlier declaration that the United States is facing a "moral emergency." McLaren avers,

> If God has predetermined that the world will get worse and worse until it ends in a cosmic megaconflict between the forces of Light (epitomized most often in the United States) and the forces of Darkness (previously centered in communism, but now, that devil having been vanquished, in Islam), why waste energy on peacemaking, diplomacy, or interreligious dialogue? Aren't those simply endeavors in rearranging deck chairs on the Titanic? And since even Jesus can't set the world right without taking up the sword and shedding swimming pools of his enemies' blood . . . what's so bad about another war, and maybe even a little torture and genocide now and then? If God sanctions it, why can't we?[22]

McLaren agrees with Harris that doomsday eschatology has profound practical consequences for how we seek to share this planet and utilize its resources. This is one reason McLaren believes that the most lethal contemporary apologetic threat to Christianity can be found within its own ranks. In particular, McLaren believes distorted versions of Christian monotheism, which promote divine determinism, exclusive privilege, and "redemptive" violence, pose a more menacing challenge to the gospel in our current postmodern, postcolonial world than any external, non-Christian foe.[23]

McLaren identifies five-point Calvinism as the chief propagator of this kind of distorted Christian narrative.[24] McLaren argues that Calvinism has

---

[22] McLaren, *NKOCY*, 193. George Marsden points out the "central cultural paradox" within the Religious Right: "In tandem with massive efforts to transform American politics and culture for the long run, ever more popular dispensational premillennial teachings suggested that for the United States there would be no long run." George M. Marsden, *Fundamentalism and American Culture* (New York: Oxford University Press, 2006), 247. While McLaren does not overtly identify this paradox, he does critique both of the Religious Right's premillennial and postmillennial impulses.

[23] In a CNN guest editorial, McLaren wrote, "If I could get one message through to my evangelical friends, it would be this: The greatest threat to evangelicalism is evangelicals who tolerate hate and who promote hate camouflaged as piety." See Brian McLaren, "My Take: It's Time for Islamophobic Evangelicals to Choose," *CNN* website, September 12, 2012, http://religion.blogs.cnn.com/2012/09/15/my-take-its-time-for-islamophobic-evangelicals-to-choose/.

[24] McLaren recognizes additional streams of Reformed theology and limits his critique to classical five-point Calvinism, which traces its heritage and authority to the writing of John Calvin, the

been shaped by modernity and colonialism, which is problematic in the postmodern, postcolonial era.[25] Additionally, the influence of Calvinism is especially troubling in the United States because of Reformed theology's dominant role in orchestrating the development of contemporary Evangelicalism and the Religious Right, which have contributed to the negative public perception of the Christian faith. In short, because of its powerful influence, Calvinistic theology and practice have played a central role in grinding and molding the lens through which the American public views evangelical Christianity.[26] Consequently, the heart of McLaren's new kind of apologetic project focuses on deconstructing the core doctrines and narrative contours of classical Calvinism and replacing them with what he contends is a fresh and faithful reconstructed biblical storyline that is morally and rationally believable. McLaren hopes this reconstructed lens will provide a more faithful vision of the goodness of God manifested most clearly in Jesus of Nazareth and his kingdom of God ethic. In turn, he hopes this renewed vision of the goodness of God will inspire a more felicitous response to the moral emergencies facing the world today.

Overview of the Book

The purpose of this study is to assess the postmodern apologetic project of Brian McLaren, who is widely recognized as the leading voice in the ECM. While much has been written about the ECM, a comprehensive treatment of McLaren's apologetic project is lacking. This study seeks to fill that gap by exploring the full range of McLaren's work—from his master's thesis[27] as a

---

Synod of Dort, and certain creedal statements, including the Westminster Confession of Faith. Consequently, when "Calvinism" is discussed in this book, the term will be associated with the five-point variety unless otherwise noted.

[25] McLaren, *GO*, 188.

[26] Ibid., 186. According to Gary Dorrien, the US "evangelical establishment is still dominated by Calvinists." Consequently, the public perception of Evangelicalism is framed by "the steady stream of books from Grand Rapids, Michigan, that have portrayed evangelicalism as monolithically middle-class, Reformed, white, Republican, and preoccupied with correct doctrine." While Evangelicalism has always included "sizable groups who do not admire the Westminster Confession or vote conservative . . . [o]nly the Calvinists were assumed to be qualified to make evangelicalism respectable in American society or to play a culture-forming role within it." See Gary Dorrien, *The Remaking of Evangelical Theology* (Louisville: Westminster John Knox Press, 1998), 153–59. For an additional discussion regarding the role of Calvinism in the development of Evangelicalism and its influence upon the Religious Right, see Marsden, who identifies the Southern Baptist Convention as "probably the largest source of the fundamentalistic Religious Right in recent decades." In Marsden, *Fundamentalism and American Culture*, 229–57, citing 239.

[27] This is the first academic engagement with McLaren's unpublished master's thesis.

graduate student at the University of Maryland in the early 1980s to the publishing of the 2016 book *The Great Spiritual Migration*. Additionally, much of the critical engagement with McLaren's work has come from Calvinist leaders. This book seeks to offer the first full-scale Arminian assessment of McLaren's theological and apologetic project.[28]

It should be noted at the outset that McLaren does not function as an academic apologist. He does not enter into the methodological debate between advocates of evidentialism, presuppositionalism, and verificationism.[29] He does not seek to undermine the truth claims of other religions, nor does he offer sustained offensive arguments utilizing natural theology or historical apologetics.[30] McLaren claims to be "an evangelist at heart," however, so introducing people to a proper picture of Jesus is a chief motivating concern.[31] McLaren believes this task is becoming increasingly problematic because the dominant evangelical narrative of five-point Calvinism is corrupted with modern and colonial "viruses."[32] Many contemporary people are rejecting this distorted picture of the Christian faith rather than the true gospel narrative. Therefore, McLaren's primary apologetic project is to debug this distorted narrative and replace it with a rationally and morally believable alternative that is more faithful to the original gospel message and

---

[28] This is not to say that Arminians have been silent in critiquing McLaren. One leading voice has been Scot McKnight, who is an outspoken critic of the New Calvinism. McKnight has engaged McLaren's thought in a critically appreciative manner, although in recent years he has become increasingly strident. Leonard Sweet, the E. Stanley Jones Professor of Evangelism at Drew University, is one of McLaren's co-authors. Sweet, however, eventually turned critical of McLaren, as this study will show. Additionally, Deirdre Brower-Latz wrote a PhD thesis on Wesley and the ECM. Latz, who is the principal at Nazarene Theological College in Manchester (UK), focuses on the broader emergent movement, rather than only McLaren, and on practical theology instead of systematic theology and apologetics, as this study will do. Gary Tyra compares McLaren's theology and missional emphases with the thinking of Marcus Borg. Tyra, who teaches at Vanguard University (an Assembly of God institution), offers his critique from a broadly evangelical perspective without discussing the finer points of either Calvinism or Arminianism. See Gary Tyra, *A Missional Orthodoxy* (Downers Grove: InterVarsity Press, 2013).

[29] For two helpful treatments of apologetic methodology, see Gordon R. Lewis, *Testing Christianity's Truth Claims: Approaches to Christian Apologetics* (Chicago: Moody, 1976) and Steven B. Cowan, *Five Views on Apologetics* (Grand Rapids: Zondervan, 2000).

[30] In *FF*, McLaren briefly discusses natural theology, including the cosmological, teleological, and moral arguments. His treatment of this subject matter is sketchy and is not central to his overall apologetic project. See *FF*, 83–98. That said, McLaren is willing to engage in apologetic conversations with people of other faiths on an ad hoc, person-to-person, context-specific basis. Ad hoc apologetics will be explored as part of McLaren's overall apologetic strategy in Chapter Six.

[31] Brian McLaren, email message to author, July 20, 2009.

[32] This metaphor of a virus is used by McLaren in *COOS*, 197–210, and will be explored in relation to Calvinism in Chapter Four.

sensitive to postmodern and postcolonial concerns. This study will consider McLaren's project an apologetic endeavor, since he is offering an alternative vision of the Christian faith to those who are questioning whether to remain within the Christian fold or to those who find the Christian faith morally and intellectually unpalatable due to a distorted presentation (in word and deed) of the true gospel message.[33]

A Personal Note

This project originated as a PhD thesis at Brunel University—London (England), and was jointly supervised at the London School of Theology and Asbury Theological Seminary. After successfully defending the thesis, I spoke with several publishers about this manuscript. I chose to publish with Abilene Christian University Press because the editorial team shared my sensibilities and vision to make this work accessible to a broad audience without sacrificing academic integrity.[34] Consequently, what follows is a book that is intended not only for scholars but also clergy and laypersons who have read McLaren and other important voices that have shaped the ECM and continue to contribute to various streams of emergence and convergence Christianity.[35] In light of this intended purpose, some sections of this manuscript have been streamlined to engage a broader audience. In such cases, the reader is directed to sources that will provide more technical, academic detail. For those interested in reading my original PhD thesis, it is readily available by conducting a "theses and dissertations" search at your local library.[36]

In researching this project, I have personally interacted with McLaren through email and in several face-to-face interviews spanning a decade. I could not have asked for a more gracious and responsive dialogue partner.

---

[33] Brower-Latz also views the ECM as "developing a public apologetic." See Deirdre Brower-Latz, "A Contextual Reading of John Wesley's Theology and the Emergent Church" (PhD thesis, Manchester, 2009), 23.

[34] The director of ACU Press, Jason Fikes, has researched and written about the ECM and is a scholar on this subject in his own right. See Jason Fikes, "Emerging Historiography: New Church Leaders Are Looking at the Past and Shaping What Is to Come," *Stone-Campbell Journal* 14, no. 2 (2011): 207–18.

[35] These terms will be defined shortly.

[36] For the original PhD thesis, see Scott R. Burson, "Apologetics and the New Kind of Christian: An Arminian Analysis of Brian D. McLaren's Emergent Reconstruction of the Faith" (PhD thesis, Brunel University—London, 2015).

He answered every question with thoughtful and helpful candor. Much of the content of these conversations is woven throughout the body of this book, which introduces aspects of McLaren's thought that have never made their way into print until now. This is particularly the case with some of McLaren's provocative statements concerning five-point Calvinism.[37]

Finally, as my research unfolded, a disconcerting pattern emerged. It became clear that many Christian leaders interacting with McLaren were less than gracious in their commentary. Instead of limiting the critique to the content of McLaren's project, these interlocutors often engaged in vicious ad hominem arguments, bordering on libel and slander. Many critics seemed to relish questioning McLaren's motives and in so doing refused to extend him the benefit of the doubt. D. A. Carson is a case in point. In *Becoming Conversant with the Emerging Church*, Carson accuses McLaren of compromising the gospel because of his overriding desire for cultural relevancy. In so doing, Carson argues that McLaren has dishonored Scripture.

While *Publisher's Weekly* religion editor Phyllis Tickle has favorably compared McLaren to Martin Luther, Carson juxtaposes the "wayward" McLaren with the courageous German reformer.

> It is impossible to find in the writings of, say, Brian McLaren, an utterance akin to that of Luther at the Diet of Worms: "Since then your Majesty and your lordships desire a simple reply, I will answer without horns and without teeth. Unless I am convicted by Scripture and plain reason . . . I do not accept the authority of popes and councils, for they have contradicted each other—my conscience is captive to the Word of God. I cannot and will not recant anything, for to go against conscience is neither right nor safe. God help me. Amen."[38]

In a 2014 *Parse* article, entitled "Wings of Wax: The Strange Yet Familiar Tale of Brian, Rob, and Don," Kevin Miller accuses McLaren, Rob Bell, and Donald Miller of flying too close to the sun.[39] Pride and desire for celebrity,

---

[37] Transcriptions of the email correspondence are available in Appendix D.

[38] D. A. Carson, *Becoming Conversant with the Emerging Church* (Grand Rapids: Zondervan, 2004), 43.

[39] Kevin A. Miller, "Wings of Wax? The Strange yet Familiar Tale of Brian, Rob, and Don," *Parse: Ministry/Culture from Leadership Journal*, February 18, 2014, http://www.christianitytoday.com

the author claims, led to the downfall of these once respected evangelical leaders and relegated them to their current status as evangelical has-beens and outcasts. McLaren's blog response to this cautionary tale is a fitting riposte not only to Kevin Miller but to Carson as well:

> I can only say that life is wonderful when you follow your con-science and aren't afraid. . . . As the Proverb says, "The fear of man brings a snare," and as Jesus said, "The truth will set you free." Several years ago, a respected older Evangelical theologian confided to me if he had it to do over again, he wouldn't have let the fear of critique by Evangelical gatekeepers have such control over him. He encouraged me to follow my conscience and not trim my sails for fear of being singled out. I have tried to follow that advice, and am glad I did.[40]

In an email exchange, McLaren revealed that this "older Evangelical theo-logian" was prolific author Stanley Grenz, who communicated this message a week before he died unexpectedly at the age of fifty-five.[41] What can be found in this blog post is precisely what Carson claims is "impossible to find" in McLaren's writings—namely, a confession of conscience and a commitment to godly conviction despite the consequences.[42] Luther could not have said it better.

Instead of rejecting the authority of "popes and councils," McLaren has rejected the authority of "Evangelical gatekeepers." McLaren is mild-man-nered and not contentious by nature. He even has the reputation of kindness and gentleness among his critics.[43] It is unconscionable to refuse the benefit

/parse/2014/february/strange-yet-familiar-tale-of-brian-rob-and-don.html?paging=off; accessed March 3, 2014.

[40] Brian McLaren, "Q & R: You, Rob Bell, Don Miller, and *Christianity Today*," *brian d. mclaren* (blog), February 21, 2014, http://brianmclaren.net/archives/blog/q-r-you-rob-bell-don-miller-and.html.

[41] Brian McLaren, email message to author, August 3, 2014.

[42] It is worth noting that Jacob Arminius (1559–1609) was likewise known for his fearless commitment to conscience in the face of Calvinist supralapsarian persecution. According to Keith Stanglin and Thomas McCall, "The motto appearing on his [Arminius's] seal, which well epitomized his life of seeking the truth despite the consequences, was 'a good conscience is paradise' (*bona conscientia paradisus*)." See Keith D. Stanglin and Thomas H. McCall, *Jacob Arminius: Theologian of Grace* (New York: Oxford University Press, 2012), 36.

[43] While Carson, Kevin DeYoung, and Ted Kluck have not met McLaren, they claim to have heard good things about him. See Carson, *Becoming Conversant*, 158, and Kevin DeYoung and Ted Kluck, *Why We're Not Emergent* (Chicago: Moody, 2008), 43.

of the doubt at this juncture. It is one thing to critique the content of an opponent's theology, but it's quite another to presume to know the content of an opponent's character or what animates his motives. Such strident ad hominem arguments do nothing to advance the cause of Christian scholarship; rather, they serve to confirm McLaren's contention that aspects of modern Evangelicalism are virulent and in critical need of debugging.[44]

David Mills surely hits the nail on the head when he writes, "Perhaps I am reading McLaren too charitably here, projecting my own desires and hopes onto the text. If so, I'd rather be guilty of a hermeneutics of charity than a hermeneutics of suspicion which is incompatible with Christian behavior."[45] While the following engagement with McLaren's apologetic project does not shy away from critique at certain key points, it is the hope and intent of this author to follow Mills in adopting a constructive and appreciative hermeneutic of charity rather than a cynical and virulent hermeneutic of suspicion.

---

[44] For a similar critique of Carson and his interaction with Grenz, see Roger E. Olson, *Reformed and Always Reforming* (Grand Rapids: Baker, 2007), 25.

[45] David M. Mills, "The Emergent Church—Another Perspective: A Critical Response to D. A. Carson's Staley Lectures," unpublished paper, n. d., 22, http://people.cedarville.edu/Employee/millsd/mills_staley_response.pdf; accessed February 26, 2014.

MCLAREN'S RISE TO PROMINENCE

In the same way that Martin Luther became the symbolic leader and spokesman for the Great Reformation, so too has Brian McLaren become the symbolic leader and spokesman for the Great Emergence. His 2005 volume *A Generous Orthodoxy* (Zondervan) is both an analog to Luther's ninety-five theses and also a clearly stated overview of many of the parts of post-Constantinian Christian theology that are now undergoing reconsideration.[1]

—Phyllis Tickle, *The Great Emergence*

IN THE INTRODUCTION TO *A NEW KIND OF CHRISTIANITY*, McLaren wonders how "a mild-mannered guy like me" got "into this swirl of controversy?"[2] Chapter Two will seek to answer this question. In what follows, McLaren's life, ministry, and publishing will be divided into three eras: "Early McLaren" (1956–1994), "Emerging McLaren" (1995–2005), and "Emergent McLaren" (2006–present). This biographical overview will trace the development of McLaren's life, influences, ministry, and publishing, as well as his effects upon the ECM and beyond.

The "Early McLaren" Era (1956–1994)

Brian McLaren experienced and explored a broad range of eclectic Christian expressions during his formative years. He grew up in the 1950s and '60s

---

[1] Phyllis Tickle, *The Great Emergence* (Grand Rapids: Baker, 2008), 164.
[2] McLaren, *NKOCY*, 2.

just outside of Washington, DC, the area he has lived most of his life.[3] He was raised in a Plymouth Brethren home, "way out on the end of one of the most conservative branches of one of the most conservative limbs of Christianity."[4] During his early years, McLaren recalls heavy doses of dispensational[5] teaching and preaching, "sometimes illustrated through huge and serious wall charts and dramatized in B-rated movies."[6]

THE PLYMOUTH BRETHREN

The Plymouth Brethren movement originated in Dublin, Ireland, in the late 1820s. The Brethren, which subsequently splintered into several competing sects, rejected the authority of the Church of England, as well as any type of ecclesiology that privileged ordained clergy. John Nelson Darby (1800-1882) was an early leader who later became known as the "father of Dispensationalism." Darby focused on eschatology and introduced the secret rapture theory, which claims that Jesus will instantaneously transport all believers to heaven to protect them from various tribulations and bring them back with Him when He returns for a second time.

When developing his famous reference Bible in the early twentieth century, Cyrus Scofield (1843–1921) appropriated Darby's eschatological teaching. More recently, Darby's dispensational teaching has informed the popular *Left Behind* book and movie franchise.

See Vern S. Poythress, *Understanding Dispensationalists* (Grand Rapids: Zondervan, 1987) and Peter E. Prosser, *Dispensationalist Eschatology and Its Influences on American and British Religious Movements* (Lewistown, N.Y.: Mellen Press, 1999), 183-98.

As a lover of science from an early age, McLaren encountered in textbooks content that often conflicted with the young-earth creationism he

---

[3] Eddie Gibbs and Ryan Bolger, *Emerging Churches* (Grand Rapids: Baker, 2012), 283. Although McLaren has lived in Maryland the majority of his life, he now resides in Florida.

[4] McLaren, *GO*, 35. See also McLaren, *FF*, 71–72.

[5] McLaren, *NS*, 24, and McLaren, *FOWA*, 56–58. John Nelson Darby, one of the founders of the Plymouth Brethren movement, was responsible for systematically developing dispensational eschatology. McLaren would later reject Darby's premillennial dispensationalism in favor of what he calls "participatory eschatology."

[6] McLaren, *NKOCY*, 263.

had been taught by his family and church.[7] Consequently, by the age of thirteen McLaren had rejected Fundamentalism, in general, and Plymouth Brethren teaching, in particular.[8] By fifteen, he was "struggling deeply with [his] faith."[9] Around that time, he was invited to a Young Life Bible study where a leader named David Miller took a special interest in him.[10] This relationship introduced McLaren to a distinctly Calvinistic interpretation of the faith at a critical time in his development. This Young Life experience was soon buttressed by a "charismatic" experience at a Southern Baptist youth retreat[11] and positive encounters with the Jesus Movement[12] during the early 1970s. McLaren claims that these experiences combined to solidly keep "both [of his] feet on the Christian path."[13] As McLaren grew in his adolescent faith, Calvinistic doctrine became deeply ingrained in his psyche.

McLaren discovered his evangelistic gifting in high school, where he led investigative Bible studies.[14] In 1974, he enrolled at the University of Maryland, originally as a philosophy major, but he soon shifted to English while maintaining an interest in the aesthetic dimensions of philosophy.[15] During his college years, McLaren read popular apologists C. S. Lewis and Francis Schaeffer, a common port of entry for many Christians in the academy today.[16] As a student in the English department, McLaren was also reading secular postmodern authors.[17] Through exposure to these early seeds of postmodernism, McLaren came to the conclusion that no

---

[7] McLaren, *FF*, 71–72.

[8] Gibbs and Bolger, *Emerging Churches*, 283.

[9] Ibid. See also Shayne Lee and Phillip Sinitiere, *Holy Mavericks* (New York: New York University Press, 2009), 89–90.

[10] McLaren, *FF*, 299. Miller is thanked in the "Acknowledgments" section in *NKOC*.

[11] McLaren, *FF*, 300–303.

[12] McLaren, *GO*, 44–45.

[13] Gibbs and Bolger, *Emerging Churches*, 283.

[14] Ibid.

[15] McLaren, *GO*, 147.

[16] McLaren, *FF*, 73. For more about how Lewis and Schaeffer inspired many young Christians to take ideas seriously and to pursue graduate studies in a wide range of fields, especially philosophy and theology, see Scott R. Burson and Jerry L. Walls, *C. S. Lewis and Francis Schaeffer* (Downers Grove: InterVarsity Press, 1998), 15–17.

[17] McLaren claims that he was originally introduced to postmodern thinking through novelist Walker Percy. See McLaren, *EMC*, 34.

Christian author, including the then-popular Schaeffer, was adequately addressing the issues raised by these writers.[18]

McLaren earned a BA and MA in English.[19] His master's thesis focused on novelist Walker Percy's subversive apologetic writing. While completing his master's degree and for a few years beyond, McLaren taught at the University of Maryland and Montgomery College. In total he would teach college-level English for eight years, from 1978 to 1986.[20]

During his college and young adult years, McLaren explored a variety of denominations, including Episcopalian, Catholic, and charismatic expressions.[21] In 1982, however, he helped form a fellowship group that crystallized into a house church.[22] In 1986, McLaren relinquished his English teaching duties to lead a transition from the original house church to a church plant. According to McLaren, "of the eighty adults who were a part of the original church, at least sixty stayed to help start the new one."[23]

The new venture, which "reoriented around evangelism," helped grow the Cedar Ridge Community Church to around two hundred people in two years. McLaren placed a special emphasis on welcoming seekers. In the spirit of Schaeffer's L'Abri Fellowship,[24] McLaren told his flock, "If your neighbor comes over and smokes, put out an ashtray." Some of his church members reacted like he was encouraging "mass fornication." During the early years of Cedar Ridge's development, McLaren and other congregational leaders learned much from mega-church pastors Rick Warren and Bill Hybels; however, they "did not fully participate in the seeker model."[25]

Cedar Ridge continued to grow in the early 1990s. McLaren's primary energies were focused on shepherding an increasingly diverse congregation,

---

[18] Gibbs and Bolger, *Emerging Churches*, 283. For a discussion of Schaeffer's positive influence on McLaren, see R. Alan Streett, "An Interview with Brian McLaren," *Criswell Theological Review* 3, no. 2 (Spring 2006): 10–11, as well as McLaren, *COOS*, 20–21.

[19] McLaren, *NKOC*, 171.

[20] McLaren, *SMJ*, 5.

[21] For a discussion of McLaren's early spiritual experiences, see McLaren, *NS*, 5–12. See also Lee and Sinitiere, *Holy Mavericks*, 90.

[22] McLaren, *NKOCY*, 10.

[23] McLaren, *RYC*, 24–25.

[24] In the 1950s, Schaeffer and his wife, Edith, opened their Swiss chalet to seekers who could explore the truth, goodness, and beauty of the Christian faith within the context of a spiritual intellectual community. This decision led to an international movement known as L'Abri, which means "shelter" in French. For more, see Edith Schaeffer, *L'Abri* (Wheaton: Tyndale, 1969).

[25] Gibbs and Bolger, *Emerging Churches*, 284.

which ranged from "highly educated rocket scientists (NASA was nearby) to addicted high school dropouts."[26] In the summer of 1990, however, he wrote a paper for the Christian Brethren Review.[27] In the article, McLaren discusses the features of John Wesley's Methodist renewal strategy as a model for rejuvenating the Brethren movement. This article is noteworthy for three reasons: it is McLaren's first published article, it demonstrates McLaren's early appreciation for the Arminian ministry of John Wesley, and it shows McLaren beginning to wrestle with the need for churches to transition into different forms of existence. This transition from an old kind of Christianity to a new way of following Christ would dominate much of McLaren's thinking and subsequent writing for the next quarter of a century.

Before McLaren published anything else, however, he experienced a spiritual crisis. While his church was showing signs of growth and health with increases not only in membership transfers but also in conversions, the foundations of McLaren's personal faith and professional confidence were cracking. In 1994, the thirty-eight-year-old McLaren wrote in his journal, "One year from today I will not be in the ministry."[28]

Several factors led to McLaren's crisis of faith. First, he was growing weary of the hubris and "absolute certainty" of many evangelical leaders and radio preachers.[29] Second, he struggled to craft and deliver sermons that simultaneously connected with parishioners and seekers.[30] Third, he noticed that an increasing number of seekers were unconvinced by his pat responses to their honest questions. Eventually, many of these probing questions became his own.[31] Fourth, his pastoral counseling sessions revealed little moral distinction between Christians and non-Christians.[32] Fifth, he was experiencing a mounting conviction that no honest systematic theology could do justice to the full range of biblical data. Sixth, he began noticing a dearth in quality Christian publishing. McLaren wondered, "Is there no Saint Francis or Soren Kierkegaard or C. S. Lewis in the house with some

---

[26] Ibid.

[27] Brian McLaren, "Rewriting Brethren Distinctives," *Christian Brethren Review* 125 (1991): 39–42.

[28] McLaren, *NKOC*, XIII.

[29] Ibid., XVII.

[30] Ibid.

[31] McLaren, *NKOCY*, 6–7. See also McLaren, "The Method, the Message, and the Ongoing Story" in *CIEC*, 194.

[32] McLaren, *NKOC*, XVII–XVIII.

fresh ideas and energy?"[33] Seventh, people both inside and outside the church began experiencing and proclaiming the end of the modern era.[34] These seven factors led McLaren to the brink of spiritual collapse.

The "Emerging McLaren" Era (1995–2005)

The insight into a significant cultural shift, however, gave McLaren the requisite resources to avert spiritual suicide and the necessary lens to begin crystallizing the problem.[35]

> Morning after morning I woke up in the brutal tension between something real and something wrong in the Christian faith. The sense of something real kept me in ministry and in the Christian faith; the sense of something wrong kept me looking for a way out. . . . And eventually, I began to get some sense of what to do to disentangle the one from the other, to hold on to the something real and let the other go.[36]

This tension between "something real" and "something wrong" is a key to understanding the early stages of McLaren's journey. McLaren was convinced that the "real" telling of the Christian story was worth retaining, but much had become ethically twisted. It took several years for McLaren to separate the ontological "something real" from the ethical "something wrong."[37]

Once McLaren started to figure it out, however, he began to write his first book, *The Church on the Other Side*.[38] He admits that authoring this

---

[33] Ibid. In response to this question asked by McLaren, *CT* columnist Mark Galli cited St. Francis, Kierkegaard, and Lewis as three paradigmatic examples of Christians who actually steered clear of novelty when communicating the gospel. Galli concludes his article by challenging McLaren's search for "fresh ideas and energy": "Early on, McLaren asks poignantly, 'Has the good news been reduced to the "good same-old same old?"' In fact, it needs to be expanded to the same-old, same-old." See Mark Galli, "The Virtue of Unoriginality," *CT* 46, no. 4 (April 1, 2002): 62.

[34] Gibbs and Bolger, *Emerging Churches*, 33–34.

[35] McLaren, *NKOC*, XIX.

[36] McLaren, *NKOCY*, 15–16.

[37] Chapter Four will explore in greater detail how the ethical "something wrong" was deeply entangled with five-point Calvinism.

[38] This book was originally entitled *Reinventing Your Church* (Grand Rapids: Zondervan, 1998). As McLaren's thinking continued to evolve during the next few years, he came to realize that the first edition of his book contained aspects of both the modern spirit and the church-growth vernacular that he was seeking to shed. In the preface to the second edition, McLaren explains that the original title expressed a modern flavor, evoking mechanical, engineering imagery which undercut the book's main thesis—namely, the need to rethink and recast Christian imagery into organic postmodern language and categories. See McLaren, *COOS*, 9.

book was also a "kind of self-therapy."[39] In this pragmatic monograph, McLaren offers thirteen strategies to assist practitioners in the shift from a modern to postmodern expression of ministry. At the start of this writing project, McLaren "didn't know a single author or pastor who saw what [he] was seeing."[40] During the writing, however, he discovered that Stanley Grenz, Sally Morgenthaler, Leonard Sweet, and Brian Walsh had all written books about ministry in postmodern culture.[41] Grenz's vision of the modern-to-postmodern shift especially influenced McLaren and other members of the ECM (see Appendix A).

In 1999, McLaren followed up with a second book, *Finding Faith*, which was an early attempt to offer a postmodern apologetic to contemporary atheists, agnostics, and seekers. Rather than writing as a scholar, McLaren states that he was attempting "to fill the role of a helpful friend."[42] The subtitle suggests McLaren's method: "A Self-Discovery Guide for Your Spiritual Quest." Instead of an evidential approach to apologetics, this book proposes a holistic, respectful strategy designed to assist rather than insist, guide rather than drive the reader to conclusions. As a central theme, McLaren distinguishes between "good faith" and "bad faith." According to McLaren, good faith is humble, teachable, integrated, curious, appreciative, communal, active, and tough, while honoring and pursuing truth, beauty, and goodness wherever it is found. Bad faith, by contrast, is arrogant, unwise, dishonest, exclusive, selfish, unteachable, coercive, needy, lacking in integrity, and based on unquestionable authority.[43] In this book, McLaren emphasizes orthopraxy over orthodoxy, a theme he continued to develop and nuance in subsequent works.

Also in 1999, McLaren wrote an article for *Mars Hill Review*.[44] In this essay, McLaren likened the transition from the modern to postmodern world to the differences between the original *Star Trek* and *Star Trek: The Next Generation*. Spock serves as the prototypical modern man, characterized by "cool, emotion-free, objective logic," while Data represents the

---

[39] Gibbs and Bolger, *Emerging Churches*, 285.
[40] McLaren, *NKOCY*, 9.
[41] Ibid.
[42] McLaren, *FF*, 21.
[43] Ibid., 27, 34–41.
[44] Brian McLaren, "Honey, I Woke Up in a Different Universe: Confessions of a Postmodern Pastor," *Mars Hill Review* 41 (Fall 1999): 35–46.

ideal postmodern individual, who is "more emotional, more involved, less detached and mechanistic."[45]

The influence of Grenz upon McLaren is evident in this article. Grenz originally used this same Star Trek analogy in a 1994 essay.[46] Spock, Data, and others from the Enterprise also were prominently featured when Grenz addressed the 1998 National Re:Evaluation Forum in Glorieta, New Mexico, the event that laid the foundation for the United States ECM.[47] Through this and similar events, McLaren was personally introduced to Grenz and many in the Young Leaders Network (YLN), an eclectic group that included Tony Jones, Andrew Jones, Doug Pagitt, Mark Driscoll, Brad Cecil, Chris Seay, Tim Conder, Dan Kimball, Karen Ward, Tim Keel, and Mark Scandrette.[48] This group showed McLaren that he was not alone in his questions and emotional turmoil.[49]

Tony Jones explains that the YLN was primarily concerned about "epistemic humility."[50] The group believed that many churches and seminaries had developed an intellectual and moral hubris in their "stands on doctrinal issues, polity, and social issues."[51] Through involvement with this group, McLaren would eventually meet several influential academicians, including Dallas Willard, John Franke, Alan Roxburgh, and Nancey Murphy.[52]

Interaction with the YLN, which transitioned into the Theological Working Group, the Terranova Project, and eventually Emergent Village,[53] proved indispensable in the production of *A New Kind of Christian*, the first installment in a trilogy of creative fiction and the book that would launch McLaren into the national spotlight.[54] In the acknowledgments section of *A New Kind of Christian*, McLaren writes, "It's hard to tell where one person's

---

[45] Ibid., 40.

[46] Stanley J. Grenz, "*Star Trek* and the Next Generation: Postmodernism and the Future of Evangelical Theology," *Crux* 30, no. 1 (March 1994): 24–32.

[47] Tony Jones, *The Church Is Flat* (Minneapolis: JoPa Group, 2011), i–ii.

[48] These young evangelicals were the leading lights of the YLN in the late 1990s. See Tony Jones, *The New Christians* (San Francisco: Jossey-Bass, 2008), 41–46.

[49] For a succinct overview of the US ECM, see Appendix A.

[50] Jones, *Church Is Flat*, ii.

[51] Ibid.

[52] Gibbs and Bolger, *Emerging Churches*, 285.

[53] Jones, *Church Is Flat*, i–ii, and Jones, *New Christians*, XVII, and 41–46.

[54] McLaren, *NKOC*, xi.

thinking ends and another's begins; I feel that these pages reflect our best thoughts, not just mine."[55]

In *A New Kind of Christian*, McLaren moved into the genre of philosophical dialogue[56] or dialogical essay.[57] *A New Kind of Christian* reflects McLaren's "semiautobiographical" quest,[58] a journey loosely illustrated in the interaction between troubled middle-aged pastor Dan Poole and Neil Oliver (aka Neo), a progressive high school science teacher and former Episcopal priest originally from the Caribbean. Neo tells Dan that he has an immigration problem. He is practicing a modern faith in a postmodern world and, consequently, suffering from an inability to transition from one-time period to another. In *The Church on the Other Side*, McLaren compares this problem to modern viruses in need of debugging.[59] In this work, however, McLaren uses the fictitious Neo as a mouthpiece to liken modern enculturation to bathing in "ten hormones," each of which represents a defining characteristic of the modern era.[60] The main contours of these characteristics can be correlated to Grenz's overview of the modern-to-postmodern shift.

MCLAREN'S TEN CHARACTERISTICS OF MODERNITY

1. Conquest and control
2. Mechanization
3. Analytical reason
4. Secular science
5. Absolute objectivity
6. Criticism
7. Modern nation-state and organization.
8. Individual human autonomy
9. Protestantism and institutional religion
10. Consumerism

See Appendix C for a summary of McLaren's marks of modernity

If these ten features of the modern era are accurate, Neo explains, then there are ten corresponding qualities or corrective "hormones" in the emerging postmodern era:

---

[55] Ibid.
[56] McLaren, *NKOC*, XXII.
[57] McLaren, *SWFOI*, xiii.
[58] McLaren, *NKOCY*, 10.
[59] McLaren, *COOS*, 197–206.
[60] McLaren, *NKOC*, 18.

MCLAREN'S TEN CORRECTIVES FOR MODERNITY

1. Postconquest
2. Postmechanistic
3. Postanalytical
4. Postsecular
5. Postobjective

6. Postcritical
7. Postorganizational
8. Postindividualistic
9. Post-Protestant
10. Postconsumeristic

See McLaren, *NKOC*, 19.

Much of McLaren's subsequent project following *A New Kind of Christian* has been an ever-crystallizing attempt to clarify what it means as a Christian to embody these corrective hormones in a postmodern, postcolonial world.

It is striking to note that Neo's presentation of modernity lacks any substantive engagement with philosophy and the key philosophers of the modern and postmodern eras.[61] As the conversation continues, Dan asks Neo, who holds a PhD in the philosophy of science, if he would be able to explain postmodern philosophy. Neo responds:

> I could, but I'm not sure it's necessary. We could go there if you want. You may have already noticed, perhaps with relief, that I've tried here to describe postmodernity without once mentioning Foucault, Derrida, Rorty, Fish, Baudrillard, or any of the other great philosophical lights of postmodernism. That omission is intentional: I believe it possible to describe postmodernity—the broad culture defined by its having moved beyond modernity—without having to go too deeply into postmodernism as a philosophy.[62]

In differentiating between *postmodernity* and *postmodernism*, McLaren is following the categorical distinction articulated by Grenz.[63] Although

---

[61] As the book continues, we find Neo addressing a group of Christian college students. He lays out chronologically how the world has advanced from the medieval mindset to our current postmodern climate. In this talk, Neo relies heavily upon C. S. Lewis's *The Discarded Image* (Cambridge: Cambridge University Press, 1964). Much of the content in this section grew out of a team-teaching experience between McLaren, John Franke, and David Dunbar at Biblical Seminary in 1998. See *NKOC*, 167–68.

[62] McLaren, *NKOC*, 19.

[63] Stanley J. Grenz, *A Primer on Postmodernism* (Grand Rapids: Eerdmans, 1996), 12.

McLaren and others in the ECM were "deeply interested in philosophy and theology,"[64] in *A New Kind of Christian* he was writing primarily to a nonacademic audience. In so doing, he was hoping to communicate the spirit of *postmodernity* without weighing down his reader with the overly technical baggage of *postmodernism*, which would likely turn some away.

A second reason for McLaren's hesitancy to wade too deeply into the philosophical minutiae surrounding the modern-to-postmodern transition would become apparent in his later writings, including the 2007 *An Emergent Manifesto of Hope*. In a contributing chapter, McLaren makes it clear where his real concern lies. Discussion of the postmodern milieu, along with all of the associated esoteric details, is for McLaren simply a means to an end. The real issue for McLaren is not postmodern epistemology, but rather the ethical implications of postcolonialism. He elaborates,

> I am not too concerned whether or not a person is a philo-
> sophical foundationalist, whether or not he or she agrees with
> (or understands) the correspondence theory of truth, or how
> enlightened he or she is about the Enlightenment, Descartes,
> Derrida, Reid, or Rorty. (Instead I'm more concerned whether
> the person is doing justice, loving mercy, and walking humbly
> with God.) . . . More important, though, I've become convinced
> that the conversation about modernity and postmodernity is
> the "tails" side of the coin, and the "heads" side is a related but
> different conversation. So I am hereby giving notice that I'm not
> interested in arguing with anyone about modernity and postmo-
> dernity, but I would very much like to engage in honest conver-
> sation about colonialism and postcolonialism.[65]

This shift from the "tails" to the "heads" side of the coin would prove to be a key factor in the transition from the "Emerging McLaren" era to the "Emergent McLaren" era. In 2001, however, McLaren was still primarily focused on the postmodern "tails" side of the coin.

---

[64] McLaren, "Introduction" in *JP*, 15.

[65] Brian McLaren, "Church Emerging: Or Why I Still Use the Word *Postmodern* but with Mixed Feelings," in *Emergent Manifesto of Hope,* eds. Doug Pagitt and Tony Jones (Grand Rapids: Baker, 2007), 142–51, citing 143.

The publishing of *A New Kind of Christian* gave McLaren a national platform. Tony Jones tells how Phyllis Tickle was holding a press conference during the 2001 Christian Booksellers Association Convention when one reporter asked her: "Other than Rick Warren's *Purpose-Driven Church*, what is one book here that you think will be around for a long time? A book we haven't heard of?" Tickle "without hesitation" endorsed McLaren's *A New Kind of Christian*.[66] Jones continues, "Legend has it that the reporters and publishers left the press conference and walked en masse to the Jossey-Bass booth, where Brian was besieged with book-signing requests."[67]

A New Kind of Christian was selected for a *CT* award of merit,[68] and it has since achieved ECM "canonical" status, according to James Bielo.[69] The success of this book also opened the door to critical engagement with McLaren's work. *Christianity Today* periodicals ran no less than six articles dealing with *A New Kind of Christian*, including three separate in-depth reviews in *Books and Culture (B&C)*, followed by a response from McLaren.[70] In his article, McLaren notes that the majority of feedback concerning *A New Kind of Christian* had been positive; in fact, "very seldom is heard a discouraging word."[71] He cites with appreciation the *B&C* reviews by Andy Crouch and Tony Jones, but he notes that Mark Dever, pastor of Capitol Hill Baptist Church in Washington, DC, found *A New Kind of Christian* to be "downright bad."[72] Dever's review was one of the first of many Calvinist critiques of McLaren's work.

McLaren's fourth solo project, *More Ready Than You Realize*, focuses on postmodern evangelism as spiritual friendship.[73] McLaren uses the example

---

[66] Jones, *New Christians*, 50.

[67] Ibid.

[68] McLaren, *NKOC*, 171.

[69] Bielo claims that *NKOC* is "one of the most often-cited as formative by my [ECM] consultants." See James S. Bielo, *Emerging Evangelicals* (New York: New York University Press, 2011), 38.

[70] The family of *CT* periodicals includes *Christianity Today*, *Books & Culture*, and *Leadership Journal*, all publications that ran articles on *NKOC*. The three *B&C* articles were: Andy Crouch, "Let's Get Personal: Yes, the Church Needs to Get Past Modernity's Impersonal Techniques. But Adding the Prefix 'Post' Doesn't Solve Anything," *B&C* 8, no. 1 (January/February 2002): 12; Mark Dever, "Reformed or Deformed? Questions for Postmodern Christians," *B&C* 8, no. 2 (March /April 2002): 26–27; and Tony Jones, "Post-Evangelicalism: Last in a Series of Responses to Brian McLaren's Book, *A New Kind of Christian*," *B&C* 8, no. 3 (May/June 2002): 32.

[71] Brian McLaren, "Faithfully Dangerous: Christians in Postmodern Times," *B&C* 8, no. 3 (May/June 2002): 33.

[72] Ibid.

[73] This should be distinguished from "friendship evangelism," something Neo rejects because it sounds like friendship is the manipulative means to an end. McLaren, *NKOC*, 103–9.

of Jesus, the conversationalist, to illustrate his understanding of the differences between modern and postmodern approaches to evangelism:

> Unlike the typical evangelist-caricature of the late twentieth and early twenty-first centuries, Jesus was short on sermons, long on conversations; short on answers, long on questions; short on abstractions and propositions, long on stories and parables; short on telling you what to think, long on challenging you to think for yourself; short on condemning the irreligious, long on confronting the religious. . . . This is the kind of evangelism we are going to explore in this book. Evangelism in the style of Jesus; evangelism that flows like a dance.[74]

As in *A New Kind of Christian*, McLaren focuses on *showing* rather than *telling* the reader how evangelism ought to be done in a postmodern setting. In *More Ready Than You Realize*, McLaren shares portions of an actual ongoing email exchange with a postmodern seeker that covers topics ranging from homosexuality to divine sovereignty as McLaren's conversation partner eventually comes to faith. Woven in between emails are commentary and suggestions to readers. The book received high praise from Sally Morgenthaler, who called it "the postmodern sequel to C. S. Lewis's *Mere Christianity*."[75]

In 2003, McLaren contributed to three co-authored volumes: *A Is for Abductive*, *Adventures in Missing the Point*, and *The Church in Emerging Culture*. In *The Church in Emerging Culture*, each contributor discussed the interrelationship between message and methodology in communicating the faith to contemporary society.[76] Leonard Sweet, who wrote the introduction, distinguished between four approaches:

- *Garden* (preserving message/preserving methods)
- *Park* (preserving message/evolving methods)
- *Glen* (evolving message/preserving methods)
- *Meadow* (evolving message/evolving methods).[77]

---

[74] McLaren, *MRTYR*, 15.

[75] Ibid., back cover.

[76] Sweet interacts with the categories introduced by H. Richard Niebuhr in his classic treatise *Christ and Culture* (San Francisco: Harper, 2001), but argues that the advent of postmodernity requires expanding Niebuhr's options.

[77] Sweet, "Introduction: Garden, Park, Glen, Meadow," in *CIEC*, 13–41.

McLaren argued for the final model, the most fluid of the four. He received the sharpest critique from Calvinist apologist Michael Horton, who defended the second model of unchanging message/ever-changing methodology.[78]

Unwilling to distill the gospel to bite-size, easy-to-deliver packaging,[79] McLaren describes the gospel as "the story of Jesus, the story leading up to Jesus, the story of what Jesus said and did, the story of what happened as a result, of what has been happening more recently, even today."[80] Because the gospel is always contextualized, and context is always changing, different facets of the story will emerge in different historical and social scenarios.[81] McLaren does not believe there is a universal, abstract, timeless essence to the gospel message that transcends each concrete situation. While sympathetic to the demands of missiological nuance, Horton finds McLaren's proposal lacking.

> While we should avoid simply repeating the words of past witnesses, Brian's own example should warn us against rewriting the gospel for each generation. Reconciliation with God through the perfect obedience, satisfaction, and victory of his Son is just the answer for those in every time and place who have been faced with the reality of God and their guilt.[82]

The second installment in the *New Kind of Christian* trilogy was released in 2003. In *The Story We Find Ourselves In*, McLaren introduces a pastor's daughter named Kerry, who rejects her faith to become an evolutionary biologist.[83] Eventually, Kerry meets Neo, who helps her reconcile the Christian faith with the facts of evolution. In so doing, Neo explains

---

[78] Sweet, "Introduction to the Contributors," in *CIEC*, 53.

[79] McLaren, "The Method, the Message, and the Ongoing Story," in *CIEC*, 195. McLaren uses the examples of "the Four Spiritual Laws," "Romans Road," and "the Bridge" to illustrate the kind of modern methodology that should be avoided in the postmodern world.

[80] Ibid., 214.

[81] Elsewhere, McLaren likens his approach to that of Marshall McLuhan, who proclaimed that the medium is the message. See McLaren, "Introduction," in *JP*, 15.

[82] McLaren, "The Method, the Message, and the Ongoing Story," in *CIEC*, 218. Horton, the editor-in-chief of *Modern Reformation*, also would devote space to McLaren and the ECM in a 2005 issue. The tension exhibited here between Horton and McLaren is described elsewhere by Grenz as the modern-to-postmodern "transition from realism to social construction and from the metanarrative to local stories." See Stanley J. Grenz, *Renewing the Center*, 2nd ed. (Grand Rapids: Baker Academic, 2006), 176–83.

[83] McLaren, *SWFOI*, 7.

how the Bible can be read as an unfolding narrative, an evolving drama of ongoing creative partnership. By viewing the Bible in this dynamic way, rather than as a modern static, inerrant, propositional answer book, Kerry finds an angle on Christianity that is compelling and satisfying. *The Story We Find Ourselves in* marked a turn in McLaren's writing from explaining the nature of postmodernity to describing the Christian story from within the postmodern framework. In other words, he shifted from deconstruction to concrete reconstruction.[84]

> The more I have written about postmodernity (and so on), the more I have wanted to get to the point where it no longer needed to be written about so much. I wanted to start writing more directly about the Christian gospel itself, from a vantage point within the emerging culture, without always having to describe, validate, and defend the vantage point.[85]

The following year proved to be pivotal for several reasons. First, Stanley Grenz, who had become a close personal friend and mentor, recommended McLaren to receive an honorary doctor of divinity degree from Carey Theological College.[86] Second, McLaren began writing for *Sojourners*, a progressive Christian social activist periodical founded by Jim Wallis. While McLaren continued to contribute to *CT* publications, this signaled a shift in his focus and affiliation. Third, *CT* published a major in-depth feature story entitled "Emergent Mystique,"[87] to which McLaren responded on his blog.[88]

Fourth, McLaren's most controversial monograph to date was released. Tickle gave McLaren another boost by drawing connections to Luther:

---

[84] It should be noted, however, that while McLaren spoke less about the modern-to-postmodern transition after this book, his deconstructive/reconstructive project did not fully crystallize until the 2010 *NKOCY*.

[85] McLaren, *SWFOI*, xii.

[86] Brian McLaren, "Foreword," in Grenz, *Renewing the Center*, 8.

[87] Phil Johnson identifies this article as the "first major story about the movement." While he was acquainted with the ECM before this article, Johnson writes that this piece "seemed to introduce the ECM to many in the evangelical mainstream for the very first time." See Phil Johnson, "Joyriding on the Downgrade at Breakneck Speed," in *Reforming or Conforming?*, eds. Gary L. W. Johnson and Ronald N. Gleason (Wheaton: Crossway, 2008), 211.

[88] See Brian McLaren, "Annotation to 'The Emergent Mystique'—CT Article," *brian d. mclaren* (blog), October 22, 2004, http://www.brianmclaren.net/archives/000271.html.

In the same way that Martin Luther became the symbolic leader and spokesman for the Great Reformation, so too has Brian McLaren become the symbolic leader and spokesman for the Great Emergence. His 2005 volume *A Generous Orthodoxy* (Zondervan) is both an analog to Luther's ninety-five theses and also a clearly stated overview of many of the parts of post-Constantinian Christian theology that are now undergoing reconsideration.[89]

McLaren did not coin the phrase "generous orthodoxy," and he acknowledges his debt to both Hans Frei and Grenz.[90] This book, which has been labeled an "Emergent Manifesto,"[91] describes an inclusive vision that weaves together salient elements from a variety of traditions to construct a shared "ancient-future" Christian tapestry for the postmodern world.[92] Operating from a stated commitment to the historic ecumenical creeds, McLaren assesses strengths and weaknesses in multiple traditions and calls for adherents to separate the gold from the dross for the collective benefit of the whole Christian tradition. While Morgenthaler had called *More Ready Than You Realize* the "postmodern sequel to C. S. Lewis's *Mere Christianity*," *A Generous Orthodoxy* more accurately mirrors what Lewis attempted to do in that classic work—namely, identify a common core around which all Christians could agreeably unite.

In the introduction, however, McLaren offers a warning: "As in most of my other books, there are places here where I have gone out of my way to be provocative, mischievous, and unclear, reflecting my belief that clarity is sometimes overrated, and that shock, obscurity, playfulness, and intrigue (carefully articulated) often stimulate more thought than clarity."[93] According to John Franke, who wrote the foreword to *A Generous Orthodoxy*, McLaren's peculiar strategy is intended to "encourage readers to think and enter into the conversation themselves."[94] This strategy is not

---

[89] Tickle, *Great Emergence*, 164. Tickle mistakenly identifies the publishing year of *GO* as 2005 instead of 2004.

[90] McLaren, *GO*, 25.

[91] McLaren, *LWWAT*, 202.

[92] McLaren, *GO*, 18.

[93] Ibid., 22–23.

[94] John R. Franke, "Generous Orthodoxy and a Changing World," Foreword to *GO*, 14.

entirely new to McLaren and can, in fact, ultimately be traced back to his master's thesis on novelist Walker Percy. In summarizing Percy's literary apologetic strategy, McLaren writes:

> Walker Percy is a religious writer incognito. He practices his evangelical craft with deceitfulness and cunning, following the model of an earlier crafty religious writer, Soren Kierkegaard. His audience generally considers the Christian message—which is Percy's message—at best an interesting body of largely irrelevant knowledge and at worst a tiresome, worn out, offensive commercial for heaven which is no longer worthy of serious consideration at all. Naturally, to communicate such a message to such an audience calls for conscious deception and calculated obliqueness.[95]

McLaren is employing a similar "crafty" strategy with "calculated obliqueness" in *A Generous Orthodoxy* for the purpose of arresting the attention of his audience and drawing them deeper into the conversation. In so doing, the spirit of his writing is intentionally paradoxical and provocative.

This book elicited strong responses. Tickle recounts the impact that *A Generous Orthodoxy* had upon the former Archbishop of Canterbury Rowan Williams, who allegedly read *A Generous Orthodoxy* on a flight and when finished expressed his desire to "buy up all the available copies of the book, hire a fleet of airplanes, and air-drop those copies all over the United Kingdom."[96] Craig L. Blomberg, distinguished professor of New Testament at Denver Seminary, also expressed support in a critically appreciative review:

> I am far more enthusiastic about this volume than worried over it. What worries me are the growing numbers of people who are worried about it. What does this portend if not an ungenerous orthodoxy that draws ever-narrowing boundaries around what counts as authentic Christianity, thereby alienating even more

---

[95] McLaren, WP, i.
[96] Phyllis Tickle, *Emergence Christianity* (Grand Rapids: Baker, 2012), 101.

onlookers from the very faith they already see as too judgmental and divisive?[97]

Among the growing numbers worried about this book were Reformed scholars John MacArthur, David Wells, and Albert Mohler. In *The Truth War*, MacArthur states that he was particularly troubled by McLaren's provocative strategy: "Advocating ambiguity, exalting uncertainty, or otherwise deliberately clouding the truth is a sinful way of nurturing unbelief."[98] In *The Courage to Be Protestant*, Wells refused to mince words: "This book is neither generous to those who take a more traditional Christian position, nor is it orthodox. The author has apparently no respect for those who have gone before him and who contributed the classical understandings of Christian faith."[99] Mohler expressed similar concerns in *The Disappearance of God:*

> This author's purpose is transparent and consistent. Following the worldview of the postmodern age, he embraces relativism at the cost of clarity in matters of truth and intends to redefine Christianity for this new age, largely in terms of an eccentric mixture of elements he would take from virtually every theological position and variant.[100]

Mohler goes on to challenge McLaren's apparent lack of resolve to take a stand on any issue, including questions surrounding eternal damnation and homosexuality. He concludes that McLaren "is a man who doesn't want to offend anyone on any side of any argument. That's why it is hard to find the orthodoxy in *A Generous Orthodoxy*."[101]

---

[97] Craig L. Blomberg, "Review of *A Generous Orthodoxy*," *Denver Journal* 7 (November 1, 2004), http://www.denverseminary.edu/article/a-generous-orthodoxy-review-by-craig-blomberg.

[98] John MacArthur, *The Truth War* (Nashville: Thomas Nelson, 2007), xi. MacArthur is a pastor and the president of the Master's College and Seminary.

[99] David. F. Wells, *The Courage to Be Protestant* (Grand Rapids: Eerdmans, 2008), 87. Wells is a distinguished senior research professor at Gordon-Conwell Theological Seminary.

[100] R. Albert Mohler Jr., *The Disappearance of God* (Colorado Springs: Multnomah, 2009), 99. Mohler is the president of Southern Baptist Theological Seminary.

[101] Ibid., 100. Carson also reports that McLaren, at the 2004 Emergent Conference in Nashville, answered a question about homosexuality by saying, "There is no good position, because all positions hurt someone, and that is always bad." See D. A. Carson, *Becoming Conversant with the Emerging Church* (Grand Rapids: Zondervan, 2004), 34–35.

It is curious that Mohler would question McLaren's hesitancy to "offend anyone on any side of any argument," since he, Wells, MacArthur, and other commentators in the Reformed tradition were clearly provoked by the treatment of Calvinism in *A Generous Orthodoxy*. While McLaren writes tentatively at times and with ambiguity in places throughout this book, he is clear and forthright in his wholesale rejection of five-point Calvinism, calling for a sweeping reformation of Reformed theology—including total depravity, unconditional election, and the penal substitutionary theory of the atonement.[102]

In *The Last Word and the Word After That*, the final installment in the *New Kind of Christian* trilogy, McLaren challenges the traditional doctrine of eternal damnation and attempts to reframe the issue of homosexuality. This novel begins with pastor Dan Poole's daughter, Jess, a college student at the University of Maryland, asking her father questions about the existence of hell. Jess laments, "If Christianity is true, then all the people I love except for a few will burn in hell forever. But if Christianity is not true, then life doesn't seem to have much meaning or hope. I wish I could find a better option."[103] This question "found the Achilles' heel, so to speak, of [Dan's] own theology."[104] While a fictional daughter raises this query, it was actually a question posed by one of McLaren's young adult sons.[105] McLaren's inability to provide a satisfying answer helped fuel the development of this book. Likewise, Dan's inability to provide satisfying answers for Jess fuels a historical research project that culminates in an alternative understanding of this doctrine.

Dan concludes that the Old Testament is silent on the subject of hell. Rather than originating as a Hebrew concept, this doctrine entered the Jewish consciousness during the intertestamental period through Mesopotamian, Egyptian, Zoroastrian, and Greek sources.[106] Additionally, Dan surmises that Jesus did not believe or teach hell as a place or state of eternal conscious

---

[102] McLaren, *GO*, 183–198.

[103] McLaren, *LWWAT*, 5.

[104] Ibid.

[105] See McLaren, *GO*, 49, and *LWWAT*, 182.

[106] McLaren, *LWWAT*, 49–73. McLaren's view of eternal damnation was informed by various sources, including the work of Jan Bonda and Edward Fudge. See Jan Bonda, *The One Purpose of God* (Grand Rapids: Eerdmans, 1998), and Edward Fudge, *The Fire That Consumes* (Carlisle: Paternoster, 1994).

torment. Rather, Jesus deconstructed the Pharisees' use of the term and turned it on its head for rhetorical effect.[107] While Dan and his family are coming to terms with an alternative interpretation of hell, they are also befriending a lesbian parishioner. Without offering a definitive answer on the homosexuality question,[108] this book seeks to humanize LGBT persons and deconstruct what McLaren believes are unhelpful dualistic categories.

The year 2005 would be the final installment in the "Emerging McLaren" era. Four factors converged to make this a pivotal year for McLaren's ministerial trajectory.

National Media Coverage

Time magazine selected McLaren as one of "the 25 most influential evangelicals in America."[109] Through the impact of *A Generous Orthodoxy* and *A New Kind of Christian*, which David Van Biema claims was "enormously popular in seminaries," McLaren gained an expanded platform.[110] His selection by *Time* led to interviews with national media and appearances on *Larry King Live, Nightline,* and *Religion & Ethics Newsweekly.*[111]

Ministry Expansion

McLaren decided to resign the pastorate after twenty-four years. The demands upon his time and schedule were unsustainable. As one of the leading voices in the ECM, he decided to become a full-time writer, speaker, consultant, and activist.

---

[107] Ibid., 74–81.

[108] In 2006, when McLaren was asked about his stance on homosexuality and the church, he offered an uncertain response, requesting time to ponder, research, and study the issue. He wrote, "Perhaps we need a five-year moratorium on making pronouncements. In the meantime, we'll practice prayerful Christian dialogue, listening respectfully, disagreeing agreeably. When decisions need to be made, they'll be admittedly provisional. We'll keep our ears attuned to scholars in biblical studies, theology, ethics, psychology, genetics, sociology, and related fields. Then in five years, if we have clarity, we'll speak. If not, we'll set another five years for ongoing reflection." See Brian McLaren, "Brian McLaren on the Homosexual Question: Finding a Pastoral Response," on *Parse* website, January 23, 2006, http://www.christianitytoday.com/parse/2006/january/brian-mclaren-on-homosexual-question-finding-pastoral.html.

[109] David Van Biema, "The 25 Most Influential Evangelicals in America," *Time* 165, no. 6 (February 7, 2005): 34–45, citing 45.

[110] Ibid., 45. See also McLaren, *NKOCY,* 11. McLaren mentions not only *NKOC* but also *GO* as the two books most popular "in reading groups, seminary classes, conferences, and retreats."

[111] McLaren, *FOWA,* 215.

The Postmodern-to-Postcolonial Shift

While the "Emerging McLaren" era began with placing a premium on the importance of the modern-to-postmodern shift, it was concluding with an increasing awareness of the need to address postmodernism less and post-colonialism more. This impulse also contributed to McLaren's decision to resign the pastorate and serve as an international ambassador for Emergent.

Critical Engagement

McLaren's expanding influence and increasingly controversial books caught the attention of evangelical church leaders and scholars. In *The Younger Evangelicals*, Robert Webber had already labeled McLaren the "guru of younger evangelical pastors."[112] Webber divides the history of American Evangelicalism into three groups or eras: Traditional Evangelicals (1950–1975), Pragmatic Evangelicals (1975–2000), and Younger Evangelicals (2000–present). Webber associates one key leader with each of these distinct phases of Evangelicalism. For the traditional evangelicals Billy Graham led the way, for the pragmatic evangelicals Bill Hybels was the iconic figure, and for the younger evangelicals Brian McLaren was identified as the face and voice of the movement.[113]

In a less favorable treatment, entitled *Reclaiming the Center,* Justin Taylor named Grenz as the professor, McLaren as the pastor, and Roger Olson and Robert Webber as the publicists of the postconservative movement that his book was seeking to challenge.[114] Two contributors to *Reclaiming the Center*, D. A. Carson and R. Scott Smith, would in 2005 publish the first book-length academic challenges to the ECM in general and McLaren in particular. Both would take aim primarily at McLaren's postmodern epistemology.

Carson's *Becoming Conversant with the Emerging Church* would serve as the touchstone critique for many in Calvinist circles. A lecture series at Cedarville University inspired the book, which critiques the ECM in general, but much of his interaction is focused on McLaren. The bulk of the

---

[112] Robert E. Webber, *The Younger Evangelicals* (Grand Rapids: Baker, 2002), 114.

[113] Ibid., 16.

[114] Justin Taylor, "An Introduction to Postconservative Evangelicalism" in *Reclaiming the Center*, ed. Millard J. Erickson et al. (Wheaton: Crossway, 2004), 17–32, citing 18–26.

critique is centered on Carson's general concerns with the ECM which are manifested in McLaren, whose writing he calls at various junctures "snide," "manipulative," "ignorant," "resoundingly false," "silly," "sly," "slippery," and "shallow."[115] Carson accuses the ECM and McLaren of misrepresenting the modern-to-postmodern shift, accommodating to postmodern culture, mishandling Scripture, and disrespecting confessional Christianity.

The other key book to surface in 2005 was Smith's *Truth and the New Kind of Christian*, in which the author interacts extensively with McLaren and Tony Jones.[116] Like Carson, Smith focuses primarily on the issue of postmodern epistemology. Unlike Carson, however, Smith exhibits a willingness to dialogue with McLaren, Jones, and others in the ECM. Smith believes "McLaren offers perhaps the most carefully nuanced, thoughtful viewpoints on the practical effects of modernity upon the church."[117] Nevertheless, Smith challenges McLaren's critique of modernity and his alleged endorsement of postmodern epistemology.

After *Truth and the New Kind of Christian* was published, Smith and McLaren contributed articles to *Criswell Theological Review*[118] and exchanged email. This dialogue changed Smith's mind on several issues. Smith realized that he had misconstrued McLaren as a hard postmodernist. He also acknowledged McLaren's lack of interest in epistemology and his shift to ethical and social issues.[119] By exhibiting a willingness to dialogue and revise his critique, Smith modeled what Carson and several other interlocutors have refused to do with the ECM in general and McLaren in particular—namely, engage in irenic, critically appreciative Christian scholarship that honors the pursuit of truth without forfeiting a charitable spirit.

This decade saw McLaren working out his theology in a public manner, often through the main protagonists of Dan Poole and Neil Oliver. By the end of 2005, however, the "emerging" McLaren was giving way to "emergent" McLaren as he began to find more definite answers to the many questions he had been raising.

---

[115] Carson, *Becoming Conversant*, 65, 162, 159, 175, and 177, respectively.

[116] R. Scott Smith, *Truth and the New Kind of Christian* (Wheaton: Crossway, 2005).

[117] Ibid., 49.

[118] See Streett, "An Interview with Brian McLaren," 5–14, and R. Scott Smith, "Some Suggestions for Brian McLaren," in *Criswell Theological Review* 3, no. 2 (Spring 2006): 67–85.

[119] See R. Scott Smith, "Reflections on McLaren and the Emerging Church," in *Passionate Conviction*, ed. Paul Copan and William Lane Craig (Nashville: B&H, 2007), 234–37.

The "Emergent McLaren" Era (2006–present)

While the "Emerging McLaren" era began with placing a premium on the importance of the modern-to-postmodern shift, it concluded with an increasing awareness of the need to address postmodernity less and postcolonialism more. While McLaren was generally aware of the connection between western European overconfidence and colonialism when he wrote *A New Kind of Christian*, he did not appreciate fully the interrelationship until African theologian Mabiala Kenzo[120] explained postmodernity and postcolonialism as opposite sides of the same coin.[121] According to Kenzo, the conversation in the West has focused on epistemology. The emergence of the postmodern critique, consequently, has helped undermine the hubris of the Enlightenment project. In the global South, however, the conversation has centered on postcolonialism and how oppressed people groups might rebuild the confidence that was stripped away by Western colonizers.[122]

This impulse also contributed to McLaren's decision to resign his position at Cedar Ridge Community Church to serve as an international ambassador for Emergent. McLaren already had been traveling extensively around the country speaking to colleges, seminaries, and churches. During the next two years, however, he expanded his travel to more than twenty countries, concentrating on international networking and issues of poverty, peace, and justice.[123] His international travel and conversations with leaders in the global South made him increasingly sensitive to postcolonial perspectives and concerns.[124]

As McLaren entered this new season of ministry, he moved from discussing the postmodern transition to exploring the temporal implications of Jesus's kingdom of God vision. In an interview with *Criswell Theological Review*, McLaren explained how this shift in understanding the kingdom was significant: "Like many people, I formerly understood kingdom of God to refer to heaven after this life, with a kind of backlight cast on this life. Now, I see kingdom as primarily being about God's will being done on

---

[120] Kenzo is the president of the Evangelical Community of the Alliance in the Congo.

[121] Brian McLaren, "Why Postcolonial Conversations Matter" in *Evangelical Postcolonial Conversations*, ed. Kay Higuera Smith et al. (Downers Grove: InterVarsity Press, 2014), 13–15.

[122] McLaren, *EMC*, 303.

[123] Ibid., 6.

[124] Lee and Sinitiere, *Holy Mavericks*, 101.

earth, in history, with a forward light cast beyond this life."[125] McLaren had long argued that evangelicals frequently are guilty of reducing the gospel message to individual salvation, shifting the focus from present social and environmental concerns to eschatology, often with a sensationalistic apocalyptic twist.[126] In so doing, Christians are prone to ignoring many problems in the contemporary world.

In his next two books, McLaren would seek to crystallize the practical, temporal implications of the gospel. In *The Secret Message of Jesus*, McLaren explored the social, political, and cultural context of first-century Palestine in order to illuminate Jesus's proclamation of the kingdom of God. This was not McLaren's first extended engagement with Scripture. In the second and third installments in the *New Kind of Christian* trilogy, McLaren explored the Bible through the lens of narrative theology and wrestled with the doctrine of eternal damnation in light of key biblical texts. In *The Secret Message of Jesus*, however, McLaren offers his first sustained treatment of Jesus of Nazareth and his kingdom vision.

McLaren argues that Jesus "concealed his deepest message,"[127] so that people would need to seek carefully and intentionally to find it. McLaren does not claim to have it entirely crystallized but is confident he is "on to something." McLaren contends that a renewed appreciation for the historical, cultural, and political context of first-century Palestine will illuminate properly Jesus's "secret" message as a countercultural revolutionary call to live out the gospel in stark contrast to the dictates of Caesar, on the one hand, and the popular Jewish strategies designed to overthrow the Roman empire, on the other. Rather than following the reclusive Essenes, judgmental Pharisees, violent Zealots, or compromising Herodians and Sadducees, the kingdom of God ethos is a call to turn the other cheek, go the second mile, overcome evil with good, and love enemies.[128]

In *Everything Must Change*, McLaren focuses on how Jesus might address some of the most critical challenges facing the world today. Coupled with the book release was a twelve-city national campaign, appropriately

---

[125] Streett, "An Interview with Brian McLaren," 7.
[126] McLaren, *SMJ*, 14–18. See also *GO*, 43–68, and *EMC*, 1–8.
[127] McLaren, *SMJ*, 4.
[128] Ibid., xii, 9–25.

called "The Everything Must Change Tour." In this follow-up work, which relies upon the paradigm introduced in *The Secret Message of Jesus*, McLaren argues that our world is caught in the clutches of a systemic "societal suicide machine,"[129] fueled by global prosperity, equity, and security crises. McLaren writes, "All attempts to resolve these systemic crises—the *prosperity* crisis of the planet, the *equity* crisis of poverty, and the *security* crisis of peacemaking—fail in solution deadlock because they fail to address the fourth crisis, the *spirituality* crisis, the crisis of hope." McLaren argues that Jesus's kingdom of God message "confronts the suicidal societal machinery and seeks to transform it from a suicidal system into a sacred global community."[130]

While McLaren relies upon paradox, hyperbole, and other playful literary techniques in *A Generous Orthodoxy* to invite the reader deeper into conversation and to encourage a person-relative pace, the strategy in these two books is more direct and urgent: "In one of my previous books, I said that clarity is sometimes overrated and that intrigue is correspondingly undervalued. But here I want to say—clearly—that it is tragic for anyone, especially anyone affiliated with the religion named after Jesus, not to be clear about what Jesus' message actually was."[131]

McLaren discloses the need for a clear, non-circuitous approach, which is a guiding force behind these two books. He believes that global peace could hinge upon a proper perception of Jesus, and calibrating that perception is a matter of extreme exigency. Despite the differences among world religions and the negative associations linked to Christians and the Christian religion, Jesus of Nazareth is still respected by Muslims "as a great prophet," by Hindus "as a legitimate manifestation of the divine," and by Buddhists "as one of humanity's most enlightened people."[132]

McLaren also underscores the importance of appreciating the Jewishness of Jesus for a proper interpretation of his teachings. McLaren concludes with the following pressing pronouncement:

> A shared reappraisal of Jesus' message could provide a unique space or common ground for urgently needed religious

---

[129] McLaren credits the term "suicide machine" to Leonard Sweet. See McLaren, *EMC*, v.
[130] Ibid., 313.
[131] Ibid., 7.
[132] McLaren, *SMJ*, 7.

dialogue—and it doesn't seem an exaggeration to say that the future of our planet may depend on such dialogue. This reappraisal of Jesus' message may be the only project capable of saving a number of religions, including Christianity, from a number of threats, from being co-opted by consumerism or nationalism to the rise of potentially violent fundamentalism in their own ranks.[133]

McLaren's engagement in interfaith dialogue[134] and turn toward the social and political dimensions of the gospel, including campaigning for the Barack Obama presidency in 2008, caused a stir.[135] Supporting the Democratic nominee would not only further alienate McLaren from conservative evangelicals, but also raise questions among some of his colleagues. In response to McLaren's political engagement, former co-author Leonard Sweet opined:

> We got to this point in the '70s where you could not tell the difference between the Democratic Party platform and the Church's portrayal of the Kingdom of God. I think that any intrusion of Christianity into politics—whether Right or Left—is ugly. So I don't see Jesus as coming with a political agenda. Yes, there are radical social and economic consequences to His message, but to claim that Jesus' message was a political one [is incorrect]. It's Jim Wallis' evangelical updating of the Social Gospel movement, or liberalism's liberation theology of the '70s and '80s.[136]

---

[133] Ibid., 7–8.

[134] McLaren's decision to join Muslim friends in celebrating Ramadan also raised several eyebrows in the Christian community. See Brian McLaren, "Ramadan 2009: Part 1 What's Going On?" *brian d. mclaren* (blog), August 13, 2009, http://www.brianmclaren.net/archives/blog/ramadan-2009-part-1-whats-going.html.

[135] McLaren's campaign trail included a stop in Marion, IN, where the author of this book and approximately fifty other people interacted with him in an informal setting. It should be noted that McLaren's political engagement did not begin with his support of the Obama campaign. In 2003, he wrote a fictitious sermon for the president. See Brian McLaren, "A Sermon for President Bush," *brian d. mclaren* (blog), n.d., accessed February 16, 2014, http://www.brianmclaren.net/emc/archives/imported/a-sermon-for-president-bush.html. In 2006, McLaren also was arrested as part of a peaceful demonstration against welfare budget cuts. See Brian McLaren, "Jim Wallis Gets It Right on Theology and Health Care Reform, Part 1," *brian d. mclaren* (blog), n.d., accessed February 16, 2014, http://brianmclaren.net/archives/blog/jim-wallis-gets-it-right-on-theo.html.

[136] Peter J. Walker and Tyler Clark, "From the Mag: Missing the Point," *Relevant* 21 (July/August 2006), posted online October 2, 2007, http://www.relevantmagazine.com/god/church/features/1360-from-the-mag-missing-the-point.

Over the next few years, McLaren would contribute essays to *An Emergent Manifesto of Hope* and *The Justice Project*, two volumes that created space for a variety of emergent voices on divergent topics, from spiritual formation, ecclesiology, and evangelism to biblical hermeneutics, postcolonialism, and social justice. McLaren would also serve as translator for the Luke and Acts contributions to the *The Voice* series, described by the publisher as a "Scripture project to rediscover the story of the Bible."[137]

This new direction or expanded emphasis prompted *CT* in 2008 to run an evaluation of McLaren's recent books. "McLaren Emerging" was a critically appreciative assessment written by Scot McKnight, who called McLaren's work "a rich source for Christian imagination, vision, and reflection."[138] He also stated that McLaren, who functions as "emergent's pastor and confessing priest," is without equal when it comes to expressing, "like a beat poet, both the ironic faith of emergents . . . and a strong sense of how the gospel should be lived today."[139] McKnight readily concurred that evangelicals often have ignored the social and political dimensions of the faith, and McLaren's call to recapture these dimensions provides a helpful corrective. That said, McKnight also offered some critical commentary that focused on the need for McLaren to be more forthright in clarifying his doctrinal views, particularly his theory of the atonement and the relationship between the kingdom of God and the church.

During the next few years, McLaren turned his attention to the relatively placid topic of spiritual formation in *Finding Our Way Again* and *Naked Spirituality*. By 2010, however, he reentered the world of turbulence with *A New Kind of Christianity*, the book that many McLaren followers and critics had eagerly awaited. In this monograph, McLaren finally offers a comprehensive and crystallized account of his emergent beliefs by addressing ten of the most important questions facing contemporary Christianity.

> In all my books to date, I feel that I've been excavating, scraping away layers of debris, trying to get to the core issues that need to be courageously addressed in our lifetimes. This is the book where I feel I've gotten down to ten bedrock issues—which,

---

[137] McLaren, *VL*, vii.
[138] Scot McKnight, "McLaren Emerging," *CT* 52, no. 9 (September 2008): 58–66, citing 60.
[139] Ibid.

as the subtitle suggests, I've articulated as ten transformative questions: What is the shape of the biblical narrative? What is the Bible and what is it for? Why does God seem so genocidal in some biblical passages? What does it mean to say Jesus is the way? What is the gospel? What future does the church have? Why are Christians so preoccupied with sexuality? How should we relate to people of other religions? How should we view the future? Where do we go from here?[140]

In assessing the importance of this controversial book, Phyllis Tickle again noted similarities between McLaren and Luther:

> Emergence Christianity's Marburg, when it happened in 2010, was in many ways the point at which Emerging and Emergent finally had to agree to disagree. . . . If *A Generous Orthodoxy* had been, as it was, the Emergence analog to Luther's Ninety-Five Theses, then *A New Kind of Christianity* was most surely the Emergence analog to Luther's "Here I Stand" declaration of faith and principles in 1521.[141]

In the author's *magnum opus*, McLaren proved to be a gadfly of unprecedented proportions. *A New Kind of Christianity* elicited waves of protest from evangelicals, many of which will be considered throughout this study.

In 2012, McLaren returned to the relationship between Christianity and other religions in *Why Did Jesus, Moses, the Buddha, and Mohammed Cross the Road?*, which won the Academy Parish Clergy Book of the Year Award.[142] In *Everything Must Change*, McLaren had argued that a shared proper perception of Jesus could play a vital role in global peace. This book expands that claim into a full-scale treatment, seeking to forge what McLaren calls a "strong-benevolent" Christian identity in a multifaith world.[143] Rather than pursuing a hard apologetic, evangelistic, or phil-

---

[140] Brian McLaren, "Big Publishing News . . . ," *brian d. mclaren* (blog), April 21, 2009, http://brianmclaren.net/archives/blog/big-publishing-news.html.

[141] Tickle, *Emergence Christianity*, 143.

[142] "Century Marks," in *Christian Century* (February 20, 2013): 8.

[143] McLaren, *JMBM*, 10–11.

osophical approach in this book, he chose a "practical," "pastoral," and "constructive" strategy instead.[144]

McLaren argues that Christians historically have struggled to find the right balance in their relationship with adherents of other religions. Believers tend to hold either a "strong-hostile" Christian identity or a "weak-benign" identity that sacrifices a faithful Christian witness on the altar of indiscriminate tolerance.[145] McLaren proposes a via media:

> So I will explore the possibility of a third option, a Christian identity that is both strong and kind. . . . [T]he stronger our Christian faith, the more goodwill we will feel and show toward those of other faiths, seeking to understand and appreciate their religion from their point of view. My pursuit . . . is a Christian identity that moves me toward people of other faiths in whole-hearted love, not in spite of their non-Christian identity and not in spite of my own Christian identity, but because of my identity as a follower of God in the way of Jesus.[146]

In *Why Did Jesus, Moses, the Buddha, and Mohammed Cross the Road?*, McLaren works to free believers from what he calls Conflicted Religious Identity Syndrome (CRIS), a condition of ambivalence concerning one's religious beliefs and affiliations. McLaren admits that many of his books have been "literary self-therapy for my own chronic case of CRIS." McLaren concludes that when it comes to religious conflict, the "root problem is neither religious *difference* nor religious *identity* nor even *strong* religious identity. Our root problem is the *hostility* that we often employ to make and keep our identities strong." McLaren spends a good portion of this book discussing strategies to squelch hostility and encourage believers to repent of an imperial Christian faith that has deeply ingrained "us versus them" thinking into the Christian DNA.[147]

In 2014, McLaren wrote *We Make the Road by Walking*. This devotional catechesis follows the liturgical calendar and seeks to discuss the full range

---

[144] Ibid., 9.
[145] Ibid., 67.
[146] Ibid., 10–11.
[147] Ibid., 21, 63.

of the biblical narrative using his *New Kind of Christianity* hermeneutic. McLaren does not break new ground here, but he does take much of the soil he has been plowing in recent years and tills it into a narrative format that is devotionally accessible. McLaren likens his most recent book, *The Great Spiritual Migration*, to a home makeover TV show. His thesis in this book is that the Christian religion is worth salvaging, but it is in need of serious renovation. We might say McLaren's literary journey, which has led to the big reveal of this book, is much like an episode of *Property Brothers*, *Extreme Makeover* or, perhaps, *This Old House*.

> Over the years, I've shown the step-by-step process of rehabbing significant aspects of the Christian home: theology, ecclesiology, spirituality, liturgy, mission, and interfaith relations, to name a few. This book could be thought of as a "big reveal" or season finale in which you get a tour of the whole house, with plenty of before-and-after shots to show what has changed. If there was a lot of deconstruction in my previous books, this one is a simple act of construction.[148]

Major McLaren Motifs

With McLaren's biographical overview in place, eight summary observations are in order.

Evolutionary Progression

A trajectory can be traced across the three McLaren eras. First, McLaren became disillusioned with the status quo of American Evangelicalism, which led to a spiritual crisis ("early McLaren" era).[149] Second, he began to address this disillusionment with largely pragmatic resources, a holdover from the church growth movement ("emerging McLaren" era). Third, McLaren started to ask more penetrating theological questions ("emerging McLaren" era). Fourth, these questions led to a rethinking of the gospel

---

[148] Brian D. McLaren, *The Great Spiritual Migration* unpublished manuscript (New York: Convergent, 2016), 15. McLaren shared an early version of this manuscript (originally titled *Converting Christianity*) with the author through email, May 13, 2015.

[149] In Chapter Four, McLaren's spiritual crisis will be connected more directly to his personal experience with Calvinism.

("emerging McLaren" era). Fifth, the quest to answer the gospel question led McLaren back to the Scriptures, especially the gospel accounts ("emergent McLaren" era). Sixth, by reading the gospel accounts with fresh eyes, McLaren claims he was confronted with the message of justice, "inextricably woven" throughout ("emergent McLaren" era).[150]

Key Transitional Moments

Closely related are several key pivotal moments in McLaren's journey. First, McLaren's spiritual crisis set him on a path that culminated in an appreciation for the modern-to-postmodern transition. Second, after several years of writing and discussing postmodernism, he shifted his attention to postcolonial concerns. Third, this increased focus on postcolonialism coincided with a rethinking of the gospel as the kingdom of God, which included a rethinking of the doctrines of Scripture, atonement, and the afterlife. This new emphasis deepened the growing divide with conservative evangelicals, especially Calvinists.

Fourth, concomitant with these shifts was a transition from writing for evangelical *CT* periodicals to more progressive magazines, such as *Sojourners*, *Christian Century*, and *Tikkun*. Fifth, coinciding with this shift was a move from speaking at evangelical colleges, seminaries, and churches to more progressive institutions. Sixth, when Tony Jones stepped down as Emergent Village national coordinator, and the original leadership team passed the baton to a new group in 2008, McLaren forged new alliances and connected to other movements, including the CANA Initiative and Convergence.[151]

Seventh, the publishing of *A New Kind of Christianity* in 2010 finally severed the tenuous connection to traditional Evangelicalism and deepened

---

[150] McLaren, "Introduction," in *JP*, 18.

[151] The CANA Initiative was a venture led by McLaren, Pagitt, and Stephanie Spellers. The organization described itself as an effort to bring "together innovative leaders from all streams of the faith to collaborate in the development of new ways of being Christian." CANA Initiative website, n.d., accessed March 3, 2014, http://www.canainitiative.org. In 2015, the CANA Initiative morphed into Convergence, accessed January 22, 2015, http://www.convergenceus.org. McLaren has longstanding connections to many other organizations as well. He has served on the board of directors for Sojourners (chairperson), Orientación Cristiana, International Teams, Mars Hill Graduate School, and Off the Map. He also is a founding member of Red Letter Christians. See McLaren, *FOWA*, 216.

the divide between emergent and emerging participants.[152] Eighth, McLaren had called for a five-year moratorium on the discussion of homosexuality in 2006. In *A New Kind of Christianity*, McLaren condemned "fundasexuality," which he described as "a reactive, combative brand of religious *fundamentalism* that preoccupies itself with *sexuality*."[153] He associated "fundasexuality," however, primarily with homophobia. Two years later, McLaren would make his gay-affirming position public and clear when he presided over his son's same-sex commitment ceremony.[154]

Evangelist at Heart

A major thread that can be traced throughout McLaren's life is a passion for outreach, especially for the disenfranchised and marginalized. He started an investigative Bible study in high school. The impulse for evangelism served as the motivating factor for reorienting Cedar Ridge Community Church in the 1980s. Two of McLaren's early books, *Finding Faith* and *More Ready Than You Realize*, as well as his master's thesis, focus on evangelism and apologetics. In these works, McLaren rejects modern evangelistic methods, such as "the Four Spiritual Laws," and advocates for creative, organic, person-relative approaches to living out and sharing the faith. It is clear that McLaren would rather offend those already within the Christian fold than those who are on the outside looking in. In so doing, McLaren confidently believes he is following in the footsteps of Jesus, who was "short on condemning the irreligious, [but] long on confronting the religious."[155]

Spiritual Formation

During his spiritual crisis in the 1990s, McLaren wrote about how spiritual practices sustained him while his belief system was crumbling.[156] As he

---

[152] For a discussion surrounding the diversity that exists within the ECM, see Appendix A.

[153] McLaren, *NKOCY*, 174.

[154] See "Trevor McLaren and Owen Ryan," *New York Times*, posted online September 23, 2012, http://www.nytimes.com/2012/09/23/fashion/weddings/trevor-mclaren-owen-ryan-weddings.html?_r=2smid=fb-share.

[155] McLaren, *MRTYR*, 15.

[156] There is an interesting symmetry and asymmetry between McLaren's spiritual crisis and Francis Schaeffer's spiritual crisis in the 1950s. Both men were repulsed by the rampant hypocrisy and lack of spiritual authenticity in their respective evangelical circles. Both men also surfaced with their faith intact. For Schaeffer, however, his spiritual crisis confirmed his traditional understanding of the gospel. He came to the conclusion that justification was the correct doctrine, but he needed to place more emphasis on sanctification. For McLaren, however, his spiritual crisis led him on a path

resurfaced, the consistent point of emphasis for McLaren would be "good faith" over "right beliefs." He would write two books on spiritual practices, *Finding Our Way Again* and *Naked Spirituality*. While some authors have tried to reduce McLaren's emphasis to "orthopraxy" over "orthodoxy,"[157] McLaren makes it clear in *A New Kind of Christianity* that he is committed to a holistic approach: "Good thinking (orthodoxy), good being (ortho-pathy), and good relating (ortho-affinity) must interact with and express themselves through good work and practice (orthopraxy) in the world."[158]

Communal Influence

Most of McLaren's works have grown out of community. When he began writing his first books, he thought he was a lone ranger. It was not long, however, before he befriended the aforementioned members of the YLN and several scholars associated with that group. McLaren's thinking and subsequent writing were shaped profoundly in community and influenced by various voices. Consequently, it is difficult to fully identify the origin of every thought and argument in his works. In this way, McLaren is fruitfully compared to Francis Schaeffer, whose thinking was deeply enriched and formed by the many voices that contributed to the intellectual stimulation of L'Abri. It is important to note, however, that as McLaren's journey has matured, the voices in his network have expanded to include increasingly progressive personalities, something that most decidedly does not mirror Schaeffer's trek.[159]

Writing as Therapy

Not only is McLaren a prolific writer, but he also has exhibited impressive range and literary dexterity, crafting both fiction and nonfiction with equal

---

that would eventually reconfigure his entire Christian faith. For an account of Schaeffer's spiritual crisis, see Francis A. Schaeffer, *True Spirituality* (Wheaton: Tyndale, 1971).

[157] For a case in point, see Mark D. Christy, "Neoorthopraxy and Brian D. McLaren," (PhD dissertation, Southwestern Baptist Theological Seminary, 2011).

[158] McLaren, *NKOCY*, 29.

[159] As Schaeffer aged, he arguably became more restrictive in his thinking and less inclusive in his communal circle. It is interesting to note that in recent years, McLaren and Schaeffer's son, Frank, have become good friends. See Frank Schaeffer, "A One Man Army for Decency (Brian McLaren)," *Huffington Post*, September 12, 2012, http://www.huffingtonpost.com/frank-schaeffer/a-one-man-army-for-decenc_b_1854431.html. See also Brian McLaren, "Why You Should Read Frank Schaeffer's New Novel . . . and . . . ," *brian d. mclaren* (blog), September 18, 2013, http://brianmclaren.net/archives/blog/why-you-should-read-frank-schaef.html.

ease. He employs direct and indirect forms of communication with effectiveness. In *A Generous Orthodoxy*, he at times uses an indirect, playful, intentionally provocative literary strategy, while in *The Secret Message of Jesus*, for instance, he employs a more direct technique. It is instructive to note, however, that writing has other benefits for McLaren, who admits his first book was a form of self-therapy. In other words, in McLaren's books, the reader is often seeing the author internally processing a wide variety of issues in a very public and incremental manner.

Social and Political Concern

An increased sensitivity to political and social issues has largely defined the "Emergent McLaren" era. In the foreword to Grenz's *Renewing the Center*, McLaren voices his concern over Evangelicalism becoming America's civil religion.

> The most significant development in American evangelicalism in our shared lifetimes [is] the nearly complete alignment of evangelicalism with the Republican Party in U.S. politics. . . . [W]hen a young religious movement without a strong sense of history, with a less than fully developed academy, and often armed with a rather bizarre eschatology becomes the civil religion of the most powerful nation with the most powerful weapons—including the most weapons of mass destruction—of any nation, not only in the world but in the history of the world, that is staggeringly important, breathtakingly important.[160]

McLaren regrets how much the Religious Right, empowered by the Calvinist evangelical establishment, has tainted the witness of the Christian church in America.[161] Elsewhere, McLaren mourns the fact that "for many people—especially young people and highly educated people the word 'Jesus' now means things it shouldn't mean: judgmental, angry, exclusive, unkind, lacking understanding, reactionary, violent, pro-war, anti-poor, and the like."[162] These words echo the Barna research considered in the introduction to this study.

---

[160] McLaren, "Foreword," in Grenz, *Renewing the Center*, 9–10.
[161] This point will be explored in greater detail in Chapter Four.
[162] Streett, "An Interview with Brian McLaren," 6.

This emphasis on political and social concerns did not suddenly appear during the "Emergent McLaren" era, but rather can be traced back to the 1980s. McLaren and his house church exhibited a "strong social concern through these years and helped a lot of refugees settle."[163] McLaren's crisis in the 1990s also was in no small part precipitated by what he claimed to be the hubris and "absolute certainty" of many evangelical leaders and radio preachers.[164] McLaren recalls, "When I saw Calvinism allying itself with Theonomy and the hard-core Religious Right . . . I began to lose confidence."[165] Therefore, it is worth noting that McLaren's focus on political and social concerns is not a recent novelty, but a key thread that can be traced back to the early days of his ministry. Likewise, it is worth reiterating McLaren's indictment of Calvinism as the driving force behind Evangelicalism's complicity with the Religious Right.

Academic Engagement

McLaren has risen to a place of prominence without a formal degree in theology, philosophy, or related field, but it would be inaccurate to classify him as a theological or philosophical neophyte. He is a voracious reader, motivated autodidact, skilled communicator, frequent collaborator with members of the academy, and former university instructor. Roger Olson even includes McLaren in a list of postconservative, evangelical academic theologians, though Olsen concedes that these individuals might not apply this label to themselves.[166]

Nevertheless, McLaren admits his initial embarrassment regarding writing books on theological topics without the expected credentials, "having snuck into ministry . . . through the back door of the English department." McLaren, who has "sat on seminary board of directors," no longer feels anxious about his "lack of 'proper credentials.'" McLaren explains,

> In fact, I can see God's guidance in it. My graduate training was
> in literature and language, which sensitized me to drama and

---

[163] Gibbs and Bolger, *Emerging Churches*, 284.

[164] McLaren, *NKOC*, XVII.

[165] Brian McLaren, email message to author, July 20, 2009.

[166] Olsen's complete list is as follows: : Stanley Grenz, Clark Pinnock, Kevin Vanhoozer, John Sanders, John Franke, Amos Young, Nancey Murphy, James McClendon, Miroslav Volf, Henry (Hal) Knight, and Brian McLaren. See Roger E. Olson, *Reformed and Always Reforming* (Grand Rapids: Baker, 2007), 65.

conflict, to syntax and semantics and semiotics, to text and con-text, to prose and to poetry. It gave me a taste, a sense, a feel for the game and science and art and romance of language. It helped me to see how carefully chosen and clear, daring words can point to mysteries and wonders beyond words. It prepared me to see how a generous orthodoxy must be mystical and poetic.[167]

McLaren's degrees in English have perhaps providentially prepared him for such a time as this. He has spoken at an eclectic mix of institutions,[168] and some of McLaren books became required reading at several of these institutions during the past decade.[169]

McLaren does not consider himself an academician in the traditional sense but rather a "reflective practitioner . . . focused on the down-and-dirty of doing ministry, but trying to have a high-altitude understanding of when, where, how, and why we are doing it."[170] Consequently, it would be a mistake to label him an academic philosopher, theologian, or apol-ogist. McLaren is a public intellectual who started as a college instructor and who has expanded into diverse cultural settings, including a broader swath of academia, for the purpose of stimulating conversation between a wide range of people both inside and outside the academy.

With this biographical summary in place, we can now explore the specific content of McLaren's new kind of apologetic project, starting with the overarching storyline of the Bible and biblical interpretation, areas in which ECM leader Tony Jones claims McLaren "is absolutely on his game."[171]

---

[167] McLaren, *GO*, 156–57.

[168] McLaren's speaking engagements have included the following: Abilene Christian University, Anderson University, Asbury Theological Seminary, Baylor University, Bethel Seminary, Biblical Seminary, Calvin College, Duke Divinity School, Eastern Mennonite University, Fuller Theological Seminary, Furman University, George Fox University, Goshen College, Harvard Divinity School, Lipscomb University, Louisville Seminary, Malone University, Mars Hill Graduate School, McCormick Seminary, Moravian Seminary, North Park University, Pepperdine University, Pittsburgh Theological Seminary, Princeton University, Samford University, Southern Methodist University, Spring Arbor University, Taylor University, Tyndale University College, Wake Forest University, Western Seminary, Wheaton College, and Yale University.

[169] McLaren has taught courses at Fuller Seminary, Biblical Seminary, Mars Hill Graduate School (now the Seattle School of Theology and Psychology), and Western Seminary. McLaren, *LWWAT*, 202. Brian McLaren's assistant provided this list of academic institutions. Laci Scott, email message to author, June 24, 2009.

[170] McLaren, *COOS*, 10.

[171] Tony Jones, "The McLaren Lectionary," *Theoblogy* (*Patheos* blog), June 10, 2014, http://www.patheos.com/blogs/tonyjones/2014/06/10/the-mclaren-lectionary/.

Chapter Three

MCLAREN AND THE BIBLE

I'm convinced that we Christians—Western Christians in particular—must acknowledge the degree to which our faith has become a syncretized faith, a compromised faith, we might even say a corrupted faith. From Constantine to Columbus to the other Conquistadors to the Colonizers to the present, we have mixed authentically Christian elements of love, joy, peace, and reconciliation with strictly imperial elements of superiority, conquest, domination, and hostility. . . . In other words, what we call Christianity today has a history, and this history reveals it as a Roman, imperial version of Christianity.[1]

—Brian McLaren, *Why Did Jesus, Moses, the Buddha, and Mohammed Cross the Road?*

WHEN MCLAREN'S CONTROVERSIAL MAGNUM OPUS, *A NEW Kind of Christianity*, was published in 2010, *Christianity Today (CT)* commissioned Scot McKnight to write a review. While McKnight had been more appreciative than critical in previous assessments of McLaren's work, his opinion of *A New Kind of Christianity* was ambivalent at best. McKnight argued that McLaren was buying into "an old saw—namely, the Constantinian Fall of the church."[2] He went on to accuse McLaren of treating Evangelicalism as his "devil" and "foil,"[3] while following the

---

[1] McLaren, *JMBM*, 84.
[2] Scot McKnight, "Rebuilding the Faith from Scratch: Brian McLaren's 'New' Christianity Is Not So Much Revolutionary as Evolutionary," *CT* 53, no. 3 (March 2010): 59–66, citing 60.
[3] Ibid., 59.

liberal teaching of Adolf von Harnack, Marcus Borg,[4] and Harvey Cox in his critique of the conventional Christian narrative.[5]

Interestingly, however, McKnight shifted his tone when discussing McLaren's proposed biblical hermeneutic. In fact, McKnight claims that McLaren's new way of reading the Bible "is one of the book's best images" and similar to his own treatment of Scripture "as a collection of inspired texts that come at things from different angles and use differing terms and speak to ever-changing contexts, but always with the ever-true truth of the gospel that leads us to Christ." In short, McKnight panned McLaren's critique of the conventional Christian narrative but offered qualified praise of his new biblical hermeneutic.[6] This chapter will focus on these two aspects of McLaren's interaction with the Bible, which is a major part of his new apologetic.

In *A New Kind of Christian*, McLaren identifies modernity as the problem facing contemporary Christianity. In *A New Kind of Christianity*, however, McLaren traces the primary problem back further to alleged compromises made by the early Christian church. More specifically, McLaren argues that an unholy union with Greek philosophy, Roman Imperialism and, later, Enlightenment foundationalism has tainted the conventional evangelical message and dominant storyline. Most troubling to McLaren is the conviction that this metanarrative, chiefly exemplified by five-point Calvinism, has fueled various expressions of colonial excessive confidence. Consequently, this storyline is in need of major deconstruction.

McLaren's reconstructive proposal to this misguided metanarrative is a three-part biblical narrative that he calls creation, liberation, and peaceable kingdom. The first part of this chapter will explore McLaren's interaction with these two different ways of telling the Christian story. The second half of this chapter turns to McLaren's new hermeneutic approach, and his

---

[4] For a comparative analysis of McLaren and Borg, see Gary Tyra, *A Missional Orthodoxy* (Downers Grove: InterVarsity Press, 2013). When Borg passed away in 2015, McLaren wrote a heartfelt tribute on his blog. See Brian McLaren, "In Honor of Marcus Borg," brian d. mclaren (blog), January 22, 2015, http://brianmclaren.net/archives/blog/in-honor-of-marcus-borg.html.

[5] McKnight, "Rebuilding the Faith," 66.

[6] Ibid., 61, 66. While McKnight resonates with much of this new hermeneutical proposal, he disagrees with McLaren's evolutionary reading of Scripture: "The flow of the Bible is not neat. It doesn't fit into an evolutionary scheme. There are as many mercy passages in the Old Testament as there are grace-and-love passages in the New."

strategy for conserving an inspired, Christocentric biblical library rather than viewing Scripture as a homogenous legal constitution.

McLaren's First Deconstructive Thrust: The Six-Line Narrative

During McLaren's spiritual crisis in the 1990s, he experienced a tension between "something real" and "something wrong."[7] For several years, he reexamined his faith and identified a lot in the "something real" category; however, putting his finger on the problem proved elusive.[8] He eventually concluded that the fundamental challenge with the Christianity he had been taught (and, in turn, taught to others), was operating out of a faulty narrative framework. McLaren elaborates,

> Up until that point, this narrative shape had been like my glasses, through which I saw everything, but of which I was largely unconscious nearly all the time. . . . Increasing numbers of us share the feeling that our theological lens is scratched. That's why this quest begins not by tweaking details of the conventional six-line narrative, but by calling the entire narrative scheme into question.[9]

So what is this "six-line narrative" to which McLaren refers?[10] In short, there are six terms that McLaren believes provide the contours of the misguided traditional Christian storyline: Eden, Fall, Condemnation, Salvation, Heaven, and Hell/Damnation.[11] McLaren argues that "nobody in the Hebrew Scriptures ever talked about original sin, total depravity, 'the Fall,' or eternal conscious torment in hell."[12] McLaren struggled to see how this story ever grew out of the sacred Hebrew texts until he had a series of epiphanies.

The first insight came during a talk in which he concluded that the conventional Western Christian storyline was in part a by-product of reading

---

[7] McLaren, *NKOCY*, 33.
[8] Ibid.
[9] Ibid., 35.
[10] Ibid., 33–45.
[11] Ibid., 34.
[12] Ibid., 37.

Jesus through the eyes of his successors rather than in light of his predecessors.[13] Additional epiphanies came in subsequent conversations with friends. McLaren recalls spontaneously drawing the six-line narrative on a napkin during a meal.[14] It dawned on him that this narrative was a syncretistic blend of Greek philosophy with the social and political narrative of the Roman Empire.[15] He labeled it the "Greco-Roman narrative."[16]

McLaren then connected these six lines with the six lines of the Greco-Roman narrative. [17]

MCLAREN'S SIX LINE NARRATIVE

1. Eden	1. Platonic ideal/being
2. Fall	2. Fall into the cave of illusion
3. Condemnation	3. Aristotelian real/becoming
4. Salvation	4. Salvation
5. Heaven	5. Platonic ideal
6. Hell/damnation	6. Greek Hades

In this Greco-Roman storyline, humans fell from an ideal state of "perfection" into the "relative darkness" of Plato's cave and the realm of Aristotelian alteration, motion, becoming, and decay—a story that *Theos* (the name McLaren gives to the god of the Greco-Roman narrative as opposed to *Elohim*, the God of the Judeo-Christian account) cannot tolerate and must judge.

One of McLaren's chief influences, N. T. Wright, corroborates this juxtaposition of Platonic and Aristotelian thought, as follows:

---

[13] Ibid., 36–37.

[14] Brian McLaren, in discussion with the author, Fort Wayne, IN, March 20, 2014.

[15] McLaren, *NKOCY*, 264n2. See also McLaren, *NKOC*, 78.

[16] McLaren, *NKOCY*, 37. McLaren clarifies that the "Greco-Roman narrative" does not represent the only way the Christian story has been told historically. He references the minority positions of "the desert fathers and mothers, the Celts, the Franciscans, the Anabaptists, the Catholic and Protestant mystics, not to mention the other main wing of the faith known as Eastern Orthodoxy." *NKOCY*, 263–264n1. For support, McLaren cites Thomas Cahill, *How the Irish Saved Civilization* (New York: Anchor, 1996).

[17] McLaren, *NKOCY*, 41. McLaren claims that while "I'm highly critical of the unintended consequences of the embrace of the Greco-Roman narrative by early Christian theologians, I must acknowledge the absolute brilliance of their move." *NKOCY*, 264n3. In other words, McLaren appreciates the short-term pragmatic cash value that was gained by incorporating both Platonic and Aristotelian insights into the Christian system of thought, despite the long-term loss.

We may say that Plato's picture was based on a rejection of the phenomena of matter and transience. The mess and muddle of the space-time-matter world was an offense to the tidy, clean philosophical mind, which dwelt upon eternal realities. It wasn't just evil that was wrong with the world; it was change and decay, the transitoriness of matter.[18]

McLaren explains that Theos is partial to Platonic dualism, in which perfection is found in the realm of the "forms," and imperfection is located in the Aristotelian material world of time and space.[19] The *telos* of this narrative is to escape punishment and achieve restoration to the perfect Platonic state.[20] Those who are not redeemed are condemned to eternal conscious torment in Hades.[21] Elsewhere, McLaren calls this the "soul-sort" narrative, in which everyone is ultimately separated into eternal binary bins.[22] McLaren argues that the conventional six-line narrative is simply a Christianized version, albeit unwittingly, of this hellenized framework.[23]

McLaren is especially concerned with the Greek concept of "perfection," which he juxtaposes with the Hebrew notion of "goodness."[24] McLaren explains, "In this way, the Greco-Roman mind transforms the Garden of Eden from its original earthy stuff into a transcendent Platonic ideal. It is no longer a *good* Jewish garden; it is a *perfect* Platonic Greco-Roman garden. In this perfect Platonic garden, nothing ever changes, because in perfection change can only be for the worse."[25]

Echoes of this argument can be found in the writing of McLaren influence Clark Pinnock, who identifies the reliance of the early church upon Greek philosophy. For instance, Pinnock argues that Perfect Being Theology[26] is deduced from our intuitive notion of perfection and comes

---

[18] N. T. Wright, *Surprised by Hope* (New York: HarperOne, 2008), 88.

[19] McLaren, *NKOCY*, 37.

[20] McLaren, *NKOC*, 129.

[21] McLaren, *NKOCY*, 42.

[22] Ibid., 195.

[23] Ibid., 34–35.

[24] Ibid., 41. Implicit in McLaren's interpretation of Jewish "goodness" is the need for ongoing evolutionary and cooperative development between Creator and creation. For McLaren, therefore, the concept of "goodness" entails the notion of "potentiality."

[25] Ibid.

[26] For a discussion of Perfect Being Theology, see Thomas V. Morris, *Our Idea of God* (Downers Grove: InterVarsity Press, 1991), 35–39, and J. P. Moreland and William Lane Craig, *Philosophical Foundations for a Christian Worldview* (Downers Grove: InterVarsity Press, 2003), 501–16.

to the conclusion that God must embody such attributes as necessary existence, omnibenevolence, omniscience, and omnipotence.[27] Embedded in this methodology is a Greek assumption of perfection that includes a resistance to change or alteration. Pinnock argues that this assumption can be traced back to Plato:

> The Christian doctrine of God was, however, shaped in an atmosphere influenced by Greek thought. . . . [Plato] had argued in the *Republic* that deity, being perfect, cannot change or be changed because any change in a "perfect" being could only be change for the worse. Whatever Plato meant by this, the power of this idea on Christian thinking has been enormous.[28]

Tethered closely to this Hellenistic six-line narrative was an alliance with the Roman Empire. McLaren believes the Greek perspective influenced the Roman mindset in three specific ways.[29] First, it converted the Roman perspective to the kind of dualism just outlined.[30] Second, through "Aristotelian resources," the Greco-Roman culture was empowered to accomplish groundbreaking "feats of engineering." Additionally, through Platonic thought, "the Greco-Romans pioneered what we might call the life of the mind." These combined resources fueled a sense of "supremacy."[31] Third, "this philosophical dualism and intellectual superiority fused in a corresponding social dualism and superiority."[32] This led to the hubris of in-grouping and out-grouping, in which the whole world was split into either refined, cultured, and enlightened or backward, barbaric, and ignorant.[33]

McLaren favorably cites Harvard University emeritus professor Harvey Cox, who proposes a tripartite historical taxonomy in *The Future of Faith*. According to Cox, Christianity began in the "Age of Faith," then transitioned into a fifteen-hundred-year period known as the "Age of Belief," and is now experiencing the "Age of the Spirit."[34] The Christian movement

---

[27] Clark Pinnock, *Most Moved Mover* (Grand Rapids: Baker, 2001), 70.
[28] Ibid., 68.
[29] McLaren, *NKOCY*, 38.
[30] Ibid., 38–39.
[31] Ibid., 39.
[32] Ibid.
[33] Ibid.
[34] Harvey Cox, *The Future of Faith* (New York: HarperOne, 2009), 4–20.

started with "a buoyant faith" and an intense desire to pursue the way of Jesus.[35] According to Cox, this "Age of Faith," however, soon capitulated to the "Age of Belief," an era in which followers of Jesus exchanged the status of persecuted minority for the favored majority. This apparent ascendency, however, had devastating consequences. Cox explains, "But for Christianity it proved to be a disaster: its enthronement actually degraded it. From an energetic movement of faith it coagulated into a phalanx of required beliefs, thereby laying the foundation for every succeeding Christian fundamentalism for centuries to come."[36] Cox contends that Emperor Constantine co-opted Christianity for his own political gain, "appointing and dismissing bishops, paying salaries, funding buildings, and distributing largesse. He and not the pope was the real head of the church."[37]

In *A Christianity Worth Believing*, Doug Pagitt provides additional support for McLaren's argument.[38]

> But then something changed. Historians and theologians debate the details, reasons, and timelines, but within a few centuries a shift took place. Christianity started moving from a faith committed to multicultural unity to one requiring monocultural uniformity. . . . Strangely that mandatory worldview was not the Hebrew worldview of the Jewish people. It was the Greek worldview of the Gentiles.[39]

Pagitt, likewise, links this syncretistic appreciation of Greek philosophy with the "story of Constantine domesticating the faith by turning it into one of control and dominance."[40] Pagitt believes the Greek worldview has permeated "Christian thought about everything from God and Jesus to sin and salvation, for the last seventeen hundred years."[41]

In conclusion, McLaren argues that this conventional six-line Greco-Roman narrative has held a powerful sway over the Western Christian

---

[35] Ibid., 5.
[36] Ibid., 6.
[37] Ibid.
[38] McLaren, *NKOCY*, 13.
[39] Doug Pagitt, *A Christianity Worth Believing* (San Francisco: Jossey-Bass, 2008), 41. McLaren favorably cites *A Christianity Worth Believing* in *NKOCY*, 13.
[40] Pagitt, *Christianity Worth Believing*, 42.
[41] Ibid., 45.

mindset. He and others have attempted to work within the parameters of this narrative by "tweaking various elements or lines in this story"; however, he now concludes the only way forward is to discard the narrative altogether and seek out a biblically faithful and "morally believable" alternative.[42] In other words, to use McLaren's earlier metaphor, the only way to see the true biblical storyline is to exchange the scratched theological lens for a new pair of glasses. McLaren avers,

> I'm convinced that we Christians—Western Christians in particular—must acknowledge the degree to which our faith has become a syncretized faith, a compromised faith, we might even say a corrupted faith. From Constantine to Columbus to the other Conquistadors to the Colonizers to the present, we have mixed authentically Christian elements of love, joy, peace, and reconciliation with strictly imperial elements of superiority, conquest, domination, and hostility. . . . In other words, what we call Christianity today has a history, and this history reveals it as a Roman, imperial version of Christianity.[43]

McLaren's First Reconstructive Thrust: The Three-Dimensional Narrative

In 1998, McLaren team-taught a course with John Franke at Biblical Theological Seminary. The two men began discussing the future of theology and agreed "new theologies probably would be less analytical in structure and more rooted in the biblical narrative."[44] Both had been independently working on a "thumbnail summary of the biblical story," which turned out to be strikingly similar. This collaboration led to McLaren's seven-episode biblical narrative introduced in *The Story We Find Ourselves In*: creation, crisis, calling, conversation, Christ, Church, and consummation.[45]

In *A New Kind of Christianity*, McLaren cites an eclectic blend of authors who have helped him develop a narrative "frontward reading" of

---

[42] McLaren, *NKOCY*, 35.
[43] McLaren, *JMBM*, 84.
[44] McLaren, *SWFOI*, xiii.
[45] Ibid., 205–15. The reader's guide located in the back of *SWFOI* is crafted around these seven themes.

the text that is informed by Jewish sensibilities.[46] These authors include N. T. Wright, Walter Brueggemann, Marcus Borg, Ched Myers, William Herzog, Rita Brock, James Cone, John Dominic Crossan, Leonardo Boff, Jon Sobrino, Gustavo Gutiérrez, Richard Rohr, and Joan Chittister. After deconstructing the conventional narrative, McLaren turns to an alternative storyline. Instead of the seven-episode outline of *The Story We Find Ourselves In*,[47] however, McLaren articulates what he believes is the authentic shape of the biblical account—the three-dimensional narrative of creation, liberation, and peaceable kingdom.[48] This is the story of the Jewish Elohim, rather than the Greek Theos, creating a good, unfinished world in need of ongoing evolutionary development and human cooperation to bring the potentiality of God's design, purpose, and dream to fruition. Instead of "Plato, Aristotle, and Caesar," McLaren primarily turns to the narratives of Genesis, Exodus, and Isaiah to provide the guiding grid for understanding the overarching biblical plotline.[49]

McLaren believes the opening book of the Bible provides a "fractal for the story as a whole and for its many parts."[50] McLaren continues, "This story begins with something better than the perfect realm of Plato: the good world of Genesis. Jewish *goodness*, it turns out, is far better than Greco-Roman *perfection*. . . . It seems far closer to the Aristotelian world of becoming than the Platonic plane of being."[51] McLaren views God through the lens of Elohim, the patient, long-suffering parent[52] rather than through the lens of the harsh, intolerant Theos, bearing the likeness of the impetuous Zeus.[53]

Central to the Genesis storyline is a non-determined world and the gift of human freedom. McLaren states, "God tells Adam and Eve they are free

---

[46] McLaren, *NKOCY*, 46. By "frontward reading," McLaren means reading Jesus in light of the Old Testament narrative rather than through the lens of those who came after him.

[47] While this is an alternative narrative structure, it makes room for the seven-episode flow as well. There are no essential contradictions between the two. The three-dimensional storyline is simply McLaren's most mature narrative expression.

[48] McLaren, *NKOCY*, 55. McLaren claims that he was well-prepared to perceive the "three-dimensional" narrative because of his academic training as an English major.

[49] Ibid., 47.

[50] Ibid., 56.

[51] Ibid., 47.

[52] Ibid., 49.

[53] Ibid., 42–43.

(this is a primary condition of their existence)."[54] The story then becomes one episode after another of humanity misusing its freedom (e.g., Adam and Eve, Cain and Abel, the tower of Babel, and Joseph's brothers) and God seeking creative ways to transform the resulting systemic and personal evil into redemptive good. In short, the narrative "begins with God creating a good world, continues with human beings creating evil, and concludes with God creating good outcomes that overcome human evil. . . . Good has the first word, and good has the last."[55]

The next key plotline for McLaren is found in the second book of the Bible. McLaren contends that the "prime narrative comes to us in the book of Exodus. If Genesis is a story of sacred creation and reconciliation, Exodus is a story of sacred liberation and formation."[56] He believes the opening pages of the book of Exodus record the story of "liberation from the external oppression of social sin," while the balance of the book chronicles "liberation from the internal spiritual oppression of personal sin."[57] In other words, the book of Exodus is largely a tale of liberation from both social and personal evil, as well as a story of ancient Jewish formation in the faith.[58] Therefore, in McLaren's narrative, salvation is not understood as escaping the punishment of eternal perdition, but rather joining God on a reconciling mission in the present world to redeem all aspects of creation from the devastating effects of individual and corporate sin, corruption, and evil.

The final narrative functions as the bookend. McLaren writes, "If Genesis is the prequel to Exodus, the third narrative is its sequel: the sacred dream of the peaceable kingdom."[59] McLaren cites passages from Isaiah, Hosea, Joel, and Micah that promote a hope-filled future of shalom.[60] While many read these passages as a glimpse of a heavenly "eternal destination *beyond* history," McLaren argues that those who are initiated into this alternative three-dimensional narrative perspective will see the peaceable

---

[54] Ibid., 49.
[55] Ibid., 54.
[56] Ibid., 56.
[57] Ibid., 58.
[58] Ibid.
[59] Ibid., 59.
[60] Ibid., 59–62.

kingdom "more as a guiding star *within*" history.[61] McLaren believes that interpreting the "third narrative" in this manner frees the reader from "a deterministic future" since "the future in this approach is waiting to be created."[62] This statement suggests McLaren's commitment to open theism, a view that will be explored in greater detail in Chapter Four. The peaceable kingdom, therefore, is the new Promised Land. It is not a future that is divinely determined from behind, but rather a potentiality to which God from the future is inviting humanity as "junior partners" to help establish in this space-time matrix rather than in an ethereal eschatological existence beyond the grave.[63]

The central plotline of the New Testament, therefore, is simply the "fulfillment of the three prime narratives of the Hebrew Scriptures."[64] Rather than solving the problem of original sin and escaping the punishment of eternal damnation, McLaren believes the gospel is about entering into this three-dimensional Hebrew narrative in a fresh way:

> First, to accept the free gift of being "born again" into "life of the ages" or "life abundant" meant participation in a new Genesis, a new creation, interrupting the downward death spiral of violence and counterviolence and joining an upward, regenerative movement. Second, to follow Jesus meant embarking on a new Exodus, passing through the waters once again (this time, baptism instead of the Red Sea), eating a new Passover meal (the Eucharist), and experiencing liberation from the principalities and powers that oppress and enslave. Third, to enter or receive the "kingdom of God" meant becoming a citizen of a new kingdom, the peaceable kingdom imagined by the prophets and inaugurated in Christ, learning its ways (as a disciple) and demonstrating in word and deed its presence and availability to all (as an apostle).[65]

---

[61] Ibid., 62.
[62] Ibid.
[63] Ibid., 47.
[64] Ibid., 140.
[65] Ibid.

In summary, McLaren believes this three-dimensional narrative provides an overarching storyline that extends from Genesis to Revelation, and offers a vision of "the wild, passionate, creative, liberating hope-inspiring God" rather than the "dread cosmic dictator of the six-line Greco-Roman framework."[66] Now that McLaren's deconstruction of the six-line narrative and reconstruction of the three-dimensional storyline are in clear view, this study can turn to his approach to biblical interpretation.

McLaren's Second Deconstructive Thrust: The Bible as Legal Constitution

In *Adventures in Missing the Point*, McLaren claims that recommending the Bible to a postmodern seeker is often like setting up a friend on a blind date, "but the introduction isn't going so well."[67] It is not that the two are mismatched, but rather his friend's expectations are askew. In other words, the Bible often fails to yield direct, mechanical answers, requiring instead a sincere organic wrestling with the narrative within the appropriate literary, historical, and cultural context.[68]

McLaren argues that a proper postmodern, postcolonial, and post-critical hermeneutic requires "debugging our software of needless modern viruses."[69] While conservative Christians are quick to point out compromises by liberals, who read the Bible "like an engineer and dismiss anything that doesn't fit [the] modern, Western, rationalistic, reductionistic mind-set,"[70] McLaren believes conservative evangelicals are often less aware of their own accommodations. In *A New Kind of Christian*, Neo explains, "Modern conservatives treat the Bible as if it were a modern book. They're used to reading modern history texts and modern encyclopedias and modern science articles and modern legal codes, and so they assume that the Bible will yield its resources if they approach it like one of those texts."[71] This modern conservative approach to Scripture, typically termed

---

[66] Ibid., 65.
[67] McLaren, *AMP*, 75.
[68] McLaren, *NKOC*, 159.
[69] McLaren, *AMP*, 78. See also McLaren, *NKOC*, 48–53.
[70] McLaren, *NKOC*, 158.
[71] Ibid., 55–56. See also McLaren, *AMP*, 78–79. McLaren is not rejecting the appropriate use of biblical commentaries, dictionaries, and encyclopedias, but rather is reacting to an exclusively "backward reading" of the text. See McLaren, *NKOCY*, 35–37.

"inerrancy,"[72] is rooted in classical epistemological foundationalism—the quest for a sturdy and certain grounding for all knowledge.[73] Key McLaren influence John Franke argues that this approach to biblical inerrancy "gives every indication that Scripture is to be viewed as just the sort of strong foundation envisioned by classical foundationalists."[74]

The problem, however, as McLaren admits, is that the Bible is not what one might have expected an all-powerful, perfectly loving God to provide. Given the fact that there is so much riding on a proper interpretation of key passages, McLaren has frequently puzzled over the kind of revelation God chose to deliver: "If God were trying to give us a holy book, a self-revelation, couldn't God have made it clearer, less controversial, more universal, less vulnerable to cultural irrelevancy?"[75] Rather than a universally accessible, systematic theological encyclopedia, however, God's Word has come to humanity in a "seemingly disorganized, patchwork form."[76] Franke laments the fact that many contemporary readers "codify the true meaning of the text in a series of systematically arranged assertions that then function as the only proper interpretive grid through which we read the Bible."[77] Pagitt concurs that contemporary evangelicals often have succumbed to the modern seduction of reducing scriptural teaching into neat, under-standable nuggets: "It is not a reference book. Far too many people—and by that I mean nearly all of us—have a tendency to use the Bible as an encyclopedia."[78]

---

[72] Representatives from the International Council on Biblical Inerrancy drafted a doctrinal declaration during a three-day summit, October 26–28, 1978. See "The Chicago Statement on Biblical Inerrancy," *Journal of the Evangelical Theological Society* 21, no. 4 (December 1978): 289–96. For a classic defense of inerrancy, see Harold Lindsell, *The Bible in the Balance* (Grand Rapids: Zondervan, 1979). For a more recent discussion, see J. Merrick and Stephen M. Garrett, eds., *Five Views on Biblical Inerrancy* (Grand Rapids: Zondervan, 2013).

[73] McLaren, *NKOC*, 54–55.

[74] John R. Franke, "Recasting Inerrancy: The Bible as Witness to Missional Plurality," in *Five Views on Biblical Inerrancy*, 259–87, citing 262. Franke associates this kind of approach to inerrancy with the Chicago Statement.

[75] McLaren, *FF*, 231.

[76] Ibid..

[77] John R. Franke, *Manifold Witness* (Nashville: Abingdon, 2009), 83. See also Franke, "Response to R. Albert Mohler Jr.," in *Five Views on Biblical Inerrancy*, 77–81.

[78] Pagitt, *Christianity Worth Believing*, 57. In a conversation with Dan Poole, Neo says something similar: "We want it [the Bible] to be God's encyclopedia, God's rule book, God's answer book, God's scientific text, God's easy-steps instruction book, God's little book of morals for all occasions." McLaren, *NKOC*, 52. See also McLaren, *LWWAT*, 44. For a discussion of various contemporary biblical hermeneutical approaches, see Scot McKnight, "Scripture in the Emerging Movement" in *Church in the Present Tense*, ed. Kevin Corcoran (Grand Rapids: Brazos, 2011), 107–11.

While the scaffolding of Scripture might not conform to preconceived modern expectations, McLaren ultimately acknowledges wisdom in the kind of special revelation God has chosen to provide: "If God is indeed having a real story unfold through history, then of course, the story has to 'happen' with freedom, and the reports of it have to come to us in their raw, unedited forms, warts and wrinkles, bizarre twists and unpredictable turns."[79] McLaren rejects the notion of a fully formed, totally determined world, opting instead for one that is charged with open possibilities, including a myriad of choices that the biblical characters and authors could execute in the flow of a real, evolving story.[80]

According to McLaren, however, an appreciation for human dignity, evolutionary development, and narrative has not adequately informed the standard conventional evangelical treatments of Scripture. He believes a new kind of Christianity requires a radically different approach because "interpretation is a moral act,"[81] and, therefore, "a matter of the heart and the conscience."[82] McLaren contends that ignoring the ethical dimension of hermeneutics has led evangelicals "into a mess with the Bible."[83] McLaren argues that the conventional evangelical constitutional approach to the Bible has created problems specifically in the realms of *science*, *ethics*, and *peace*.[84]

The Bible and Science

McLaren believes treating the Bible "as a divinely dictated scientific textbook" has placed Christians historically on the wrong side of a host of issues, "from Galileo's time, to Darwin's, to our own."[85] Consequently, the church has often wrongly vilified believers who courageously pursued the truth at great personal cost. Renouncing sound scientific research not only

---

[79] McLaren, *FF*, 232.

[80] Ibid., 236.

[81] Brian McLaren, "A New Kind of Bible Reading," *brian d. mclaren* (website), unpublished paper, 7, n. d., accessed May 25, 2014, http://www.brianmclaren.net/A%20New%20Kind%20of%20Bible%20Reading.pdf.

[82] McLaren, *JMBM*, 205.

[83] McLaren, *NKOCY*, 68.

[84] Ibid., 68–69.

[85] Ibid., 68. For a glimpse into McLaren's own childhood dissatisfaction with juxtaposing Scripture and science, see McLaren, *FF*, 71–72.

undermines the credibility of the Christian community, but it also can lead to personal and social calamity.[86]

The Bible and Ethics

McLaren argues that the Bible cannot be used as a straightforward, self-interpretive, inerrant guide to adjudicate every contemporary ethical controversy since many of these issues, including abortion, schizophrenia, affirmative action, genetic engineering, and biological warfare are not mentioned in Scripture.[87] Regrettably, the Christian community has a history of lifting "verses from the Bible to justify unjustifiable ethical positions."[88]

The Bible and Peace

One of the most urgent concerns for McLaren is finding a way to responsibly interpret violent passages. He laments the fact "that the Bible is becoming a box cutter or suitcase bomb in the hands of too many preachers, pastors, priests, and others."[89] McLaren believes that many Old Testament passages "are lying around like loaded weapons waiting for some fearful or angry interpreters to pick them up and use them for genocidal purposes."[90]

Pagitt reflects McLaren's unease: "Yet many of the Christians I know truly believe that we are at war with the human enemies of our faith. They use the Bible to stab and shred and rip into what they believe to be faulty theology. They wield that weapon in a way that brings pain, suffering, and humiliation."[91] Franke, likewise, acknowledges that Christianity has a regrettable legacy of "erroneous and destructive understandings of the Bible that have led to the oppression and marginalization of others."[92]

With these motivating concerns in mind, McLaren proceeds to deconstruct what he believes to be the dominant conventional Western evangelical approach to biblical hermeneutics—namely, treating the Bible as a

---

[86] McLaren, *NKOCY*, 68.
[87] Ibid., 68–69.
[88] Ibid., 69. McLaren specifically references the way the Bible has been used to justify slavery, segregation, mistreatment of homosexuals, and "government-sanctioned torture."
[89] Ibid.
[90] McLaren, *JMBM*, 199.
[91] Pagitt, *Christianity Worth Believing*, 56.
[92] Franke, "Recasting Inerrancy," 275. While agreeing with McLaren on this point, Franke admits he is not a pacifist, but rather an advocate of "just war theory." See Franke, "Recasting Inerrancy," 285–86.

legal constitution. McLaren extends the metaphor accordingly: "Lawyers in the courtroom quote articles, sections, paragraphs, and subparagraphs to win their case, and we do the same with testaments, books, chapters, and verses."[93] In so doing, evangelicals cite precedents and "distinguish 'spirit' from 'letter' and argue the 'framers' intent,' seldom questioning whether the passage in question was actually intended by the original authors and editors to be universal, eternally binding law."[94] Consequently, seminaries become law schools and ecclesiastical leaders are elevated to judges overseeing their courtrooms.[95] Roger Olson concurs: "Like the U.S. Constitution the Bible serves as the evangelical 'highest court of appeal' in matters of belief and practice."[96] This approach empowers those who have been trained to read the Scriptures in a legal manner, strengthening their authority and reinforcing a built-in disincentive to challenge from within the "constitutional system" that provides compensation, prestige, and job security.[97]

McLaren, however, believes the legal system is actually more accommodating to reform than the evangelical ecclesiastical and academic guilds. Constitutions are open to amendment, and lawyers can challenge each other. This is not the case with many ecclesiastical and educational bodies, where "challenging an authority figure's interpretation can lead to excommunication."[98] Additionally, the biblical authors did not envision contributing to a universal constitution that would serve to enforce religious law "hundreds or thousands of years in the future and thousands of miles away"; rather, they were addressing concrete issues in their own particular culture and in their own historical time period.[99] Therefore, McLaren is confident that treating the Bible as a constitution is a category error,[100] and embracing it in this manner perpetuates the aforementioned scientific, ethical, and violent abuses.

---

[93] McLaren, *NKOCY*, 78.
[94] Ibid.
[95] Ibid.
[96] Roger E. Olson, *How to Be Evangelical without Being Conservative* (Grand Rapids: Zondervan, 2008), 40. It should be noted, however, that while McLaren is critiquing the use of Scripture in a constitutional manner, Olson is utilizing this metaphor in a non-pejorative way.
[97] Ibid., 80.
[98] Ibid.
[99] Ibid., 81.
[100] McLaren, *JMBM*, 204.

McLaren's Second Reconstructive Thrust: The Bible as Inspired Library

If the Bible is not like a constitution, then to what can this collection of books be compared? McLaren, the literary scholar, believes the answer is "a library filled with diverse voices making diverse claims in an ongoing conversation."[101] Or, as Franke frames it: "The Bible is not so much a single book as it is a collection of authorized texts written from different settings and perspectives. . . . In other words, the Bible is polyphonic, made up of many voices."[102] McLaren points out that not only are there multiple voices, but multiple genres and literary techniques are employed by a diverse team of authors, including "poets, protestors, storytellers, activists, priests, and mystics."[103] Instead of understanding the Bible "as one tidy story with many chapters," McLaren argues that it is better viewed "as a wild and fascinating library with many stories told from many perspectives."[104] By properly classifying and respecting Scripture, "the Bible is liberated from its constitutional captivity to be the wild, inspired, and impassioned collection of literary artifacts that it is."[105]

Different types of libraries house various kinds of specialized collections. In this case, McLaren claims the Bible "is a carefully selected group of ancient documents of paramount importance for people who want to understand and belong to the community of people who seek God and, in particular, the God of Abraham, Moses, David, the prophets, and Jesus."[106] While there is much wisdom to be gleaned from reading the church fathers, contemporary theologians, and sagacious leaders from other religions, McLaren insists that the Bible maintains a special status and an "unparalleled role that none of these other voices can claim."[107]

One of the key differences between a constitution and a library relates to the matter of internal consistency. Constitutions are neat, orderly, and

---

[101] Ibid. While he does not fully develop his idea of the Bible as an inspired library until 2010, one can find McLaren as early as 1999 likening the Bible to a "library for lifelong learning." See McLaren, *FF*, 71.

[102] Franke, *Manifold Witness*, 85. See also Franke, "Recasting Inerrancy," 275.

[103] McLaren, "New Kind of Bible Reading," 4. See also McLaren, *WMRBW*, 59.

[104] McLaren, *WMRBW*, 7.

[105] Ibid.

[106] McLaren, *NKOCY*, 81.

[107] Ibid., 83.

well organized so that the proper precedent can be located efficiently and the correct ruling meted out with regularity. Libraries, on the other hand, safeguard differing viewpoints and are more concerned with preserving conversation and debate rather than ensuring ideological homogeneity. Old Testament scholar Peter Enns believes an examination of Jewish tradition demonstrates an approach to Scripture that embraces healthy debate and diversity of opinion rather than a single monolithic voice. Enns explains:

> The history of Judaism is a lively tradition of wrestling openly with scripture and coming to diverse conclusions about how to handle it. More so than the Christian tradition, Judaism embraces debate as a vital part of its faith. Disagreements are preserved (not silenced or marginalized) in official core texts of Judaism, like the Talmud and medieval commentaries on the Bible. Opposing opinions sit side by side as monuments to this wrestling match with Scripture—and with God.[108]

McLaren argues that "a culture is messy and full of internal tension, and those characteristics would be reflected in a good library."[109] The community as a whole benefits "when we listen humbly to all the different voices arising in the biblical library. Wisdom emerges from the conversation among these voices."[110] Franke believes the plurality of the sacred text should be safeguarded; therefore, it is critical to make sure that "none of the texts of Scripture [are] forced into conformity with others for the sake of systematic unity."[111]

McLaren is indebted in part to the work of Walter Brueggemann at this juncture. At the time a conservative evangelical with a built-in bias against liberals, McLaren first encountered Brueggemann's progressive thinking in a short article. He began the article with suspicion, but he concluded it with keen appreciation. McLaren recalls the article accordingly:

---

[108] Peter Enns, *The Bible Tells Me So* (New York: HarperCollins, 2014), 23. In September 2014, Enns and McLaren posted a conversation focused on their most recent books dealing with biblical hermeneutics. The first of three parts can be found here: http://www.patheos.com/blogs/peterenns/2014/09/my-interview-with-brian-mclaren-part-1/; accessed January 25, 2015.

[109] Ibid., 81.

[110] McLaren, *WMRBW*, 59.

[111] Franke, "Recasting Inerrancy," 277.

It talked about the argument in the Bible about the monarchy. Some biblical voices said the monarchy was a rejection of God, while others said it was a gift from God. In my biased understanding, "liberals" were supposed to then say, "The Bible is full of contradictions. So don't listen to it." But Walter said something very different—something along the lines of this: "Aren't we better off having both of these perspectives in tension, so that we see both the upsides and downsides of centralized power?"[112]

This insight from Brueggemann transformed McLaren's understanding of biblical internal consistency. McLaren learned that the reader need not dismiss the authority of the text just because internal tensions exist. Rather, the most faithful approach is to acknowledge and honor both sides of the argument as part of an ongoing communal conversation.

McLaren believes respecting this plurality of perspectives works best within a dynamic community in which the Bible is heard and discussed, rather than simply studied by a "solitary scholar with furrowed brow."[113] This includes voices that have gone before, "listening respectfully to the ways our ancestors interpreted the text in centuries past."[114] Brueggemann concurs: "There is not one voice in Scripture, and to give any one voice in Scripture or in tradition authority to silence other voices surely distorts the text and misconstrues the liveliness that the text itself engenders in the interpretive community."[115]

Indeed, while holding diverse opinions, a culture or community ironically is united at a deeper level by a plurality of perspectives concerning key issues, because "certain questions are so important that it keeps struggling with them over many generations."[116] Franke, who believes the Bible reflects the "plurality-in-unity and unity-in-plurality"[117] of the Trinity, agrees.

---

[112] Brian McLaren, "Brian McLaren on Walter Brueggemann," *Walter Brueggemann* (blog), June 3, 2013, http://www.walterbrueggemann.com/2013/06/03/brian-mclaren-on-walter-brueggemann/. See also Walter Brueggemann, "Biblical Authority: A Personal Reflection," in *Struggling with Scripture*, Walter Brueggemann, et al. (Louisville: Westminster John Knox Press, 2002), 5–31, and McLaren, *AMP*, 86–87.

[113] McLaren, *NKOCY*, 84.

[114] McLaren, "New Kind of Bible Reading," 6–7. McLaren insists that this should include a variety of minority voices rather than just the privileged Greco-Roman and Euro-American perspectives.

[115] Brueggemann, "Biblical Authority," 16.

[116] Ibid.

[117] Franke, "Recasting Inerrancy," 276.

"What is indicative of community is a shared interest in being involved in an ongoing conversation as to the nature of the communal identity."[118] If this is the case, then McLaren believes "we judge internal tension and debate as flaws or failures in the components of a constitution, but we see them as a sign of vitality and vigor in the literature of a culture. . . . An authoritative library preserves key arguments; an authoritative constitution preserves enforceable agreements."[119]

As mentioned, McLaren is quick to point out that this cultural library is inspired in a unique way.[120] McLaren proposes a via media between those who advocate for a divinely inspired constitution on the one hand and those who consign the Bible to the shelf of merely great historical literature, on the other. McLaren's third-way proposal holds up the Bible "as an inspired library [that] preserves, presents, and inspires an ongoing vigorous conversation with and about God, a living and vital civil argument into which we are all invited and through which God is revealed."[121] In other words, McLaren claims that the conservative constitutional hermeneutic puts us "*under* the text," the liberal approach "lifts us *over* it," but his inspired portable library proposal "puts us *in* the text."[122]

In addition to being an inspired portable library, McLaren believes the Bible houses progressive revelation of God's dealings with humanity. This is one of the key ways in which McLaren addresses the three problems of science, ethics, and peace. If God has chosen to reveal aspects of the divine nature progressively, then not every passage in Scripture carries the same authoritative weight for contemporary readers, who must "wisely interpret Bible stories with science, art, and heart."[123] McLaren argues that the biblical authors' vision of God progressively develops throughout the biblical narrative. To be clear, that does not mean God's ontological being evolves over time,[124] but rather the epistemic perspective of the biblical authors

---

[118] Franke, *Manifold Witness*, 32.

[119] McLaren, *NKOCY*, 82.

[120] Ibid., 83.

[121] Ibid.

[122] Ibid., 96. See also McLaren, "New Kind of Bible Reading," 9. McLaren cites the subject of his master's thesis when offering the following exhortation: "The reader must always remember, to use Walker Percy's terms, that the reader is himself or herself in the predicament that text addresses."

[123] McLaren, *WMRBW*, 51–52.

[124] While appreciating aspects of process theology, especially the writing of John Haught and John Cobb, McLaren distinguishes his position from process theology and pantheism. Brian McLaren, email message to author, July 20, 2009.

matures and crystallizes in much the same way a student's understanding of mathematics develops from lower-level arithmetic to higher-level calculus after years of rigorous engagement with the relevant subject matter.[125] McLaren also likens stories in ancient oral traditions to modern-day scientific hypotheses.

> For ancient people in oral cultures, a story is like a hypothesis. A good and helpful story, like a tested hypothesis, would be repeated and improved and enhanced from place to place and generation to generation. Less helpful stories would be forgotten like a failed theory, or adjusted and revised until they become more helpful. . . . In all these ways, storytelling was, like the scientific method, a way of seeking the truth, a way of grappling with profound questions, a way of passing on hard-won insights. As our ancestors deepened their understanding, their stories changed—just as our theories change.[126]

McLaren believes this evolutionary development takes place in five distinct areas.

God's uniqueness. McLaren proposes that the biblical account begins with viewing Elohim as supreme among many deities.[127] Over time, however, the Jewish authors come to embrace monotheism.

God's ethics. The Old Testament God is initially concerned with "religious and ceremonial fidelity," which is centered in the priesthood. Eventually, however, God is seen as "passionately committed to social justice,"[128] the message associated with the prophetic tradition.

God's universality. It is not unusual for the Hebrew authors to portray God as partial to their own clan. A deeper understanding that the Jewish people are elect for service, rather than exclusive favor, however, eclipses this sense of privilege.

---

[125] McLaren, *NKOCY*, 105.

[126] McLaren, *WMRBW*, 20.

[127] Ibid. This position is known as Henotheism, which allowed for the worship of multiple gods with one deity seen as supreme. See J. Goldingay, "Monotheism," in *New Dictionary of Theology*, ed. Sinclair B. Ferguson et al. (Downers Grove: InterVarsity Press, 1988), 443–44.

[128] McLaren, *NKOCY*, 100.

God's agency. McLaren notes that God, at times, is depicted as "generally outside and uninvolved in the universe until certain moments" of intervention are required. In other parts of the biblical narrative, however, God acts "like a cosmic chess master moving pieces from square to square or a live-in mother-in-law who hovers judgmentally over her daughter-in-law's every move." The more mature perspective on divine agency, however, frames "God's work and wisdom [as] gently but firmly present in the dynamic and unfolding processes of creation and history themselves."[129]

God's character. Herein lies McLaren's biggest concern: namely, how humans understand the character of God. Despite shifting from the Greco-Roman god of Theos to the Jewish God of Elohim, and from the constitutional to library hermeneutical lens, McLaren acknowledges unresolved Old Testament stories in which "God appears violent, retaliatory, given to favoritism, and careless of human life."[130] In light of the Genesis flood account, McLaren speaks with stark candor when he ponders, "One would think God would have more creativity, moral finesse, and foresight than to create a good world only to destroy it because it went so bad so (relatively) quickly. Shouldn't God be better than this?"[131] McLaren wonders, "How can you ask your children—or nonchurch colleagues and neighbors—to honor a deity so uncreative, overreactive, utterly capricious regarding life?"[132] Fortunately, however, as the narrative evolves and moves toward its climax, the biblical portrait of the divine character gravitates toward "justice, kindness, reconciliation, and peace; God's grace gets the final word."[133]

McLaren contends that conservative evangelicals who are bound to the six-line Greco-Roman narrative and constitutional reading of the Bible never grow beyond seeing God as "a competitive warrior," "superficially exacting," "exclusive," "deterministic," and "violent."[134] This hermeneutical stagnation has profound practical implications since there is evidence that the human brain is shaped by or, one might say, made in the image of the

---

[129] Ibid., 101.
[130] Ibid., 101–02.
[131] McLaren, *WMRBW*, 20.
[132] McLaren, *NKOCY*, 109.
[133] Ibid., 102. See also McLaren, "New Kind of Bible Reading," 8.
[134] McLaren, *NKOCY*, 102–3. Without directly naming him, McLaren holds up Mark Driscoll as a paragon of this kind of stagnated and dangerous fundamentalist hermeneutic. See *NKOCY*, 119–20.

kind of God we choose to love, worship, and follow.[135] McLaren expresses his concern accordingly: "In recent years though, I began thinking about how some might use the story as a 'constitutional precedent'—if God single-handedly practiced 'ethnic cleansing' once, and if God cannot do evil, then there is apparently a time and place when genocide is justified."[136] This is hardly hypothetical. American colonization, the Holocaust, the Rwandan genocide, and Darfur are examples of how the Bible has been misused to justify indefensible and horrific acts of violence and oppression.[137]

If progressive revelation, therefore, is an accurate rendering of God's plan of disclosure, then all biblical texts do not possess equal weight and authority. Consequently, every reader and interpreter must make responsible choices, "faithfully picking and choosing—subverting hostility in the strong pursuit of love."[138] McLaren underscores the sober nature of this endeavor: "Ultimately, in choosing how to interpret our sacred texts, we pick and choose between 'compassion and murder.'"[139] While "picking and choosing" might sound arbitrary,[140] McLaren believes there are three sound hermeneutical principles that can guide a progressive[141] and responsible reading of Scripture.

The Bible should be read as a narrative rather than as a constitution. McLaren argues that the Bible must be read "in [the] context of the nested series of stories it is telling."[142] Scot McKnight concurs: "Had God wanted us

---

[135] See Newberg and Waldman, *How God Changes Your Brain*, 131–46. A glimpse of this insight can be seen in an email from Neo to Casey: "Even though we all live on the same planet, we live in different universes—depending on the kind of God we believe in and on our understanding of the master story we are a part of." McLaren, *NKOC*, 161.

[136] McLaren, *NKOCY*, 108–9.

[137] Ibid., 109.

[138] McLaren, *JMBM*, 203.

[139] Ibid., 198. The quote within the quote is attributed to Richard Kearney, *Anatheism* (New York: Columbia University Press, 2010), 160. See also McLaren, "New Kind of Bible Reading," 7–8.

[140] For another discussion related to "picking and choosing" or "adopting and adapting," see Scot McKnight, *The Blue Parakeet* (Grand Rapids: Zondervan, 2008), 13–21. For a critique of McLaren's handling of Scripture, see Richard Mayhue, who asserts, "It appears that McLaren has designed his own version of Christianity in general and of Jesus in particular by picking and choosing what he likes from what he dislikes." Richard L. Mayhue, "The Emerging Church: Generous Orthodoxy or General Obfuscation?" *The Master's Seminary Journal* 17, no. 2 (Fall 2006): 191–205, citing 195, and Tyra, *Missional Orthodoxy*, 172–73.

[141] William Webb calls this "a 'redemptive-movement' hermeneutic because it captures the redemptive spirit *within* Scripture." He equates this interpretive approach with what also might be called "a 'progressive' or 'developmental' or 'trajectory' hermeneutic." See William J. Webb, *Slaves, Women & Homosexuals* (Downers Grove: InterVarsity Press, 2001), 31.

[142] McLaren, "New Kind of Bible Reading," 1.

to read the Bible as the Grand System, I suspect God would have given us a Systematic Theology. He did not, and I suspect we need to learn to read the Bible *as God gave it—as a collection of books from Genesis to Revelation.*"[143] McKnight believes this collection of books is best understood as an ongoing telling of "wiki stories" within the larger framework of "the Story."[144] N. T. Wright, likewise, reinforces the narrative fabric of the textual tapestry: "The Bible, rather obviously, not only offers some fairly substantial individual stories about God, the world and humankind, but in its canonical form, from Genesis to Revelation, tells a single overarching story."[145]

The Bible should be read following the eschatological vision of the biblical prophets. Stories have different plotlines and trajectories, so which ones should be followed and which ones left behind "like fossils in layers of sediment?"[146] McLaren argues that the sacred biblical narrative is best seen as "a series of trade-ups, people courageously letting go of their state-of-the-art understanding of God when an even better understanding begins to emerge."[147] This means that some of the stories in the Old Testament are not literal descriptions of the deity, but rather an approximation or best attempt on the part of the biblical authors given the personal and communal level of spiritual and moral insight at the time.

This view allows McLaren to identify God as a "character"[148] rather than a metaphysical reality in some of the "wiki stories," such as in the negotiations with Satan in the book of Job[149] or the infliction of genocide through mass drowning in the book of Genesis.[150] McLaren argues that the missional message of the peaceable kingdom preached by the biblical prophets provides an orientation for determining which plotlines to embrace and

---

143 McKnight, "Scripture in the Emerging Movement," 109.
144 Ibid., 117. McKnight explains that the "gospel Story is so deep and wide, *God needed a variety of expressions to give us a fuller picture of the Story.*" For a fuller treatment of McKnight's discussion of "wiki stories," see *Blue Parakeet*, 55–79.
145 N. T. Wright, *The Last Word* (New York: HarperCollins, 2005), 7.
146 McLaren, *NKOCY*, 103.
147 Ibid., 111.
148 McKnight finds this a "titillating suggestion." McKnight, "Rebuilding the Faith," 66.
149 McLaren, *NKOCY*, 87–97.
150 Ibid., 98–99. McLaren recognizes the similarities and differences between the Jewish flood narrative and other Ancient Near East accounts. He argues that the biblical narrative should be read in light of the Gilgamesh story, for instance. In so doing, the biblical account can be honored as progress without ignoring its shortcomings. McLaren argues, "In this way of reading the Bible as an ongoing conversation about the character of God, we not only look to the antecedents of the Noah story; we also consider its descendants." See McLaren, *NKOCY*, 108–10.

which ones to cast aside.[151] While McLaren admits that this evolutionary approach is "somewhat complex and nuanced," it does not leave the believer "cast adrift in an 'anything goes' theological sea" of relativism.[152]

The Bible ultimately should be read in light of the character and teaching of Jesus of Nazareth. McLaren recounts a conversation he once had with a former student of Quaker theologian Elton Trueblood. This student told McLaren that Trueblood often said, "The historic Christian doctrine of the divinity of Christ does not simply mean that Jesus is like God. It is far more radical than that. It means that God is like Jesus."[153] This means the life, teachings, and example of Jesus carry more authoritative weight than other scriptural passages.[154] Instead of fitting Jesus into "a predetermined, set-in-stone idea of God derived from the rest of the Bible," Greek philosophy, or natural theology, McLaren believes the iconoclastic Jesus shatters and redefines the human understanding of the divine.[155] The life, character, teaching, and actions of Jesus, therefore, become the ultimate lens and orientation for McLaren's progressive, evolutionary hermeneutic.

McLaren believes Trueblood's statement "is the best single reason to be identified as a believer in Jesus, and it is an unspeakably precious gift that can be offered to people of all faiths."[156] While much theology is abstract and obscure, reflecting upon the disposition of Christ moves the activity into the realm of the concrete and clear. "The stories of Jesus' life and teaching," McLaren notes, "wisely told, can help us imagine and create a more peaceful future."[157] McLaren continues,

> The character of Jesus, we proclaim, provides humanity with a
> unique and indispensable guide for tracing the development of
> maturing images and concepts of God across human history and
> culture. It is the North Star, if you will, to aid all people, what-
> ever their religious background, in their theological pilgrimage.
> The images of God that most resemble Jesus, whether they

---

[151] See McLaren, "New Kind of Bible Reading," 3.
[152] McLaren, *NKOCY*, 113.
[153] Ibid., 114.
[154] McLaren, "New Kind of Bible Reading," 11–13.
[155] McLaren, *NKOCY*, 114.
[156] Ibid.
[157] McLaren, *WMRBW*, 49.

originate in the Bible or elsewhere, are the more mature and complete images; the ones less similar to the character of Jesus are the more embryonic and incomplete, even though they may be celebrated for being better than the less complete images they replaced.[158]

McLaren acknowledges that "violence, like slavery and racism, was normative in our past, and it is still all too common in the present."[159] This, however, does not mean that such realities must be embraced as definitive expressions of the Judeo-Christian story.[160] Neither should these stories be covered up, "hiding them like a loaded gun in a drawer that can be found and used to harm."[161] Rather, McLaren recommends "exposing these violent stories to the light of day. And then we must tell new stories beside them, stories so beautiful and good that they will turn us toward a better vision of kindness, reconciliation, and peace for our future and for our children's future."[162]

How can this project advance within the framework of biblical fidelity? In response to this question, McLaren favorably cites the exemplary work of Derek Flood, who argues "for a way that allows us to remain faithful to Scripture without needing to defend and promote violence in God's name."[163] He describes how Jesus and Paul both engaged in this kind of evolutionary, faithful "picking and choosing"[164] or the "artful and deliberate reshaping" of Old Testament passages.[165] For example, Flood notes how in Romans 15, Paul cites Psalm 18 and Deuteronomy 32, but "the language of divine violence and vengeance is gone."[166] Likewise in Romans 3, Paul's

---

[158] McLaren, *NKOCY*, 114.

[159] McLaren, *WMRBW*, 49.

[160] See Webb, *Slaves, Women & Homosexuality*, 32–33.

[161] McLaren, *WMRBW*, 49.

[162] Ibid.

[163] McLaren, *JMBM*, 200. McLaren quotes Flood but doesn't provide a reference.

[164] For a discussion between Neo and Dan Poole on biblical "picking and choosing," see *NKOC*, 46–53. Additionally, in a talk at the 2014 Wild Goose Festival, McLaren favorably cited Tom Boomershine, former United Theological Seminary professor and founder of the Network of Biblical Storytellers, as another example of one who is faithfully "picking and choosing." According to McLaren, Boomershine claims that violent and exclusive biblical stories should not be told in isolation, but rather in tandem with related biblical accounts that communicate an alternative, redemptive message and complete the totality of the narrative. Brian McLaren, ".@BrianMcLaren: We Make The Road By Walking #wgf14," *YouTube*, June 30, 2014, https://www.youtube.com /watch?v=Ll8LWIrLIhk.

[165] McLaren, *JMBM*, 204. Derek Flood, *Healing the Gospel* (Eugene: Cascade, 2012).

[166] McLaren, *JMBM*, 200.

selective interaction with several Old Testament passages leads Flood to observe, "Paul is making a very different point from the original intent of these Psalms. In fact, he is making the opposite point—we should not cry out for God's wrath and judgment [on the other], because we are all sinners in need of mercy."[167] Paul here is apparently following in the footsteps of his master, who was not shy about redacting the ethnically hostile, exclusive, and vengeful language from the sacred Jewish text as can be seen throughout the Gospels, but preeminently in the Sermon on the Mount.[168] Franke concurs: "In this teaching, Jesus is inviting a radical openness to the other in a way that revises and overturns the instruction in Deuteronomy."[169] McLaren concludes,

> The more I read the New Testament, the more clearly I realize that this other-aversion is at the heart of what the gospel calls us to repent of. The old era of us-them thinking and oppositional identity is coming to an end, the gospel declares. In Christ, God is calling us to a path of reconciliation. Walking that path requires us to go back and reread our Scriptures and 'flip them,' faithfully picking and choosing—subverting hostility in the strong pursuit of love.[170]

This chapter has explored McLaren's deconstructive and reconstructive interaction with the biblical narrative and hermeneutics. With his position on Scripture in clear view, we can now take a closer look at why he believes Calvinism, as the chief expression of bad Christian monotheism, poses a major threat to the gospel in our postmodern, postcolonial world.

---

[167] Ibid., 201.
[168] Flood, *Healing the Gospel*, 14–16.
[169] Franke, "Recasting Inerrancy," 287.
[170] McLaren, *JMBM*, 203.

Chapter Four

MCLAREN AND CALVINISM

I think a terrible convergence occurred, something like the Perfect Storm, when the massive low-pressure system of theistic determinism (Calvin-the-next-generation via Beza & Co.) synergized with the strengthening hurricane of mechanical determinism (Sir Isaac Newton) and then drew strength from the high-pressure system of rationalistic philosophy (Descartes and others). This perfect storm produced a whole new landscape where mechanisms were seen as the ultimate reality and where God was promoted to chief engineer, controlling the whole machine. I do not believe in this modern mechanistic God or this closed, mechanistic universe. I do not believe that this universe is a movie that's already "in the can," having been "produced and shot" already in God's mind, leaving us with the illusion that it's all real and actually happening. I find it hard to imagine worshiping or loving a deterministic, machine-operator God.[1]

—Brian McLaren, *A Generous Orthodoxy*

R. C. SPROUL ASSERTS THAT THERE IS NOTHING MORE OBNOX-ious than an Arminian who has converted to Calvinism.[2] In this statement, Sproul specifically references his own conversion to Reformed theology and the subsequent passion for "the cause of predestination" that has made him a popular apologist for five-point Calvinism.[3] This kind of zeal, however, can work in the opposite direction as well. Consider former Sproul disciple Brian McLaren, who believes bad Christian monotheism is more threatening to the Christian faith than any external foe.

---

[1] McLaren, *GO*, 187.
[2] R. C. Sproul, *Chosen by God* (Wheaton: Tyndale, 1986), 13.
[3] Ibid. Classical Arminianism affirms predestination as well, albeit a conditional rather than unconditional form. Arminian theology will be considered in Chapters Seven and Eight.

The next two chapters will demonstrate that McLaren views Calvinism as the chief expression of the kind of bad Christian monotheism that must be deconstructed for a new kind of Christianity to flourish.[4] After tracing McLaren's personal trek from five-point Calvinism to open theism, this chapter will evaluate his critical engagement with the Reformed view of divine sovereignty and human freedom. Additionally, McLaren's concerns with aspects of the Calvinistic TULIP will be introduced, but deferred until Chapter Five.

McLaren's Journey from Calvinism to Open Theism

Young Life leader David Miller introduced McLaren to Calvinism during high school.[5] Miller explained the doctrine of unconditional election and reprobation to McLaren, who "thought (and maybe said), 'If that's what the Bible teaches, I don't believe the Bible.'"[6] Despite initial resistance to the Reformed vision of divine sovereignty and its soteriological implications, Calvinistic doctrine took root in McLaren's psyche through listening to "hundreds of hours of tapes" by Reformed teachers such as Sproul and Albert Martin, a Baptist pastor from New Jersey.[7] Several Calvinist authors, including Francis Schaeffer and J. I. Packer, also influenced McLaren's thinking.[8] Consequently, McLaren "became a card-carrying (should I say 'tulip-toting'?) Calvinist" during his teens.[9]

Into the early part of his Cedar Ridge ministry, McLaren held to a broadly Reformed framework, appreciating its "appeal from the inside, because it's a highly coherent (from the inside), self-reinforcing closed system, and it gives its defenders a feeling of true superiority, in a

---

[4] McLaren's rejection of five-point Calvinism and movement toward a more relational conception of God parallels in some respects the spiritual journey of Clark Pinnock. See Clark H. Pinnock, "From Augustine to Arminius: A Pilgrimage in Theology," in *The Grace of God and the Will of Man*, ed. Clark Pinnock (Bloomington, MN: Bethany House, 1995), 15–30. This essay is especially germane since Pinnock is one of McLaren's influences in the realm of divine sovereignty and free will.

[5] Brian McLaren, email message to author, July 20, 2009.

[6] Ibid. Dan Poole's daughter, Jess, says something similar when a classmate explains to her the doctrine of unconditional election. See McLaren, *LWWAT*, 30.

[7] Brian McLaren, email message to author, July 20, 2009.

[8] R. Alan Streett, "An Interview with Brian McLaren," *Criswell Theological Review* 3, no. 2 (Spring 2006): 6.

[9] Brian McLaren, "Q&R: Why Do Evangelicals Dislike You?" *brian d. mclaren* (blog), n. d., accessed March 7, 2014, http://brianmclaren.net/archives/blog/q-r-why-do-evangelicals-dislike.html.

OPEN THEISM
(A.K.A. PRESENTISM)

In 1994, *The Openness of God* introduced this view to mainstream evangelicalism.[1] Several books and articles have been written in support and critique,[2] however, arguably the apologetic *magnum opus* is *The God Who Risks* by John Sanders. Sanders outlines four features of this model as follows: (1) God is fundamentally defined by love and it is this love that motivates the creation of humans who are capable of reciprocal relations. Clark Pinnock concurs, "Love and not freedom was our central concern because it was God's desire for loving relationships which required freedom."[3] (2) God sovereignly chose to create a world in which some divine actions are contingent upon and responsive to human choice. (3) General providence is employed to allow humanity the space to cooperate with God in this unfolding creative project. (4) God endows humanity with genuine freedom, a necessary ingredient for authentic relationships.[4]

While the above characteristics resonate with aspects of traditional Arminian theology, advocates of open theism believe two tenets need to be modified for the sake of scriptural faithfulness and rational clarity. (1) Open theists believe God should be understood as temporal rather than atemporal to allow for true divine relationality.[5] Sanders and other open theists argue that a God who experiences the sequence of time is necessary to do justice to the portions of Scripture that portray God as relational, interactive, and responsive. The God of open theism reacts to and is changed by relationships without disturbing God's essential nature and character.[6] (2) Open theism affirms what Sanders calls "dynamic omniscience," and rejects the doctrine of complete foreknowledge.[7] Many open theists

---

[1] Clark H. Pinnock, et al., *The Openness of God* (Downers Grove: IVP, 1994). While the contributors to this volume are among the most recent spokespersons for open theism, predecessors include Peter Geach, J. R. Lucas, George Schlesinger, and Richard Swinburne. See William Hasker, *Providence, Evil and the Openness of God* (London: Routledge, 2004), 97.

[2] Pinnock discusses the reaction to *Openness* in *Most Moved*, 10-18.

[3] Pinnock, *Most Moved*, 3.

[4] John Sanders, *The God Who Risks* (2nd edn; Downers Grove: IVP, 2007), 14f.

[5] John Sanders, "An Introduction to Open Theism," *Reformed Review* 60/2 (Spring 2007): 37.

[6] For a critique of divine temporality and the dynamic view of time, see Laurence Wood, "Boethius or Open Theism?" *Wesleyan Theological Journal* 45/2 (Fall 2010): 41-66. For a response to Wood's concerns in the same issue, see John Sanders "The Eternal Now and Theological Suicide: A Reply to Laurence Wood," 67-81.

[7] Sanders, *Risks* (2nd edn), 15f.

endorse "dynamic omniscience" because they are convinced that exhaustive foreknowledge is incompatible with libertarian freedom. Advocates of open theism argue that God has exhaustive knowledge of all true propositions concerning the past and present, however, future free human choices are not yet part of the furniture of reality so such choices cannot in principle be known.[8] As Thomas Morris explains, "The forward edge of determinant reality is the present, and what comes next is no more than a realm of the possible and the probable."[9] The future is brought about in large part through divine-human cooperation. God does not know the future in its entirety since some aspects of the future are determined by the choices of free agents who have not yet deliberated and made up their respective minds.[10] Morris continues, "On this view, God's knowledge is as complete as it is possible for a state of knowledge to be, *given the sort of world which exists to be known*."[11]

Open theists, however, claim this does not diminish God's glory.[12] If divine omnipotence is not compromised by logical impossibilities, so the argument goes, then the absence of exhaustive foreknowledge from the divine repertoire should in no way diminish God's omniscience, either.[13] Gregory Boyd likens God to "an infinitely intelligent chess player," who is incomparably wise, cunning, resourceful, and never caught off guard.[14] Hasker emphasizes that God could have created "a world in which everything that happens is fully controlled by his sovereign decrees," but apparently a live, open, organic world was preferable, allowing for authentic, loving intersubjectivity and true becoming.[15] Finally, open theists believe this model is faithful to the dynamic biblical depiction of God, whereas many classical theologies unwittingly show their allegiance to the static god of Greek philosophy.[16]

[8] Ibid., 199.

[9] Thomas V. Morris, Our *Idea of God* (Downers Grove: IVP, 1991), 100.

[10] David Basinger, *The Case for Freewill Theism* (Downers Grove: IVP, 1996), 40.

[11] Ibid., 101.

[12] Sanders, *Risks* (2nd edn), 206.

[13] Jerry L. Walls, *Hell: The Logic of Damnation* (Notre Dame, Ind.: Notre Dame University Press, 1992), 47. For a discussion about God's limitations, see Sanders, *Risks* (2nd edn), 238-42.

[14] Boyd, *God of the Possible*, 127.

[15] Hasker, *Providence, Evil and Openness*, 101.

[16] See Pinnock, "Augustine to Arminius," 23-26, and Boyd, *God of the Possible*, 130-32. For an alternative view, see Paul Helm, *Eternal God* (Oxford: Oxford University Press, 1988), 1-22.

humble-yet-exclusively-privileged sort of way."[10] His appreciation for Reformed theology, however, began to wane in the 1990s as he observed "Calvinism allying itself with Theonomy and the hard-core Religious Right."[11]

McLaren also found that his evangelistic attempts were suffering. He diagnosed the problem as follows:

> "God" became the product of the Religious Right. I started to see that the slaughter/land theft/apartheid of the Native Americans, the enslavement of Africans, segregation in the Deep South, Apartheid in South Africa, and now the anti-gay, anti-Muslim, we're-gunning-for-world-war-3, culture war-mentality of American Evangelicals all had something in common . . . and it was the hyper-confidence of Calvinism.[12]

A periodical entitled *Credenda/Agenda*, edited by Reformed pastor and theologian Douglas Wilson, was particularly disconcerting.[13] McLaren recalls, "Every time I read it, I was pushed not only away from Calvinism, but toward atheism. That anybody could be so arrogant, critical, pompous, derisive, dismissive, and utterly sure of themselves struck me as dangerous. . . . So it wasn't arguments against Calvinism [that drove me away], it was the behavior and manner of Calvinists themselves."[14]

During his mid-90s spiritual crisis, McLaren eventually "drifted away from Calvinism without disavowing it."[15] In the late 1990s, however, McLaren began reading Lesslie Newbigin on the recommendation of Young Leader Network colleague Chris Seay.[16] McLaren observed a recurring

---

[10] Ibid. Calvinist pastor Greg Dutcher describes his own conversion to Calvinism in a similar manner: "For me, 'getting' Calvinism was like a pizza secret taken to cosmological levels. It definitely provided a powerful sense of belonging to the right club. A person needs to think like this for only five minutes before seeing himself as fundamentally better than his uninitiated brothers and sisters in Christ." Greg Dutcher, *Killing Calvinism* (Adelphi, MD: Cruciform Press, 2012), 83.

[11] Brian McLaren, email message to author, July 20, 2009.

[12] Ibid.

[13] See http://www.credenda.org; accessed March 7, 2014. Wilson pastors Christ Church in Moscow, Idaho. This magazine is published by Christ Church, which is affiliated with the Confederation of Reformed Evangelical Churches.

[14] Brian McLaren, email message to author, July 20, 2009.

[15] Ibid.

[16] Brian McLaren, "Annotation to 'The Emergent Mystique'—CT article," *brian d. mclaren* (blog archive), October 22, 2004, http://www.brianmclaren.net/archives/000271.html.

theme in Newbigin's works—namely, the claim that "the most stubborn heresy in the history of monotheism is the belief that God chooses people for exclusive privilege, not for missional responsibility."[17] McLaren linked this statement to much of the Calvinism he had personally witnessed and experienced. This insight from Newbigin gave him "permission to leave the whole [Calvinistic] system behind. It was an important breakthrough in my life. I see Newbigin as my primary liberator from Calvinism."[18]

McLaren's drift away from and final break with Calvinism parallels the ascendency of open theism. The controversial *Openness of God* was published in 1994, and several other related volumes soon followed.[19] McLaren acknowledges that he "gradually moved to a more or less open theism position (before [he] really heard of the term) simply out of fatigue with the intellectual gymnastics (and ethical ugliness) of keeping the Calvinist boat afloat in [his] mind."[20]

Clark Pinnock, Gregory Boyd, John Haught, Jürgen Moltmann, and Thomas Jay Oord have influenced McLaren, who prefers to use the phrase, "'the openness of God's universe,' suggesting that a good and creative God would want to create an open universe, not a deterministic one."[21] While resonating with many core tenets of open theism, McLaren did not become a public apologist for this controversial theology for two reasons: first, he discerned a spiritual warfare emphasis in the writing of some open theists, particularly Boyd. McLaren struggled with both the warfare language and the emphasis upon a literal Satan.[22] Second, McLaren perceived among some early open theists a proof-texting hermeneutic that he personally

---

[17] McLaren, *GO*, 195–96. For more, see Lesslie Newbigin, *The Open Secret*, revised ed. (Grand Rapids: Eerdmans, 1995), 66–90.

[18] Brian McLaren, email message to author, July 20, 2009.

[19] Clark Pinnock et al, *The Openness of God* (Downers Grove: InterVarsity Press, 1994). Subsequent books included David Basinger, *The Case for Freewill Theism* (Downers Grove: InterVarsity Press, 1996); John Sanders, *The God Who Risks* (Downers Grove: InterVarsity Press, 1998 and 2007); Gregory A. Boyd, *God of the Possible* (Grand Rapids: Baker, 2000); and Pinnock, *Most Moved Mover* (Grand Rapids: Baker, 2001).

[20] Brian McLaren, email message to author, January 6, 2006.

[21] Ibid. It is worth noting that in this statement, McLaren seems to present a false dichotomy by suggesting that the only two options are an open universe or a deterministic one. This fallacy will be considered in Chapter Eight.

[22] See Gregory A. Boyd, *Satan and the Problem of Evil* (Downers Grove: InterVarsity Press, 2001).

rejected. More recently, McLaren finds these two emphases less apparent, especially with Oord.[23]

Nevertheless, in *A New Kind of Christian*, McLaren inserts a prayer into the mouth of Dan Poole. In this prayer, Poole links the Calvinist view of God's providence to deeply ingrained modern sensibilities.

> I was thinking about the statement "God is in control." I know that the question of what that statement means has been under hot debate in recent years, with the "openness of God" camp suggesting new interpretations and traditionalists crying "heresy" in response. Now I realize that this debate really reflects some thinking people questioning their own modernity, not your ultimate power.[24]

In defense of the open theism movement, McLaren explains "new interpretations" of divine sovereignty not as accommodations to culture, or rationalistic self-sufficiency, or rejecting the clear teaching of Scripture,[25] but rather as "some thinking people questioning their own modernity, not [God's] ultimate power."[26] McLaren claims that this modern mechanistic understanding of control would have been foreign to the original biblical authors. For them, "control was associated with farmers controlling animals or parents controlling children or perhaps a king controlling subjects—all very different from an operator controlling a machine 'like clockwork.'" Failing to exegete the original text and context runs the risk of "importing and imposing all our modern conceptions of clockwork, operation, and mechanism" onto God.[27]

In *The Story We Find Ourselves in*, Neo explains how a movement toward "the openness of God's universe"[28] is a rejection of the mechanistic mentality associated with modernity and an embracing of more organic

---

[23] Brian McLaren, email message to author, January 9, 2014.
[24] McLaren, *NKOC*, 23. This study will explore the Arminian conception of divine sovereignty in Chapters Seven and Eight.
[25] Several books have critiqued open theism along these lines, including Millard J. Erickson, *What Does God Know and When Does He Know It?* (Grand Rapids: Zondervan, 2003) and John Piper et al., *Beyond the Bounds* (Wheaton: Crossway, 2003).
[26] McLaren, *NKOC*, 23.
[27] Ibid.
[28] McLaren, *SWFOI*, 160.

descriptive language. Neo expounds, "So the new universe, or the emerging conception of the universe, is more poetry than machine, more story than gears and levers. In this new universe, to call God a machine operator or engineer feels like an insult, a demotion, a blasphemy even. It feels trivial and restricting. That's what they're getting at in the open theism argument."[29]

What can be discerned here is the connection that exists between McLaren's shift from Calvinism to open theism and his shift from modernism to postmodernism. In both cases, McLaren is exchanging a mechanistic and controlling view of the world for an organic and relational outlook. In *A New Kind of Christianity*, McLaren claims that this deterministic way of understanding divine providence did not originate with modernity, however. McLaren traces it through the Reformers to Augustine, and ultimately back to Platonic Greek philosophy and even parts of Scripture itself.[30] This point of view is consistent with other open theists who have made the case that the god of classical Christian theism has more in common with the god of the Greeks than the God of Jesus.[31]

While McLaren avoided front-line combat surrounding the open theism controversy,[32] his apparent resonance with the movement became one objection among many for several Reformed critics. Many conservative Calvinists already had been fighting open theism for a solid decade when *A Generous Orthodoxy* was published in 2004.[33] As McLaren developed into a prolific author and one of *Time* magazine's most influential evangelicals, the battle with conservative Calvinist critics intensified on multiple fronts.

McLaren and the "New Calvinism"

By the end of the 1980s, just before the open theism controversy ignited, Clark Pinnock saw a thinning in the Calvinist ranks. He observed, "It is hard to find a Calvinist theologian willing to defend Reformed theology. . . . The laity seem to gravitate happily to Arminians like C. S. Lewis for their

---

[29] Ibid.

[30] McLaren, *NKOCY*, 34–45, 101.

[31] See Pinnock, *Most Moved Mover*, 65–111, and Sanders, "Historical Considerations" in *Openness*, 59–100.

[32] While McLaren did not publicly advocate for open theism, fellow ECM founder Doug Pagitt was vocal in his support. See Tony Jones, *The New Christians* (San Francisco: Jossey-Bass, 2008), 46.

[33] For a description of the 1990s battle over open theism, see Pinnock, *Most Moved Mover*, 1–24.

intellectual understanding. So I do not think I stand alone. The drift away from theological determinism is definitely on."[34]

Nearly ten years later, McLaren made a similar pronouncement in *The Church on the Other Side*, identifying Calvinism as "the strongest and most virile of all" the modern systematic theologies. He observed, "The old systematic theologies are fading. Calvinism (or Neo-Calvinism) is . . . showing signs of defensiveness in many quarters that expose its decline."[35] Six years later, when *A Generous Orthodoxy* was published, McLaren followed with the prediction that Calvinism "as the highest expression of modern Christianity" will face "the most trouble . . . and a major identity crisis in the next few decades."[36]

More than a decade has passed since this 2004 doomsday pronouncement, and it appears, at least initially, that McLaren's prediction could not have been more mistaken. Instead of slipping into disarray, Calvinism has crystallized into a dominant renewal movement in the US. Between 2006 and 2009, *CT* published two substantive articles on the "New Calvinism," or the young, restless, reformed movement (YRRM). The September 2006 issue featured an excerpt from Collin Hansen's book, *Young, Restless, Reformed*,[37] which offers an exploration into the organizations, institutions, and key leaders—including John Piper, Albert Mohler, and Mark Driscoll—fueling this movement.[38] Three years later, *CT* published another essay entitled "John Calvin: Comeback Kid, Why the 500-year-old Reformer retains an enthusiastic following today."[39]

It is one thing for the flagship journal of Evangelicalism to cover the revival of Calvinism. It is a different matter altogether when *Time* magazine starts paying attention. *Time* ran a 2009 cover story entitled "10 Ideas That Are Changing the World Right Now,"[40] which introduced a new segment of

---

[34] Pinnock, "From Augustine to Arminius," 26–27.

[35] McLaren, *COOS*, 72.

[36] McLaren, *GO*, 188.

[37] Collin Hansen, *Young, Restless, Reformed* (Wheaton: Crossway, 2008). Jones's book, *The New Christians*, also was published in 2008. *CT* devoted space to a conversation between Hansen and Jones. See "Emergent's New Christians and the Young and Restless Reformed," *CT* (web-only article), May 1, 2008, http://www.christianitytoday.com/ct/2008/mayweb-only/118-51.0.html.

[38] Collin Hansen, "Young, Restless, Reformed," *CT* 50, no. 9 (September 2006): 32–38.

[39] Timothy George, "John Calvin: Comeback Kid," *CT* 53, no. 9 (September 2009): 26–32.

[40] David Van Biema, "10 Ideas That Are Changing the World Right Now: #3, The New Calvinism," *Time* 173, no. 11 (March 23, 2009): 45–66, citing 50.

THE FIVE POINTS OF CALVINISM

The Calvinism-Arminianism conflict can be traced to the Canons of Dort.[1] The Synod of Dordrecht consisted of Reformed international delegates who convened during the winter of 1618–19 to respond to an internal protest movement known as the Remonstrants. The Remonstrants, led by Simon Episcopius (1583–1643), carried on several of the concerns previously voiced by Calvinist pastor and theologian Jacob Arminius (1560–1609). These concerns were enumerated in a document entitled the "Remonstrance," published in 1610. The Remonstrants, who were not included in the Dordrecht deliberation, were deemed Reformed heretics and Arminianism was repudiated as an aberrant doctrinal system. Consequently the following Canons of Dort or five points of Calvinism were developed to repudiate the Arminian challenge:

(1) **Total Depravity:** Every aspect of humanity is tainted by sin. Consequently, humans cannot please God in their own strength.

(2) **Unconditional Election:** God unconditionally predestines (apart from divine foreknowledge of any human act) those who are eternally elect for heaven and passes over the rest, leaving the reprobate in their sins to suffer eternal punishment in hell.

(3) **Limited Atonement:** Christ died on the cross for the unconditionally elect only.

(4) **Irresistible Grace:** God shares His saving grace with the elect only. Since they are unconditionally predestined for salvation, the elect cannot refuse the necessary means (divine grace) leading to the predetermined end.

(5) **Perseverance of the Saints:** The unconditionally elect cannot lose their salvation.

---

[1]While not all Calvinists affirm every aspect of the dividing line established by the Canons of Dort, it remains a useful tool for locating the classical theological and philosophical fault line that runs between Calvinism and Arminianism. Authors who have defined Calvinism by these five points or TULIP include Loraine Boettner, *The Reformed Doctrine of Predestination* (Philadelphia: P&R, 1976); Edwin H. Palmer, *TULIP: The Five Points of Calvinism* (Grand Rapids: Baker, 1972); and James Boice and Philip Ryken, *The Doctrines of Grace* (Wheaton: Crossway, 2002). For a challenge to defining Calvinism solely along these lines, see Kenneth J. Stewart, *Ten Myths About Calvinism* (Downers Grove: IVP, 2011), 75–96; Richard A. Muller, *Calvin and the Reformed Tradition* (Grand Rapids: Baker, 2012), 58–69; and Oliver D. Crisp, *Deviant Calvinism* (Minneapolis: Fortress, 2014).

the population to this Reformed resurgence: "Calvinism is back. . . . John Calvin's 16th century reply to medieval Catholicism's buy-your-way-out-of-purgatory excesses is Evangelicalism's latest success story, complete with an utterly sovereign and micromanaging deity, sinful and puny humanity, and the combination's logical consequence, predestination."[41]

In 2014, *The New York Times* ran a feature on the YRRM with extensive space devoted to pastor Mark Dever, whose congregation worships near McLaren's Cedar Ridge Community Church.[42] As noted in Chapter Two, Dever had written one of the first Calvinist critiques of *A New Kind of Christian* in 2002. The *Times* article included an interview with University of Notre Dame student Brad Vermurlen, the author of a doctoral dissertation on the YRRM. Vermurlen is unclear whether this movement will maintain traction or be seen through the eyes of history as a blip on the screen.

> Ten years ago, everyone was talking about the "emerging church." . . . And five years ago, people were talking about the "missional church." And now "new Calvinism." I don't want to say the new Calvinism is a fad, but I'm wondering if this is one of those things American evangelicals want to talk about for five years, and then they'll go on living their lives and planting their churches.[43]

While the future of the YRRM remains uncertain, McLaren's prediction of a Calvinistic identity crisis has apparently missed the mark.

McLaren's Critique of Calvinism in A Generous Orthodoxy

Questionable predictions notwithstanding, it is important to engage McLaren's characterization of Reformed theology. His most direct and aggressive critique of Calvinism can be found in Chapter Twelve of *A Generous Orthodoxy*.

---

[41] Ibid.

[42] Mark Oppenheimer, "Evangelicals Find Themselves within the Midst of a Calvinist Revival," *New York Times* (January 4, 2014): A13.

[43] Ibid. Vermurlen seems to believe the ECM has passed away. The ongoing relevance and vitality of emergence Christianity is a matter of dispute. For a more positive assessment of the ECM's ongoing presence and viability, see Phyllis Tickle, *Emergence Christianity* (Grand Rapids: Baker, 2012), 112–13, and Gerardo Marti and Gladys Ganiel, *The Deconstructed Church* (Oxford: Oxford University Press, 2014), 193–95.

In Calvin's defense, McLaren claims that the Geneva reformer did not invent theological determinism but was merely "reflecting a widely held belief that went back to at least Augustine."[44] McLaren, who "values Calvin but not determinism," argues that Calvin's followers elevated God "to chief engineer, controlling the whole machine." Additionally, McLaren credits Reformed authors, including Francis Schaeffer, R. C. Sproul, J. I. Packer, Ravi Zacharias, and Os Guinness, for giving him the "permission to think."[45] Moving forward, McLaren believes Calvinism can contribute to the emergence of a generous orthodoxy in three specific ways.

Honor the young Calvin. Contemporary believers should look to the bold example of the early Calvin rather than the mature Calvin. McLaren argues that the "brilliant, bold, young Calvin" faced the problems of his day by filling the void left by the demise of the "corrupt medieval establishment" with "a lean and pure intellectual system: a logically rigorous system of doctrine that would effectively reindoctrinate" the masses. McLaren wonders if a young Calvin today would "identify a completely different need and boldly meet it with similar skill and passion?"[46]

Always be reforming. Citing John Franke and Jürgen Moltmann as two contemporary exemplars of the Reformed movement, McLaren suggests the second contribution that Calvinists can offer is a commitment to ongoing reformation. McLaren believes the concept "of continual reformation is essential for any understanding of a generous orthodoxy." McLaren references his contribution to *The Church in Emerging Culture*, in which he defends the view that Christians should be open to changing both the message and methodology in different cultures and time periods. Consequently, he argues that Calvinists should be willing to evolve not only in terms of methodology, but also in message.[47]

---

[44] McLaren, *GO*, 187.

[45] Ibid. McLaren notes that the Calvinism presented to him during his teen years, which included a commitment to intellectual rigor, seemed like a move toward freedom out of his fundamentalist and anti-intellectual Brethren background. See Frank Schaeffer, "The New Brian McLaren Interview with Frank Schaeffer & Schaeffer Interviews McLaren," video posted at *Why I Still Talk to Jesus—In Spite of Everything* (*Patheos* channel), July 12, 2014, http://www.patheos.com/blogs/frankschaeffer/2014/07/the-new-brian-mclaren-interview-with-frank-schaeffer-schaeffer-interviews-mclaren-the-58-min-video-watch. While McLaren identifies these authors as Reformed, not all of them embrace five-point Calvinism.

[46] McLaren, *GO*, 189.

[47] Ibid., 190–94.

Model repentance and humility. McLaren charges the Reformed tradition with the unfortunate "legacy of horrible mistakes, misjudgments, and even atrocities." In support of this accusation, McLaren claims that Calvinistic teaching has given its adherents "a strange confidence and certainty, [which] while comforting and productive, also proved dangerous at times." Such confidence inspired Calvin "to oversee the execution of fellow Christians," some of the early Puritan settlers to "steal the lands of the Native Peoples," the Calvinist colonists to justify slavery, and South African Calvinist settlers "to create and defend apartheid." But these are not just isolated, unrelated events. McLaren is convinced that "Calvinism is a racist ideology," especially the Kuyperian stream.[48] If this is the case, then McLaren believes it is not surprising that Calvinist orthopraxy (logically consistent practice of five-point Calvinist teaching) naturally leads to these kinds of atrocities. Consequently, McLaren argues correct Calvinist orthopraxy must start with reforming what counts as correct Calvinist orthodox doctrine. And if Calvinists are truly committed to continual reform, then they should repudiate "their legacy of confidence" and "learn from these tragic mistakes."[49]

With a mixture of playful hyperbole and gritty disregard for one of the prized steer in the Reformed pasture, McLaren then proposes the following revisions to the five points of Calvinism.[50]

Instead of total depravity, McLaren proposes triune love. McLaren claims to repudiate the doctrine of total depravity on biblical grounds, but he does not reject the doctrine of original sin. Rather, he redefines it in light of René Girard's mimetic theory.[51] McLaren suggests here exchanging the predominant legal metaphor of "judge" for the intersubjective metaphor of "community" when discussing God's fundamental relationship to humanity.

---

[48] Ibid., 194–95. Brian McLaren, in discussion with the author, Fort Wayne, IN, March 20, 2014. By "Kuyperian," McLaren is referring to Dutch Calvinist theologian and politician Abraham Kuyper (1837–1920) and the role that his political theology played in the development of the Afrikaner culture in South Africa. According to Alan T. Davies, Kuyper's ideology included the belief that "the highest form of religion, i.e., Calvinist Christianity, and the highest kind of human being on a creaturely scale, i.e., the white race (*not* the children of Ham) belonged naturally together." See Alan T. Davies, *Infected Christianity* (Montreal: McGill-Queens University Press, 1988), 93. McLaren also associates Calvinism with the metaphor of an infectious virus, as we will see shortly.

[49] McLaren, *GO*, 194.

[50] This study will consider McLaren's interaction with the first three points of the TULIP (total depravity, unconditional election, and limited atonement) in Chapter Five.

[51] See McLaren, *JMBM*, 105–14. Girard's views will be discussed in the next chapter.

Instead of unconditional election, McLaren proposes unselfish election. As noted earlier in this chapter, Lesslie Newbigin was McLaren's "chief liberator from Calvinism."[52] The key insight that enlightened McLaren was Newbigin's claim that election is for service rather than privilege.[53] In this affirmation, McLaren sees the opportunity for contemporary Calvinists to redeem the doctrine of election.

Instead of limited atonement, McLaren proposes limitless reconciliation. McLaren rejects both exclusive doctrine and the traditional Reformed priority on legal imagery in favor of an alternative bank of metaphors.[54] In Chapter Five, this study will turn to McLaren's mature understanding of the cross in terms of relational betrayal and reconciliation rather than an objective forensic transaction associated with the favored penal substitutionary view.[55]

Instead of irresistible grace, McLaren proposes inspiring grace. McLaren rejects the picture of a "mechanistic force" operating upon the human will in such a way that resistance is rendered futile. In its place, McLaren suggests divine grace "as a passionate, powerful personal desire to shower the beloved with healing and joy and every good thing."[56]

Instead of perseverance of the saints, McLaren proposes passionate, persistent saints. In this final point, McLaren does not discuss whether a believer can lose personal salvation. Instead, he focuses on the term "perseverance," purifies it of the original Calvinistic emphasis upon individual eternal security, and infuses the term with new temporal meaning. By emphasizing the first four revised TULIP terms, McLaren insists, "Reforming Christians would be indefatigable in their attempts to live and share the gospel, resilient after failure, persevering in adversity, persistent over centuries and across generations."[57]

In summary, McLaren believes that Calvinism is rife with modern viruses, which must be debugged. The term "virus" can be used in both organic and inorganic ways.[58] *The Oxford English Dictionary* defines a virus

---

[52] Brian McLaren, email message to author, July 20, 2009.
[53] McLaren, *GO*, 196.
[54] Ibid.
[55] McLaren, *JMBM*, 108–14.
[56] McLaren, *GO*, 196.
[57] Ibid., 197.
[58] McLaren, *COOS*, 197–99.

as "a moral or intellectual poison."[59] In light of McLaren's interaction with five-point Calvinism in *A Generous Orthodoxy,* and elsewhere in his corpus, this would seem to be an apt rendering of what McLaren has in mind. He clearly has identified what he believes are aspects of Reformed theology that have poisoned and corrupted both the morals and the intellect of many of its followers, and by extension have damaged countless lives in their wake.

An alternative definition of virus is equally germane: "A computer program that is usually hidden within another seemingly innocuous program and that produces copies of itself and inserts them into other programs and usually performs a malicious action."[60] This definition of a virus is equally poignant since McLaren asserts, "Before we set ourselves to reboot the new church on the other side, we must be sure to debug it of the viruses it picked up during modernity."[61]

McLaren's Strategy for Debugging the Calvinistic Viruses

Before turning to McLaren's strategy for debugging the modern viruses[62] of Calvinism, we should note his ambivalence concerning the Calvinism-Arminianism debate.[63] In a contribution to *A New Evangelical Manifesto,* McLaren states, "It's not that free-willers are becoming predestinarians or vice versa, although both are occurring. No, it's that new questions are being raised—questions that render the concepts of predestination and free will equally irrelevant or uninteresting."[64] Elsewhere, McLaren elaborates:

> It seems to me that both traditional Arminianism and Calvinism
> are (currently) framed as answers to the question, "Why do
> some people end up in heaven and some people in hell?" They
> end up talking about Divine Agency and larger issues, but they
> do so to answer a question about who is "saved," with saved

---

[59] *The Oxford English Dictionary,* 2nd ed. (Oxford: Clarendon, 1989), 681.

[60] *Merriam-Webster's Collegiate Dictionary,* 11th ed. (Springfield, MA: Merriam-Webster, 2003), 1,398.

[61] McLaren, *COOS,* 197.

[62] McLaren also uses the virus metaphor in *NKOC,* 24. Dan Poole records in his journal, "Neo's thinking is really infecting me. I feel like I've been invaded by a computer virus that's corrupting all my data—or at least reorganizing my data."

[63] It is worth noting that McLaren is also critical of the Arminian contribution to this soteriological debate.

[64] Brian McLaren, "Church in America Today," in *A New Evangelical Manifesto,* ed. David P. Gushee (St. Louis: Chalice, 2012), 4.

being defined as being saved from the eternal consequences of original sin.[65]

During the 1990s, McLaren stopped wondering "whether Calvinism or Arminianism was the right answer to the question; I started wondering if they were answering the right question in the first place."[66]

McLaren argues that the Calvinism-Arminianism debate is historically about *individual* eternal salvation. By focusing inordinate attention on the eternal destiny of the individual soul, more pressing temporal social issues, such as matters of justice, peace, and creation care are often marginalized.[67] In fact, these oft-ignored present-day social issues are central to McLaren's own soteriology, which is properly situated within the broader framework of a kingdom-of-God theology that focuses on the temporal salvation of the entire planet. Therefore, the problem here is not technically one of soteriology, but rather a certain type of soteriology: *eternal individualistic* soteriology.

Another factor fueled McLaren's unease with the Calvinism-Arminianism debate. As he was letting go of Calvinistic theology, McLaren came to the conclusion that "one either begins with a system or a narrative."[68] McLaren had been reading Harvard philosopher W. V. O. Quine, who used the metaphor of a web to describe how all of our beliefs are connected.[69] McLaren came to interpret Quine's metaphor of a web as a narrative, "facts and beliefs arranged as a storyline."[70] McLaren was moved to the conviction "that narratives form us before systems do, and that systems are often apologetics for a covert narrative."[71] In an interview at the 2013 Wild Goose Festival, McLaren stated, "We're probably at our worst when we present our faith as a system instead of as a story."[72] In light of

---

[65] Brian McLaren, email message to author, January 21, 2014.
[66] Ibid.
[67] McLaren, *GO*, 99–100.
[68] Brian McLaren, email message to author, July 20, 2009.
[69] W. V. O. Quine and J. S. Ullian, *The Web of Belief* (New York: Random House, 1970). Many in the ECM were introduced to Quine through Nancey Murphy, who promotes "Quinean Holism" as an alternative to modern foundationalism. See Nancey Murphy, *Beyond Liberalism and Fundamentalism* (Valley Forge: Trinity Press International, 1996), 85–109.
[70] Brian McLaren, email message to author, July 20, 2009.
[71] Ibid.
[72] Krista Tippett, "Transcript for Brian McLaren—The Equation of Change," *On Being* (website), March 13, 2014, http://www.onbeing.org/program/transcript/6174.

McLaren's commitment to narrative rather than systematic theology, it is not hard to see why he "lost interest in solving the [logical] issue [of free will and determinism]."[73]

Nevertheless, when seen from another angle, this debate takes on tremendous value for McLaren. When viewing the Calvinism-Arminianism debate as an eternal, individualistic soteriological struggle for solving the problem of original sin (i.e., the six-line narrative), McLaren considers this matter passé. When understanding this dispute as a struggle concerning the nature of the character of God and the dignity of humanity (in fact, the entire planet), however, this debate becomes central to McLaren's project.[74] In *A Generous Orthodoxy*, McLaren identifies the "fundamentals of the faith" as the two great commandments: "To love God and to love our neighbors."[75] When understood as a dispute over the nature of divine and human love, dignity, and authenticity, therefore, the Calvinism-Arminianism debate radiates with urgent meaning and purpose. So, despite objections to the debate, this is why McLaren continues to engage Calvinism.

With the reason for McLaren's ongoing interest in this subject matter established, this study can explore in greater detail his strategy for debugging the Calvinistic viruses. Based on our survey in this chapter, we can summarize McLaren's view of five-point Calvinism as follows:

> *Calvinism is a tightly formulated, highly rationalistic systematic theology that provides a universalized explanation of how the divine judge and king unconditionally determines all individuals to either eternal salvation or eternal damnation.*[76] *This ideology has infused excessive confidence into the hearts and minds of many who have viewed themselves as a member of the chosen elect, which, in turn, has often fueled colonizing superiority and oppression.*

In this summary statement, we can discern how McLaren links Calvinism to several modern viruses, including individualism, rationalistic systematic

---

[73] Brian McLaren, email message to author, July 20, 2009.
[74] Brian McLaren, email message to author, January 21, 2014.
[75] McLaren, *GO*, 184.
[76] Ibid., 188.

thinking, divine mechanistic control, and an imperialistic, colonizing spirit.[77] The remainder of this chapter will explore the virus of divine mechanistic control and how it has infiltrated the Calvinistic system in ways that poison the human perception of the character of God and the dignity of creation. Chapter Five will examine the other modern Calvinistic viruses in greater detail.

Throughout his books, McLaren is univocal in his condemnation of all forms of mechanistic control or determinism,[78] which create four specific problems. While McLaren does not overtly identify the following problems with Calvinistic determinism in precisely these terms, an exploration of his corpus can locate these concerns, often inchoately.[79] Each problem can be addressed by positing a commitment to genuine human freedom, something McLaren argues is eliminated by the total determinism of Calvinistic sovereignty.

The Problem of Dignity and Authenticity

Total determinism appears to indiscriminately eliminate freedom, and consequently, dignity and authenticity for all. Throughout his corpus, McLaren is a defender of creational dignity. He connects Calvinism's endorsement of comprehensive determinism to the modern virus of mechanization. In *Everything Must Change*, McLaren argues that the modern mind believed the most secure truth of the universe could be seen through a mechanistic lens. "Machines are the quintessential modern metaphor, meaning they reflect the habit of the mind in modern Western societies to describe things by comparing them to machines or mechanisms. As modern Western people, when we find objective, impersonal, universal laws—the kind that run machines—we tend to feel we have found the deepest truth about things."[80]

McLaren argues that modern humanity was most impressed with airtight, systematic, mechanistic explanations and characterizations.

---

[77] All of these modern characteristics were discussed in Chapter Two. For a summary of McLaren's marks of modernity, see Appendix C.

[78] For a brief critique of Marxism and Skinnerian behaviorism, see McLaren, *COOS*, 170.

[79] McLaren confirmed that he had all four of these problems in mind when writing against divine determinism. Brian McLaren, in discussion with the author, Fort Wayne, IN, March 20, 2014.

[80] McLaren, *EMC*, 53–54.

Therefore, it is not surprising that the Calvinistic system, as a product of its culture and age, would "view the universe as a great machine," and exalt the deity to the position of "the Great Modern Machine Operator."[81] In *The Story We Find Ourselves In*, Neo makes this point as well: "In the modern world, the universe was a machine. . . . So, the highest promotion we could give to God was the position of designer and operator of the machine."[82]

Nevertheless, McLaren argues that this mechanistic virus, while in some ways an understandable missiological accommodation to modernity, is particularly malicious because it strips creation of its freedom and, consequently, its inherent dignity and authentic ability to participate as co-creators in the evolutionary development of the planet.

In *A Generous Orthodoxy*, McLaren emphasizes another nefarious modern virus associated with determinism—namely, control.

> Ironically, though, when many modern Christians use the word sovereignty (another form of "kingship" or "lordship"), they make matters worse, much worse, because for them, sovereignty means absolute control. . . . [I]t's not good news at all if you live, as we do, at the end of modernity, a period that told us in a hundred different ways how we're already controlled. . . . Against this backdrop theistic determinism is just another determinism, and in that case, talking about God as the all-powerful, all-controlling Lord/King is just more bad news.[83]

The connection between this quotation and Calvinism is worth amplifying. McLaren believes theistic determinism cannot escape the critique that is due other determinisms. Likewise, the roles that Calvinists most prefer in discussing God's sovereign reign—namely, God as "king" and "judge"—do not resonate as good news with postmodern people, since control is an unwelcome concept. Elsewhere, McLaren writes, "This view of reality folds much (not all) of today's Calvinism into a broader way of thinking called Determinism, which says that ultimately, our freedom is an

---

[81] McLaren, *COOS*, 200–201.
[82] McLaren, *SWFOI*, 160.
[83] McLaren, *GO*, 81.

illusion, and that we're just puppets of one sort or another."[84] Consequently, it is clear that McLaren equates Calvinism with determinism, determinism with the modern virus of "control," and control with an "illusion" of freedom.

This tight association between theological determinism, control, and Calvinism also can be seen in *The Secret Message of Jesus,* in which McLaren argues that Jesus employed the genre of parable as a vehicle to respect human liberty:

> But if it's the heart that counts, then hearts can't be coerced; nobody can be forced, they can be invited, attracted, intrigued, enticed, and challenged—but not forced. And that, perhaps, is the greatest genius of a parable: it doesn't grab you by the lapels and scream in your face, "Repent, you vile sinner! Turn or burn!" Rather, it works gently, subtly, indirectly. It respects your dignity. It doesn't batter you into submission but leaves you free to discover and choose for yourself.[85] In *Finding Faith,* McLaren also claims that Jesus understood the connection between human freedom and authentic faith. McLaren argues that Jesus's noncoercive "approach makes perfect sense in the development of a faith that is real. It has to be free and unforced, a choice rather than a necessity."[86] In the same book, McLaren offers determinism as one possible solution to what he calls the "divine-human dilemma": "Determinism resolves it by saying that, yes, people are hopelessly disconnected from God, and that, yes, God cares for some and shows it by forgiving them and reconnecting them."[87]

This quote demonstrates McLaren equating Calvinism with an all-controlling determinism. Consequently, if determinism eliminates human

---

[84] Ibid., 186.

[85] McLaren, *SMJ*, 48.

[86] McLaren, *FF*, 297.

[87] Ibid., 121. In this case, it appears McLaren has mistakenly asserted that theological determinism is synonymous with unconditional election and reprobation. This, however, clearly is not true. No such entailment exists. It is not difficult to imagine God determining all that comes to pass, including the eternal salvation of every soul.

freedom, dignity, and authenticity, then Calvinism likewise leads to the same unfortunate condition.

In *A Generous Orthodoxy*, McLaren tells of a teenager who explained his understanding of divine and human agency using a gaming analogy: "God is the video game creator and player, and we're characters in a game God plays for personal entertainment. Being 'good' means not resenting that we're jerked around in this way."[88] Of course, one wonders how fully determined video game characters could choose whether or not to resent how they are being treated. Nevertheless, in light of these demeaning metaphors, which strip God, humanity, and the rest of creation of the appropriate dignity and life itself of authenticity, McLaren finds it "hard to imagine worshiping or loving a deterministic, machine-operator God."[89]

METAPHORS OF CALVINISM

McLaren uses several metaphors to describe the kind of artificial world and vacuous semblance of freedom that Calvinistic determinism would create if true. The Calvinistic deity is likened to a *chief engineer*,[a] movie producer,[b] puppet master,[a] behavioral scientist,[c] *chess master*,[d] and *Great Modern Machine Operator*.[e]

Correspondingly, McLaren believes that a mechanistic, deterministic, controlling Calvinism empties humanity of its inherent dignity, reducing humans to impersonal *robots*,[c] actors,[a] *puppets*,[a] *rats*,[c] and chess pieces.[a] Likewise, if Calvinism were true, McLaren believes creation would be reduced to a *vast machine*,[f] movie set,[a] and *chessboard*,[a] as well as a *fantasy, simulation, test*, or *dream universe*.[g]

Italicized terms appear directly in McLaren's primary texts. Non-italicized terms summarize key metaphors.

McLaren's Writings: [a]*GO*, 186-187; [b]*MRTYR*, 118; [c]*FF*, 121; [d]*NKOCY*, 101; [e]*COOS*, 201; [f]*NKOC*, 16; [g]*SWFOI*, 46.

---

[88] McLaren, *GO*, 186.
[89] Ibid., 187.

The common element in each of these inorganic metaphors (see sidebar) is a lack of genuine human agency. Chess pieces, robots, actors,[90] puppets, video game characters, and rats all suffer from an inability to make real, live, first-cause choices. For McLaren, genuine agency, rather than the artificial appearance of freedom, is essential to human dignity and authentic existence. Therefore, any domineering portrait of God is inconsistent with the type of human dignity that comes from being created in the image of a personal deity.

The Problem of Relationality

Closely related is the question of how organic relationships are possible apart from genuine human freedom. Rather than "a group of fish trying to learn about camels," McLaren claims, "we're sons and daughters who want to get to know our father—someone with whom we have an essential relationship. We're creations in the universe God created—we're part of God's universe, and God is therefore part of ours. We're related."[91] In *A New Kind of Christianity*, McLaren likens the divine-human relationship to "a parent guiding a child with a will of her own. The universe, in this view, isn't just an object upon which God acts by dominating fiat; it is a subject endowed by its Creator with millions of real minds and wills, a community with which God relates intersubjectively."[92]

In *Speaking of a Personal God*, fellow open theist Vincent Brümmer underscores the importance of symmetrical reciprocity in relationships, without which one is left with an asymmetrical causal event rather than a true personal interrelationship. Brümmer expounds:

> For the realization of a personal relationship the initiative of
> both partners in the relationship is necessary. Given that both
> partners in such a relationship are persons, both have by defini-
> tion the freedom of will, by which it must be factually possible
> for both of them to say no to the other and so prevent the rela-
> tionship from coming into existence. It is only by means of the

---

[90] McLaren has in mind an actor who must stick to the exact script rather than improvising.
[91] McLaren, *FF*, 128.
[92] McLaren, *NKOCY*, 196.

"yes" of one partner that the other receives the freedom of ability to realize the relationship.[93]

This need for relational symmetry is why McLaren underscores the importance of divine personality. In *The Last Word and the Word After That*, McLaren shares through Dan Poole a common belief among open theists: "The early church believed that God was impassible—incapable of feeling or experiencing or suffering sadness or pain. Now we see God's empathy and compassion as part of the beauty of God's character."[94] In other words, McLaren believes that this relational God is emotionally responsive to the choices humans make in this real, dynamic theater of experience.[95]

In *The Secret Message of Jesus*, McLaren contrasts the preferred modern metaphors of God as a machine-operator or engineer with the premodern New Testament metaphors of God as a good parent or king. McLaren writes, "So the universe was less like a machine and more like a family, less like a mechanism and more like a community. . . . The king may make laws, but the citizens may ignore them. Then the king may respond to their incivility and so on, in an ongoing interactive relationship."[96]

Central to McLaren's organic vision of the universe is an affirmation of theistic evolution, rather than a static, fully determined, ready-made creation. Neo states, "It's God's ongoing creative process; it's not a mechanistic process taking place apart from God, and it's not a simulation being run in the mind of God." Rather, creation is situated in a "matrix of space and time."[97] Within this framework, McLaren envisions a live unfolding of shared relational creative activity between God, humanity, and nature. Neo expounds:

> God needs to create time, so that the universe can be itself,
> become itself, with some kind of freedom and authenticity.
> Otherwise, it's just a puppet universe, just a simulation. . . . So
> if God wants to make a universe that's real, I think we would

---

[93] Vincent Brümmer, *Speaking of a Personal God* (Cambridge: Cambridge University Press, 1992), 75.

[94] McLaren, *LWWAT*, 93.

[95] The early church's position on impassibility will be discussed in Chapter Eight.

[96] McLaren, *SMJ*, 52–53.

[97] Ibid., 53, 30.

expect it to happen just as evolution says: the universe would develop, over time, writing its own story, so to speak. It's a story of becoming, of unfolding, of novelties emerging and possibilities being explored and diversity flowering.[98]

McLaren is lobbying not only for genuine human freedom but also for "some kind of freedom and authenticity" for the rest of the natural world. For this to happen, McLaren contends that Calvinistic determinism, rooted in the modern virus of mechanistic control, must be purged from the Christian narrative.

The Problem of Evil

In 2013, an earthquake triggered a devastating tsunami that killed tens of thousands of people in Japan. John Piper blogged about the tragedy, stating that God determines natural disasters for a reason.[99] Piper confidently proclaimed, "Earthquakes are ultimately from God. Nature does not have a will of its own. And God owes Satan no freedom." Piper reasons that this disaster could have "hundreds of thousands of purposes," but the biblical purposes appear to be a "call to repentance," "warning," "wake-up call," "loud declaration . . . that life is a loan from God," and a "thunder-clap summons to fear God."[100]

Piper and McLaren, the elder statesmen of the YRRM and ECM, respectively, have never met, but Piper had critiqued McLaren five years earlier[101] In a lunch meeting between Tony Jones, Doug Pagitt, and Piper, Jones recalls, "[Piper] really didn't have anything against Emergent Christians per se. His beef is with Brian McLaren and Steve Chalke."[102] As Jones wrote on his blog, "I didn't get the impression that Piper has read anything by McLaren, but Brian's endorsement of Chalke's book was enough to concern

---

[98] Ibid., 98.

[99] John Piper, "Japan: After Empathy and Aid, People Want Answers," *Desiring God* (website), March 17, 2011, http://www.desiringgod.org/blog/posts/japan-after-empathy-and-aid-people-want-answers.

[100] Ibid.

[101] McLaren confirmed that he has never met Piper. Brian McLaren, in discussion with the author, Fort Wayne, IN, March 20, 2014.

[102] Jones, *New Christians*, 77.

him."[103] While McLaren did not respond publicly to these lunch comments, he did respond to Piper's attempt at explaining evil.[104]

McLaren claims Piper delivers "exactly what he believes is wanted—answers: clear, direct, and free of nuance . . . sentimentality and equivocation." McLaren acknowledges that Piper's theodicy "brings great comfort and security to some," but he is not personally persuaded or consoled. In fact, if Piper's answers were the only available theodicy, then McLaren "would be driven away" from the Christian faith. McLaren continues,

> Dr. Piper inhabits a religious universe where it must be deeply satisfying to respond to catastrophes in the way he has, for he has done so on a number of occasions—an earthquake in Turkey, a bridge collapse in Minneapolis, and a tornado that seemed to him to single out liberal, gay-friendly Lutherans. I doubt he, or many like him, will ever change course because this kind of explanation for them, is fidelity—to their way of reading the Bible, to their understanding of God, to their tradition of strict Calvinism.[105]

Instead of conceding that God is the unilateral determining force behind such disasters, McLaren instead asks the preliminary question, "What is God's relationship with the universe?" While "Piper and his colleagues would [answer] 'Sovereignty,' and sovereignty would mean absolute, unilateral control," McLaren offers a different perspective: "The kingdom or sovereignty of God that Jesus proclaims, then, doesn't come with the power of unilateral control but with a radically different kind of power: the gentle power (Paul dares call it 'weakness') of love."

Rather than a "totalitarian" form of providence that is grounded in "absolute control," McLaren believes that God has sovereignly chosen to enter into a different kind of relationship with the universe—namely, one

---

[103] Tony Jones, "My Lunch with John Piper," *Theoblogy* (blog), October 5, 2006, http://theoblogy .blogspot.com/2006/10/my-lunch-with-john-piper.html. The book in question was Chalke's *The Lost Message of Jesus* (Grand Rapids: Zondervan, 2003). Piper's concern, according to Jones, was with "Chalke's characterization of the penal substitutionary theory of the atonement 'as cosmic child abuse.'"

[104] Brian McLaren, "Faith Beyond All Answers: A Response to John Piper's Theodicy," *The Other Journal* (website), Seattle School of Theology and Psychology, March 23, 2011, http://theotherjournal .com/2011/03/23/faith-beyond-all-answers-a-response-to-john-piper%E2%80%99s-theodicy.

[105] Ibid.

in which creation has the freedom "to become, to unfold in its own story, its own evolution." This freedom for the planet presumably includes God allowing natural forces, such as the shifting of tectonic plates, to function according to their own essences without divine interference. God, however, does not leave creation alone, but is engaged relationally: "God's kingship is God's absolute commitment to be with us, whatever happens, always working to bring good from evil, healing from suffering, reconciliation from conflict, and hope from despair."[106] Elsewhere, McLaren explains, "God comes to us in intersubjectivity, in relationship, in history, in an environment, in the stuff of our day-to-day lives."[107]

While earthquakes and tsunamis fall under the rubric of natural evil, elsewhere McLaren addresses the problem of moral evil with an overt appeal to the free will defense.[108] In *Finding Faith*, McLaren explains that humans are created in the image of a personal God who bestowed upon humanity a "mysterious endowment" of "freedom, wisdom, creativity, love, communication, civilization, [and] virtue."[109] This endowment of personality, however, contained a potential underbelly, making humans "vulnerable to rebellion, pride, foolishness, destructiveness, hatred, division, and vice." Since "being neither robots nor prisoners, these free human beings early on failed to fulfill the full promise of their primal innocence and natural nobility." In other words, if God is to honor the personality of humanity, then humans must ultimately be capable of making real, live, first-cause choices for which they are responsible. Unfortunately, humans have not always exercised this gift of freedom responsibly; consequently, humanity possesses "a self-destructive bent."[110]

In a prayer offered by pastor Dan Poole in *A New Kind of Christian*, the essence of McLaren's argument becomes clear:

---

[106] Ibid.

[107] Brian McLaren, "Honey, I Woke Up in a Different Universe: Confessions of a Postmodern Pastor," *Mars Hill Review* 41 (Fall 1999): 41.

[108] This theodicy can be traced back to Augustine. Ironically, it is unlikely that Augustine articulated a sufficient notion of freedom to advance this argument in a consistent manner. See John Hick, *Evil and the God of Love*, rev. ed. (San Francisco: Harper & Row, 1977), 64–69.

[109] McLaren, *FF*, 235.

[110] Ibid. While McLaren discusses the doctrine of original sin, he disagrees with Augustine's account of "the Fall." This subject will be examined in Chapter Five.

In one way, Lord, this makes me want to praise you, because many of our intellectual problems with faith, like the whole issue of how evil can exist in your universe, seem to disappear or shrink when we step outside the mechanistic model. In other words, if a company designs a plane and it crashes due to design failure, we hold the designer liable. Or if a person drives a car drunk and kills a pedestrian, we hold the driver responsible. In both cases, the machine designer or operator is the only sentient being capable of being held responsible. But if a parent raises a child with all appropriate guidance and the child grows up and rejects his parents' teaching and commits a crime, we don't hold the parent responsible in the same way. So I can see how limiting ourselves as moderns to a mechanistic view of the universe and of you—really creates problems for us.[111]

In summary, McLaren insists that when human agents exercise their personal freedom in irresponsible ways, God is not to blame, but rather the culpability rests with the individual who possessed the categorical power to have chosen differently. God has a "good dream" for this world, but selfishly exploiting the gift of freedom can turn that dream into a "nightmare."[112] While the discussion in this section does not exhaust McLaren's theodicy, it does demonstrate his strong resistance to deterministic solutions to the problem of evil, as well as his affinity to lines of reasoning that highlight the importance of human freedom.

The Problem of Reliability

As already demonstrated, McLaren believes that theistic determinism leaves humanity with an illusion of freedom.[113] If all things are comprehensively, unconditionally determined, then life lacks authenticity. Instead, this world would be a divine "mind game,"[114] "simulation,"[115] "fantasy,"[116] or "movie

---

[111] McLaren, *NKOC*, 23–24. This explanation, however, does not address some of the problems that open theism still must face, such as why God intervenes at some times, but not at other points in history.

[112] Ibid.

[113] McLaren, *GO*, 186.

[114] McLaren, *MRTYR*, 118.

[115] McLaren, *SWFOI*, 46.

[116] Ibid.

that's already 'in the can.'"[117] Therefore, if theistic determinism is true, then the world is in tension with the deep-seated human intuitive belief that our environment is a real, authentic time-space arena in which genuine freedom is not only possible, but essential.

As disconcerting as this would be, there is perhaps an even more unsettling problem for the believer. Christians of all stripes view God as both omnibenevolent and omnicompetent. If the world lacks authenticity, however, then questions are raised not only concerning deep-seated human intuitions but also about the faithfulness and credibility of the designer who created such intuitions. In other words, it would appear that the creator either lacks the competence to design a world that corresponds to our deepest, most certain intuitions, or the creator is intentionally deceptive. Neither horn of the dilemma is especially attractive for the Christian.

As stated, McLaren's arguments are often suggestive and inchoate. This is a case in point, and, consequently, this argument requires some teasing out. It should be noted, however, that in conversation, McLaren confirmed the following formal structure as faithful to his implicit line of reasoning.[118] That said, the problem of reliability can be understood as follows.

Several theologians and philosophers have argued that humans are naturally wired to believe we possess genuine freedom. Clark Pinnock explains:

> There is an intuition in us that is difficult to shake. I refer to the deep sense that human behavior is not entirely shaped by causal factors but is partially self-determining. It is an intuition that people hold in practice even when they deny it intellectually. For example, we hold others responsible for their actions, whether praiseworthy or blameworthy; we do not believe God is the only significant agent; we do not consider the fact that a person holds a different viewpoint than ours as something they were predestined to do; and we exhort one another because we assume that people can change their ways. Freedom is, in Griffin's words, "a hard-core common sense notion," a notion presupposed in practice, even when denied verbally. Life itself requires us to posit it

---

[117] McLaren, *GO*, 187.
[118] Brian McLaren, in discussion with the author, Fort Wayne, IN, March 20, 2014.

and we all live as if it were true. God has given us the experience of voluntary action in which alternative possibilities present themselves and we hold to it, unless some clever person talks us out of it.[119]

Austin Fischer, author of *Young, Restless, No Longer Reformed*, was "talked out of [belief in genuine freedom]," but has since rejected Reformed theology and returned to a position of trusting this intuition of freedom. In agreement with Pinnock, Fischer writes, "But we certainly experience ourselves as free, if nothing else, which is why no one starts out a Calvinist."[120]

Many philosophers argue that the human conscience and natural sense of morality, as well as the experience of regret and deliberation all appear to assume a genuine form of freedom.[121] William Hasker insists that this "human intuitive conviction of freedom . . . is one that we are entitled to take seriously and treat with respect."[122] Jerry Walls and Joe Dongell agree that "it seems intuitively and immediately evident that many of our actions are up to us in the sense that when faced with a decision, both (or more) options are within our power to choose."[123] In other words, it is a commonly held belief that genuine freedom is a deep-seated intuition that appears to be hard-wired into the human apparatus.

Walls and Dongell continue, "This is a basic moral intuition, and we do not believe that there are any relevant moral convictions more basic than this one that could serve as premises to prove it."[124] The concept of moral intuition will be explored more fully in Chapter Seven. For now, it is sufficient to establish the plausibility of the basic belief in the moral intuition of genuine human freedom. The key point here has nothing to do

---

[119] Pinnock, *Most Moved Mover*, 160–61.

[120] Austin Fischer, *Young, Restless, No Longer Reformed* (Eugene: Cascade, 2014) Kindle edition, 7. It is worth pointing out that Calvinists typically affirm some kind of human freedom, as will be discussed in the final section of this chapter.

[121] One might argue moral standards vary from culture to culture. This is a debatable point, however, irrelevant to the argument here. What is being argued is not that every human culture shares the identical ethical system, but rather that nearly all people in all cultures share some sense of morality and an intuition of genuine freedom. For an interesting investigation into the relationship between universal moral intuitions and cultural considerations, see Jonathan Haidt, *The Righteous Mind* (New York: Pantheon Books, 2012), 112–54.

[122] William Hasker, *Metaphysics* (Downers Grove: InterVarsity Press, 1983), 45.

[123] Jerry L. Walls and Joseph R. Dongell, *Why I Am Not a Calvinist* (Downers Grove: InterVarsity Press, 2004), 104.

[124] Ibid., 105.

with whether or not humans are actually free, but rather that human beings appear to be hardwired to act *as if* they are free and capable of making real, live, nondetermined choices.

Closely related to this intuitive assumption of human freedom is the intuitive assumption that a real external world metaphysically exists.[125] In order to freely choose between two or more live options, one must have a metaphysical context or time-space matrix in which real, live choices could take place. Therefore, it would seem that the intuitive assumptions of genuine human freedom and belief in an actual external world, while neither can be proven, are sturdy, basic beliefs and more plausible than alternative skeptical theories.[126]

If humans are justified in trusting their intuitions regarding human agency and the existence of an external world, then one must ask why these intuitions are part of the human apparatus in the first place. Walls and Dongell contend that "our moral intuitions are an aspect of the image of God, so God himself is their author."[127] McLaren concurs. In fact, this is where his critique of modernism is especially germane. One of his chief criticisms of the modern project is that it tended to suppress all human faculties, with the exception of "objective" analytical reason. The postmodern response is to holistically reempower the full range of human faculties, including the human experience of intuition.[128] Consequently, if intuition is part of the divine design, then God is the designer and presumably intended this gift of intuition to be a faithful guide to exploring, discovering, and navigating the environment in which humans find themselves.

---

[125] Even solipsists function practically as metaphysical realists. Some in the ECM, however, seem to have adopted an anti-realist position. McLaren, as a soft postmodernist, however, affirms the existence of a real external metaphysical world. Kevin Corcoran argues persuasively that epistemic humility does not require an anti-realist posture. See Kevin Corcoran, "Philosophical Realism," in *Church in the Present Tense*, ed. Kevin Corcoran (Grand Rapids: Brazos, 2011), 3–21.

[126] Properly basic belief is one in which individuals are justified without evidence or proof. Philosophers, especially different kinds of foundationalists, disagree over what counts as properly basic. In the absence of a defeater, there are basic beliefs—in this case the beliefs that humans possess genuine freedom and that an external world actually exists—that are properly justified without evidence and proof, since evidence and proof are unavailable in such matters. What makes these beliefs properly basic is that they appear to function according to their design and in the environment in which they have been placed. For more, see Alvin C. Plantinga, *Warrant and Proper Function* (Oxford: Oxford University Press, 1993), 3–20.

[127] Walls and Dongell, *Why I Am Not a Calvinist,* 105.

[128] McLaren, *NKOC,* 16–17.

McLaren's problem of reliability can now be seen more clearly. For if humans are justified in trusting the intuition of human agency (and the corresponding intuited belief that the external world is real), and if God is a competent and faithful designer of such intuitions, as well as of the external world in which humans find themselves, then it follows that God would engineer an organic consonant fit between the most basic and certain human intuitions and the world as it actually exists. If theistic determinism is true, however, there is a radical dissonance between the world that humans intuitively believe to be real and the world that actually exists. Such radical dissonance would lead humans to question either the omnicompetence or the omnibenevolence of the deity to equip humanity with the basic apparatus to faithfully and authentically navigate the environment for which humanity has been designed. In short, if God has created a world that only *appears* to be real, live, and authentic, but actually is fully determined, then it raises the ominous specter of whether or not humans can trust both their deepest intuitions and their designer.

In *The Story We Find Ourselves in*, Neo describes what he believes to be the true organic condition of this world in contradistinction to a contrived world that has been determined: "The universe that God created is a real one. It isn't a fantasy universe, a simulation universe, a test universe, or a dream universe. It's real, and what happens here is real."[129] If the world is as the five-point Calvinist has described, however, fully, unconditionally, and unilaterally determined by God, then the normal, intuitive understanding of freedom and moral responsibility is impossible and therefore misleading. For if God has determined precisely what comes about, then humans are incapable of choosing other than what God has determined, despite possessing the *illusion* of genuine freedom. If this is so, then much of the world as humans experience it lacks authenticity. If theistic determinism is a true depiction of reality, McLaren argues, then humans are reduced to a misleading existence, believing in real, live freedom but in actuality functioning as no more than "plastic chessmen on a board of colored squares, puppets on strings in a play we don't write, characters in a video game that we aren't even playing, cogs in a contraption whose levers and buttons

---

[129] McLaren, *SWFOI*, 46.

God and God alone pulls and pushes."[130] In other words, the deep human intuition of genuine freedom is entirely misleading, and the designer of that shared intuition is either incompetent or deceptive. Either way, God cannot be trusted and considered good in any meaningful sense of the word. Moreover, our own experience of and deeply held intuitive conviction of human freedom is specious and contrived.[131]

In summary, each of the four problems identified in this section can be attributed to theistic determinism, in general, and Calvinistic sovereignty, in particular. McLaren contends that a Reformed notion of total, unconditional sovereignty undermines genuine human freedom, which in turn eliminates the full range of human personality and dignity, as well as the authenticity of the external world. Additionally, it calls into question the character, relationality, competency, and faithfulness of God. This study will now turn to assessing whether McLaren's critique of Calvinistic sovereignty and human significance is sound.

Evaluating McLaren's Arguments

As seen, McLaren believes total determinism eliminates genuine human freedom. Up to this point, we have simply used the term "freedom" without careful nuance. To properly assess McLaren's evaluation of Calvinistic sovereignty and human freedom, however, we must spend the next few pages summarizing one of the most contentious and enduring debates in philosophy of religion—namely, the free will problem.[132] This will require an introduction to three different models of free will and determinism: *hard determinism*, *libertarianism*, and *soft determinism* (aka *compatibilism*).[133]

---

[130] McLaren, *GO*, 81.

[131] One potential way for the Calvinist to sidestep this critique is to suggest that Adam and Eve were originally endowed with the power of genuine freedom, but after the Fall it was lost. The human race, therefore, has a built-in genetic memory of this type of freedom, but due to original sin it is no longer within our grasp. It is worth noting that both Calvinists and Arminians recognize the existence of common grace which restores human faculties, including the faculty of intuition, to a point of allowing humanity to function in common civil society. See Walls and Dongell, *Why I Am Not a Calvinist*, 105.

[132] Timothy O'Connor, *Persons and Causes: The Metaphysics of Free Will* (New York: Oxford University Press, 2000), xi. According to David Hume, the question of free will is the most contentious in metaphysics. See Kevin Timpe, *Free Will: Sourcehood and Its Alternatives*, 2nd ed. (New York: Bloomsbury, 2013), 3–4.

[133] These three models are the generally accepted options in contemporary philosophy of religion. For an accessible introduction to these models, see Hasker, *Metaphysics*, 29–55, and Scott R. Burson and Jerry L. Walls, *C. S. Lewis and Francis Schaeffer* (Downers Grove: InterVarsity Press, 1998),

Once these models have been nuanced, we can properly analyze McLaren's engagement with Calvinistic sovereignty and human freedom.

While adherents to these three models disagree over the proper definition of freedom (as we will see shortly), they agree on the definition of total determinism. One common definition comes from Hasker, who defines total determinism as "the view that for every event which happens, there are previous events and circumstances which are its sufficient conditions or causes, so that, given those previous events and circumstances, it is impossible that the event should not occur."[134] Determinism can come in naturalistic and theological expressions, but the key unifying consideration is that every event is ultimately necessitated and, given the relationship between the previous causes and conditions, the event in question must occur. With this definition of total determinism in clear view, we can now summarize the aforementioned models.

Hard Determinism

Hard determinism assumes the veracity of total determinism. Adherents to this view claim that everything in the world—including all human thoughts, feelings, and choices—is fully determined by either God or nature. Hard determinists also believe that human freedom is illusory. This can be seen clearly by how a free act is defined. **According to hard determinism, freedom is an event without a cause.** Since every event in a completely determined world has a cause, human freedom is therefore eliminated.[135] Additionally, hard determinists reject the concept of moral responsibility since freedom is a necessary ingredient for a morally culpable act.

Libertarianism

Hard determinism and *libertarianism* find common ground on one point— total determinism and human freedom cannot be harmonized.[136] This means that hard determinism and libertarianism are both expressions of

---

66–69. For a more advanced discussion, see Robert Kane, ed., *The Oxford Handbook of Free Will* (Oxford: Oxford University Press, 2002).

[134] Hasker, *Metaphysics*, 32.

[135] Walls and Dongell, *Why I Am Not a Calvinist*, 108.

[136] One should take care to distinguish between philosophical libertarianism and political libertarianism.

incompatibilism. But this is where the agreement ends. In contrast to hard determinism, libertarians deny the existence of comprehensive determinism, particularly in the realm of human agency.

While acknowledging genetic and environmental *influences*, libertarians believe that humans are capable of real, live, nondetermined choices, at least some of the time. More specifically, libertarians define freedom as **the ability to choose between two or more live options,** also known as **the power of contrary choice**.[137] This libertarian definition of freedom is consistent with our natural assumption that certain choices and decisions are truly up to us without any predetermining cause. As long as a person has the live option of choosing differently in a given situation, then the person is free and morally responsible for that particular action.

This interpretation of freedom is an intuitively appealing model because much of life appears to be grounded in the assumption of libertarian freedom. While deliberating and planning one's day, one generally assumes at least two or more real options; otherwise, the process of deliberation between alternative plans would be seemingly meaningless. Additionally, legal systems in the Western world generally assume libertarian freedom. A convicted murderer is sentenced to life in prison or even death because judges and juries believe the defendant's actions were **not fully determined**, but rather the defendant had the ability to either fire the weapon *or* resist firing the weapon at the key moment.[138]

Soft Determinism

Whereas hard determinists and libertarians both claim that determinism and free will are incompatible, adherents to *soft determinism* assert that total determinism and free will can be logically harmonized, which is why this position is also called *compatibilism*. Now, on the surface, this is quite puzzling. If some kind of external force has determined every thought, desire, and choice, then how can humans be free and morally responsible for their thoughts and actions? As we have seen, the hard determinist and

---

[137] Some libertarians opt to ground freedom in the source of the choice rather than having alternative live options available. See Timpe, *Free Will,* 25–31.

[138] See Roger E. Olson, "The Classical Free Will Theist Model of God" in *Perspectives on the Doctrine of God,* ed. Bruce A. Ware (Nashville: B&H, 2008), 157.

A CASE STUDY IN FREEDOM:
JIMMY AND THE ROCK CONCERT

The following illustration is offered to illuminate the differences between *hard determinism*, *libertarianism*, and *soft determinism*. Let us say that Jimmy, a 20-year-old college student, wants to attend a rock concert. He goes to the arena several hours in advance, only to find that the concert is sold out. Disappointed, but undeterred, Jimmy walks around the perimeter of the arena and notices a door by the loading dock is propped open with a stick. While Jimmy is not generally prone to unethical behavior, the more he stares at the stick, the more tempted he is to enter. Finally, Jimmy approaches the door, looks both ways and moves briskly inside. He quickly hides in a closet. As the concert begins, Jimmy cautiously exits the closet and watches the full performance without any challenges from security.

Now, let us evaluate Jimmy's scenario in light of each model. First, consider *hard determinism*. Was Jimmy's decision to sneak into the concert a free choice? The hard determinist would say "No." According to hard determinism, every event has been caused by prior events and conditions stretching back in an incalculably lengthy chain. Whether it is the result of one's genetic composition, environmental factors, or divine determinism, Jimmy could not have chosen differently. Since a free act (as defined by the hard determinist) is an event without a cause in a universe in which everything is caused, Jimmy was not free and morally responsible for this unlawful act.

Libertarianism offers a considerably different perspective on what happened. According to this position, there are events in life, such as the rising and falling of the tides, that are determined, but humans possess the power to transcend the causal nexus and make real, self-determined choices. In this case, it appears that Jimmy had the power to resist the unlawful entry to the concert, but he chose to pursue an immoral act. So unless it can be demonstrated that Jimmy was unable to resist sneaking into the concert due to physiological, mental, emotional, or environmental determining factors, he should be considered free and morally culpable for this act.

Soft determinism (a.k.a. Compatibilism) offers a final interpretation. According to this view, all events are fully determined so Jimmy could not have avoided sneaking into the concert. Yet Jimmy was still free and morally responsible for his action because he did what he wanted to do. Nothing forced or coerced Jimmy to act against his will. Consequently, Jimmy freely, in a compatibilistic sense, made the choice and is morally responsible even though he could not have chosen differently. When asked if Jimmy was determined to sneak into the concert or if he entered of his own volition, the soft determinist can answer, "Both." The legitimacy of this compatibilistic definition of freedom will be considered in Chapter Seven. For now, it is sufficient to point out that compatibilism affirms both determinism and freedom, albeit a highly counterintuitive form of freedom.

the libertarian would both say that total determinism and freedom are logically incompatible, but the soft determinist disagrees with the definitions of freedom suggested up to this point. Instead, soft determinists offer an alternative, counterintuitive way of thinking about freedom.

According to the soft determinist, **a free act is simply one in which a person does what she wants to do, even though she can't do otherwise**. According to this model, the person is not coerced or forced to do something against her will, but rather she is determined to do what she wants to do. As long as she acts in a way that is consistent with her inner states (thoughts, feelings, wishes, desires, and so on), then she is free and morally responsible for that action, even though she was fully determined to perform the action in question. In short, this position offers a view that attempts to harmonize both total determinism and human freedom (and moral responsibility).[139]

With these definitions in place, we can now see how these models apply to the theological systems of Arminianism and Calvinism. Libertarianism

---

[139] William Hasker summarizes the three criteria necessary for a free compatibilistic act: "(1) It is not caused by compulsion [against the agent's will] or by states of affairs external to the agent. (2) Instead, the *immediate cause* of the action is a psychological state of affairs internal to the agent—a wish, a desire, intention or something of the sort. (3) The situation is one in which it was *in the agent's power* to have acted differently, *if he had wanted to*." Hasker, *Metaphysics*, 34. These criteria will be evaluated more carefully in Chapter Seven.

is the consistent Arminian view because total unconditional determinism is incompatible with our normal understanding of moral responsibility and intuitive view of freedom (the power of contrary choice). [140] Soft determinism is the consistent Calvinist position because this view affirms the logical consistency of total, unconditional divine determinism and a counterintuitive understanding of human freedom and moral responsibility. [141] The one position, however, that is not embraced by either Arminians or Calvinists is hard determinism. The reason hard determinism is not attractive to the Christian is because it does not allow for human freedom and moral responsibility. Instead, this is the position of behaviorists such as B. F. Skinner, who believed that humans can be conditioned in the same manner as lower animals. [142]

It should now be apparent that McLaren affirms a libertarian form of freedom and in so doing is aligned with orthodox Arminianism on this point. Libertarians reject total determinism because they believe it eliminates concepts such as human freedom, responsibility, dignity, authenticity, and relationality, as well as divine faithfulness along the lines of the arguments presented in the previous section. But don't most Calvinists believe in some form of human freedom, responsibility, dignity, authenticity, and relationality, as well as divine faithfulness? In fact, they do. This is why soft determinism rather than hard determinism is an attractive model for the Calvinist. But if Calvinists are soft determinists, then why does McLaren believe Calvinistic sovereignty eliminates human liberty, dignity, and relationality? The answer appears to be that McLaren has not carefully distinguished between these two different deterministic models.

In *A Generous Orthodoxy*, McLaren states that he is seeking to engage the more popular, on-the-street formulation of Calvinism rather than "scholarly understandings of predestination [that] are finely nuanced." [143] So he believes the on-the-street version of Calvinism can be summed up simply as "Determinism," which seems to have all of the features of hard determinism,

---

[140] Prominent historical and contemporary libertarians include Jacob Arminius, John Wesley, Thomas Reid, William Lane Craig, and Jerry Walls.

[141] Prominent compatibilistic Calvinists will be introduced in the main text shortly.

[142] See B. F. Skinner, *Walden Two* (Englewood Cliffs: Prentice Hall, 1976).

[143] McLaren, *GO*, 186.

including the elimination of human freedom and moral responsibility.[144] This maneuver, however, is problematic since hard determinism eliminates aspects of the Christian narrative affirmed by Calvinism. It is not enough to simply equate Calvinism with a generic form of determinism, because soft determinism and hard determinism define freedom in very different ways. A more carefully nuanced assessment is needed.

To compound the problem, McLaren also associates the doctrine of predestination with fatalism. In *The Secret Message of Jesus*, McLaren argues that God's "goal is not to place us in a fatalistic, determined universe that makes us succumb to can't-win disempowerment, fatalism, despair, and resignation."[145] In a similar passage, located in *A New Kind of Christianity*, McLaren writes, "If we take this third narrative in this way, we are immediately freed from arguments about a deterministic future . . . because the future in this approach isn't waiting to be created; it is not fatalistically predetermined."[146] This conflation of fatalism with determinism, however, is also problematic for McLaren. As Kevin Timpe points out, the technical concepts of determinism and fatalism are critically distinct:

> This initial worry is misplaced for it confuses determinism with fatalism, the view that future events—including an agent's action—are inevitable and will happen no matter what the agent does. . . . The truth of determinism is completely compatible with our actions being in part determined by our choices such that if we had not made a particular choice, we would not have done a particular action. Of course, if determinism is true, then our choices are themselves causally necessitated by earlier factors in a way that one might think threatens free will. But the worry that determinism rules out the causal efficiency of our volitions is misguided.[147]

Linking Calvinism with either a generic or hard form of determinism on the one hand or fatalism on the other is unlikely to please most

---

[144] Ibid.

[145] McLaren, *SMJ*, 175.

[146] McLaren, *NKOCY*, 62. See also Terrance L. Tiessen, *Providence and Prayer* (Downers Grove: InterVarsity Press, 2000), 271–85.

[147] Timpe, *Free Will*, 20.

Calvinistic scholars.[148] This is a common misunderstanding of Reformed theology, and responses from Calvinist authors are plentiful. D. A. Carson avers, "Christians are not fatalists. The central line of Christian tradition neither sacrifices the utter sovereignty of God nor reduces the responsibility of his image-bearers. In the realm of philosophical theology, this position is sometimes called *compatibilism*."[149] Anticipating the kind of objections that McLaren has raised, John Feinberg implores, "Before you conjure up notions of robots, mechanistic universes and fatalism, withhold judgment long enough to let me explain my position."[150] Robert Peterson and Michael Williams likewise labor to dispel caricatures that claim "divine ordination of history turns human beings into chess pieces who do not make meaningful choices."[151] Paul Helm also distinguishes between the Reformed notion of predestination and fatalism:

> The thought of men and women being directly controlled raises in some minds the spectre of fatalism, of the idea that men and women are blindly destined, perhaps by the stars, for a particular fate irrespective of their own wishes and plans. But such a conception is quite at variance with divine providence. For in providence the controller is not blind, nor is the control exercised apart from what men and women themselves want. The controller is God, who is the supreme purposer of the universe. He exercises his control, as far as men and women are concerned, not apart from what they want to do, or (generally speaking) by compelling them to do what they do not want to do, but through their wills.[152]

---

[148] One cannot help but feel that Calvinist critics such as Michael Horton, who claims that many of McLaren's "criticisms are based on caricatures," and Kevin DeYoung, who argues that McLaren's books are "full of overgeneralizations," are not entirely unjustified in their objections when it comes to McLaren's treatment of the finer points of Reformed sovereignty and human freedom. See Michael Horton, *For Calvinism* (Grand Rapids: Zondervan, 2011), 190, and Kevin DeYoung and Ted Kluck, *Why We're Not Emergent* (Chicago: Moody, 2008), 43.

[149] D. A. Carson, *The Difficult Doctrine of the Love of God* (Wheaton: Crossway, 2000), 51–52.

[150] John S. Feinberg, "God Ordains All Things," in *Predestination and Free Will*, ed. David Basinger and Randall Basinger (Downers Grove: InterVarsity Press, 1986), 17–41, citing 19.

[151] Robert A. Peterson and Michael D. Williams, *Why I Am Not an Arminian* (Downers Grove: InterVarsity Press, 2004), 137.

[152] Paul Helm, *The Providence of God* (Downers Grove: InterVarsity Press, 1994), 22.

It is not clear whether McLaren's critique of Calvinism is best associated with hard determinism or fatalism. What is clear is that neither of these options is a carefully nuanced and faithful representation of Reformed theology. Calvinism cannot be equated with a hard form of determinism that defines freedom as an event without a cause in a world in which everything is caused. Neither is it synonymous with an impersonal fatalistic vision of reality in which a definite outcome will obtain despite our thoughts, feelings, wishes, or choices. While distinct paradigms, neither hard determinism nor fatalism can accommodate the kind of human freedom, responsibility, and dignity upon which exemplary five-point Calvinists typically insist. Either way, McLaren has not summarized Calvinism in a manner that the leading Reformed advocates would recognize, which surely explains some of the Calvinist backlash to McLaren's works.

As seen in the previous section, McLaren charges Calvinistic determinism with creating four problems. For McLaren's charges to stick, however, it is crucial to accurately represent the Calvinist view of divine sovereignty and human freedom. As mentioned, the majority report position for Calvinist philosophers and theologians is soft determinism (or compatibilism).[153] This position is affirmed by Calvinist scholars and popularizers such as Carson, Feinberg, Helm, Peterson, Williams, Bruce Ware, and Wayne Grudem, whose *Systematic Theology* has been called "the unofficial textbook of the [New Calvinism] movement."[154] This also is the position of Sproul, the chief Calvinistic influence upon McLaren during his formative years.[155]

---

[153] J. I. Packer and Francis Schaeffer defended a minority report position called paradoxical Calvinism. Both men argued that Scripture teaches the mystery of total, unconditional predestination on the one hand and first-cause human freedom (libertarianism) on the other. Advocates of this position claim that humans cannot presently see how these two apparently contradictory realities can be harmonized, but from the perspective of eternity they are self-consistent. For a challenge to the coherence of this view, see Burson and Walls, *C. S. Lewis and Francis Schaeffer*, 81–98.

[154] See Morgan Lee, "Where Do John Piper, Mark Driscoll and Russell Moore Appear in 'The New Calvinism' Timeline?" *Christian Post*, March 12, 2014, http://www.christianpost.com/news/where-do-john-piper-mark-driscoll-and-russell-moore-appear-in-the-new-calvinism-timeline-infographic-116036. Since Piper is a key leader in the New Calvinism movement, it is worth noting that he is not easily classified because he does not use precise language when it comes to this subject matter. He clearly affirms both total, unconditional predestination and human moral responsibility. Whether he is best considered an inconsistent compatibilist or a paradoxical Calvinist, such as Packer and Schaeffer, remains an open issue.

[155] Sproul, *Chosen by God*, 54.

Therefore, since compatibilism is the majority position for five-point Calvinism, the onus is upon the critic to demonstrate how this model fails in its attempt to safeguard God's character and human significance. Condemning a generic form of determinism lacks the necessary nuance for McLaren's argument to get off the ground. It is not sufficient to assert that the theological determinism of Calvinism reduces humanity to "puppets," "robots," or "characters in a [video] game God plays for personal entertainment."[156] Rather, McLaren must show *how* the Calvinist view of divine sovereignty entails the loss of human freedom, moral responsibility, and dignity. In order to do this, McLaren would need to challenge the compatibilistic definition of freedom rather than assuming that either hard determinism or fatalism accurately represents the Calvinist perspective. If there are good reasons to believe that the compatibilistic definition of freedom is unsound, then McLaren arguably is justified in drawing the conclusions that he has. Until such an argument is offered, however, McLaren's engagement with Calvinistic sovereignty and human freedom is incomplete.

This chapter has traced McLaren's journey from five-point Calvinism to a broadly open theistic position. McLaren credits Lesslie Newbigin as his primary liberator from five-point Calvinism, which he critiqued heavily in *A Generous Orthodoxy*. Throughout his corpus, McLaren informally identifies four problems with theistic determinism, and although McLaren does not use the technical terminology, it is clear that he proposes a libertarian form of freedom as the solution to each of these problems.

In evaluating McLaren's engagement with Calvinistic sovereignty and human significance, however, we have seen that he has mistakenly equated Calvinistic providence with either hard determinism or fatalism rather than with compatibilism (a.k.a., soft determinism), the position held by most of the Reformed philosophers and theologians surveyed in this book. In Chapters Seven and Eight, this study will turn to an evaluation of McLaren's project in light of Arminian theology. In Chapter Seven, a cluster of arguments against compatibilism will be offered as a way of strengthening McLaren's critique of the Calvinistic conception of divine sovereignty and human freedom.

---

[156] McLaren, *GO*, 186.

For now, this chapter will end on a practical note. As demonstrated, McLaren has not engaged the Calvinist view of sovereignty and free will with rigor; however, he seems to be saying that "although scholarly understandings of predestination are finely nuanced," they all lead to the same practical conclusion—namely, that human freedom and significance are eliminated. Pinnock expresses this same insight:

> Conventional theism struggles with fatalism. Fatalism and predestination are not the same thing—one is impersonal, the other is personal—but they imply much the same thing for practical purposes, i.e. the certainty of future events. For example, if I am to die today, I will die; if not, I will continue to live. Nothing I do can change anything at all. All incentives are removed. I can only pretend to be making a difference. Divine control rules out free agency and any responsibility. How can a person be a free and responsible agent if their actions have been foreordained from eternity? They are only nominally free. Genuine agency contemplates the future as open, not settled. There's room to make a difference by what we do now.[157]

---

[157] Pinnock, *Most Moved Mover*, 162–63.

Chapter Five

MCLAREN'S DOCTRINAL REVISIONS

The great missiologist Lesslie Newbigin claimed that the most stubborn heresy in the history of monotheism is the belief that God chooses people for exclusive privilege, not for missional responsibility. A Reforming Reformed tradition would grasp this powerful insight and preserve the Reformed emphasis on election—but not the exclusive election that, like a popular credit card, offers elite privileges to possessors. Rather a Reforming Reformed faith would see election as a gift that is given to some for the benefit of all others. To be chosen means to be "blessed to be a blessing," to be healed to heal, to be chosen to serve, to be enriched to enrich, to be taught to teach. This reformation in the Reformed understanding of election would be truly revolutionary and, I think, liberating.[1]

—Brian McLaren, *A Generous Orthodoxy*

In *The Last Word and the Word After That*, McLaren recounts a time in the late 1990s when he joined Todd Hunter[2] and Dallas Willard[3] to help mentor some "young Vineyard leaders."[4] One pastor asked Willard which elements of Christian theology need rethinking. Willard responded, "Our doctrine of atonement, doctrine of Scripture, and doctrine of heaven and hell."[5] McLaren recalls, "I was especially surprised to

---

[1] McLaren, *GO*, 195–96.
[2] Todd Hunter was a national leader in the Vineyard movement when this took place. He is now an Anglican priest.
[3] In this account, McLaren refers to "a well-known theologian." In a personal interview, McLaren confirmed the identity of this theologian as Dallas Willard. Brian McLaren, in discussion with the author, Fort Wayne, IN, March 20, 2014. McLaren was especially influenced by Willard's *The Divine Conspiracy* (New York: HarperCollins, 1998). For the sequel to this influential work, see Dallas Willard and Gary Black Jr., *The Divine Conspiracy Continued* (New York: HarperOne, 2014).
[4] McLaren, *LWWAT*, 186.
[5] Ibid.

hear him say 'atonement.' I thought, 'Well, if that is what Dallas is saying, I need to take it seriously.'"[6]

That conversation set McLaren on a path to reconsidering all three of these doctrines. While Chapter Three explored McLaren's reconsideration of Scripture, this chapter will examine McLaren's rethinking of the atonement and eschatology. Additionally, McLaren's engagement with other aspects of the Calvinist TULIP, including total depravity and unconditional election, will be considered.

McLaren and Total Depravity

McLaren believes the doctrine of total depravity[7] is extracanonical.[8] As noted, he claims the doctrine of "the Fall" is a Greco-Roman accretion rather than a teaching that emerged out of special revelation. While McLaren rejects doctrines such as the Fall and total depravity, he does not reject what he believes to be a "proper understanding" of original sin.[9] McLaren renounces the conventional view, which claims that the first sin introduced an onto-logical shift in human nature resulting in universal "inbred sin,"[10] as well as extreme enmity between God and creation.[11] McLaren argues, "According to this popular understanding, God's particular form of perfection requires God to punish all imperfect beings with eternal conscious torment in hell. So in this popular view of original sin, God's response to anything that is less than absolutely perfect must be *absolute and infinite hostility*."[12]

Instead of the conventional view, McLaren relies upon René Girard's mimetic theory.[13] McLaren summarizes the doctrine of original sin as a

---

[6] Brian McLaren, in discussion with the author, Fort Wayne, IN, March 20, 2014.

[7] Michael Horton defines total depravity as follows: "Our bondage to sin in Adam is complete in its extensiveness, though not in its intensity." In other words, Horton argues that humans are not individually and collectively as bad as they could be; however, no aspect of humanity can escape the effects of the Fall. Michael Horton, *For Calvinism* (Grand Rapids: Zondervan, 2011), 15. See also Wayne A. Grudem, *Systematic Theology (Grand Rapids: Zondervan, 1994)*, 497.

[8] McLaren, *LWWAT*, 134. Tony Jones also rejects the traditional formulation of total depravity and original sin. See Tony Jones, *A Better Atonement* (Minneapolis: JoPa, 2012), Kindle edition.

[9] McLaren, *JMBM*, 106. See also McLaren, *LWWAT*, 134–35.

[10] Roger E. Olson, *Arminian Theology* (Downers Grove: InterVarsity Press, 2006), 33.

[11] McLaren, *NKOCY*, 42.

[12] McLaren, *JMBM*, 106.

[13] Ibid, 108. McLaren also favorably cites the work of Catholic theologian James Alison, James Warren, and Paul Nuechterlein. See James Warren, *Compassion or Apocalypse? A Comprehensible Guide to the Thought of René Girard* (Winchester, UK: Christian Alternative, 2013), and Paul Nuechterlein's website, *Girardian Reflections on the Lectionary*, http://girardianlectionary.net.

five-step process: imitation, rivalry, anxiety, scapegoating, and ritualization. From birth, humans fundamentally learn by imitation, "from speaking to using spoons to driving." This mimetic desire undergirds trivial longings, as well as the deepest human yearnings. What begins as innocent mimicry, however, soon transforms into competition in a world with finite resources. McLaren explains, "You start as my model for imitation, but when I compete with you to achieve the object of our now-shared desire, I become your rival (or visa versa)."[14] Girard further amplifies the concept of competitive triangulation in this manner: "Rivalry does not arise because of the for- tuitous convergence of two desires on one single object; *rather the subject desires the object because the rival desires it.*"[15]

The next step in this archetypal process is the experience of anxiety. Since humans imitate those with whom they spend the most time—namely, family and friends—it stands to reason that these are the same people who "can most easily become rivals."[16] This rivalry, unfortunately, can spiral into violence. Instead of experiencing hostility only from enemies, it turns out that enmity can, for this emulous reason, also erupt from within one's own household or close circle of friends.[17] Such violence produces a swelling sense of societal angst. This collective feeling of anxiety and dread must find an outlet. Either society can experience "an explosion of social disin- tegration" or "one member (or one subgroup)" can be identified to serve as a scapegoat.[18]

This latter maneuver leads all members of society to "imitate one another in shared aversion toward and violence against the victim—or scapegoat—and in so doing, all experience a catharsis of anxiety and a euphoria of unity."[19] Since this scapegoat mechanism serves its purpose with such efficacious utility, societies began to ritualize this maneuver, leading to regularly scheduled rites of human or animal sacrifices or banishments.

---

[14] McLaren, *JMBM*, 108–9.

[15] René Girard, *Violence and the Sacred*, trans. Patrick Gregory (Baltimore: Johns Hopkins, 1972), 145.

[16] McLaren, *JMBM*, 109.

[17] Ibid.

[18] Girard identifies Oedipus as the archetypal sacrificial martyr. Girard writes, "In the myth, the fearful transgression of a single individual is substituted for the universal onslaught of reciprocal violence. Oedipus is responsible for the ills that have befallen his people. He has become a prime example of the human scapegoat." See Girard, *Violence and the Sacred*, 77.

[19] McLaren, *JMBM*, 109.

McLaren points out that in our contemporary society, "religious and political systems (and sports leagues) become the curators of our rivalry-management mechanisms."[20]

Rather than understanding original sin as a genetic condition that is transmitted from our literal, time-space aboriginal parents[21] via human physiological DNA,[22] McLaren argues that this doctrine is best explained in light of the universal hominine phenomenon known as mimesis. McLaren avers, "All human beings are caught in these subtle webs of destructive imitation, rivalry, anxiety, scapegoating, and ritualization. No sphere of life is untouched by these mechanisms."[23]

This mimetic understanding of original sin explains how in the Genesis account Adam and Eve, who "bear the image of God—loving, generous, harmonious, beautiful, hospitable, creative, good," turned from "a constructive imitation" of their Creator to a destructive form of mimesis.[24] Instead of "imitating God as a model," they "become God's rivals, imitating the serpent's desire for the forbidden fruit."[25] According to James Warren, the divine curse of the seditious serpent was fundamentally an act of "cursing mimetic rivalry itself."[26]

This mimetic rivalry unfolds in biblical proportions between Adam and Eve, Cain and Abel, Sarah and Hagar, Isaac and Ishmael, Jacob and Esau, Joseph and his brothers,[27] and down through history in countless subsequent relational conflicts. Warren continues, "Human history thus becomes the kaleidoscopic reflection of a thousand variations of this kind of 'knowledge of good and evil,' with human activity characterized by wars and interpersonal hostilities based upon each side's claimed possession of

---

[20] Ibid., 110.

[21] Girard interprets the Genesis creation account metaphorically. Warren, *Compassion or Apocalypse*, 40. McLaren, likewise, reads the opening chapters of Genesis figuratively.

[22] For a discussion concerning the debate over the transmission of original sin, see J. E. Colwell, "Sin" in *New Dictionary of Theology*, ed. Sinclair B. Ferguson et al. (Downers Grove: InterVarsity Press, 1988), 641–43, and Grudem, *Systematic Theology*, 494–96.

[23] McLaren, *JMBM*, 110.

[24] Ibid.

[25] Ibid., 111. Warren explains the nature of this divine prohibition not as an attempt by God "to safeguard his own 'stash,' but to prevent Adam and Eve from tasting mimetic rivalry and its consequences." Warren, *Compassion or Apocalypse*, 50.

[26] Warren, *Compassion or Apocalypse*, 46.

[27] According to McLaren, however, Joseph is an exception to this mimetic virus since he "refuses to imitate the hatred of his rival brothers." McLaren, *JMBM*, 112.

the 'good,' along with a labeling of the other side as evil."[28] Consequently, McLaren believes original sin is transmitted generationally, but through the sociological mechanism of mimesis rather than through the biological mechanism of genetics.

McLaren and Unconditional Election

Another troubling dichotomy according to McLaren is the social dualism that emerges from the second point in the Calvinist TULIP: unconditional election. As defined in Chapter Four, unconditional election is the Reformed doctrine that claims, "God chooses some humans to save before and apart from anything they do on their own."[29]

Some Calvinists have been hesitant to affirm the apparent negative side of this coin—namely, the assertion that God unconditionally elects the reprobate for eternal damnation. In order to safeguard God's character, unconditional damnation is often explained by invoking concepts such as God's "permissive will" or "passing over the reprobate." Jerry Walls and Joe Dongell, however, argue that the use of permission language (when God has supposedly unconditionally determined every detail) "does not sit well with serious Calvinism."

> Indeed, John Calvin himself noted this and warned against any
> use of the term permission that might deny that everything
> happens exactly as willed by God. This means that, for Calvin,
> everything that happens does so necessarily; thus, to speak of
> God's permitting things is misleading.[30]

Walls and Dongell's point is confirmed by going directly to Calvin, who placed the emphasis upon the total, unconditional sovereignty of God over all matters, especially the eternal destiny of every person. In the *Institutes of the Christian Religion*, Calvin asserts,

> By predestination we mean the eternal decree of God, by which
> he determined with himself whatever he wishes to happen with
> regard to every man. All are not created on equal terms, but some

---

[28] Warren, *Compassion or Apocalypse,* 47.
[29] Roger E. Olson, *The Story of Christian Theology* (Downers Grove: InterVarsity Press, 1999), 460.
[30] Jerry L. Walls and Joseph R. Dongell, *Why I Am Not a Calvinist* (Downers Grove: InterVarsity Press, 2004), 125–26.

are preordained to eternal life, others to eternal damnation; and, accordingly, as each has been created for one or other of these ends, we say that he has been predestinated to life or to death.[31]

As with original sin, McLaren does not deny the doctrine of election, but rather defines it differently than five-point Calvinism. McLaren argues that the doctrine of unconditional election has led to "all kinds of mischief and hostility,"[32] and, ultimately, to what Lesslie Newbigin calls the "the most stubborn heresy in the history of monotheism."[33] Newbigin points out that Abraham and his descendants were chosen as "bearers—not exclusive beneficiaries. There lay the constant temptation. Again and again, it had to be said that election is for responsibility, not for privilege."[34] John Franke agrees that election must stay tethered to the mission of God: "It begins with the call to Israel to be God's covenant people and the recipient of God's covenant blessings for the purpose of blessing the nations."[35] David Bosch discusses election in relation to the Jonah account. Bosch believes the primary point of this biblical story is to highlight the "call to Israel to allow themselves to be converted to a compassion comparable to that of Yahweh. Election primarily conveyed neither privilege, nor favouritism, but rather responsibility."[36]

McLaren believes reorienting one's perspective regarding the doctrine of election "gets us beyond the us-them and in-grouping and out-grouping that lead to prejudice, exclusion, and ultimately to religious wars."[37] This goes directly to the heart of McLaren's project. He believes a misappropriation of the doctrine of election has contributed to Calvinism's "legacy of horrible mistakes, misjudgments, and even atrocities."[38] McLaren admonishes Reformed believers to adopt a posture of humility in light of this regrettable track record.

---

[31] John Calvin, *Institutes of the Christian Religion*, book 3, chap. 21, trans. Henry Beveridge (Grand Rapids: Eerdmans, 1989), 206.

[32] McLaren, *JMBM*, 119.

[33] McLaren, *GO*, 195–96. See also McLaren, *LWWAT*, 169, and McLaren, *WMRBW*, 24–27.

[34] Lesslie Newbigin, *The Open Secret*, rev. ed. (Grand Rapids: Eerdmans, 1995), 32.

[35] John R. Franke, *Manifold Witness* (Nashville: Abingdon, 2009), 60.

[36] David J. Bosch, *Witness to the World* (Atlanta: John Knox Press, 1980), 52–53.

[37] McLaren, *GO*, 109.

[38] Ibid., 194. McLaren also cites how some Jews and Christian Zionists have been fueled by "a distorted doctrine of chosen-ness" in the territorial dispute concerning the West Bank and Gaza Strip. See *JMBM*, 119. See also Brian McLaren, "Chosen for What?" *Tikkun* 23, no. 3 (May/June 2008), accessed June 5, 2014, http://www.tikkun.org/article.php/McLaren-Chosenforwhat.

Such a reorientation and posture of humility is easier said than done, however. McLaren acknowledges the organic connection between one's view of God's character and one's own brain physiology, citing Michael Gerson's review of *How God Changes Your Brain*: "Contemplating a loving God strengthens portions of our brain—particularly the frontal lobes and the anterior cingulate—where empathy and reason reside. Contemplating a wrathful God empowers the limbic system, which is 'filled with aggression and fear.' It is a sobering concept: The God we choose to love changes us into his image, whether he exists or not."[39] If this is true, then there is good reason to believe that one's portrait of God must change before one's attitude toward others can change. This insight reinforces McLaren's project, which focuses not only on changing methodology but on changing the content of one's beliefs, as well.

Newbigin also points to this tendency toward superiority in the Calvinistic tradition. Instead of advancing "self-confident imperialism,"[40] he proposes the remedy of viewing election as communal connectivity. Salvation does not "come to each, direct from above, like a shaft of light through the roof."[41] Rather, individuals are chosen for the collective benefit of the whole.[42] As such, Newbigin's interpretation of the doctrine of election is rooted in Trinitarian *terra firma*, "because God is no solitary monad. . . . Interpersonal relatedness belongs to the very being of God."[43] Newbigin expounds,

> There is no salvation except in a mutual relatedness that reflects
> that eternal relatedness-in-love which is the being of the triune
> God. Therefore salvation can only be the way of election: one
> must be chosen and called and sent with the word of salva-
> tion to the other. . . . It has in view not "the soul" conceived as
> independent monad detached from other souls and from the
> created world, but the human person knit together with other

---

[39] As quoted in McLaren, *NS*, 70–71. See Michael Gerson, "Neuroscientist Andrew Newberg on the Brain and Faith," *Washington Post*, April 15, 2009, http://www.washingtonpost.com/wp-dyn/content/article/2009/04/14/AR2009041401879.html.

[40] Newbigin, *Open Secret*, 72.

[41] Ibid., 70–71.

[42] McLaren, *LWWAT*, 169.

[43] Newbigin, *Open Secret*, 70.

persons in a shared participation in and responsibility for God's created world.[44]

While the doctrine of the Trinity has been used at times as a "sinister tool of mind and speech control,"[45] it is not beyond redemption, according to McLaren. Instead, a proper understanding of the Trinity can serve as a "bridge, rather than a barrier." McLaren echoes the writing of Social Trinitarian advocates, such as Jürgen Moltmann, Stanley Grenz, and Miroslav Volf, when he describes God as "a dynamic unity-in-community of self-giving persons-in-relationship."[46] The notion of three persons with one shared essence is deepened by the concept of "being in relationship."[47] Relationships are not expendable or an external "accessory," but rather that which defines "what and who that person is." McLaren further clarifies, "*Being*, then, for God as for us, means 'interbeing,' being in relationship, so the three persons of the Holy Trinity are not merely one *with* each other: they are one *in* each other. We might say they are *interpersons*, or *interpersonalities*. And, as creatures made in the image of God, so are we."[48]

Grounding election in Trinitarian soil, therefore, provides powerful resources for addressing the "us versus them" dichotomy created by some interpretations of the doctrine of election. McLaren characterizes God's calling of Abraham as a pilgrimage to "become 'other.'" Abraham leaves the security of his homeland, which includes the familiarity and comforts of his ethnic, political, and religious affiliations, and sets out on an uncertain journey into foreign territory. It is within this context of "otherness" that "God promises to make of Abraham's descendants 'a great nation' with a great name."[49] McLaren elucidates this narrative:

> But that great or strong identity isn't cast in hostility to other
> nations. Abraham's identity is not greatness exploiting others
> (domination), greatness overthrowing others (revolution), great-
> ness absorbing others (assimilation), greatness excluding others

---

44 Ibid., 77.
45 McLaren, *JMBM*, 128.
46 Ibid. See also Franke, *Manifold Witness*, 43–52.
47 McLaren, *JMBM*, 129.
48 Ibid.
49 Ibid., 120.

(purification), greatness resenting others (victimization), greatness separated from others (isolation), or greatness at the expense
of others (competition). Abraham's greatness is for the sake of
others: And all nations on earth will be blessed through yo*u*.[50]

McLaren claims that all three monotheistic religions, which trace
their heritage back to Abraham, often have misused their mimetic freedom and failed to embrace the other. Rather, "Christians, Muslims, and
Jews, for all their differences, have imitated one another again and again
in misunderstanding and misapplying this doctrine of chosen-ness." In
fact, McLaren believes the entire Bible "struggles with this issue of 'us-ness'
and 'otherness.'" Nevertheless, while this doctrine has been "abused as a
vicious weapon of hostility," McLaren contends it is possible to "rediscover
it as an instrument of peace."[51]

McLaren and Limited Atonement

Roger Olson defines limited atonement as "Christ died only to save the elect,
and his atoning death is not universal for all of humanity."[52] In recent years,
some Calvinist authors have recast this doctrine into more positive language. Michael Horton believes "limited atonement (the 'L' in the TULIP)
is an unfortunate label. . . . Alternate terms such as 'definite atonement'
or 'particular redemption' seem more useful in clarifying this position."[53]
Additionally, Richard Mouw opts for the rather colloquial "mission accom-
plished,"[54] while Robert Peterson and Michael Williams prefer "particular
atonement."[55] In each case, what appears on the surface to be a negative
characterization of the doctrine has been reframed euphemistically.

Nevertheless, McLaren rejects the claim that Christ's atonement is
salvifically efficacious solely for the unconditionally elect. In *A Generous
Orthodoxy*, McLaren writes,

---

[50] Ibid., 121.

[51] Ibid., 121–124.

[52] Olson, *Story of Christian Theology*, 460.

[53] Horton, *For Calvinism*, 80.

[54] Richard J. Mouw, *Finding Calvinism in the Las Vegas Airport* (Grand Rapids: Zondervan,
2004), 34.

[55] Robert A. Peterson and Michael D. Williams, *Why I Am Not an Arminian* (Downers Grove:
InterVarsity Press, 2004), 203.

Instead of speculating on the limited scope of legal atonement
(as the original 'L' in the acrostic did), a Reforming Reformed
faith would concentrate on the missio dei of relational reconciliation, a reconciliation that never isolates divine from human
healing, and therefore always prays to be forgiven by God as
we forgive others, that always loves God and neighbor, and that
never, ever asks the question, 'Who is my neighbor?' to contract
the scope of love.[56]

As noted at the beginning of this chapter, Dallas Willard encouraged
McLaren to rethink the atonement, in general, and the penal substitutionary theory, in particular—a position often associated with five-point
Calvinism.[57] McLaren did not enter lightly into this journey of reconsideration because "growing up evangelical meant growing up believing the
gospel *was* the theory of penal substitutionary atonement."[58] He recalls, "I
had two great fears when I began rethinking my inherited understanding
of the gospel and the atonement. First, I was afraid that I would get into
trouble with my authority figures and peers: I lived in circles where honest
difference of opinion is not easily tolerated. Second, I was afraid that I would
end up somewhere that was less biblical than where I started."[59]

In the *CT* article entitled "McLaren Emerging," Scot McKnight associated McLaren's developing position on the atonement with the scapegoat
theory proposed by Girard, who believes that God, through the cross, "identified with the victim and both unmasked and undid evil, systemic violence,
and injustice."[60] McKnight, who has written extensively on the atonement,[61]

---

[56] McLaren, *GO*, 196.

[57] McLaren identifies Carson and Albert Mohler as two Calvinists who "identify this theory of the
atonement with the Christian gospel." See McLaren, *JMBM*, 210n6. It is worth noting that McLaren
apparently still accepted the penal view when *FF* was written in 1999. In the section on the biblical
story, he wrote, "In some mysterious way, as Jesus suffered and died, he was absorbing and paying
for the wrongs of the whole human race." See McLaren, *FF*, 240. Likewise, in *NKOC*, Neo offers an
invitational prayer at the end of a sermon: "I believe Jesus was your way of reaching out to me, and I
believe that when he died, he paid for all of my wrongs." McLaren, *NKOC*, 93.

[58] McLaren, "Foreword," in Derek Flood, *Healing the Gospel* (Eugene: Cascade, 2012), ix.

[59] Ibid., xi.

[60] Scot McKnight, "McLaren Emerging," *CT* 52, no. 9 (September 2008): 58–66, citing 63–64.

[61] McKnight has authored the following books on the Atonement: *Jesus and His Death* (Waco:
Baylor University Press, 2005), and *A Community Called Atonement* (Nashville: Abingdon, 2007),
which was nominated for the Grawemeyer Award.

asserted that McLaren (and Girard) are offering a valuable insight into the nature of the cross, but it is incomplete in its current formulation.[62]

This chapter has already demonstrated McLaren's affinity with Girard's thinking, especially his insight into how mimetic theory illuminates the doctrine of original sin. McLaren, however, does not embrace the full scope of Girard's scapegoat theory of the atonement, because McLaren admits he no longer has a theory of the atonement.[63] In a personal interview with the author of this book, McLaren explained that his journey of rethinking the atonement has led him to the position of rejecting all atonement theories, because the idea of atonement does not make sense within his three-dimensional narrative.[64] In *We Make the Road by Walking*, McLaren explains, "God isn't the one who is angry and hostile and needs appeasement. We humans are the angry ones! Our hostile, bloodthirsty hearts are the ones that need to be changed!"[65]

McLaren's rejection of atonement theories, however, does not mean that he finds the work of the cross to be irrelevant to the gospel. On the contrary, McLaren understands the cross as the paramount moment in which "God's self-giving being is most clearly displayed. Instead of control, we have relinquishing control.[66] McLaren believes "there could be no other way to show us what God is truly like. God is not revealed in killing and conquest . . . in violence and hate. God is revealed in this crucified man—giving himself to the very last breath, giving and forgiving."[67] Instead of emulating the way of Caesar, Jesus models the inverse. McLaren continues, "While Caesar gains and holds power and enforces Pax Romana by shedding the blood of all who resist him, Jesus exercises his sovereignty and brings the Pax Christi by shedding his own blood."[68]

In light of this nonviolent Christological vision, McLaren is especially critical of the penal substitutionary theory and other narratives that portray God as an imperial, wrathful, domineering monarch or magistrate in need

---

[62] McKnight, "McLaren Emerging," 63–64.

[63] Brian McLaren, in discussion with the author, Fort Wayne, IN, March 20, 2014.

[64] While McLaren does not embrace any particular "atonement theory," he does value holding on to these theories "as an artifact of theological history." McLaren, *JMBM*, 210n6.

[65] McLaren, *WMRBW*, 30.

[66] Brian McLaren, in discussion with the author, Fort Wayne, IN, March 20, 2014.

[67] McLaren, *WMRBW*, 160.

[68] McLaren, *JMBM*, 137. See also McLaren, *WMRBW*, 103–4.

of appeasement or satisfaction.[69] In *Why Did Jesus, Moses, the Buddha, and Mohammed Cross the Road?*, McLaren articulates his understanding of the penal substitutionary theory:

> The popular idea of penal substitution works like a rather complex equation. God cannot forgive sin without inflicting punishment and shedding blood, the doctrine teaches, so God is obliged to punish all sinners. Because their offense is against an infinitely holy God, their punishment must be absolute, irrevocable, and eternal. All human beings will therefore be damned to eternal conscious torment in hell if God does not provide a substitute upon whom God's infinite wrath can be vented. For those who hold these assumptions, it makes sense to say that God tortured and killed Jesus on the cross so as to be able to vent divine wrath upon a single divine-human representative or substitute rather than all of us.[70]

Within the context of the Eucharist, McLaren opts for a table-centered approach that focuses on "reconciliation and fellowship"[71] rather than on "a sacrificial altar . . . a place where God's hostility toward sinners is pacified by body-and-blood sacrifice. In this understanding, we bond not to Jesus' original gospel of the kingdom of God, but to another gospel, the gospel of penal substitutionary atonement."[72] McLaren argues that a sacrificial approach strengthens the misconception that God is "hostile toward sinful humanity" and reinforces the social dualism which presents Christians as "acceptable and pleasing to God" and non-Christians "as deserving utter and eternal punishment."[73]

Rather than describing an objective "forensic transaction,"[74] McLaren offers a picture of relational betrayal and ultimate forgiveness and reconciliation in an essay entitled, "The Cross as Prophetic Action." In this article, which

---

[69] For a recent full-scale treatment of the atonement along similar lines, see Tony Jones, *Did God Kill Jesus?* (New York: HarperCollins, 2015). McLaren provides an endorsement on the back cover.
[70] Ibid., 210.
[71] McLaren, *JMBM*, 211.
[72] Ibid., 209–10. See also McLaren, *WMRBW*, 43–44.
[73] McLaren, *JMBM*, 212.
[74] Brian McLaren, "The Cross as Prophetic Action," in *Proclaiming the Scandal of the Cross*, ed. Mark D. Baker (Grand Rapids: Baker, 2006), 118.

was originally a sermon delivered in 2003, McLaren suggests an alternative to "substitutionary theory entirely."[75] McLaren links the account of Gomer's betrayal and Hosea's faithful longsuffering to the passion narrative, as follows:

> Contemporary pop atonement theology is an interpretation, and therefore a choice, as is this alternate view. Do we choose to see God as the distanced judge, or as the involved victim and friend? Is God the offended potentate who needs somewhere to vent his revenge? Or is God the fellow victim who suffers, endures, accepts the ugliest and fiercest of human rage and injustice—as Hosea suffered and endured Gomer's wandering lusts?[76]

In *The Story We Find Ourselves In*, McLaren paints a similar picture. After Dan has introduced multiple atonement theories to Kerry, Neo shares from his own life the betrayal he endured at the hands of his unfaithful wife. That painful experience provided new insight into the cross. Neo explains,

> When I think of the cross, I think it's all about God's agony being made visible—you know, the pain of forgiving, the pain of absorbing the betrayal and forgoing any revenge, of risking that your heart will be hurt again, for the sake of love, at the very worst moment, when the beloved has been least worthy of forgiveness, but stands most in need of it. It's not just something legal or mental. It's not just words; it has to be embodied, and nails and thorns and sweat and tears and blood strike me as the only true language of betrayal and forgiveness.[77]

In summary, McLaren rejects the doctrine of limited atonement, as well as all atonement theories in general, and the penal substitutionary theory especially, since his three-dimensional narrative does not accommodate appeasement of an angry and wrathful deity. McLaren is particularly suspicious of atonement theories that reinforce a social dualism between insiders and outsiders. McLaren does, however, find meaning in the cross because it reveals divine solidarity with human suffering, as well as the correct

---

[75] Ibid., 110.
[76] Ibid., 119.
[77] McLaren, *SWFOI*, 107.

pathway to reconciliation which is not found in domineering power and control, but rather in selfless longsuffering and forgiveness.

McLaren and Eschatology

While McLaren has spent most of his energy discussing the present-day aspects of the gospel message, he is acutely aware that one's views about eternity have important practical consequences. Therefore, McLaren has covered a range of eschatological issues with an eye on contemporary implications. The final section of this chapter will summarize McLaren's views on three topics under the banner of eschatology: the second coming of Christ, the afterlife, and the fate of the unevangelized.

The Second Coming of Christ

N. T. Wright implicates McLaren's denominational ancestors for much of the North American preoccupation with "the second coming of Jesus Christ."[78] Wright expounds, "Growing out of some millenarian movements of the nineteenth century, particularly those associated with J. N. Darby and the Plymouth Brethren, a belief has arisen, and taken hold of millions of minds and hearts, that we are now living in the end times, in which all the great prophecies are to be fulfilled at last."[79]

McLaren was raised in a Plymouth Brethren dispensationalist community in which end-times speculation was common. At the age of eight, McLaren once came home to find a locked, empty house. He spent the next hour on the back porch in emotional angst, wondering whether his raptured family had left him behind to face the tribulation alone.[80] This extreme focus on eschatological conjecture left a bad taste in McLaren's mouth, which explains in part his preference for a preterist approach to eschatology. As McLaren puts it, "I am worried that a misunderstanding of the second coming of Jesus is edging out the priority of the first coming of Jesus."[81]

---

[78] N. T. Wright, *Surprised by Hope* (New York: HarperOne, 2008), 118.
[79] Ibid.
[80] McLaren, *NKOCY*, 192. See also McLaren, *NS*, 11.
[81] Brian McLaren and Jon Stanley, "Why Everything Must Change: A Conversation with Brian McLaren," *The Other Journal (website)*, Seattle School of Theology and Psychology, October 15, 2007, http://theotherjournal.com/2007/10/15/why-everything-must-change-a-conversation-with-brian-mclaren/.

Henry Knight has observed, "Dispensationalism is as much a hermeneutic as it is an eschatology."[82] Consequently, McLaren had to find a new way of reading the Bible if he was to escape the grip of his childhood religion. This included a new way of understanding the prophetic and apocalyptic sections of Scripture. For instance, in *A New Kind of Christianity*, McLaren repudiates the popular dispensationalist concept of the Rapture, arguing that the second coming or *parousia* is commonly misunderstood. Regarding this Greek term, McLaren cites Wright, who emphasizes its "political connotations, being used 'in relation to the visit of a royal or official personage.'"[83] McLaren also looks to Andrew Perriman, who adds, "The word *parousia* appears especially suited to denoting the *presence* that is the immediate result of the arrival of a figure of significance."[84] Therefore, instead of a "second coming" or literal bodily return of Christ, McLaren argues that this term refers to the fullness of Christ's royal presence working through the church, the figurative body of Christ.

According to McLaren, rather than expecting to meet the glorified Christ in the clouds, the New Testament writers were anticipating "a new age or era—a new season of growth."[85] McLaren continues, "*Parousia*, in this way, would signal the full arrival, presence, and manifestation of a new age in human history. It would mean the presence or appearance on earth of a new generation of humanity, Christ again present, embodied in a community of people who truly possess and express his Spirit, continuing his work." McLaren believes this new age was ushered in by the temple destruction in AD 70, when the old era of sacrifice and priesthood was dismantled and "the new age, new covenant, new testament, or new era was brought to full term, and its *parousia* had come."[86] Therefore, Christ-followers are to enter into this existing "new age" and actively participate in the holistic restoration of the planet.

This emphasis upon the present-day dimensions of the gospel, coupled with McLaren's persistent reluctance to amplify his views pertaining

---

[82] Henry H. Knight III, *A Future for Truth* (Nashville: Abingdon, 1997), 29.

[83] McLaren, *NKOCY*, 198. McLaren cites N. T. Wright, *Jesus and the Victory of God* (Minneapolis: Fortress, 1996), 360.

[84] Andrew Perriman, *The Coming of the Son of Man: New Testament Eschatology for an Emerging Church* (London: Paternoster, 2005), 53.

[85] McLaren, *NKOCY*, 198.

[86] Ibid., 198–99.

to life after death, led fellow ECM colleague Andrew Jones[87] to once ask McLaren if he still believes in the afterlife. The question engendered an emphatic response:

> Just to be super clear . . . YES! I believe in life after death! I find it hard to line up my views with conventional pre, post, or amillenial views because I think they are all based on an assumption I don't share, i.e. that the book of Revelation is intended to tell us how the world will end. This view presupposes a deterministic view of history, which I don't share. I suppose I'm more Wesleyan and Anabaptist in this regard than Calvinist. . . . In this, I follow N. T. Wright's general line of thought so if I am off the ranch, so is he.[88] I see Biblical prophecy in terms of warnings and promises, which are different from prognostications. If I had to put a name on my eschatology, I suppose I would call it "Participatory"—meaning that God invites us to participate in God's ultimate victory of all that is good and the ultimate defeat of all that is evil.[89]

McLaren believes "there is no single fixed point toward which we move, but rather a widening space opening into an infinitely expanding goodness."[90] The future is unsettled and could go a number of different directions; however, an "eschatology of participation produces an ethic of anticipation: we seek to have our present way of life shaped by our vision of God's desired future."[91] This desired future has not been predetermined by Theos, the god of the Greco-Roman six-line narrative, but is waiting to emerge out of the "participatory" evolutionary project that is a composite of divine,

---

[87] New Zealand native Andrew Jones blogs under the pseudonym "Tall Skinny Kiwi."

[88] Wright seems to distance himself from the kind of truncated interpretation that McLaren offers here: "Nor will it do to say, as do some who grasp part of the point but have not worked it through, that the events of A.D. 70 were themselves the second coming of Jesus so that ever since then we have been living in God's new age and there is no further coming to await. . . . Let me say it emphatically for the sake of those who are confused on the point . . . the second coming has not yet occurred." See Wright, *Surprised by Hope*, 127.

[89] Brian McLaren and Andrew Jones, "Brian McLaren Responds to *Everything Must Change* Concerns," *Tall Skinny Kiwi* (blog), March 26, 2008, http://tallskinnykiwi.typepad.com/ tallskinnykiwi/2008/03/brian-mclaren-r.html.

[90] McLaren, *NKOCY*, 195.

[91] Ibid., 200. Elsewhere, McLaren asserts, "There is a trajectory to history, a flow to creation, a moral arc to the universe that slowly but surely tends toward justice, as Dr. King used to say." McLaren, *NKOCY*, 194.

human, and creational decisions and forces. Instead of driving determin-istically from behind, Elohim, the God of the three-dimensional narrative, is calling "to us from the future, toward which we reach an outstretched and hopeful hand."[92]

McLaren's view is similar to Hans Küng's "improvisational escha-tology"[93] and follows the thinking of John Haught, Jürgen Moltmann, Wolfhart Pannenberg, and Karl Rahner, who all view "God as essentially future."[94] Haught elaborates, "The sense of where the reality of God is to be 'located' can also begin to shift from the One who abides vertically 'up above' to the One who comes into the world from 'up ahead,' out of the realm of the future."[95]

Another reason for McLaren's resistance to conventional eschatologies can be attributed to their inherent violence. Mark Driscoll is a case in point. The former ECM colleague and YRRM trendsetter once character-ized McLaren and some other Emergent Village participants as wanting "to recast Jesus as a limp-wrist hippie in a dress with a lot of product in His hair, who drank decaf and made pithy Zen statements about life while shopping for the perfect pair of shoes."[96] Driscoll juxtaposes this "emergent" Jesus with his eschatological vision of a macho, out-for-blood warrior: "In Revelation, Jesus is a prize-fighter with a tattoo down His leg, a sword in His hand and the commitment to make someone bleed. That is the guy I can worship. I cannot worship the hippie, diaper, halo Christ because I cannot worship a guy I can beat up."[97]

McLaren links this vision of a violent, imperial, warrior Jesus with contemporary evangelical warmongering, because "if God sanctions it, why can't we?"[98] McLaren has a hard time believing that Jesus was engaged in a bait and switch tactic, preaching the triumph of evil through peaceful

---

[92] Ibid., 28. See also Franke, *Manifold Witness*, 79, for a discussion of eschatological realism. Neo also briefly mentions eschatological realism in McLaren, *SWFOI*, 159.

[93] McLaren also links Wright and Kevin Vanhoozer to this position. See *NKOCY*, 196, 283–84n6.

[94] John F. Haught, *God after Darwin* (Boulder: Westview, 2008), 224n29.

[95] Ibid., 42.

[96] McLaren, *NKOCY*, 119–20.

[97] Ibid. McLaren does not overtly identify Driscoll; however, Driscoll's comments can be located in an article in *Relevant* magazine. See Mark Driscoll et al, "From the Mag: 7 Big Questions," *Relevant* 24 (Jan/Feb 2007), August 28, 2007, http://www.relevantmagazine.com/god/church /features/1344-from-the-mag-7-big-questions.

[98] McLaren, *NKOCY*, 193.

means while on earth the first time, only to return a second time under the banner of imperial force, coercion, and control.

The Afterlife

This participatory or collaborative eschatology motivated McLaren to write *Everything Must Change*, a book focused on some of the most pressing problems facing the planet today. However, McLaren was chagrined to find that, rather than discussing the questions raised in this book, many of his evangelical interlocutors persistently redirected the conversation to his views on the atonement and the afterlife.[99] Instead of joining him on the mission to bring Jesus's kingdom vision to bear on contemporary concerns, many appeared to be on a single-minded witch-hunt to excommunicate McLaren from the evangelical fold. McLaren had little interest in participating in this evangelical inquisition and often refused to give his interrogators straight answers to questions that were foreign to his emergent narrative.

One reason McLaren is hesitant to discuss the afterlife is how this issue is framed by many conservative evangelicals. The matter of personal salvation can appear self-centered and excessively individualistic—a modern characteristic, as seen previously in this study. It also can distract people from the present-day dimensions of the gospel.[100] Nevertheless, a review of McLaren's corpus reveals discussion of the afterlife, including opinions related to judgment, eternal damnation, and eternal life. As noted, Willard had suggested the need for an evangelical rethinking of the afterlife. The fruit of this rethinking begins with the *New Kind of Christian* trilogy. The subject of judgment and eternal life surfaces as Kerry is approaching death in *The Story We Find Ourselves In*.[101] Neo explains that everyone will be judged, but that does not entail condemnation.[102] Neo amplifies,

> Can you imagine what it means to say that God forgets forever?
> So when you leave this life, and you meet God, up ahead, up

---

[99] Brian McLaren and Scot McKnight, "Brian McLaren: 'Conversations on Being a Heretic,'" *Q Ideas* website, n.d., accessed June 21, 2014, http://qideas.org/articles/brian-mclaren-conversations-on-being-a-heretic/.

[100] McLaren, *NKOC*, 82–83.

[101] One also can find hints of McLaren's developing eschatological thoughts regarding judgment and the afterlife in *COOS*, 157–64.

[102] McLaren, *SWFOI*, 153, and McLaren, *LWWAT*, 138.

in the future, the little sliver of who you are in that moment
meets the you from all the past moments, and the full you that
is reconstituted there in God is fully and completely judged, and
all the wrong has been named and judged, forgiven and forgot-
ten, and there you are: full and substantial and free and pure and
complete. Can you imagine that?[103]

Neo's explanation of judgment appears to suggest that all will be judged
and forgiven, irrespective of one's faith in Christ or libertarian free choice.

In *The Last Word and the Word After That*, Dan asks Neo's mentor,
Markus, if one could possibly freely "refuse redemption" for all of eternity.[104]
In other words, "if God's love is always there, waiting, would they be able
to hold out longer than God?"[105] Dan is told that such a question is off-limits;[106] nevertheless, he goes on to say, "It's hard for me to imagine somebody being more stubbornly ornery than God is gracious."[107] This position
seems to suggest that no sin or resistance can match God's overwhelming
goodness, love, resourcefulness, ingenuity, and patience. Consequently,
everyone will end up in heaven, which would make hell as an eternal place
or state superfluous.

In *A New Kind of Christianity*, McLaren points out that the six-line
narrative "starts with one category of things—good and blessed—and then
ends up with two categories of things: good and blessed on the top line
and evil and tormented on the bottom."[108] This soul-sort narrative does
not mesh with McLaren's moral intuitions of a good God. In fact, one of
the key aphorisms in the entire McLaren corpus is found at the beginning
of *The Last Word and the Word After That*: "No thought I have ever had of
God is better than God actually is."[109]

This bedrock belief in the goodness of God inspired McLaren to explore
the history of the doctrine of hell. He concluded that the concept of eternal

---

[103] McLaren, *SWFOI*, 154.

[104] McLaren, *LWWAT*, 138.

[105] Ibid.

[106] This notion of "off-limits" questions among members of the open-minded ECM is curious and
will be explored in Chapter Eight.

[107] McLaren, *LWWAT*, 138.

[108] McLaren, *NKOCY*, 34.

[109] McLaren, *LWWAT*, xi.

damnation was borrowed from non-Hebrew sources[110] and that Jesus never taught a literal hell, but rather used the term against Jewish religious leaders for rhetorical effect.[111] McLaren argues,

> Again and again, Jesus took conventional language and imagery for hell and reversed it. We might say he wasn't so much teaching about hell as he was un-teaching about hell. . . . Those fire-and-brimstone passages that countless preachers have used to scare people about hell, it turns out, weren't intended to teach us about hell: Jesus used the language of hell to teach us a radical new vision of God![112]

This "radical new vision" offered compassion and hope to society's rough-and-tumble marginalized outcasts and turned the tables on the religious authorities who, from the perch of self-righteous superiority, condemned the least of these.

McLaren's most explicit exposition of the afterlife can be found in an unpublished paper entitled "Making Eschatology Personal," in which he affirms a literal existence with God for all people beyond the grave.[113] McLaren believes "in death we join God in the vast, forever-expanding future" that is a continuation and culmination of the three-dimensional narrative. McLaren elaborates, "This approach locates heaven—or the center or headquarters, so to speak, of [the] presence of God—not in another realm (like the realm of Platonic forms), and not above us (as if God were in the sky), but instead ahead of us in time, or perhaps better said, in the flow of possibility which the future constantly brings to us."[114] McLaren explains judgment as "setting things right, dealing decisively with evil and freeing good to run wild. . . . [I]n the end, that's good news for everyone." Since God's judgment is never fundamentally retributive, but always redemptive,

---

[110] Ibid., 49–73. See also McLaren, *WMRBW*, 112. McLaren believes the concept of hell was imported from neighboring cultures, including the Mesopotamians, Egyptians, Greeks, and Persian Zoroastrians.

[111] McLaren, *LWWAT*, 74–81. See also McLaren, *WMRBW*, 113–14.

[112] McLaren, *WMRBW*, 113.

[113] Brian McLaren, "Making Eschatology Personal," *brian d. mclaren* (blog), unpublished paper, n. d., accessed May 10, 2014, link found at the end of the post "Q&R:Afterlife" at http://brianmclaren .net/archives/blog/q-r-afterlife.html.

[114] Ibid., 3–4.

there is good reason to hope that all will be saved, albeit some "by the skin of [their] teeth."[115]

McLaren seems to concur with Dan Poole's daughter, Jess, who declares, "I could never be happy in a party upstairs in the heavenly living room knowing that so many people were being tortured in the basement."[116] Therefore, in the final assessment, the purpose of damnation language for McLaren is not to predict actual divine punishment, but rather to offer a stern warning. "As in the ancient story of Jonah, God's intent was not to destroy but to save. Neither a great big fish nor a great big fire gets the last word, but rather God's great big love and grace."[117]

The Fate of the Unevangelized

On the back cover of *A New Kind of Christianity* is the query, "What Would Christianity Look Like If We Weren't Afraid of Questions?"[118] Indeed, the ECM has been characterized by honest and open inquiry in which questions of all kinds are encouraged. An exception for McLaren, however, comes in the form of arguably the most asked apologetic question of our day—namely, "What happens to people who die without hearing the gospel message?"[119]

This question surfaces in several of McLaren's works and is frequently met with either apparent evasion or an uncharacteristically harsh, off-limits response. In *A New Kind of Christian*, Dan asks Neo if "people of other religions will go to heaven." Neo is disappointed with Dan's obsession with this issue and refers him to one of the final sermons he preached before leaving the pastorate.[120] Later in the story, Neo writes an email to Dan and lays out three responses to this question—Universalism, Exclusivism,

---

[115] Ibid., 4, 6.

[116] McLaren, *LWWAT*, 30. Philosopher Eric Reitan articulates this argument as follows: "The eternal damnation of anyone is incompatible with the salvation of any because knowledge of the sufferings of the damned would undermine the happiness of the saved." See Eric Reitan, "Eternal Damnation and Blessed Ignorance: Is the Damnation of Some Incompatible with the Salvation of Any?," *Religious Studies* 38 (2002): 429, quoted in Jerry L. Walls, *Heaven, Hell, and Purgatory* (Grand Rapids: Brazos, 2015), 154.

[117] McLaren, *WMRBW*, 114.

[118] See also an epigraph at the beginning of *NKOCY* that quotes Vincent J. Donovan without a reference: "Never accept and be content with unanalyzed assumptions, assumptions about the work, about the people, about the church or Christianity. There is no question that should not be asked or that is outlawed."

[119] Sanders writes, "According to some estimates this is the most asked apologetic question." John Sanders, "Evangelical Responses to Salvation Outside the Church," *Christian Scholar's Review* 24, no. 1 (September 1994): 45.

[120] McLaren, *NKOC*, 85.

and Inclusivism—each of which he spurns. Neo unpacks each position accordingly: Christian universalists believe "that Jesus is the only way and the Savior of the whole world and that everyone is already saved regardless of whether they believe in him."[121] Exclusivists argue "that Jesus is the only way, but he is the Savior of only those who choose (or are chosen) to believe in him. Only they will go to heaven." Inclusivists affirm Jesus as the only way to heaven, but salvation "extends to everyone who in some way (known only to God) accepts the grace of God."[122]

Neo likewise rejects the view of "pluralism and relativism" as patently modern due to its claim of absolute objectivity. While on the surface pluralism might appear magnanimous, in actuality "it may be the least tolerant position of all, since behind the scenes it must admit that every other position's claim to legitimacy is bogus."[123] Neo places each of these inadequate options below a line. Above the line, however, he offers his favored position entitled "predicamentalism." It is the view that "refuses to let anyone speculate about other people's eternal fate but instead focuses you on your own."[124] In other words, questions concerning the eternal destiny of others are considered by McLaren to be idle conjecture and a deterrent to focusing on temporal social concerns and one's own personal spirituality. This commitment to predicamentalism can be traced to Newbigin, "who leaves the issue open. In fact, he suggests that it is improper and disobedient to try to speculate on the eternal destiny of others."[125]

Our survey of McLaren's doctrinal revisions is complete. Chapters Seven and Eight will assess McLaren's emergent theology in light of Arminianism. But before evaluating McLaren's doctrinal claims, this study will first turn to the charge of Liberalism in Chapter Six. It is not surprising, in light of McLaren's deconstruction of five-point Calvinism, that many Reformed apologists would seek to classify McLaren as a contemporary advocate for modern liberal teaching. The following chapter will explore whether or not this charge is warranted.

---

[121] Ibid., 125. Neo acknowledges that there are other forms of universalism; however, in this context he is limiting the conversation to the Christian variety.

[122] Ibid. Similar definitions are offered in McLaren, *LWWAT*, 103.

[123] McLaren, *NKOC*, 126.

[124] Ibid.

[125] McLaren, *LWWAT*, 103.

Chapter Six

MCLAREN, EVANGELICALISM, AND LIBERALISM

Among the young stand arrayed two groups of evangelicals. On the one hand are those increasingly committed to a fairly aggressive form of Reformed theology with a strongly Puritan flavor, influenced by J. I. Packer, R. C. Sproul, John Piper, D. A. Carson, and other "confessing evangelicals." On the other hand are those fascinated with the experimentation of worship found in the "emerging church network" led by Brian McLaren and influenced by Stanley Grenz.[1]

—Roger E. Olson, *Reformed and Always Reforming*

WHEN MCLAREN WAS NAMED ONE OF *TIME*'S MOST INFLUENTIAL evangelicals in 2005, the author of the article, David Van Biema, offered a promising prediction: "If his movement can survive in the politicized world of conservative Christianity, McLaren could find a way for young Evangelicals and more liberal Christians to march into the future together despite their theological differences."[2] Within a few years, however, McLaren had fallen out of favor in the "politicized world of conservative Christianity," and many suggested the term "liberal" as a more accurate designation than "evangelical." For instance, commenting on a 2012 *New York Times* article that reported McLaren's involvement in leading his son's gay commitment

---

[1] Roger E. Olson, *Reformed and Always Reforming* (Grand Rapids: Baker, 2007), 31.
[2] David Van Biema, "The 25 Most Influential Evangelicals in America," *Time* 165, no. 6 (February 7, 2005): 34–45, citing 45.

ceremony, Terry Mattingly wondered if this represents "a final 'jumping the shark' moment for those who want to use the word 'evangelical' to describe McLaren?"[3]

Long before this definitive act of public solidarity with his son and the LGBT community, however, many conservative critics were questioning McLaren's fitness for the evangelical label. For instance, Stephen Wellum compared McLaren to the father of modern liberal theology, Friedrich Schleiermacher.[4] Jeremy Bouma traced McLaren's lineage through the "liberal *Kingdom* grammar" of Paul Tillich, Walter Rauschenbusch, and Albrecht Ritschl back to Schleiermacher.[5] Kevin DeYoung agreed, "McLaren stands in the tradition of Ritschl, Harnack, Rauschenbusch, and Whitehead, plain and simple."[6] Mark Christy accused McLaren of trading in the true orthodox message of the Christian faith for a liberal "neoorthopraxy."[7] Scot McKnight identified the influence of not only Harnack, but contemporary liberals Marcus Borg and Harvey Cox as well.[8]

John Armstrong noted the shift in endorsements of McLaren's books from "respected evangelicals" to "fairly liberal Christian leaders and authors."[9] Larry Dixon affectionately labeled McLaren a "friendly heretic."[10] Tim Challies declared McLaren's journey "has taken him into outright, rank,

---

[3] Terry Mattingly, "Time to Pin New Label on Brian McLaren?" *Get Religion* (*Patheos* blog), September 26, 2012, http://www.patheos.com/blogs/getreligion/2012/09/time-to-pin-new-label-on -brian-mclaren/. In response to Mattingly's blog, McLaren admits to pondering whether or not he is still properly considered an evangelical, as well. See Brian McLaren, "An Interesting Discussion, Somewhat Peripherally about Me . . ." *brian d. mclaren* (blog), September 29, 2012, http:// brianmclaren.net/archives/blog/an-interesting-discussion-somewh.html.

[4] R. Albert Mohler Jr., Bruce Ware, Gregory Wills, Jim Hamilton, and Stephen Wellum, "Panel Discussion—New Kind of Christianity?—Brian McLaren Recasts the Gospel," Southern Baptist Theological Seminary, March 11, 2010, http://www.sbts.edu/resources/chapel/chapel-spring-2010 /panel-discussion-a-new-kind-of-christianity-brian-mclaren-recasts-the-gospel/.

[5] Jeremy Bouma, *Reimagining the Kingdom* (Grand Rapids: Theoklesia, 2012), 27–30.

[6] Kevin DeYoung, "Christianity and McLarenism (1)," *Kevin DeYoung* (*The Gospel Coalition* blog), February 17, 2010, http://www.thegospelcoalition.org/blogs/kevindeyoung/2010/02/17/christianity -and-mclarenism-1/.

[7] Mark D. Christy, "Neoorthopraxy and Brian D. McLaren" (PhD dissertation, Southwestern Baptist Theological Seminary, 2011), 15–16.

[8] Scot McKnight, "Rebuilding the Faith from Scratch: Brian McLaren's 'New' Christianity Is Not So Much Revolutionary as Evolutionary," *CT* 53, no. 3 (March 2010): 59–66, citing 66.

[9] John H. Armstrong, "Whither Brian McLaren?" *John H. Armstrong* (blog), March 3, 2010, http:// johnharmstrong.typepad.com/john_h_armstrong_/2010/03/whither-brian-mclaren.html.

[10] Larry Dixon, "Whatever Happened to Heresy? Examples of Heresy Today," *Emmaus Journal* 19 (2010): 219.

unapologetic apostasy."[11] Albert Mohler,[12] D. A. Carson,[13] John Frame,[14] and Michael Wittmer[15] all independently referenced J. Gresham Machen's *Christianity and Liberalism* in their critique of McLaren. This illustrative list clearly demonstrates that several critics, many of whom embrace five-point Calvinism, have charged McLaren with the "heresy" of Liberalism.

Charges are one thing, but the real question is: Do they stick? If so, which kind of Liberalism is McLaren guilty of embracing? This chapter will seek to provide some answers. The previous chapters have explored McLaren's deconstructive and reconstructive thrusts, as well as his key doctrinal revisions. In this chapter, McLaren's apologetic methodology will naturally emerge as this study considers his new kind of apologetic project in light of modern Liberalism, postliberalism, and postconservative evangelical theology.

As Stanley Grenz and Roger Olson point out, "Liberal theology is notoriously difficult to define"[16] and is a term that is "much abused."[17] John Franke agrees that liberal theology is more variegated than often is recognized. Franke claims that contemporary liberal theologians tend to split into either revisionist or postliberal camps, with a range of diversity under each rubric.[18] The revisionist camp sees its project in continuity with some of the nineteenth-century Protestant liberal concerns and value the "*public* character of theology,"[19] while postliberals reject the foundationalism of the revisionist camp and understand theology in narrative terms and as an "act of communal self-description."[20] Postliberals also seek to coalesce around

---

[11] Tim Challies, "Book Review: A New Kind of Christianity," *American Theological Inquiry* 5, no. 2 (July 15, 2012): 106.

[12] Mohler, "Panel Discussion—New Kind of Christianity."

[13] D. A. Carson, *Becoming Conversant with the Emerging Church* (Grand Rapids: Zondervan, 2004), 161.

[14] John M. Frame, "The Road to Generous Orthodoxy," *Reformation and Revival Journal* 14, no. 3 (2005): 101.

[15] Michael Wittmer, "Don't Stop Believing: A Theological Critique of the Emergent Church," *Reformed Review* 61, no. 3 (Fall 2008): 129–33.

[16] Stanley J. Grenz and Roger E. Olson, *20th-Century Theology* (Downers Grove: InterVarsity Press, 1992), 51.

[17] Roger E. Olson, *The Journey of Modern Theology* (Downers Grove: InterVarsity Press, 2013), 125.

[18] John R. Franke, *The Character of Theology* (Grand Rapids: Baker, 2005), 29. See also Timothy R. Phillips and Dennis L. Okholm, "The Nature of Confession: Evangelicals & Postliberals," in *The Nature of Confession: Evangelicals and Postliberals in Conversation*, ed. Timothy R. Phillips and Dennis L. Okholm (Downers Grove: InterVarsity Press, 1996), 10.

[19] William C. Placher, *Unapologetic Theology* (Louisville: Westminster John Knox Press, 1989), 154.

[20] Franke, *Character of Theology*, 29–30.

an ecumenical "generous orthodoxy," a term that McLaren seems to have borrowed from Hans Frei. Liberal theology also has been developed in more radical directions in response to social concerns. Liberation theology and feminist theology both seek to give voice to historically marginalized groups, as does postcolonial theology. In short, the term "liberal theology" requires careful nuance, something that many conservative evangelicals have struggled to acknowledge.

Some of the same "conservative evangelicals"[21] who have engaged McLaren also struggle to recognize and accept diversity within their own ranks, often calling anyone a "liberal" who does not conform to their strict style of conservative Evangelicalism.[22] As Olson puts it, "Some conservative evangelicals seem to want to enforce a greater degree of conformity if not uniformity on all evangelicals."[23] While evangelicals typically adhere to what is known as Bebbington's quadrilateral[24]—conversionism, activism, biblicism, and crucicentrism—conservative evangelicals can be classified further as either biblicist or paleo-orthodox.[25] According to Olson, biblicist evangelicals typically believe that revelation is "primarily propositional," and it is "relatively easy with training and skill to move from biblical exegesis to establishment of sound doctrine without the aid of other sources and norms such as tradition, philosophy, or culture," while adherents to paleo-orthodoxy focus on "the consensus of the early church fathers, including the ancient ecumenical creeds."[26] Carl Henry, Norman Geisler, Wayne Grudem, J. I. Packer, and David Wells represent the former group, while Thomas Oden, D. H. Williams, and Robert Webber exemplify the latter.

That said, Olson makes a case for even greater diversity within the evangelical camp: "My purpose is to explain how a person can be evangelical and not conservative, let alone fundamentalist, in the contemporary

---

[21] Wayne Grudem is a prominent evangelical who labels his tradition "conservative evangelicalism." See Wayne A. Grudem, *Systematic Theology* (Grand Rapids: Zondervan, 1994), 38–39.

[22] Olson, *Journey of Modern Theology*, 125. Olson claims that "many people call any religious view they disagree with and think is somehow modern, as opposed to traditional, liberal theology." In so doing, these critics often reduce the term for all functional purposes to a mere expletive.

[23] Olson, *Reformed and Always Reforming*, 9.

[24] See David Bebbington, *Evangelicalism in Modern Britain* (Grand Rapids: Baker, 1989), 2–17.

[25] Olson, *Reformed and Always Reforming*, 20–22.

[26] Ibid.

sense of that term."[27] Olson lists leading evangelical abolitionists William Wilberforce and Charles Finney, Free Methodist Church founder and social progressive B. T. Roberts, and Jim Wallis's Sojourners community as historical exemplars. He believes this social awareness is alive and well in sectors of Evangelicalism and contributes to the movement's overall health and vitality. He labels the contemporary expression of this progressive evangelical stream "postconservative."[28]

Franke also observes the latest iteration of this stream within the evangelical community and notes the range of terms used to describe it: "Reformist evangelicals, the evangelical left, the younger evangelicals, postmodern evangelicals, postconservatives, and even post-evangelicals."[29] He notes that a defining unifying trait amidst this diverse set of labels is "the identification of postmodernity as one of the decisive factors in accounting for the changes described and sought."[30] Franke favors the term "postconservative" because it underscores the point Olson also has made; namely, conservativism and Evangelicalism are not and have not been historically identical. Additionally, Franke believes this label also helps identify the parallelism and common project that postconservatives and postliberals share: challenging the tenets of modernity.[31]

In this study's quest to map the location of McLaren's emergent apologetic abode, there is good reason to believe that it can be located somewhere in the recently constructed postliberal and postconservative neighborhoods, as will be seen shortly. There is no disputing that McLaren left the conservative evangelical suburbs years ago. Instead of migrating to a newly built neighborhood, however, some insist he is best seen as renovating an existing nineteenth-century Germanic domicile in an established liberal part of town. What follows is an attempt to locate the most appropriate address for McLaren's emergent home.

---

[27] Roger E. Olson, *How to Be Evangelical without Being Conservative* (Grand Rapids: Zondervan, 2008), 18–23. Other evangelicals such as Donald Dayton, John Alexander, Clark Pinnock, and Ron Sider have made similar statements. See Gary J. Dorrien, *The Remaking of Evangelical Theology* (Louisville: Westminster John Knox Press, 1998), 153–54.

[28] Olson, *Reformed and Always Reforming*, 10.

[29] Franke, *Character of Theology*, 37. See also Justin Taylor, "An Introduction to Postconservative Evangelicalism" in *Reclaiming the Center*, ed. Millard J. Erickson et al. (Wheaton: Crossway, 2004), 17–32, citing 17–18.

[30] Franke, *Character of Theology*, 37–38.

[31] Ibid.

McLaren and Modern Liberal Theology

Many outspoken critics have tied McLaren to the historic stream of modern liberal theology, and in so doing have perpetuated the old conservative-liberal divide that McLaren and others in the ECM have sought to leave behind. Albert Mohler and his colleagues at Southern Baptist Theological Seminary represent well the kind of strident biblicist critique that is common among McLaren critics. Mohler facilitated a panel discussion when *A New Kind of Christianity* was released. A vitriolic spirit was on full display in this panel discussion, as McLaren was called "self-serving," "a wolf in sheep's clothing," and "the craftiest of the serpents of the field . . . following in the train of his father, the devil."[32]

Mohler initiated the conversation by favorably citing Machen's view that conservative and liberal forms of Christianity are not different members of the same family, but rather "two rival religions."[33] Therefore, McLaren is not proposing a new kind of Christianity, but rather a different religion altogether. Mohler then explained a common teaching strategy that he employs to expose McLaren's alleged liberalism. He places sections of McLaren's writings alongside excerpts from early twentieth-century liberals, such as Harry Emerson Fosdick and Shailer Mathews, and "dares his students" to distinguish the older liberal quotes from the words of McLaren. Not surprisingly, the students are unable because "they are all saying basically the same thing."

Mohler summarizes his thesis as follows: "When you reach the conclusion of the book, you land right back into twentieth-century Protestant Liberalism."[34] On cue, each Southern Seminary professor fell in line with Mohler's thesis by connecting McLaren's project—despite possessing a superficial postmodern gloss—to classical modern liberal theology.

---

[32] In order, these statements can be attributed to professors Gregory Wills, Bruce Ware, and Jim Hamilton. See Mohler, et al., "Panel Discussion—New Kind of Christianity."

[33] J. Gresham Machen, *Christianity and Liberalism* (Grand Rapids: Eerdmans, 1923), 7. As an instructive aside, it is worth recalling that McLaren believes the greatest rival to "good monotheism" is not an outside competing religion, but rather "bad monotheism." In other words, McLaren seems to agree at this juncture with Mohler (and Machen) that the chief concern for their respective worldviews is not a marauder that attacks from without, but rather a very different rival that emerges from within.

[34] Mohler, et al., "Panel Discussion—New Kind of Christianity."

These charges of liberalism are familiar to McLaren, who is well aware that some conservative evangelicals "wish that people like me would simply declare ourselves liberal so that they could finally be done with us (Farewell, liberals!)."[35] McLaren is "continually intrigued by the deep antipathy that many Evangelicals have for Mainliners, Liberals, or Progressives." He notes how calling someone a liberal "simply wipes a person off the map in terms of serious consideration among Evangelicals." While he chooses not to self-identify as a liberal, McLaren explains that his view of what it means to be an evangelical "does not assume an eternal hostility towards liberals, nor does it assume the word 'conservative' means 'absolutely good.'"[36] In other words, McLaren does not attach all of the same baggage to the term "liberal" that appears to be part of the freight for many conservative biblicist evangelicals.

THE CONTOURS OF CLASSICAL MODERN LIBERAL THEOLOGY

- Reconstruction of Christian belief in light of modern knowledge.
- Empowerment of the individual to challenge and rethink traditional Christian teaching.
- Focus on the practical and ethical dimension of Christianity with a special premium placed upon kingdom of God teaching.
- Rejection of the absolute authority of the Bible as the foundation for Christian teaching and practice.
- A drift away from divine transcendence toward divine immanence.

See Grenz and Olson, *20th-Century Theology: God and the World in a Transitional Age (InterVarsity Press, 1992)*, 52. For comparable descriptions, see Claude Welch, *Protestant Thought in the Nineteenth Century: 1870–1914*, vol. 2 (New Haven: Yale University Press, 1985), 232–33, and Gary Dorrien, *The Making of Modern Liberal Theology: Imagining Progressive Religion, 1805–1900* (Louisville: Westminster John Knox Press, 2001), xxiii.

---

[35] Brian McLaren, "Evangelicals? Mainliners? Conservatives? Progressives?," *brian d. mclaren* (blog), August 8, 2011, http://brianmclaren.net/archives/blog/evangelicals-mainliners-conserva .html.

[36] Ibid.

That said, is McLaren's project best characterized as a recent expression of classical modern liberal theology? Before answering this question, we must first identify the major traits of this movement. In *20th-Century Theology*, Grenz and Olson offer a list of five features that describe the contours of classical modern liberal theology (See above sidebar).

Grenz and Olson associate classical modern liberal theology with a "specific movement in Protestantism that dominated academic theology around the turn of the [twentieth] century. It arose in Germany among students and followers of Schleiermacher and Hegel, and it took on its most influential form in the school of Albrecht Ritschl."[37] While Grenz and Olson recognize diversity within this movement, they believe the "essence of late nineteenth- and early twentieth-century liberal theology" is most clearly embodied in the teaching of Ritschl, Adolf Harnack, and Walter Rauschenbusch. Consequently, classical modern liberal theology is historically informed by Enlightenment concerns and sensibilities, and it possesses a strong Germanic flavor.

With this description of modern liberal theology in mind, McLaren's project will now be evaluated in light of the five characteristics of this movement.

Reconstruction of Christian Belief in Light of Modern Knowledge

As seen, McLaren's project includes major deconstructive and reconstructive thrusts. For instance, *A New Kind of Christian* details his deconstructive engagement with the excesses of modernity,[38] while *The Story We Find Ourselves In* marks the early stages of reconstruction.[39] In *A New Kind of Christianity*, McLaren deconstructs the six-line Greco-Roman narrative and the propositional, constitutional hermeneutic before proposing the reconstructed three-line narrative and an evolutionary, Christocentric, dialogical library approach to interpreting Scripture.[40] Nevertheless, McLaren's project is in conversation with postmodern knowledge rather than modern

[37] Grenz and Olson, *20th-Century Theology*, 51.
[38] McLaren, *NKOC*, 16–20.
[39] McLaren, *SWFOI*, xii.
[40] McLaren, *NKOCY*, 33–97.

knowledge, which was the case with the modern liberal theologians. Claude Welch defines modern liberal theology as "maximal acknowledgement of the claims of modern thought."[41] In other words, the modern liberal theologians embraced the spirit of modernity and sought to rework the Christian message accordingly.

It is true that McLaren views postmodernity as moving beyond modernity rather than as a fundamentally "anti-modern" mindset.[42] Consequently, his project naturally includes appreciation for aspects of the modern bank of knowledge. Yet, on the whole, McLaren is a critic of modernity rather than an advocate, unlike the modern liberal theologians who based their projects on modern assumptions. For instance, Schleiermacher did not reject foundationalism;[43] he simply grounded indubitable universal certainty in human experience rather than reason.[44] McLaren, on the other hand, rejects all forms of modern foundationalism and opts for a nonfoundational, coherentist epistemology.[45]

Additionally, the deconstructive and reconstructive endeavors of the modern liberal theologians included stripping away the miraculous and supernatural elements from the text for the purpose of identifying the universally enduring ethical kernel. While McLaren eschews the dualism of the natural/supernatural divide, he does not deny the existence of miracles. Tony Jones observes, "What McLaren is not is an unredeemed liberal, bent on demythologizing the text."[46] Likewise, when once asked if he still believes in the resurrection of Christ, McLaren responded quickly and categorically, "Not only do I believe in the resurrection of Jesus Christ, I base my life on it."[47]

While McLaren personally retains this orthodox belief, it is true that the literal time-space bodily resurrection of Christ is not a centerpiece of his

---

[41] See Olson, *Journey of Modern Theology,* 126. The original quote can be found in Claude Welch, *Protestant Thought in the Nineteenth Century: 1799–1870,* vol. 1 (New Haven: Yale University Press, 1972), 142.

[42] McLaren, *NKOC,* 22.

[43] For a discussion of foundationalism, see Appendix B.

[44] Murphy, *Beyond Liberalism and Fundamentalism,* 22–23.

[45] See McLaren, *NKOC,* 55–56.

[46] Tony Jones, "The McLaren Lectionary," *Theoblogy* (*Patheos* blog), June 10, 2014, http://www.patheos.com/blogs/tonyjones/2014/06/10/the-mclaren-lectionary/.

[47] Greg Metzger, "Brian McLaren Responds to Terry Mattingly's Scurrilous Question," *Faith and the Common Good* (blog), September 27, 2012, http://debatingobama.blogspot.com/2012/09/brian-mclaren-responds-to-mattinglys.html.

corpus, nor are miracles emphasized. In *We Make the Road by Walking*, in response to the traditional conservative and liberal approaches to miracles, McLaren writes, "There is a third alternative, a response to the question of miracles that is open to both skeptics and believers in miracles alike. Instead of 'Yes, miracles actually happened,' or 'No, they didn't really happen,' we could ask another question: *What happens to us when we imagine miracles happening?*"[48] McLaren's suggestion will be considered more carefully later in this study. For now, it is sufficient to note that McLaren's affirmation of miracles, especially the resurrection, does not manifest itself in ways that conventional conservative evangelicals recognize with comfort; however, it does separate him from the modern liberal project.

Empowerment of the Individual to Challenge and Rethink Traditional Christian Teaching

In *A New Kind of Christian*, Neo identifies modernity as "the age of individualism."[49] As communities disintegrated, individuals had never been so "free of all social constraint and connection as they [were] in late modernity."[50] Henry Knight explains this emphasis on individualism, saying, "The autonomous individual [was] free to think for him or herself, released from bondage to community or tradition."[51] While not all modern thinkers exercised their freedom in radical ways, and many maintained "a profound appreciation for the communal nature of Christian truth"; nevertheless, there was willingness, if not a sense of obligation, to break with tradition when necessary.[52]

From a young age, McLaren possessed an inquisitive mind.[53] This willingness to question and ponder traditional teaching and inherited stock answers led to the first phase of his reconstructed faith in the 1990s,[54] but it blossomed during the decade that opened with *A New Kind of Christian* (2001) and closed with *A New Kind of Christianity* (2010). As this study has shown, McLaren took the advice of mentors Stanley Grenz and Dallas

---

[48] McLaren, *WMRBW*, 97.
[49] McLaren, *NKOC*, 18.
[50] Ibid.
[51] Henry H. Knight III, *A Future for Truth* (Nashville: Abingdon, 1997), 38.
[52] Grenz and Olson, *20th-Century Theology*, 52.
[53] McLaren, *FF*, 267–68.
[54] McLaren, *NKOCY*, 6–8.

Willard to rethink large swaths of the Christian faith. In so doing, he is in tune with the liberal spirit of trailblazers such as Schleiermacher, Ritschl, Harnack, and Rauschenbusch.

There are important differences, however. First, instead of placing the autonomous rational individual at the center of his project, McLaren's proposals have emerged from within the confines of community.[55] McLaren's project cannot be understood apart from the emergent community, what he has called his "soul tribe."[56] In this type of foment, sometimes it is difficult to tell where ideas begin and where they end. Therefore, the function of community in McLaren's project is indispensable.

Second, McLaren claims that his commitment to the classical ecumenical creeds has not wavered. While McLaren de-emphasizes the doctrinal distinctives of individual denominations and traditions, he argues that his questioning has been "consistently, unequivocally, and unapologetically" tethered to an affirmation of the Apostles' and Nicene Creeds.[57] At least that is what McLaren stated in *A Generous Orthodoxy*, which was published in 2004. When the more radical proposals of *A New Kind of Christianity* surfaced in 2010, however, Scot McKnight asked McLaren in an interview if he still affirmed the ancient ecumenical creeds. McLaren responded, "As I see it there is nothing I wrote in *A Generous Orthodoxy* and nothing I wrote in *A New Kind of Christianity* that aren't in harmony."[58]

McLaren goes on to state that what he is "advocating goes back through church history all the way to the beginning" in minority report traditions such as the Celts, the Anabaptists, the Radical Reformation, and more recently the Social Gospel Movement, liberation theology, black theology, Latino theology, feminist theology, and eco-theology. Ultimately, he argues that the Greco-Roman storyline, which has been the majority report narrative among Western evangelicals, "is the ungenerous thing that has been

---

[55] Operating out of the conservative biblicist paradigm, David Wells believes "the autonomous self" is not unique to the modern mindset, but is shared by the postmodern perspective as well, "despite all the postmodern chatter about the importance of community." See David F. Wells, *Above All Earthly Powers* (Grand Rapids: Eerdmans, 2005), 67–68.

[56] McLaren, *JP*, 15.

[57] McLaren, *GO*, 32.

[58] Brian McLaren and Scot McKnight, "Brian McLaren: 'Conversations on Being a Heretic,'" *Q Ideas* (website), n. d., accessed June 21, 2014, http://qideas.org/articles/brian-mclaren-conversations-on-being-a-heretic/.

wrapped up with orthodoxy" down through history.[59] Therefore, the goal of *A New Kind of Christianity* was to disentangle this six-line narrative from what he believes to be true orthodoxy. In sum, while McLaren's radical doctrinal proposals resonate with the spirit of modern liberal theology, his commitment to the dynamic of Christian community and the classic creeds[60] sets his project apart in important ways.

Focus on the Practical and Ethical Dimension of Christianity with a Special Premium Placed upon Kingdom of God Teaching.

In John MacArthur's opinion, "McLaren presents Jesus' Kingdom message in a way that most closely aligns with the non-eschatological social activism of twentieth-century liberalism."[61] As seen, McLaren is often linked to classical modern liberals, such as Ritschl and his followers, who avoided metaphysical speculation and employed the Kantian fact-value divide in an effort to safeguard the Christian faith from the acids of modernity. In so doing, religious knowledge and language were distilled to kingdom of God ethics.

McLaren's emphasis upon the kingdom of God as the central message of the gospel reached full bloom at the beginning of the "Emergent McLaren" era, with the publishing of *The Secret Message of Jesus* and *Everything Must Change*. While McKnight suggested that these two books might provide "what could become an evangelical social gospel,"[62] not everyone welcomed McLaren's proposal.[63] For instance, in a published email exchange with Ed Stetzer, former McLaren co-author Leonard Sweet lamented, "The emergent church has become another form of social gospel. And the problem with every social gospel is that it becomes all social and no gospel. All social justice and no social gospel. It is embarrassing that evangelicals have

---

[59] Ibid.

[60] While McLaren claims to have maintained a commitment to the ancient ecumenical creeds, this statement appears to be in tension with his assertion that the post-Constantinian church compromised with Greek philosophy. Since the creeds rely heavily upon Greek philosophical categories, it is not clear how McLaren neatly resolves these two apparently conflicting commitments.

[61] John MacArthur, "Perspicuity of Scripture: The Emergent Approach," *The Master's Seminary Journal* 17, no. 2 (Fall 2006): 148.

[62] McKnight, "Rebuilding the Faith," 59.

[63] For a treatment of the ECM as a "new social movement," see Tony Jones, *The Church Is Flat* (Minneapolis: JoPa Group, 2011), 11–22.

discovered and embraced liberation theology after it destroyed the main line, old line, side line, off line, flat line church."[64]

McLaren explains that his old gospel paradigm "specialized in dealing with 'spiritual needs' to the exclusion of physical and social needs."[65] The paradigm shift into understanding the gospel in more practical and ethical terms required coming to a "place of cynically doubting much of what I had been told about Jesus," which eventually included rejecting not only the penal substitutionary theory of the atonement, but the doctrine of atonement itself.[66] It was the work of contemporary scholars such as N. T. Wright, however, rather than the Protestant liberal theologians of the nineteenth and early-twentieth centuries that introduced McLaren to the kingdom of God as a fundamentally temporal rather than exclusively eternal reality.[67]

Over time, McLaren became increasingly open to other voices and their explication of the kingdom vision. These voices included liberal scholars such as Walter Rauschenbusch, Harvey Cox, John Dominic Crossan, and Marcus Borg. As a result, many conservative evangelicals declared McLaren guilty by association. In his own defense, McLaren explains his willingness to read widely on this subject and others: "When I read a book by Anne Lamott or Walter Wink or listen to music by Bruce Cockburn or Sheryl Crow or somebody like that I am not always asking the question, 'What do they believe?' I am asking the question, 'What do they have to say to me?' I am not requiring me to agree with them or them to agree with me to be stimulated by what they have to say."[68]

With this explanation in mind, it would be unfair to assume that anyone who appears on McLaren's reading list or in his footnotes automatically

---

[64] Ed Stetzer, "The Emergent/Emerging Church: A Missiological Perspective," in *Evangelicals Engaging Emergent*, ed. William D. Henard and Adam W. Greenway (Nashville: B&H Publishing, 2009), 58–59. See also Tony Jones, *The New Christians* (San Francisco: Jossey-Bass, 2008), 82. For McLaren's response to these charges, see Brian McLaren and Andrew Jones, "Brian McLaren Responds to *Everything Must Change* Concerns," *Tall Skinny Kiwi* (blog), March 26, 2008, http://tallskinnykiwi.typepad.com/tallskinnykiwi/2008/03/brian-mclaren-r.html.

[65] McLaren, *EMC*, 33.

[66] McLaren, *SMJ*, 34.

[67] Brian McLaren and Jon Stanley, "Why Everything Must Change: A Conversation with Brian McLaren," *The Other Journal* (website), Seattle School of Theology & Psychology, October 15, 2007, http://theotherjournal.com/2007/10/15/why-everything-must-change-a-conversation-with-brian-mclaren/.

[68] McLaren and McKnight, "Conversations on Being a Heretic."

receives his full endorsement on all matters. While this is true, McLaren in recent years has cited Rauschenbusch enthusiastically.[69] For example, in an interview at the 2013 Wild Goose Festival, McLaren explained,

> So, one hundred years ago . . . this German Baptist pastor Walter Rauschenbusch goes back and reads the Gospels and realizes, wow, Jesus had this message called the Kingdom of God. And for so many Christians, Kingdom of God had been reduced to going to heaven after you die and he made this slight observation that, in the Lord's Prayer, it says, "May your kingdom come, your will be done down here on earth." In other words, the direction of the Bible was downward, not upward. I mean, that changes the world.[70]

Rauschenbusch's final book, *A Theology for the Social Gospel*, was a comprehensive attempt to develop a systematic theology for his practical and ethical social program. He reinterpreted each of the classic Christian doctrines in light of the central unifying theme of the kingdom of God. McLaren's *We Make the Road by Walking* is a similar project. Instead of casting his three-dimensional storyline (i.e., creation, liberation, and peaceable kingdom) into systematic theology,[71] however, McLaren offers a narrative overview of Scripture using a similar kingdom of God integrative motif. Consequently, it seems fair to draw connections between McLaren and the theological father of the US Social Gospel movement.

Rejection of the Absolute Authority of the Bible as the Foundation for Christian Teaching and Practice.

The modern liberal theologians rejected *sola scriptura*, but they did not discount the Bible entirely. Rather, they employed historical-critical methods to strip away what they believed to be the husk, which often included the supernatural, apocalyptic, and miracle accounts, in order to extract from

---

[69] For an example, McLaren writes, "Later reform movements grew up around people like Menno Simons, Martin Luther, John Wesley, and Walter Rauschenbusch." To place Rauschenbusch in the favorable line of Luther and Wesley is noteworthy. See McLaren, *WMRBW*, xvii.

[70] See Krista Tippett, "Transcript for Brian McLaren—The Equation of Change," *On Being* (website), March 13, 2014, http://www.onbeing.org/program/transcript/6174.

[71] McLaren's most systematic treatment of his social gospel can be found in *NKOCY* and *JMBM*.

the text the kernel of universally applicable moral teaching. Scripture was a means to an end and was subordinated to modern sensibilities, as well as personal experience.[72]

McLaren's handling of Scripture has likewise received extensive critique. According to Douglas Blount, while McLaren's interpretation of certain Old Testament passages "may soothe the postmodern conscience, it does so in defiance of historic Christian orthodoxy."[73] Blount also asserts that McLaren's rejection of violent Old Testament passages is "no less heretical than Marcion himself."[74] In response to McLaren's preference for narrative theology, Norman Geisler and Thomas Howe claim, "It seems here that power of story involves manipulating the facts to suit one's point."[75] D. A. Carson accuses McLaren of "almost never engag[ing] with the Scriptures except occasionally in prooftexting ways."[76] Gregory Wills believes that McLaren's culturally compromised reading of the Bible gives his followers "a God who can assuage their guilt without any violence, without any judgment, and without any moral demands placed on them."[77] All of these critics agree that McLaren's treatment of Scripture lacks conservative evangelical fidelity.

It is true that McLaren employs a radically different hermeneutic than the constitutional model utilized by conservative biblicist evangelicals. He also rejects *sola scriptura* and inerrancy as artifacts of modernity.[78] McLaren's methodology, however, can be distinguished from the modern liberal theologians in some important ways. First, McLaren affirms the miraculous and does not demythologize the text for the purpose of locating the naturalistic truth behind the mythological facade. In *Adventures in Missing the Point*, McLaren avers,

---

[72] Grenz and Olson, *20th-Century Theology*, 52.

[73] Douglas Blount, "A New Kind of Interpretation: Brian McLaren and the Hermeneutics of Taste," in *Evangelicals Engaging Emergent*, 125.

[74] Ibid., 115n18.

[75] Norman L. Geisler and Thomas Howe, "A Postmodern View of Scripture," in *Evangelicals Engaging Emergent*, 102.

[76] Carson, *Becoming Conversant*, 180.

[77] Wills, "Panel Discussion—New Kind of Christianity."

[78] See McLaren, ".@BrianMcLaren: We Make The Road By Walking #wgf14," *YouTube*, June 30, 2014, https://www.youtube.com/watch?v=Ll8LWIrLIhk. McLaren argues that infallibility was an advantage in the past for believers but is a detriment in our current postmodern milieu.

We presented the Bible as a repository of sacred propositions and abstractions. Which was natural, for we were moderns—children of the 18th century European Enlightenment—so we loved abstractions and propositions. Our sermons tended to exegete the texts in such a way that stories, poetry, and biography (among other features of the Bible)—the "chaff"—were sifted out, while the "wheat" of doctrines and principles were saved. Modern people loved that approach; meanwhile, however, people of a more postmodern bent (who are more like premodern people in many ways) find the doctrines and principles as interesting as grass clippings.[79]

Second, McLaren displays literary skill in handling the text, which is not surprising given his academic training. This means he seeks to read the text according to its historically appropriate literary genre rather than viewing it through a modern grid.

Third, while McLaren has moral concerns with aspects of the text, he does not jettison the Old Testament, as Harnack and Marcion did.[80] Rather, McLaren has employed a hermeneutic that allows for "faithful picking and choosing" and looks to the precedents of Jesus and Paul in doing so. McLaren's Christocentric lens is also central to his hermeneutic. Consequently, McLaren is committed to the Bible, despite its violent and genocidal passages. He rejects foundationalism in favor of coherentism and uses a very different hermeneutic. So, suggesting that McLaren is using the same hermeneutic as the modern liberal theologians is misrepresenting his project.

A Drift Away from Divine Transcendence toward Divine Immanence

Grenz and Olson claim that this final characteristic is perhaps the unifying motif or "underlying" feature of modern liberal theology. Whereas pre-Enlightenment theologians tended to underscore a radical disconnect between a "holy, transcendent God and sinful, finite humans," with the

---

[79] McLaren, *AMP*, 77.
[80] Adolf von Harnack, *Marcion: The Gospel of the Alien God*, trans. John E. Steely and Lyle D. Bierma (Grand Rapids: Baker, 1990).

"Incarnation as the dramatic event whereby God bridged this gulf," modern theologians emphasized continuity between God and humanity, with an emphasis on the temporal realm and "Jesus as the exemplary human rather than the invading Christ."[81]

While McLaren does not deny the existence of miracles, the afterlife, the transcendence and sovereignty of God (understood in open theistic terms), or the deity of Christ, he believes the Bible's "direction is downward, not upward."[82] In other words, his focus is clearly on an earthly kingdom of God understood in temporal categories with an emphasis upon Christ's teaching and example rather than his divinity. Instead of an escape plan to another realm, salvation is a restorational and transformational plan for all of God's current creation. This accent on immanence, while the details differ from the modern liberal theologians, clearly aligns him with classical liberal theology on this final point.

In summary, it is understandable why some critics place McLaren squarely in the modern liberal camp. His willingness to rethink classic Christian doctrine and respond with deconstructive and reconstructive projects; his rejection of *sola scriptura* and biblical inerrancy; his emphasis on the practical and ethical teachings of Jesus understood through the lens of a temporal kingdom of God theology; and his repudiation of a wrathful deity and eternal conscious torment all resonate with the spirit and teaching of classical modern liberal theology. Nevertheless, there are significant differences.

McLaren does not reject miracles and classic creedal claims, such as belief in the Trinity and the divinity and resurrection of Christ. He does, however, reject the experiential foundationalism of classical modern liberal theology, as well as the individualism that characterized the modern era. In fact, McLaren is a keen critic of the full range of modernity, as this study has shown. Modern liberal theologians, on the other hand, tended to embrace modernity and attempted to conform Christianity to modern tastes. This is decisively not McLaren's project. He is employing postmodern insights, not modern ones, without succumbing to hard postmodernism. Consequently, while there are important areas of resonance, it would be a

---

[81] Ibid., 52–53.
[82] See Tippett, "Transcript for Brian McLaren—The Equation of Change."

categorical mistake to locate McLaren's abode in the center of the classical modern liberal neighborhood.

McLaren and the Postconservative/Postliberal Convergence

McLaren began his ministerial work as a conservative evangelical, but his crisis in the 1990s precipitated a paradigm shift, or move out of the conservative suburbs. As seen, some critics have suggested McLaren moved to a liberal "side of town." Olson explains that conservative evangelicals have a tendency to think in the strict dualistic categories of conservative and liberal, so anyone who does not pass the "conservative" litmus test is often branded a "liberal." This is why some conservative evangelicals have struggled to fairly evaluate McLaren's project in light of postconservative and postliberal theology.[83] Olson explains:

> Conservative Evangelical theology tends to be done in the grip of fear of liberal theology. It is not uncommon to hear or read a conservative evangelical theologian warning of Friedrich Schleiermacher, the father of liberal theology, when discussing more progressive or postconservative evangelicals and their theological work. Conservatives tend to insist on placing every theologian and theological proposal on the spectrum of left to right as defined by attitudes toward modernity, with liberal theology representing maximal accommodation to modernity within a Christian theological framework. By and large, conservatives have trouble conceiving of any theology that is not tied to modernity in this way and thus neither "left" nor "right." Postliberalism (the Yale School of Theology) is a case in point; conservatives hardly know what to do with it and it is often ignored because it cannot be placed on their spectrum.[84]

---

[83] To clarify, this study is not suggesting that the previously mentioned critics of McLaren are unaware of the "postliberal" and "postconservative" terminology; rather, because of their dualistic thinking on this matter, they are unable to expand to include additional categorical possibilities. Consequently, both postconservatives and postliberals are tagged "liberal."

[84] Olson, *Reformed and Always Reforming*, 25–26.

Some conservative evangelicals, however, have correctly discerned the distinction between classical modern liberal theology and postconservative theology. Justin Taylor is a case in point. He does not consider McLaren a classic modern liberal but rather a postconservative. In fact, Taylor called McLaren the "pastor" of the postconservative movement.[85] Olson, likewise, identified McLaren as a leader in the postconservative conversation—one of two groups (the other being the New Calvinism) that younger evangelicals find attractive.[86] McLaren also identifies his comfort zone in this neighborhood. He lists several scholars and practitioners who are doing fruitful bridge-building work in this part of town, including Walter Brueggemann, Stanley Hauerwas, Diana Butler Bass, Doug Pagitt, James Cone, and Leonardo Boff. He then adds, "I think they represent a convergence of what we might call post-conservatives and post-liberals. It is among them that I feel most at home."[87] Franke believes McLaren is not only at home in this neighborhood, but he is making a "potentially significant" contribution to the postconservative/postliberal convergence.[88]

James Fodor associates three goals with the postliberal movement:

- Faithful yet creative retrieval of the Christian tradition.
- Ecumenically open renewal of the church.
- Compassionate healing and repair of the world.[89]

These three broad aims also represent much of the postconservative impulse and serve as an excellent template for framing McLaren's emergent project. In what follows, this study will nest McLaren's affinity with various postconservative/postliberal convergent characteristics under these three headings, which correlate well with McLaren's doctrines of Scripture, ecclesiology, and mission. This section will conclude by identifying some potential tension

---

[85] Taylor, "Introduction to Postconservative Evangelicalism," in *Reclaiming the Center*, 18. Wittmer is another critic who correctly discerns the emergent project as a blend between "postconservative" and "postliberal" thought. See Wittmer, "Don't Stop Believing," 119.

[86] Olson, *Reformed and Always Reforming*, 31.

[87] Brian McLaren, "Q&R: A Nasty Piece about You," *brian d. mclaren* (blog), May 6, 2014, http://brianmclaren.net/archives/blog/q-r-a-scathing-piece-about-you.html.

[88] John R. Franke, "Generous Orthodoxy and a Changing World," foreword to McLaren, *GO*, 12.

[89] James Fodor, "Postliberal Theology," in *The Modern Theologians*, ed. David F. Ford with Rachel Muers (Oxford: Blackwell, 2005), 229.

points between McLaren's project and the postconservative/postliberal convergence.

Faithful yet Creative Retrieval of the Christian Tradition

A centerpiece of McLaren's emergent project has been the attempt to cultivate an ancient-future faith, which he likens to a child playing on a swing: "kicking-back/leaning-forward, kicking-forward/leaning-back."[90] McLaren's project of "creative retrieval" is in tune with the postliberal/post-conservative vision that is centered on rediscovering the ancient ecumenical creeds and the treasures of Scripture for fruitful, faithful contemporary application.[91]

Through his interaction with the Young Leaders Network during the late 1990s, McLaren was exposed to postliberal fathers Hans Frei and George Lindbeck, and he read Stanley Hauerwas with ambivalence.[92] Chris Seay introduced McLaren to the works of Lesslie Newbigin and David Bosch.[93] The fruit of this exposure is seen clearly in *A New Kind of Christian,* which features a dialogue between a postliberal former episcopal priest turned science teacher (Neo) and a conservative evangelical pastor (Dan Poole), who is moving toward postconservatism. The main plotline is about post-modernism, but postliberalism and postconservativism are an ever-present subtext.

While discussing the modern-to-postmodern shift, Neo makes it clear that "postmodern doesn't mean being anti-modern or non-modern, and it is certainly different from being premodern (although it is similar in some ways). To be postmodern means to have experienced the modern world and to have been changed by the experience—changed to such a degree that one is no longer modern."[94] In a similar way, as Olson explains, "Postliberalism is an attempt to move beyond the confines of liberal theology without rejecting everything about it. Postconservatism is an attempt

---

90 McLaren, *GO,* 18.
91 Ibid., 28. Lindbeck was explicit about his "emphasis on creeds, confessions and dogmas." See George Lindbeck, et al. "A Panel Discussion," in *Nature of Confession,* 247.
92 McLaren's ambivalence will be explained later in this chapter.
93 Brian McLaren, email message to author, June 25, 2014.
94 McLaren, *NKOC,* 16–17.

to move beyond the limitations of conservative theology without rejecting everything about it."[95]

The tension between Liberalism and Evangelicalism is a frequent topic in *A New Kind of Christian*; however, Neo explains that both conservative evangelicals and liberals read the Bible with an unholy allegiance to modernity. Conservatives are focused on "factual accuracy, corroborating evidence, or absolute objectivity,"[96] or as Lindbeck put it, a "cognitive" reading of Scripture.[97] The modern liberals are equally off-base by rejecting the Bible's binding authority (other than in the realm of social ethics) because "it doesn't fit in with a modern Western mind-set that reveres objectivity, science, democracy, [and] individualism."[98] Or, to use Lindbeck's terminology, the liberals employ "experiential-expressivist" methodology.[99] Both conservatives and liberals ground their indubitable certainty in modern foundationalism: the conservatives in an inerrant Bible and the liberals in experience.[100] Neo proposes a coherentist alternative using the image of a web with multiple anchor points rather than the single foundation of a building.[101]

Neo argues the alternative to the conservative and liberal approaches is to approach the Bible in a "postanalytical and post-critical" manner by viewing the text as "the family story—the story of the people who have been called by the one true God to be his agents in the world, to be his servants to the rest of the world." Instead of using the Bible for modern purposes, it is retrieved as "a book that calls together and helps create a community, a community that is a catalyst for God's work in the world."[102]

Viewing the Bible as a story resonates with Frei's suggestion that the Bible should be read as "realistic narrative."[103] By resisting the modern tendencies to either spiritualize or moralize the text as the liberals have been prone to do or to fixate on its time-space factuality in the vein of the

---

[95] Olson, *Reformed and Always Reforming*, 16.
[96] McLaren, *NKOC*, 56.
[97] George A. Lindbeck, *The Nature of Doctrine* (Louisville: Westminster John Knox Press, 1984), 16.
[98] McLaren, *NKOC*, 56.
[99] Lindbeck, *Nature of Doctrine*, 17.
[100] McLaren, *NKOC*, 53.
[101] Ibid., 54–55.
[102] Ibid., 56, 52, and 53.
[103] Hans W. Frei, *The Eclipse of Biblical Narrative* (New Haven: Yale University Press, 1974), 149.

conservatives, postliberal theology seeks to rediscover the text as a narra-tive—as Neo says, "the story we find ourselves in."[104]

In *We Make the Road by Walking*, McLaren models narrative theology. When discussing the issue of miracles, he writes, "Some of us find it easy and exciting to believe in miracles. Others of us find them highly problem-atic."[105] After discussing some strengths and weaknesses associated with each perspective, he offers a third way: "Instead of 'Yes, miracles actually happened,' or 'No, they didn't really happen,' we could ask another ques-tion: *What happens to us when we imagine miracles happening?*" He goes on to suggest, "Perhaps a miracle story is meant to shake up our normal assumptions, inspire our imagination about the present and the future, and make it possible for us to see something we couldn't see before. Perhaps the miracle that really counts isn't one that happened to *them* back then, but one that could happen in *us* right now as we reflect upon the story."[106]

It is significant to note the similarities between McLaren's approach and Frei's "realistic narrative" methodology.[107] In discussing the phenom-enon of miracles, McLaren does not take the traditional conservative or liberal route. He does not argue for the time-space factuality of each New Testament miracle, nor does he demythologize the text by stripping away the husk in order to locate the true moral kernel behind the miracle myth. Instead, he asks the reader to enter imaginatively into the text without judgment and read it as realistic narrative. By setting the historical ques-tions to the side, he challenges the reader to "imagine miracles happening."

As this study has demonstrated, McLaren's quest for "creative retrieval" has led to several deconstruction and reconstruction projects. Here, the spirit of McLaren's apologetic project resonates with the ethos of postcon-servatives, "who are," as Olson puts it, "willing to subject any doctrine or practice . . . to new scrutiny in light of God's word."[108] While postconser-vatives do not uniformly endorse the content of every constructive proj-ect, they support the spirit of creative constructive theology exemplified by McLaren's proposals. According to Olson, one of the key differences

---

[104] McLaren, *NKOC*, 52.
[105] McLaren, *WMRBW*, 97.
[106] Ibid.
[107] Brian McLaren, email message to author, June 25, 2014.
[108] Olson, *Reformed and Always Reforming*, 17.

between conservative and postconservative evangelicals is a willingness to engage in this kind of creative and constructive theology.

> The essence of conservatism in theology is a determined—if often implicit and unacknowledged—adherence to tradition. It is the establishment of a magisterium, whether formal or informal, that exercises prior restraint over the critical and constructive tasks of theology. Very few evangelical theologians admit that they recognize or follow such a magisterium and most deny it. But their conservatism shows in their tendency to slam down any and every new proposal for revisioning Christian doctrine by appeal to what has always been believed by Christians generally or by what evangelicals have traditionally believed.[109]

Ecumenically Open Renewal of the Church

In *A Generous Orthodoxy*, McLaren pursued a post-critical method that sought "to find a way to embrace the good in many traditions and historic streams of Christian faith, and to integrate them, yielding a new, generous, emergent approach that is greater than the sum of its parts."[110] McLaren credits Frei (and Grenz) for the title, which he claims is not "a simple merging, mixing, conflating, or reconciling of the two schools of thought [Evangelicalism and Liberalism]." In taking his lead from Grenz, McLaren goes on to say that generous orthodoxy must challenge the modern hubris and foundationalism of both traditions and encourage a renewing of the theological center, around which both postconservatives and postliberals can coalesce.[111]

McLaren affirms the classic creeds but cautions against using them "as a club to batter into submission people with honest questions and doubts."[112] McLaren is not naïve concerning the history of creedal formation. He avers, "'Those who win the battles write the history,' it's easy to see the danger of describing orthodoxy by looking in the rearview mirror."[113] Rather than

---

[109] Ibid.
[110] McLaren, *GO*, 18.
[111] Ibid., 24.
[112] Ibid., 28. See also McLaren, *FOWA*, 33.
[113] McLaren, *GO*, 29.

defining orthodoxy strictly as "correct thinking," McLaren believes ortho-doxy should be a means to orthopraxy, "right practice of the gospel."[114]

At this juncture, McLaren is fully in tune with the postliberal project, which assigns doctrine a second-order, regulative function. The purpose of doctrine is to define and explain the "language games" of the Christian community.[115] Doctrine explains the rules of the game, it is not the game itself, and each community possesses its own cultural-linguistic regulations. McLaren likens it to a game of basketball: "You want to know the rules, not so you can blow whistles as a referee, but so you can have a lot of glorious good clean fun as a player, throwing passes and making assists and sinking three-pointers and layups without fouling out."[116]

The postliberal approach for which McLaren is advocating stands in opposition to the cognitive-propositional model used by many conservative evangelicals, who believe, according to McLaren, that orthodoxy and ortho-praxy "could and should be separated, so that one could at least be proud of getting an A in orthodoxy even when one earned a D in orthopraxy, which is only an elective class anyway."[117] Or to return to our basketball metaphor, "Defenders of orthodoxy [conservative evangelical proposition-alists] were seen more like referees than basketball players; nobody cared if they could pass, dribble, or shoot, as long as they could blow a whistle and name an infraction in their black-and-white striped shirts."[118] In other words, McLaren suggests that conservative evangelical propositionalists have been more focused on officiating and producing referees (someone who knows the rules but can't play the game) than they have been on playing the game and producing others who can dribble, pass, and shoot (someone who knows the rules in order to play the game). And when it comes to the Christian faith, nobody is called to only officiate; we are all called to play the game.

This emphasis on playing the game rather than just knowing the rules stands at the heart of McLaren's latest book, *The Great Spiritual Migration*, in which he claims Christianity needs to be converted from a system of

---

[114] Ibid., 30–31.
[115] Lindbeck, *Nature of Doctrine*, 4.
[116] McLaren, *GO*, 31.
[117] Ibid., 30.
[118] Ibid., 31.

beliefs (only knowing the rules) to a way of life (playing the game well). McLaren believes the emphasis needs to move away from blowing whistles, calling fouls, and arguing over the rulebook to proper methods of practice and becoming a competent member of the team. In short, spiritual formation (orthopathy) and missional service (orthopraxy) must replace one-dimensional doctrinal head knowledge (bad orthodoxy) as the centerpiece of the Christian life.

In discussing the pathway to Christian orthopathy and orthopraxy, Tony Jones also uses a sports metaphor to explain the importance of developing spiritual muscle memory. Committing oneself to spiritual disciplines, habits, or practices, he says, is like a soccer player developing "a feel for the game."[119] Jones argues, "A player who knows the game (practice) of soccer so well that she reacts to the plays and the movement of the ball at a prereflective level; she has internalized the game."[120] Likewise, a Christ-follower who commits herself to the practices of the Christian community will eventually develop a "feel" for the Christian life. McLaren also likens becoming a skilled Christ-follower to learning a musical instrument, which requires a diligent dedication to practice. McLaren here follows the postliberal theologians in favorably citing Michael Polanyi's theory of tacit knowledge: "In this vein, orthodoxy in this book is seen as a kind of internalized belief, tacit and personal, that becomes part of you to such a degree that once assimilated, you hardly need to think of it. We enter it, indwell it, live and love through it. . . . Orthodoxy in this book is similarly caught up in the practice (orthopraxy) of love for God and all God's creations."[121] The spiritual practices, rather than doctrinal cognitive knowledge, therefore, become the defining and enduring essence of the Christian faith. Thus, McLaren is in tune with Grenz's notion of "convertive piety."[122]

A final point of resonance between McLaren and postconservative theology can be located in the arena of boundary maintenance. One of the chief distinctions between conservative and postconservative camps relates to

---

[119] Jones, *Church Is Flat*, 90.
[120] Ibid.
[121] McLaren, *GO*, 33.
[122] For more on spiritual practices, see McLaren, *FOWA*. See also Olson, *Reformed and Always Reforming*, 28. For additional reading on "convertive piety," see Stanley J. Grenz, *Revisioning Evangelical Theology* (Downers Grove: InterVarsity Press, 1993).

campsite management. Conservatives operate out of a "bounded set" mentality, while postconservatives function with a "centered-set" approach.[123] In other words, conservative evangelicals tend to post gatekeepers who enforce strict boundaries around the edges of the camp. This bounded-set approach explains why many conservative evangelicals feel the need to patrol the borders of Evangelicalism on a fairly regular basis.[124]

Postconservative evangelicals, on the other hand, propose a gathering around the center of a few key doctrines that centripetally pull believers toward the middle of the camp. This campsite functions without explicit exterior boundaries.[125] Olson claims the set of beliefs in the center include Jesus Christ, the gospel, Bebbington's quadrilateral (with priority given to Scripture as the norming norm), and "respect for historic, Christian orthodoxy."[126] He envisions, "People gathered around the center or moving toward it are authentically evangelical; people or institutions moving away from it or with their backs turned against it are of questionable evangelical status. But it is not a matter of being 'in' or 'out' as there is no evangelical magisterium to decide that."[127] McLaren clearly affirms this centered-set approach, and *A Generous Orthodoxy* is an attempt to describe an ecumenically shared center.

Compassionate Healing and Repair of the World

This final section corresponds to McLaren's missional approach to interaction with people outside the Christian tradition and his concern for creation care. The end of this chapter will focus primarily upon McLaren's apologetic strategy and methodology, which he calls a "strong-benevolent" approach centered on Jesus's kingdom of God message.[128] Three of McLaren's early books—*The Church on the Other Side*, *Finding Faith*, and *More Ready Than You Realize*—discuss and model his approach to apologetics and

---

[123] Olson, *Reformed and Always Reforming*, 58.

[124] Albert Mohler, D. A. Carson, John MacArthur, and David Wells are excellent examples of this kind of behavior.

[125] Roger E. Olson, "Postconservative Evangelicalism," in *Four Views on the Spectrum of Evangelicalism*, eds. Andrew David Naselli and Collin Hansen (Grand Rapids: Zondervan, 2011), 163–64.

[126] Ibid., 175.

[127] Olson, *Reformed and Always Reforming*, 60.

[128] McLaren, *JMBM*, 40–45.

evangelism, but many of these characteristics are woven throughout the fabric of the entire McLaren tapestry.

McLaren's motivation to engage in apologetics diverges from conventional catalysts. Rather than defending the "right faith," McLaren advocates for what he calls "good faith."[129] McLaren avers, "'Right faith that isn't good faith isn't really right faith.' (Faith that believes true things, but does so in an ugly or inappropriate way, isn't justified just because it is conceptually correct.)"[130] Once again, McLaren elevates the importance of orthopathy and orthopraxy over orthodoxy. That is not to say that McLaren finds right thinking to be irrelevant. Instead, he believes a good faith will inevitably lead to a right faith because "a good faith will, by definition, be humble enough to admit it is wrong and self-correct, and active enough to keep pursuing the truth and learning, thus leading over time to an increasingly accurate, truth-reflecting faith."[131]

McLaren also differs from typical conservative approaches to apologetics in another way. Instead of saving souls from eternal conscious torment, which has animated much of conservative evangelical apologetic work, McLaren is on a pragmatic mission to save the planet (in every sense of the word).

McLaren's Apologetic Methodology

In *A Primer on Postmodernism*, Grenz outlines three major postmodern proposals in response to the modern Enlightenment project: cooperation instead of conquest, holism rather than rationalism, and particulars in the place of universals.[132] These three proposed shifts provide the necessary rubric to make sense of McLaren's apologetic methodology as well. Consequently, different facets of his apologetic strategy will be nested under these headings.

---

[129] McLaren, *FF*, 31.
[130] Ibid.
[131] Ibid., 154. See also McLaren, *SMJ*, 6–7.
[132] Grenz, *Primer on Postmodernism*, 7–8.

Cooperation Instead of Conquest

As this study has discussed, McLaren believes the modern age was an "era of conquest and control."[133] It was an era of dominance and subjugation. In the realm of evangelism and apologetics, this often translated into debate and "us-versus-them," triumphalistic, universal arguments supposedly driving the Christian cause forward with imperialistic fervor. As McLaren became increasingly sensitized to postcolonial concerns, this particular characteristic of modernity moved into the center of his deconstructive crosshairs. Grenz explains why the concept of conquest is especially problematic in the current milieu.

> In the postmodern world, people are no longer convinced that knowledge is inherently good. In eschewing the Enlightenment myth of inevitable progress, postmodernism replaces the optimism of the last century with a gnawing pessimism. Gone is the belief that every day, in every way, we're getting better and better. Members of the emerging generation are no longer confident that humanity will be able to solve the world's great problems. . . . They view life on earth as fragile and believe that the continued existence of humankind is dependent on a new attitude of cooperation rather than conquest.[134]

McLaren recalls a time when one of his mentors, Dallas Willard, said to him, "Remember, Brian: in a pluralistic world, a religion is judged by the benefits it brings to its nonmembers."[135] Instead of a "religion of the closed fist," which offers a confrontational posture toward other faiths, Willard was advocating a "religion of the open hand," which seeks dialogue and service alongside other faiths.[136] Instead of "us versus them" and excluding the other, this approach advocates a "withness" as a complement to Christian witness.[137]

---

[133] McLaren, *NKOC*, 16.

[134] Grenz, *Primer on Postmodernism*, 7.

[135] McLaren, *JMBM*, 40. McLaren does not identify the name of this mentor in *JMBM*, but he confirmed the man's identity in correspondence. Brian McLaren, email message to author, July 24, 2014.

[136] Brian McLaren, "Christian Identity in a Multi-faith Context," video recorded at Greenbelt 2011 on August 29, 2011, http://www.greenbelt.org.uk/media/talks/14513-brian-mclaren/.

[137] McLaren, *JMBM*, 239–47.

These postcolonial themes of solidarity, conversation, benevolence, and open-handed cooperation between people of different faiths (and non-faiths) are evident in McLaren's works, but they are presented no more clearly and forcefully than in *The Secret Message of Jesus*. McLaren lays out his bold, collaborative, interfaith project accordingly:

> In an age of global terrorism and rising religious conflict, it's sig-
> nificant to note that all Muslims regard Jesus as a great prophet,
> that many Hindus are willing to consider Jesus as a legitimate
> manifestation of the divine, that many Buddhists see Jesus as
> one of humanity's most enlightened people, and that Jesus him-
> self was a Jew. . . . A shared reappraisal of Jesus' message could
> provide a unique space or common ground for urgently needed
> religious dialogue—and it doesn't seem an exaggeration to say
> that the future of our planet may depend on such dialogue.[138]

McLaren is here offering a prophetic pragmatic pronouncement. In his interaction with people of other faiths, he does not opt for the modern triumphalistic apologetic strategy of logically restricting Jesus to a liar, a lunatic, or Lord in the tradition of C. S. Lewis's famous trilemma.[139] Rather, within the framework of his temporally focused, kingdom of God, three-dimensional narrative, McLaren focuses on the most pressing practical problems in the world today: the "prosperity crisis," the "equity crisis," and the "security crisis."[140] The failure of the world religions to adequately address these crises has led to a "spirituality crisis."[141] McLaren believes that the conventional Christian Greco-Roman six-line narrative has exacerbated these crises since it is a narrative of imperialistic conquest and domination rather than a narrative of liberation, reconciliation, and expanding peaceable kingdom. McLaren argues that the framing story of Jesus centered on the Sermon on the Mount could provide the necessary resources for the healing and reconciliation the world needs.

---

[138] McLaren, *SMJ*, 7–8; emphasis mine.
[139] See C. S. Lewis, *Mere Christianity*, 3rd ed. (New York: Macmillan, 1952), 51–56.
[140] McLaren, *EMC*, 5–6, and McLaren, *NKOCY*, 253.
[141] McLaren, *EMC*, 5–6, and McLaren, *NKOCY*, 254.

As McLaren sees it, this is not an optional theoretical exercise, but rather a pressing pragmatic call to action. In *Why Did Jesus, Moses, the Buddha, and Mohammed Cross the Road?*, McLaren asserts, "We are increasingly faced with a choice . . . not between kindness and hostility, but between kindness and nonexistence."[142] Consequently, it is up to those who are engaged in "subversive," interfaith friendships to resist the impulse to proselytize and to view the other person as a colleague instead of a competitor.[143] McLaren is engaged in many such interfaith relationships, and "in each case, our friendships are conspiratorial . . . seeking to overthrow the current regimes of hostility, opposition, exclusion, fear, and prejudice, not only dreaming of that better world but rehearsing for it, practicing it through the give and take of our friendship. Together we [are] plotting goodness."[144]

That is not to say that McLaren is an advocate for ignoring conflicting beliefs or truth claims, but that rather than debate and conquest, he promotes dialogue and a shared journey, which is a point of clear resonance with postconservative thought. This approach is well illustrated in an experience McLaren recounts in *The Church on the Other Side*. He recalls a time when he addressed a group of visiting scholars from the People's Republic of China. The topic was "the existence of God."[145] Instead of arguing in favor of the existence of the Christian God, however, McLaren chose to explain how one might go about thinking through available options, exploring strengths and weaknesses of each perspective. He concluded his talk with a personal story about how his own faith helped him through a difficult time. The response was overwhelmingly positive. One person in the audience said, "Instead of telling us what to believe, you have told us how to believe, and this is very good for us." McLaren claims that the remainder of the evening included "some of the most honest and perceptive questions I have ever heard about faith."[146]

---

[142] McLaren, *JMBM*, 12.
[143] McLaren, *COOS*, 84.
[144] McLaren, *JMBM*, 230.
[145] McLaren, *COOS*, 77.
[146] Ibid.

This approach of helping people "discover how to believe" rather than "what to believe" serves as the blueprint for *Finding Faith*.[147] In this work, McLaren guides rather than drives his readers by: first, posing thought-provoking questions instead of providing pat answers; second, utilizing storytelling rather than propositional arguments; and third, designing the book for multiple types of people and uses. These three features provide a template for his apologetic strategy, which will be amplified shortly.

Much of the modern era was characterized by a commitment to hard apologetics, rather than soft apologetics. Stephen T. Davis defines hard apologetics as the position that seeks to triumph over one's competitor by demonstrating the irrationality of rejecting Christian truth claims, while soft apologetics is the more modest view of simply attempting to demonstrate the rationality of embracing Christian truth claims without insisting that all other perspectives are irrational.[148]

McLaren's discussion of Christian truth claims falls into the soft apologetic camp. He argues for a "proper confidence," a third way that seeks a middle ground between the hubris of absolute certainty on one end of the spectrum and radical uncertainty on the other end. That said, when it comes to advocating "good faith," McLaren slips into hard apologetics. He is a forceful, persuasive apologist for a good form of faith that transcends the Christian religion and extends to other faiths as well. This is possible for McLaren because "good faith" is not fundamentally about doctrinal beliefs but rather about practices, dispositions, attitudes, and character formation, which are not the exclusive property of the Christian faith.

Holism Rather Than Rationalism

According to Grenz, the postmodern mind chooses holism rather than "the second Enlightenment assumption—namely, that truth is certain and hence purely rational."[149] By rejecting "human intellect as the arbiter of truth," postmodern people elevate other epistemological pathways, "including the

---

[147] McLaren, *FF*, 19.

[148] Stephen T. Davis, *Risen Indeed* (Grand Rapids: Eerdmans, 1993), 1. In this context, Davis is discussing hard and soft apologetics in relation to the resurrection; however, these categories can be extended to include Christian truth claims in general.

[149] Grenz, *Primer on Postmodernism*, 7.

emotions and the intuition."[150] In *A New Kind of Christian*, Neo reflects these words: "The fact that to us *thinking* and *analyzing* seem to be synonymous suggests how successful modernity has been at marginalizing all other forms of thought—imagination, intuition, pattern recognition, systems thinking, and so on."[151]

It appears as though some leaders in the ECM, however, have thrown the rational baby out with the Enlightenment bathwater.[152] For example, Peter Rollins has declared "the end of apologetics."[153] Rollins argues that apologetics, in the form of both "word and wonder,"[154] should be rejected in the postmodern world since both are expressions of "power discourses," which are designed "to forcibly bring people to their knees." This kind of imperialistic discourse is misguided since it "endeavors to compel individuals to bow their knee regardless of their motives or the nature of desire." Instead, Rollins commends a "powerless discourse," in which "the believer ought to be seen as the poem, parable and salt of God in the world rather than God's proposition to the world."[155]

McLaren offers similar sentiments, "In the modern world we could wield a proposition like a sword, a concept like a hammer. In the postmodern world we have to hold a mystery like a lover, and a story like a child."[156] Nevertheless, it would be a mistake to equate McLaren's position entirely with the view espoused by Rollins. While he resonates with aspects of the creative and noncoercive strategy proposed by Rollins, McLaren is best seen as a defender of holism rather than as antirational.[157] Likewise, he is an advocate of soft apologetics, rather than the kind of hard apologetics that Rollins is rightly rejecting.

In *Finding Faith*, McLaren writes, "Though a healthy faith is bigger than the intellect, the search for faith cannot bypass the intellect. The sincere

---

[150] Ibid.

[151] McLaren, *NKOC*, 17.

[152] Deirdre Brower-Latz, "A Contextual Reading of John Wesley's Theology and the Emergent Church" (PhD thesis, Manchester, 2009), 184.

[153] Peter Rollins, *How (Not) to Speak of God* (London: Paraclete, 2006), 37.

[154] Ibid. By "word and wonder," Rollins means rational argument and miracles.

[155] Ibid., 37–38. See also McLaren, *SMJ*, 34.

[156] McLaren, *COOS*, 185.

[157] In the foreword to Rollins's book, McLaren writes, "I would say this is one of the two or three most rewarding books of theology I have read in ten years." See Brian McLaren, "Foreword," in *How (Not) to Speak of God*, ix.

spiritual seeker must engage the mind fully, even while transcending cold or calculating rationalism."[158] McLaren goes on to point out that "the search for faith also involves noncognitive parts of us—emotions, longings, aspirations, dreams and hopes and fears, drives, desires, intuitions."[159] In *The Church on the Other Side*, McLaren advocates for both credibility and plausibility. "Credibility answers the intellectual questions: Is this message logical, intelligent, believable, supported by sufficient evidence? Plausibility explores additional social and emotional questions."[160] In short, the faith journey requires the full engagement of the entire person: mind, will, emotions, imagination, intuitions, and relationships. In this quest, McLaren underscores the importance of both questions and stories.[161]

As seen, narrative is a central feature of the postconservative/postliberal convergence. Likewise, McLaren believes the power of story is central to a postmodern apologetic. This includes viewing the Bible fundamentally as a narrative; it also means adopting all of the literary tools at one's disposal for apologetic purposes. At times, direct communication is valuable and effective. McLaren employed this communication style in *The Secret Message of Jesus* when he wrote, "It is tragic for anyone, especially anyone affiliated with the religion named after Jesus, not to be clear about what Jesus' message actually was."[162] At other times, indirect forms of communication are preferable. In *A Generous Orthodoxy*, McLaren used a variety of literary techniques, including hyperbole, caricature, strategic self-effacement, and "conscious deception and calculated obliqueness."[163] McLaren points to the example of Jesus, who "spoke pithily and often about religious absurdity. . . . His whole ministry was a kind of guerilla theatre, playing—can we say devilishly?—on irony, overturning figuratively as well as literally the money-laden tables of the religious elite."[164]

McLaren's employment of various literary techniques in the service of evangelism and apologetics can be traced back to Walker Percy's "adaptation

---

[158] McLaren, *FF*, 13.
[159] Ibid.
[160] McLaren, *COOS*, 83.
[161] Ibid., 19. See also McLaren, *AMP*, 104.
[162] McLaren, *SMJ*, 7.
[163] McLaren, *WP*, i.
[164] McLaren, *JMBM*, 7.

of Kierkegaard's indirect communication."[165] In his master's thesis on Percy, McLaren writes, "To say it bluntly, [Percy's] tricky. . . . One naturally asks, 'Why be so slippery? Why be so evasive? Why so indirect?'" Percy chooses this enigmatic approach, "this subterfuge," because Christianity is no longer palatable to his readers. He must "find new words for old truths," and use "craft and cunning to cover his tracks, yet ironically [he] wants his 'hunter' [the reader] to catch scent and in fact find him out."

McLaren also references Flannery O'Connor, whose "very large, simple caricatures"[166] and "bizarre characters" have the power "to jolt us into the realization that we routinely tolerate the intolerable."[167] Likewise, McLaren utilizes this literary apologetic strategy of drawing large and simple carica-tures and of employing indirect communication in various ways. McLaren argues, "The genius of the indirect attack . . . lies in its ability to 'capture' the man under illusion by surprise, so that he has had time neither to 'cross to the other side of the street' in avoidance nor to willfully shut his eyes in defensiveness."[168] McLaren's willingness to employ both direct and indirect forms of communication signals his commitment to a holistic approach in the apologetic arena. As McLaren puts it, "To be a good apol-ogist today, you need to offer both standard and innovative responses to common questions."[169]

Particulars in the Place of Universals

According to Grenz, postmodern thinkers reject "the Enlightenment quest for any one universal, supracultural, timeless truth." Rather, "truth con-sists in the ground rules that facilitate the well-being of the community in which one participates."[170] In the realm of apologetics, this means that there are no one-size-fits-all approaches that are universally compelling. In *A Generous Orthodoxy*, McLaren states, "We must realize that each religion

---

[165] McLaren, WP, i.

[166] Ibid., 15–18. See also McLaren, COOS, 96.

[167] McLaren, "Foreword" in Rollins, How (Not) to Speak of God, x.

[168] McLaren, WP, 23. This technique is described by Os Guinness as "subversion through surprise." Guinness believes this is the primary way in which Jesus used parables. See Os Guinness, Fool's Talk (Downers Grove: InterVarsity Press, 2015), 22.

[169] McLaren, AMP, 102.

[170] Grenz, Primer on Postmodernism, 8.

is its own world, requiring very different responses from Christians."[171] This is why McLaren rejects prepackaged attempts at sharing the gospel. Instead, McLaren aligns with the postliberal commitment to ad hoc apologetics, which is person-relative, situational, and culturally sensitive, and which helps seekers advance at a "healthy pace."[172]

William Placher describes how ad hoc apologetics could provide a via media that preserves a vigorous form of pluralism.

> One side would claim that the Enlightenment was right, and we really do have to find universally acceptable common ground for rational conversation. The other side would insist that we cannot find such common ground, and as a result people from different traditions cannot talk to one another at all. Either way, genuinely pluralistic conversation would become impossible. I want to argue for some kind of middle position between those extremes of universalism and radical relativism to see what it implies for Christian theology.[173]

In the service of this third-way, person-relative apologetic position, Placher proposes three rules for Christians who engage in interfaith dialogue. First, the person must always "remain aware that [he or she] is speaking from a Christian point of view." Every person involved in the dialogue is operating from a perspective, and this must remain clear and overt. Rules of the dialogue can be negotiated, but no one should presume to be an objective "authoritative moderator of the whole discussion."

Second, "the most interesting conversation partners may well be those persons who have entered most deeply into the particularities of their own traditions." Consequently, any attempt to exclude persons of traditions not "shaped by the assumptions of Western modernity" should be rejected.

---

[171] McLaren, *GO*, 260. This does not mean that McLaren affirms metaphysical antirealism as R. Scott Smith seems to suggest, but rather that each religious community requires a customized approach to dialogue. See R. Scott Smith, "Reflections on McLaren and the Emerging Church" in *Passionate Conviction*, 227–41, citing 232.

[172] McLaren, *COOS*, 88–89. While McLaren aligns with the postliberal ad hoc approach to apologetics, he does not resonate with the postliberal tendency to shy away from cultural engagement.

[173] Placher, *Unapologetic Theology*, 12–13.

Third, interfaith dialogue will typically take place as one concrete tradition in conversation with another specific tradition, rather than engaging "some sort of generic 'non-Christian religion.'" Naturally, different conversations will focus on different points of contact and common ground. That said, Placher is open to the possibility of broader common ground as long as it is not predicated upon the mistaken notion of a "common core of religion."[174]

It is worth revisiting McLaren's interfaith project in light of Placher's guidelines. McLaren claims that a renewed appreciation for the life and teaching of Jesus could serve as a rich resource in the service of interfaith dialogue and in the pursuit of global peace. He points out how many religious traditions outside of Christianity hold Jesus and his teachings in high regard, even though they do not view him as divine in the way orthodox Christians do. McLaren's project seems to be in line with Placher's proposal.

First, McLaren engages in conversation without muting his Christian commitments. Likewise, he encourages his dialogue partners to maintain and strengthen their respective religious beliefs by virtue of the engagement.[175] Second, McLaren is committed to bringing all cultural and religious perspectives to the table. He is sensitive to modern imperialistic attempts to exclude non-Western voices from the conversation. Third, McLaren is missiologically aware of the need to respect the particularities of each culture and religion rather than stir all non-Christian religions into a generic soup. McLaren avers, "There is no such thing as interreligious dialogue in general, rather there is a dialogue between this Christian individual or community and that Jewish or Buddhist or Hindu individual or community."[176]

Placher's final statement seems to be especially poignant in light of McLaren's pressing project. McLaren is suggesting a broader common ground—namely, the person and teaching of Jesus. This proposal transcends the typical one-to-one correspondence and engagement between religions that Placher proposes; however, the final caveat above makes room for it. It is worth reiterating that McLaren is not insisting that adherents of other religions embrace Jesus in a Christian manner, but rather they are to

---

[174] Ibid., 147 and 19.
[175] McLaren, *JMBM*, 11.
[176] McLaren, *GO*, 260.

focus on the facet that their respective religious tradition honors him (e.g., as prophet, great teacher, moral exemplar, and so on). Of course, if a person from another religion wants to learn more about the full Christian teaching regarding the person of Jesus, that conversation is not out of bounds.[177] This strategy allows for interfaith dialogue with a universal common ground; however, it respects the plurality of perspectives that reside in each enculturated religion. In so doing, it is fully in line with the kind of ad hoc postliberal apologetic approach proposed by Placher.

Tension Points with the Postconservative/Postliberal Convergence

While this chapter has demonstrated that McLaren's project has much in common with the postconservative/postliberal convergence, a few tension points are worth highlighting. McLaren shows no particular allegiance to any theological and apologetic school of thought. He is not an academic apologist nor scholarly theologian by trade, so it is not surprising that occasional tension points with postliberalism and postconservativism might emerge. McLaren is interested in practical approaches to accomplish his goals, regardless of how well his methodology meshes with academic postliberal or postconservative concerns. Three points of tension will be considered.

Resistance to Sectarianism

One of the common charges against postliberalism is the movement's tendency toward sectarianism. While resonating with much of the ecclesiology described by the postliberal project, including the commitment to subordinate orthodoxy to orthopraxy, McLaren is not an isolationist. He is fully engaged with culture and interfaith dialogue. This is where McLaren's discomfort with some of Stanley Hauerwas's thinking surfaces. Rather than engaging culture apologetically, Hauerwas calls for the church to serve as a radical counterexample to the world.[178] While McLaren would not disagree entirely, he argues that this tendency toward withdrawal is dangerous at a

---

[177] Ibid., 245–66.

[178] Stanley Hauerwas and William H. Willimon, *Resident Aliens* (Nashville: Abingdon, 1989), 15–29.

time when the Religious Right has become the dominant religious voice in public society. McLaren expounds,

> I think Stanley [Hauerwas] had the right prescription for main-
> line Protestantism of the 50's–90's. His call to "sectarianism" and
> to be the alternative community that doesn't concentrate much
> on "the world" was probably what the mainline church needed
> during that era. But then the Religious Right took up that
> mantle—trying to in a sense own and run society. If mainline
> Protestants continue to withdraw/isolate/etc., they abandon the
> field, so to speak, to the religious right. I think that's a mistake.[179]

In a *Christian Century* article written in honor of the twenty-fifth anniversary of Hauerwas and William Willimon's co-authored book *Resident Aliens*, McLaren argues that the model of Christ and culture the authors offered was "an important corrective medicine to *chaplaincy to empire, helping institution* or *conquering army*."[180] McLaren is in full agreement with the notion that "Jesus did not come to be the mascot, watchdog, or spiritual cheerleader for the American project of pursuing happiness."[181] Nevertheless, he believes engagement models and images are more appropriate in the contemporary milieu: "*Yeast, salt, doctor,* and *light,* for example, are alternative images that suggest a concern for 'transforming the world'—while also requiring a unique, counter-cultural identity."[182] McLaren's emphasis on "transforming the world," while not in contradistinction to the postliberal impulse, is in tension with streams of the movement, especially those who resonate most clearly with Hauerwas.

The Role of Christian Community in Discipleship

One of the chief postliberal claims is that the way to become a skilled follower of Christ is through apprenticing oneself to a community of fellow Christ-followers. It is within the confines of such a community that one learns "how rightly to speak, think, feel, and act in ways that cohere and

---

[179] Brian McLaren, email message to author, June 25, 2014.
[180] Brian McLaren, "*Resident Aliens* at 25: State of the Colony," *Christian Century* 131, no. 20 (October 1, 2014): 23.
[181] Ibid. See also McLaren, *GO*, 80.
[182] McLaren, "*Resident Aliens* at 25," 23.

are consistent with Christian convictions as a whole."[183] McLaren expresses this paradigm well:

> Tradition means a whole way of practice or way of life that includes systems of apprenticeship, a body of knowledge (of terms, history, lore), a wide range of know-how (skills, technique, ability), and something else—a kind of "unknown knowledge" that philosopher Michael Polanyi calls personal knowledge: levels of knowledge that one has and knows but doesn't even know one has and knows.[184]

In other words, following Jesus takes place within the context of a community of like-minded Christ-followers.

This paradigm, however, seems to be in tension with something McLaren claims elsewhere. Following the lead of missiologist David Bosch, McLaren believes it is possible for a person to become a follower of Jesus without converting to the Christian faith or apprenticing oneself to a community of Christ-followers. In other words, he believes that in some cases, it is advisable for the new follower of Jesus to remain in her existing non-Christian religious community. McLaren puts it this way: "I don't believe making disciples must equal making adherents to the Christian religion. It may be advisable in many (not all!) circumstances to help people become followers of Jesus and remain within their Buddhist, Hindu, or Jewish contexts." Elsewhere, McLaren expands, "In this light, I don't hope all Buddhists will become (cultural) Christians, I do hope all who feel so called will become Buddhist followers of Jesus; I believe they should be given that opportunity and invitation. I don't hope all Jews or Hindus will become members of the Christian religion. But I do hope all who feel so called will become Jewish or Hindu followers of Jesus."[185]

This tension is intensified by the postliberal idea that each religious community operates according to its own "language games." In fact, McLaren himself makes the claim that "each religion is its own world."[186]

---

[183] Fodor, "Postliberal Theology," 232.
[184] McLaren, *GO*, 87.
[185] Ibid., 260, 264.
[186] Ibid., 260.

If this is the case, then it is difficult to see how the follower of Jesus can simultaneously apprentice herself to two separate "worlds" and carefully learn the nuances of two distinct "language games." It is difficult to see how such a syncretistic model can mesh with the postliberal program, which is moving away from a universal shared common core toward distinct particularity.

What is the Buddhist, Jewish, Hindu, or Muslim follower of Jesus to do with the statement, "Jesus is Lord"? Perhaps each individual should focus on what his respective parent religion can accommodate. This, however, will not satisfy the postliberal vision of forming a faithful countercultural community in which all followers are to honor Jesus as the name above all other names. How should followers of Jesus in other religions faithfully and skillfully practice their faith when two different sets of incongruent rules are operating at the same time? These are not easy questions to answer.

Turning Away from the Postconservative Center?

The final point of tension is on the postconservative side of the convergence. Olson describes postconservative Evangelicalism without boundaries. Rather, those in the fold are held together by a magnetic pull toward a set of centered beliefs. According to Olson, "people gathered around the center or moving toward it are authentically evangelical; people or institutions moving away from it or with their backs turned against it are of questionable evangelical status."[187]

At one point in time, McLaren was viewed not only as a postconservative evangelical, but also as a leader of this movement. In the wake of *A New Kind of Christianity*, however, Scot McKnight declared, "McLaren has grown tired of evangelicalism. In turn, many evangelicals are wearied with Brian."[188] McKnight went on to call into question McLaren's status as a postconservative as well, by virtue of the following comments: "If evangelicalism is characterized by David Bebbington's famous quadrilateral—that is, biblicism, crucicentrism, conversionism, and activism—then

---

[187] Ibid.
[188] McKnight, "Rebuilding the Faith," 59.

Brian has poked and, to one degree or another, criticized, deconstructed, and rejected each."[189]

Of course, each point of Bebbington's quadrilateral is open to interpretation. Does biblicism require inerrancy or infallibility? Does it require a constitutional hermeneutic? Does crucicentrism require affirming a particular theory of the atonement? Does it make room for a table-centered understanding of the cross instead? Does conversionism require understanding salvation within the six-line narrative with two distinct eternal destinies, or does it make room for understanding salvation fundamentally as liberation in the temporal realm? Does activism require working alongside only fellow Christians, or is there room for interfaith service as well? Since the centered-set postconservative approach does not accommodate gatekeepers and boundary police, it is not clear who should answer these questions.

That said, McKnight appears to argue that McLaren is no longer gravitating toward the postconservative center, as Olson has described it, but instead has turned his back and is "moving away," leaving him "of questionable evangelical status."[190] At the end of the day, it is a judgment call as to whether McLaren is moving away from the postconservative evangelical center since, as Olson reminds us, there are no boundaries. Nevertheless, McLaren appears to prefer the postliberal side of the convergence, since they have "a broader canvas, so to speak, to paint on."[191] Therefore, in the final assessment, it is fair to conclude that McLaren's home is properly situated in the postconservative/postliberal neighborhood, but perhaps on the postliberal side of the street.

With McLaren's message and methodology in place, this study is now in position to evaluate his new kind of apologetic project in light of Calvinism's chief dialogue partner, Arminianism.

---

[189] Ibid.
[190] Olson, *Reformed and Always Reforming*, 60.
[191] Brian McLaren, email message to author, June 25, 2014.

Chapter Seven

MCLAREN AND ARMINIAN AFFINITY

I believe that God is good. No thought I have ever had of God is better than God actually is. . . . I am confident of this: I have never overestimated how good God is because God's goodness overflows far beyond the limits of human understanding.[1]

—Brian McLaren, *The Last Word and the Word After That*

THIS STUDY BEGAN WITH THE ASSERTION THAT BRIAN MCLAREN'S postmodern apologetic project is fundamentally a critique of "bad monotheism," of which five-point Calvinism is the chief Christian representative. This book has explored several facets of McLaren's challenge to confessional Calvinism. In Chapter Six, McLaren's project was evaluated in light of various streams of Evangelicalism and Liberalism, while highlighting his apologetic methodology. In the next two chapters, the focus will turn to an assessment of McLaren's apologetic project in light of orthodox Arminian theology, which historically has been Calvinism's primary dialogue partner.

In the previous chapter, Evangelicalism was divided into two broad camps: conservatives and postconservatives. Additionally, conservatives were separated into biblicist and paleo-orthodox subgroups. This study joins Roger Olson in affirming the position that the pietistic stream of Evangelicalism is broad enough to include both conservative and

---

[1] McLaren, *LWWAT*, xi.

postconservative expressions of orthodox Arminianism.[2] The conservative form most in tune with the spirit of orthodox Arminianism is paleo-orthodoxy. John Wesley, C. S. Lewis,[3] and Thomas C. Oden are exemplars of this stream. The postconservative features articulated by Olson in *Reformed and Always Reforming* express well the sensibilities of this second subgroup.[4] Olson, Clark Pinnock, and Henry Knight are primary exemplars of post-conservative Arminianism.[5]

Several scholars in the Wesleyan-Arminian tradition have recognized connections between the ECM and the writings of Wesley, in particular. According to Knight, the kind of generous orthodoxy proposed by Hans Frei, Stanley Grenz, and Brian McLaren was central to the teaching and the ethos of John Wesley, who was careful to distinguish between essentials and opinion in his quest to foster Christian unity.[6] As demonstrated in this study, the ECM likewise has focused on the shared tradition of the church rather than the doctrinal emphases that often divide rather than unify.

In an essay entitled "John Wesley in Conversation with the Emerging Church," Patrick Franklin argues that John Wesley "is something of a kindred spirit to the Emerging Church since he shared similar passions and faced comparable challenges."[7] According to Franklin, those affinities include a rejection of "Enlightenment rationalism," an affirmation of "religious experience," a "passion for evangelism," an appreciation for Jesus's kingdom of God teaching, and a "spirit of ecumenism."[8] Deirdre

---

[2] This is not to say that all creative theological projects flying under the banner of Postconservativism are in tune with orthodox Arminianism. Rather, the freedom to engage in creative theological thinking that is properly tethered to the authority of Scripture is respected by orthodox postconservative Arminians. See Roger E. Olson, *Reformed and Always Reforming* (Grand Rapids: Baker, 2007), 43. Also see Roger E. Olson, "Is Open Theism a Type of Arminianism?" *Roger E. Olson* (*Patheos* blog), November 10, 2012, http://www.patheos.com/blogs/rogereolson/2012/11/is-open-theism-a-type-of-arminianism/.

[3] For a defense of understanding Lewis as an Arminian, see Scott R. Burson and Jerry L. Walls, *C. S. Lewis and Francis Schaeffer* (Downers Grove: InterVarsity Press, 1998), 51–105; Clark Pinnock, *Most Moved Mover* (Grand Rapids: Baker, 2001), 14; and Gary Dorrien, *The Remaking of Evangelical Theology* (Louisville: Westminster John Knox Press, 1998), 173–75.

[4] Aspects of Postliberalism also will be discussed in this chapter. This study does not discount the possibility of significant convergence between postliberal thought and orthodox Arminianism.

[5] Olson represents a Baptist form of Arminianism, Pinnock was a leading open theist, and Knight is Wesleyan.

[6] Henry Knight, "John Wesley and the Emerging Church," *Preacher's Magazine* (Advent/Christmas 2007–2008), 5, http://www.nph.com/nphweb/html/pmol/emerging.htm.

[7] Patrick S. Franklin, "John Wesley in Conversation with the Emerging Church," *The Asbury Journal* 63, no. 1 (2008): 75–93, citing 76.

[8] Ibid., 76.

Brower-Latz, who focused her PhD thesis on connections between Wesley and the ECM in the arena of ecclesiology and the poor, agrees: "Wesley, in my view, is uniquely placed to be a source of comparison with the ecm."[9] Brower-Latz argues that a fruitful intersection occurs when comparing "eighteenth century society/the Enlightenment/Wesley's theology in the light of poverty" with "twenty-first century society/postmodernity/emergent theology in the light of poverty."[10] While the next two chapters will not explore all of these connections, a specifically Wesleyan-Arminian emphasis shows promise for this section's comparison with McLaren. Consequently, Wesley will receive pride of place in what follows.

This study's primary purpose is not to argue for the superiority of the Arminian vision of reality, but rather to identify where McLaren is and is not in line with orthodox Arminian theology and practice. A secondary purpose will be to suggest ways in which McLaren's apologetic project could be strengthened by the application of orthodox Arminian teaching.

Defining Relevant Terminology

Before exploring McLaren's resonance with Arminianism, we should clarify what is meant by orthodox Arminian theology. As detailed in Chapter Four, Jacobus Arminius (1560–1609) was a Reformed pastor and theologian who objected to several aspects of John Calvin's teaching. After Arminius died, his followers drafted a document entitled the "Remonstrance," which outlined the primary soteriological Arminian emphases. Keith Stanglin and Thomas McCall summarize the five articles as follows:

1. God chose to save through Jesus Christ all those who through grace would believe in him and persevere to the end.
2. Jesus Christ obtained forgiveness of sins sufficient for all.
3. Fallen humanity can think or do nothing that is truly good by free will.
4. God's grace, which is not irresistible, is necessary for thinking or doing any good.

---

[9] Deirdre Brower-Latz, "A Contextual Reading of John Wesley's Theology and the Emergent Church" (PhD thesis, Manchester, 2009), 18.

[10] Ibid., 29.

5. True believers are enabled by grace to persevere to the end, and it may be possible to lose this grace.[11]

These five points were countered with the Calvinist TULIP at the Synod of Dort (1618–1619). We can now summarize the main points of soteriological contention between Calvinism and Arminianism.

Classical Arminianism and five-point Calvinism both claim that all human faculties have been tainted by sin. While Adam was created good and guiltless, the Fall introduced an ontological shift that left humanity impotent to naturally please God. Arminianism claims that God universally extends prevenient grace, which frees the will sufficiently to cooperate with God's saving grace.[12] Calvinism, on the other hand, rejects the Synergism made possible by prevenient grace, and opts for Monergism,[13] which claims that God is the sole agent and determining factor in salvation. While common grace is extended to all humanity, Calvinism teaches that humanity remains dead and unregenerate in its sins, and salvation can only be secured by God's unconditional choice. This divine unconditional decree elects some for salvation and passes over the rest, leaving the reprobate to pay the penalty for his or her sin in the form of eternal damnation.

Arminianism rejects the doctrine of unconditional election and endorses the view that God conditionally elects individuals based on divine foreknowledge of who will respond favorably to the gospel message. Consequently, the soteriological merits of the atoning death of Christ are universally available to all who will freely, in a libertarian sense, cooperate with God's grace and receive the gospel. Calvinism teaches that the salvific efficacy of Christ's atonement is sufficient for the elect alone. Since humans remain dead in their sins, God extends saving irresistible grace to the elect while withholding that grace from the non-elect.

Arminianism teaches that saving grace is available to all humanity, and it is ultimately up to each person to either cooperate with it or reject it. Since salvation in the Calvinist scheme is a unilateral decision made by

---

[11] Keith D. Stanglin and Thomas H. McCall, *Jacob Arminius: Theologian of Grace* (New York: Oxford University Press, 2012), 190.

[12] For more on prevenient grace, see Stanglin and McCall, *Jacob Arminius*, 151–57.

[13] For a discussion of Synergism and Monergism, see Roger E. Olson, *Arminian Theology* (Downers Grove: InterVarsity Press, 2006), 17–19.

God, rather than contingent upon human choice, then it is impossible to fall away from grace. The unconditionally elect will persevere to the end and spend eternity in heaven. Arminianism maintains that God honors the gift of human libertarian freedom, especially in the realm of soteriology, and it remains possible until death to repudiate divine grace and to be separated from God for eternity.[14]

It should be noted that Arminianism is often incorrectly associated with either Pelagianism or semi-Pelagianism. Pelagianism denies original sin and believes humans are capable of realizing their moral and spiritual potential apart from grace, while semi-Pelagianism affirms a "modified version of original sin"; however, humans in their natural state are capable of "initiat[ing] salvation by exercising a good will toward God."[15] As mentioned, orthodox Arminianism is properly understood as an expression of Synergism, which means God and humans are both involved in the act of salvation. This dual agency, however, recognizes an asymmetrical relationship between divine and human activity, with God always serving as the initiating and primary agent in the relational equation. According to Stanglin and McCall, "God initiates conversion . . . the operation of prevenient and subsequent grace is an on-going process, never leaving humanity to make an autonomous decision."[16] With these terms clarified, this study can now consider the resonance between McLaren's project and orthodox Arminianism.

The Character of God

The first point of agreement centers on the foundational importance of the character of God, in general, and the goodness of God, in particular. In the introduction to *The Last Word and the Word After That*, McLaren expresses faith in the goodness of God, as well as faith in his own relative ability to recognize such goodness:

---

[14] Olson states, "Arminius did not deny perseverance (eternal security of the saints), but argued that it is an unsettled issue and warned against false security and assurance." Roger E. Olson, *The Story of Christian Theology* (Downers Grove: InterVarsity Press, 1999), 471.

[15] Ibid., 17–18. For a discussion of the Pelagian-Augustinian controversy, see Mildred Bangs Wynkoop, *Foundations of Wesleyan-Arminian Theology* (Kansas City, MO: Beacon Hill, 1967), 24–34.

[16] Stanglin and McCall, *Jacob Arminius*, 154.

I believe that God is good. No thought I have ever had of God is better than God actually is. True, my thoughts—including my assumptions about what good means—are always more or less inaccurate, limited, and unworthy, but still I am confident of this: I have never overestimated how good God is because God's goodness overflows far beyond the limits of human understanding.[17]

McLaren has written often about the importance of human freedom; however, his concern is not fundamentally about human liberty, but rather the goodness of God. As an advocate for the free-will defense, for instance, McLaren argues that without human libertarian freedom, God is responsible for all of the evil, injustice, pain, and suffering in the world.[18] Freedom plays an instrumental role; it is not the ultimate concern.

This core commitment to the goodness of God can be found in the theology of Arminius, as well as subsequent theologians within the Arminian tradition. Stanglin and McCall underscore the vital importance of this doctrine: "The goodness of God is a theological non-negotiable for Arminius; he is deeply convinced that the loss of a proper vision of God's goodness leads straight to heresy."[19] Despite R. C. Sproul's charge that Arminians "guard the tree of human liberty with more zeal and tenacity than Patrick Henry,"[20] Olson makes it clear that freedom is not the fundamental issue at stake: "The issue is most emphatically not a humanistic vision of autonomous free will, as if Arminians were in love with free agency for its own sake. Any fair-minded reading of Arminius, Wesley or any other classical Arminian will reveal that this is not so. Rather, the issue is the character of God and the nature of personal relationship."[21]

Later in the same book, Olson suggests a succinct summary of the Arminian priorities: "Arminianism begins with God's goodness and ends by affirming free will."[22] Jerry Walls and Joe Dongell offer similar observations: "Although we would agree that a portion of the [Calvinist and Arminian]

---

[17] McLaren, LWWAT, xi.
[18] For instance, see McLaren, NKOC, 23.
[19] Stanglin and McCall, Jacob Arminius, 60.
[20] R. C. Sproul, Chosen by God (Wheaton: Tyndale, 1986), 9.
[21] Olson, Arminian Theology, 38.
[22] Ibid., 99.

dispute swirls around the topic of sovereignty and human freedom, we contend that the truly fundamental dispute is not over power but rather over God's character."[23] In "Predestination Calmly Considered," Wesley leaves no doubt about his unbridled confidence in the goodness of God:

> But do they not agree least of all with the scriptural account
> of his love and goodness? That attribute which God peculiarly
> claims, wherein he glories above all the rest. It is not written,
> "God is justice," or "God is truth:" (Although he is just and
> true in all his ways:) But it is written, "God is love," love in the
> abstract, without bounds; and "there is no end of his goodness."
> His love extends even to the evil and the unthankful; yea, with-
> out any exception or limitation, to all the children of men. For
> "the Lord is loving" (or good) "to every man, and his mercy is
> over all his works."[24]

In Chapter Four, this study explored McLaren's ambivalence concerning the Calvinism-Arminianism debate. In light of his reconstructed temporal kingdom of God vision, it is not surprising that McLaren finds the traditional soteriological dispute between Calvinists and Arminians "irrelevant" and "uninteresting."[25] When viewed from another angle, however—as a dispute concerning the nature of God's character—this subject matter feeds into the heart of McLaren's project.

While some might consider the Calvinism-Arminianism debate a dispute over power or control, McLaren is in sync with the Arminian perspective that this disagreement is fundamentally a struggle over a proper understanding of the character of God. Is God loving and good to all of creation or does God play favorites? From McLaren's perspective, this question not only has eternal consequences but also pressing present practical social implications, because if God can choose some people for privilege

---

[23] Jerry L. Walls and Joseph R. Dongell, *Why I Am Not a Calvinist* (Downers Grove: InterVarsity Press, 2004), 8.

[24] John Wesley, "Predestination Calmly Considered," in *The Works of John Wesley*, vols. 9 and 10, 3rd ed. (Grand Rapids: Baker, 2002), 227.

[25] Brian McLaren, "Church in America Today," in *A New Evangelical Manifesto*, ed. David P. Gushee (St. Louis: Chalice, 2012), 4.

and others for fodder, then as humans who is to say we do not also have a divine precedent and edict to do the same?

Moral Intuition

Of course, how are finite, sinful, limited human beings capable of discerning what is truly good and loving? God possesses an infinite, perfect, eternal vantage point. What might appear cruel from a finite point of view could turn out actually to be loving, kind, and benevolent from the infinite perspective of the divine judge and sovereign ruler. McLaren is keenly sensitized to this kind of chastened epistemology. Modernity overestimated the ability of autonomous human reason to see and judge clearly. The post-modern turn recognizes the value of other faculties, including intuition, but these other faculties are just as fallible as reason.

It is equally arrogant to christen intuition as the infallible universal pathway to correct knowledge as it was during the modern era to elevate reason to such a status. McLaren sounds almost like an apologist for total depravity in the following word of caution: "We need to be careful and humble because, as Scripture says, God's ways are above our ways and God's thoughts are above our thoughts. We must acknowledge from the outset that we, like the Pharisees in the Gospels, can never underestimate our power to be wrong about God and God's view of things."[26]

While McLaren underscores the human propensity for missing the point, he is not a radical skeptic. Moral intuition is a God-given human faculty, just as much as reason, imagination, and emotions. It is therefore best to view McLaren in the tradition of Lesslie Newbigin, as an adherent to a chastened, humble, or "proper confidence."[27] McLaren affirms the basic reliability and soundness of our human faculties in the hermeneutical process with the caveat that absolute certainty is never within our grasp and we are always operating from an incomplete reference point.

This kind of proper confidence includes faith in one's moral intuitions as a generally reliable guide. Jerry Walls argues that this approach to moral intuition is the route taken in the Arminian approach to interpreting the Bible. According to Walls, Arminianism affirms a basic continuity between

---

[26] McLaren, "What Is Justice?" in *JP*, 21–22.
[27] Lesslie Newbigin, *Proper Confidence* (Grand Rapids: Eerdmans, 1995), 105.

divine and human moral categories. Human moral intuition was fashioned by a loving and good God to function faithfully within a God-given environment designed for human flourishing. Sin and finitude can skew the faithful deliverances of moral intuition (as it can all human faculties); however, with appropriate care and openness to scriptural guidance and correction, there is good reason to believe that humans possess "a basically sound grasp of God's love and justice."[28] Walls explains,

> The believer's positive feeling for kindness and revulsion for cruelty are independent of God in the sense that he instinctively forms these attitudes apart from any awareness that God commands the one and forbids the other. These attitudes are naturally present in normal persons and are fundamental components of their most basic moral intuitions. It is because the believer naturally values kindness that he readily resonates to the claim that God loves us. His fundamental moral intuitions are part of the background in his willing acceptance of the will of a loving God as the measure of right and wrong.[29]

The five-point Calvinist approach to biblical interpretation, on the other hand, rejects essential continuity between God's moral categories and human moral intuition. In other words, because of the effects of the Fall, there is a radical disconnect between God's morality and human moral intuition. Consequently, the human faculty of moral intuition is a questionable guide, and "the deliverances of the Christian faith may be sharply at odds with even our clearest moral judgments."[30]

Walls identifies Wesley as someone who trusted his most certain moral intuitions when engaging Scripture and John Calvin and Martin Luther as skeptics concerning the positive role moral intuition can play in biblical interpretation. To illustrate, Walls selects the doctrine of unconditional election as a test case. According to Walls, "it was axiomatic for [Wesley]

---

[28] Jerry L. Walls, "Divine Commands, Predestination, and Moral Intuition," in *The Grace of God and the Will of Man*, ed. Clark Pinnock (Bloomington, MN: Bethany House, 1995), 273.

[29] Ibid., 270.

[30] Ibid., 272.

that our clearest moral intuitions are reliable. He forcefully rejected the suggestion that our most deeply rooted moral judgments may be deceptive."[31]

The notion that God created some individuals for the purpose of eternal damnation struck Wesley as "worse than the devil; more false, more cruel, and more unjust."[32] In fact, the doctrine of unconditional reprobation, which Wesley argued was the logical entailment of unconditional election, was so repulsive and offensive to his fundamental moral sense of justice and love that he was willing to declare certain controverted scriptural passages[33] nonsense rather than "to say it had such a sense as this."[34] In other words, the concept of God's universal love toward all people "was as certain as anything [Wesley] believed," and any interpretation of Scripture to the contrary must be mistaken.[35] It is worth reiterating that both Walls and Wesley recognize that moral intuition is subject to correction; however, they are advocating for a basic continuity between human and divine categories of morality.

On the other hand, Luther and Calvin embraced both unconditional election and unconditional reprobation. Walls argues that Luther and Calvin were committed to a rather extreme form of divine-command ethics; therefore, "God's will is the standard for right, so whatever He wills is right by definition."[36] Consequently, if the Bible teaches the unconditional eternal damnation of the non-elect for the glory of God, this doctrine should be accepted regardless of how our moral intuitions react to such a proposal.

Identifying McLaren's resonance with the Arminian position is not difficult. In *A New Kind of Christianity*, when discussing the shape of the biblical narrative, McLaren writes, "Good has the first word, and good

---

[31] Ibid., 273.

[32] John Wesley, "Free Grace," *The Works of John Wesley*, vol. 7, 3rd ed. (Grand Rapids: Baker, 1978), 373–86, citing 383. Stanglin and McCall also point out that Arminius believed the doctrine of unconditional election (especially when expressed in a supralapsarian manner) was "inspired by Satan and is a doctrine quite compatible with the kingdom of darkness." See Stanglin and McCall, *Jacob Arminius*, 129.

[33] In "Predestination Calmly Considered," 217–20, Wesley specifically discusses Romans 9–11.

[34] Wesley, "Free Grace," 383.

[35] Walls, "Divine Commands," 266.

[36] Ibid., 263. For more on the divine command theory of ethics, see David Baggett and Jerry L. Walls, *Good God* (New York: Oxford University Press, 2011), 103–23, and J. P. Moreland and William Lane Craig, *Philosophical Foundations for a Christian Worldview* (Downers Grove: InterVarsity Press, 2003), 531–32.

has the last."[37] McLaren is convinced that God is good and that all will be well for everyone in the end. His entire apologetic project is motivated by an attempt to replace "right faith" with "good faith," and to combat "bad monotheism" with "good monotheism."[38] If anything, McLaren is a hard apologist for the goodness of God, which serves as his integrative apologetic motif. McLaren is convinced that he has "never overestimated how good God is because God's goodness overflows far beyond the limits of human understanding."[39] He is fully aware of the power of sin and finitude to distort human perception, so our ability to comprehend divine goodness is relative and limited. Nevertheless, he clearly recognizes that his understanding of goodness and God's concept of goodness are not at odds, but rather on the same trajectory. The difference is not one of kind, but of degree.

As this study has demonstrated, some critics have argued that McLaren is captive to his own subjective feelings rather than the dictates of Scripture. For instance, Gregory Wills charges McLaren with "trying to make the faith acceptable to modern morality."[40] Similarly, Douglas Blount accuses McLaren of simply following his own "tastes" rather than "historic Christian orthodoxy" in an effort to "soothe the Postmodern conscience."[41] This charge from Blount is especially egregious, however. To characterize McLaren's concept of God's goodness and loving character as arbitrary personal "taste" is profoundly mistaken. Blount writes,

> In short, they [McLaren and Emergent Christians] have a taste for a certain understanding of love as well as its attendant understanding of divine love—of what it means for God to be "a God of love"—and this taste leads them to reject not only readings of the Bible with which it cannot be squared but also to

[37] McLaren, *NKOCY*, 54.
[38] McLaren, *FF*, 27–45.
[39] McLaren, *LWWAT*, xi.
[40] Gregory Wills, "Panel Discussion—New Kind of Christianity?—Brian McLaren Recasts the Gospel," Southern Baptist Theological Seminary, March 11, 2010, http://www.sbts.edu/resources/chapel/chapel-spring-2010/panel-discussion-a-new-kind-of-christianity-brian-mclaren-recasts-the-gospel/.
[41] Douglas Blount, "A New Kind of Interpretation," *Evangelicals Engaging Emergent*, ed. William D. Henard and Adam W. Greenway (Nashville: B&H Publishing, 2009), 125. See also R. Scott Clark, "Whoever Will Be Saved: Emerging Church, Meet Christian Dogma," in *Reforming or Conforming?*, ed. Gary L. W. Johnson and Ronald N. Gleason (Wheaton: Crossway, 2008), 117.

deny the truthfulness of those passages that cannot in their view be interpreted in harmony with it.[42]

Blount here is likening McLaren's abhorrence of ethnic cleansing, genocide, and unconditional reprobation to an arbitrary personal "taste," such as one's preference for Pepsi over Coke or coffee to tea. This clearly is categorical confusion. Surely, preferring the teaching of the Sermon on the Mount to the divinely commanded slaughter of women and children is hardly a matter of arbitrary personal "taste." In fact, such a preference for Christ's teachings over Old Testament brutality and radical inclusion instead of ethnic exclusion should be considered profoundly Christian rather than an expression of accommodation to cultural "taste." In *A New Kind of Christianity*, McLaren anticipated this critique:

> We pursue this new approach to the Bible not out of capitulation to "moral relativism," as some critics will no doubt accuse, but because of a passion for the biblical values of goodness and justice. Our goal is not to lower our moral standards, but rather raise them by facing and repenting of habits of the mind and heart that harmed human beings and dishonored God in the past.[43]

Additionally, it should be noted that McLaren does not "deny the truthfulness" of biblical passages; rather, he attempts to reinterpret such passages in a manner that is faithful to both the teachings of Jesus and one's most certain moral intuitions. It would be a mistake to suggest that McLaren believes moral sensibilities are free to stand in judgment of Scripture. Rather, there is a dynamic interplay between one's best and most certain moral intuitions and the biblical narrative, particularly the stories of Jesus. There is a mutual reinforcement at work.

As McLaren reads the gospel accounts, his deepest and most certain moral intuitions are stirred. Yet, without the preexistence of active, discerning moral intuitions, one would not be able to recognize the exemplary nature of Christ's ethical teachings and actions. What is important here

---

[42] Ibid., 115.
[43] McLaren, *NKOCY*, 76–77.

is not determining priority, but rather noticing how McLaren's deepest moral intuitions cohere with the life, teachings, and example of Christ. McLaren describes this "fitness" accordingly: "The image of God conveyed by Jesus as the Son of God, and the image of the universe that resonates with this image of God best *fit* my deepest experience, best resonate with my deepest intuition, [and] best inspire my deepest hope."[44] There is a special kind of satisfying resonance, electricity, coherence, and fitness that emerges between McLaren's experience, intuition, and desires on the one hand and the story of Jesus on the other.

C. S. Lewis discussed something similar when considering the criteria for judging the probability of miracles, particularly the resurrection of Jesus. Lewis suggested the criterion of our "innate sense of the fitness of things."[45] Lewis used the illustration of possessing fragments of a novel or symphony while missing the central part. How should someone's claim to have located the key central element be judged? Lewis suggests, "Our business would be to see whether the new passage, if admitted to the central place which the discoverer claimed for it, did actually illumine all the parts we had already seen and 'pull them together.'"[46] The resurrection of Jesus was for Lewis the key missing part that when put into the central location pulled together the rest of the fragments into a satisfying, unified whole. For McLaren, on the other hand, it would appear that the moral teachings and example of Jesus serve as the missing centerpiece that unites the fragments of experience, desire, moral intuition, and the rest of the biblical narrative.

This commitment to a basic trust in one's deepest and most certain moral intuitions is one of the fundamental ways in which Arminians diverge from their Calvinist brethren. McLaren is fully and completely orthodox Arminian in this regard.

Libertarian Freedom

As this study has shown, McLaren's writings are laced with challenges to determinism. In fact, this is a unifying apologetic motif, as he has forcefully critiqued modern mechanization. In Chapter Four, this study identified

---

[44] McLaren, *GO*, 76–77; emphasis mine.
[45] C. S. Lewis, *Miracles* (New York: Macmillan, 1978), 106.
[46] Ibid., 109.

four problems with theological determinism, in general, and Calvinistic sovereignty, in particular: the problem of dignity and authenticity, the problem of relationality, the problem of evil, and the problem of reliability. In response to each problem, McLaren offers libertarian freedom as the solution.

This insistence upon libertarian freedom is in sync with orthodox Arminianism. Olson asserts, "Because of their vision of God as good (loving, benevolent, merciful), Arminians affirm libertarian free will."[47] Wesley, in particular, was a staunch advocate of libertarian freedom and utilized the fourth argument listed above to defend it. Walls explains,

> Wesley forcefully rejected the suggestion that our most deeply rooted moral judgments may be deceptive. This is quite obvious in his critical discussion of some of the theories of determinism that were popular in his day. Those defenders of determinism conceded that we have a deeply held ingrained sense that we are free, and that freedom is an essential presupposition of moral blame and commendation. Nevertheless, they maintained, we are not really free, for all our actions are determined, down to the last detail. If this is the case, Wesley charged, God is "the father of lies! Such you doubtless represent him, when you say . . . that feelings which he has interwoven with our inmost nature are . . . illusive!"[48]

While McLaren is in tune with the Arminian defense of libertarian freedom, his diagnosis of the problem with Calvinistic sovereignty requires a more nuanced treatment. As demonstrated in Chapter Four, McLaren associates the Calvinistic view of sovereignty and human freedom with either hard determinism or fatalism. Yet, soft determinism (aka compatibilism) is the model of choice among exemplary Calvinist philosophers and theologians, such as Paul Helm, John Feinberg, D. A. Carson, Robert Peterson, Michael Williams, Bruce Ware, and Wayne Grudem. Consequently, for McLaren's

---

[47] Olson, *Arminian Theology*, 75.
[48] Walls, "Divine Commands," 273. The quote from Wesley originally comes from "Thoughts Upon Necessity," in *Works of Wesley*, vol. 10, 3rd ed., 457–74, citing 471.

critique of theological determinism and advocacy for libertarian freedom to gain traction, an engagement with compatibilism is unavoidable.

Several contemporary Arminian philosophers and theologians have argued that compatibilism fails to offer a sufficient definition of freedom to account for a robust understanding of God's glory, character, relationality, and faithfulness on the one hand and human moral responsibility, authenticity, and dignity on the other. Since the contention between compatibilists and libertarians is well documented, multifaceted, and ongoing in contemporary philosophy, it is beyond the scope of this chapter to offer an account of all of the maneuvers both sides make in this dispute.[49] This section is not intended to settle the debate but rather will offer four Arminian arguments that would strengthen McLaren's apologetic case against the Calvinistic conception of sovereignty and human responsibility.

Compatibilism Impugns God's Character by Failing to Secure Human Moral Responsibility

One such Arminian philosopher who has argued against compatibilism along these lines is William Abraham. According to Abraham, there is a great deal at stake: "Everything hangs at this point on its [compatibilistic] account of human freedom. Without this, God becomes accountable for all moral evil, and he seems unjust for punishing the reprobate."[50] In other words, Abraham argues that compatibilistic freedom cannot exonerate God from evil if humans cannot truly avoid the choices that they make. Olson concurs, "Under no circumstances in human situations would a person be held accountable and punished for something he or she could not avoid doing."[51]

In the compatibilist account, the proximate or immediate cause of a free action is the inner state of the agent (e.g., thought, wish, desire); however, the ultimate cause is outside the agent—namely, God. Abraham likens God to a hypnotist who controls the thoughts, feelings, desires, and wishes (i.e.,

---

[49] For standard arguments and counterarguments in this debate, see Robert Kane, ed., *The Oxford Handbook of Free Will* (Oxford: Oxford University Press, 2002), and Kevin Timpe, *Free Will: Sourcehood and Its Alternatives*, 2nd ed. (New York: Bloomsbury, 2013).

[50] William F. Abraham, *An Introduction to the Philosophy of Religion* (Englewood Cliffs: Prentice-Hall, 1985), 146.

[51] Roger E. Olson, *Against Calvinism* (Grand Rapids: Zondervan, 2011), 176.

the inner states) of the person for the purpose of bringing about the choice that God desires.[52] While the choice might not be coerced since the agent is willingly making the choice, the choice is still manipulated by God, and there is no real possibility of doing otherwise. Therefore, Abraham argues that the compatibilist definition of freedom fails to offer a sufficient base for human moral responsibility and dignity. God, as the remote cause, is ultimately responsible for all human activity—good, bad, or otherwise.

The compatibilist might object at this juncture and suggest the agent hypothetically could have chosen otherwise had the agent wanted to.[53] The libertarian, however, argues that this is the point: the only way the agent could have wanted or willed something differently is if the previous causes and conditions also had been different. The only way such causes and conditions could have been different is if the prior events and circumstances also had been different. The only way such prior events and circumstances could have been different is if God had ordained a different set of events and circumstances. In short, the agent could have chosen differently only if God had either directly or indirectly caused the agent to have different thoughts, wishes, or desires. As J. P. Moreland and William Lane Craig point out:

> Libertarians claim that this [hypothetical] notion of ability is really a sleight of hand and not adequate to give the freedom we need to be responsible agents. For libertarians, the real issue is not whether we are free to do what we want, but whether we are free to want in the first place. In other words, a free act is one in which the agent is ultimately the originating source of the act

---

[52] Abraham, *Philosophy of Religion*, 146.

[53] It is important to recognize at this point a distinction between *categorical* and *hypothetical* ability. Libertarians insist that for an act to be free the agent must possess the actual categorical ability to choose between two or more live options in a given situation. The compatibilist, on the other hand, claims that for the agent to be free she simply needs to possess the hypothetical ability to have chosen differently, even though this is possible only if an antecedent variation in the causal chain obtained prior to the development of the agent's pertinent thoughts, wishes, or desires. Paul Helm explains the compatibilist perspective: "The sort of power or control that is in view here is the power of the agents to do, or to have done, otherwise in a situation if they had chosen to do so; it is a hypothetical power. Had X wished or willed to do A, an action over which X has power, then X could have done A. But the fact is that in that particular situation, X did not overridingly wish or will to do A, and therefore did B." See Paul Helm, *Providence of God* (Downers Grove: InterVarsity Press, 1993), 189.

itself. Freedom requires that we have the categorical ability to act, or at least, to will to act.[54]

Compatibilism Undermines God's Glory in Salvation

A look at the Westminster Confession will amplify a second libertarian charge. Walls and Dongell argue that the Westminster Confession requires a compatibilistic reading to be coherent.[55] The Westminster divines crafted this confession in part for the purpose of safeguarding divine glory. While the intent was noble, the result is questionable. Rather than safeguarding God's glory, the confession arguably undermines it. The first article of the third chapter, entitled "Of God's Eternal Decrees," reads: "God from all eternity, did, by the most wise and holy counsel of His own will, freely, and unchangeably ordain whatsoever comes to pass: yet so, as thereby neither is God the author of sin, nor is violence offered to the will of the creatures; nor is the liberty or contingency of second causes taken away, but rather established."[56] The framers of the confession sought to establish the total sovereignty of God over all human affairs.

Walls and Dongell state, "Now this is a rather strong claim of all-embracing determinism. Everything is ordained by God's unchangeable will from all eternity. This is not a matter of impersonal fate but rather of a determinism flowing out of the will of a personal being who is most holy and wise."[57] God is the first or ultimate cause of "whatsoever comes to pass," including human "liberty." At the same time, however, humans are the second, or proximate, cause of their choices, and as such, are responsible for the "sin," "violence," or whatever other kind of moral evil happens to exist in the world. Walls and Dongell continue, "Although God causes all things, the responsibility for the evil rests with the creatures because they are the proximate causes who actually perform it."[58] The asymmetrical attempt here is to give God the glory for all that is good in the world, but to

---

[54] Moreland and Craig, *Philosophical Foundations*, 271.
[55] Walls and Dongell, *Why I Am Not a Calvinist*, 114.
[56] John H. Leith, ed., *Creeds of the Church* (Chicago: Aldine, 1963), 198.
[57] Walls and Dongell, *Why I Am Not a Calvinist*, 111.
[58] Ibid.

exonerate God from all of the evil that is brought about by the second-cause actions of compatibilistically free human creatures.

The libertarian argues, however, that this maneuver is problematic. If humans are culpable for their second-cause sinful actions, then should not humans also be credited for their second-cause good deeds? If compatibilism is true, then the reprobate engage in the evil deeds they desire, even though they cannot choose otherwise; the elect pursue the righteous path they desire, but they likewise cannot choose otherwise. As Abraham puts it, "Now if the reprobate must take the credit for the evil actions, so the elect must take the credit for the good acts. Good acts stem from within; therefore the elect are responsible for them; therefore they can have pride in them, boast about them, and claim merit for them."[59] In other words, either all proximate-cause actions are the responsibility of human agents or none of them are. Either God is unjust in punishing the reprobate for sins they could not have avoided, or God has provided a way for the elect to boast in their own salvation. Neither horn of this dilemma is biblical. Abraham concludes, "Rather than safeguard divine glory, the Calvinist tradition, therefore, destroys it at its foundation."[60]

Compatibilism Misappropriates Causal Language

Abraham identifies a third problem for Calvinists who rely upon compatibilism; namely, its adherents often are misled by the "surface grammar of the language."[61] Causal language can be used in both broad and narrow ways. When using "causation" in a broad sense, we "mean a complete specification of the antecedent, sufficient conditions of an event." When discussing the cause of an event in a narrow sense, however, all that is meant is the most significant or primary factor. Abraham explains, "Calvin ignores this crucial point. He conflates both senses of cause in his analysis of divine causality." Abraham argues that Calvinists often are guilty of the same categorical confusion at this juncture. He elaborates, "What we need to see is that language ascribing salvation to God is indeed causal language, but it should be interpreted in a narrow sense. When believers say that it is God alone

---

[59] Abraham, *Philosophy of Religion*, 147.
[60] Ibid.
[61] Ibid., 148.

who saves, they are simply picking out the most crucial agent at work in the whole process of salvation. This does not rule out the activity of other agents, nor does it preclude human freedom."[62]

In other words, while God is the primary agent in salvation, God is not the *only* agent. Humans are secondary agents as well. There is a dual agency at work. This, however, does not mean that God has left room for humans to take pride in their salvation. Abraham likens the situation to an alcoholic who willingly checks into a rehabilitation clinic. While the alcoholic cannot unilaterally cure himself, he never would have been in position to kick the habit had he not pursued the resources the clinic offers. The alcoholic's choice was not meritorious; he simply allowed the team at the clinic to administer the treatment. Abraham concludes, "For him to take pride in his cure ignores the complexity of his problem and makes moral nonsense of the facts of the situation."[63]

There is a similar kind of dual agency at work in the mysterious experience of salvation. The Arminian claims that God, as the primary agent, always initiates with prevenient and saving grace, seeking to convict and draw the lost to a point of repentance and reconciliation. Humans, as the secondary agents, however, must freely cooperate with God's grace to be saved. This act of cooperation hardly amounts to works-righteousness; as Olson states, "What is faith? Simply trusting God; it is not a 'good work' or anything meritorious of which the saved sinner could boast."[64] Dual agency explains how God and humans are both involved in the saving act, but God alone receives the glory.[65]

Compatibilism Undermines God's Perfect Love and Goodness

Walls and Dongell identify a fourth challenge to compatibilism from an entirely different angle. Rather than dismantling the compatibilistic definition of freedom, the authors here assume the soundness of compatibilism for the sake of argument in order to explore some "far-reaching

---

[62] Ibid.
[63] Ibid., 151.
[64] Olson, *Against Calvinism*, 170.
[65] For counterproposals, see Paul Helm, "Grace and Causation," *Scottish Journal of Theology* 32 (1979): 101–12.

implications."[66] Walls and Dongell draw the logical conclusion that "if freedom and determinism are compatible, then it is possible that God could determine all persons to freely do good at all times."[67] In fact, if compatibilism were an accurate depiction of reality, then seemingly there would be no reason for anybody to experience eternal damnation since God would possess the ability to determine all persons to freely receive the gospel and spend eternity in heaven.

If compatibilism were true and God is a perfectly loving creator who desires the flourishing of all creatures, universal salvation—rather than unconditional election—would seem to be the logical conclusion. Since one of the central tenets of classical Calvinism, however, is the eternal damnation of the reprobate, there must be a problem with either compatibilism or with the Calvinist conception of God. Or both. Walls and Dongell insist "the breathtaking vision of God's trinitarian love is obscured by the Calvinist claim that God passes over persons he could just as easily save and thereby consigns them to eternal misery."[68]

Relational View of God

In *We Make the Road by Walking*, McLaren writes, "Perhaps we can agree that whoever and whatever God is, our best imagery can only point toward God like a finger. We can never capture God in our concepts like a fist."[69] Nevertheless, McLaren is convinced that some imagery is more faithful and helpful than others in representing the nature of God. Mechanical, forensic, violent, and oppressive metaphors are repulsive to McLaren, while relational, organic, familial, and communal images resonate with his deepest intuitions and careful reading of the Gospels.

Allan Coppedge argues that a holistic approach to the roles of God helps the reader avoid picking and choosing imagery to suit cultural or personal preferences. "Such a holistic theology must not be content with the parts of Scripture accented by a particular tradition, nor must it focus only on those portraits of God that are most naturally attractive."[70] Nevertheless,

---

[66] Walls and Dongell, *Why I Am Not a Calvinist*, 116.
[67] Ibid.
[68] Ibid., 220.
[69] McLaren, *WMRBW*, 29.
[70] See Allan Coppedge, *Portraits of God* (Downers Grove: InterVarsity Press, 2001), 27.

Coppedge recognizes that while Calvinists and Arminians at their best affirm the full range of biblical metaphors and roles of God, each system utilizes a different fundamental guiding grid that influences their respective hermeneutic. In other words, Calvinists typically understand God primarily as a sovereign king and righteous judge, while Arminians view God fundamentally in relational terms, often expressed as a loving parent.[71]

The implications of a holistic understanding of God are vast. Seeing God not only as a king and judge, but also as a father, alters the entire grid through which all other doctrines are viewed. In relation to salvation, the distant, objective language of pardon and justification is offset by the imagery of adoption into the family of God. Christians are children of God and are brothers and sisters in the faith. There is a promised inheritance. God reaches down in grace, like a great parental physician bent on the recovery of his children. For Wesley, therefore, God not only pardons but also heals and empowers his children to become all they were created to be—namely, like their father in heaven.[72]

Wesley also rejected the Calvinistic understanding of unconditional election in large part due to his view of God as a loving parent. In Wesley's mind, a good and just divine parent would never condemn a child to hell without offering a legitimate chance to respond. According to Walls, Wesley was convinced "that a God who loved all people would not unconditionally damn any of them. The very nature of love is such that this is simply unthinkable."[73] Wesley asks the question, "Now, I beseech you to consider calmly, how is God good or loving to this [unconditionally elect] man? Is not this such love as makes your blood run cold?"[74] Instead, Wesley believed that a loving parent would extend a legitimate offer of salvation to all of his children, while respecting their libertarian free will.[75] To ignore

---

[71] Allan Coppedge, *John Wesley in Theological Debate* (Wilmore, KY: Wesley Heritage Press, 1987), 128. Elsewhere, Gary Tyra asks, "From what source would McLaren's *post-Christian* readers most likely have derived the image of God as a 'judge' and 'potentate,' if not from the Old Testament?" Gary Tyra, *A Missional Orthodoxy* (Downers Grove: InterVarsity Press, 2013), 166. In posing this question, Tyra does not seem to consider the role that some influential expressions of Calvinism have played in portraying God as a "judge" and "potentate." McLaren addresses this point directly in *GO*, 195.

[72] Ibid., 128–30.

[73] Walls, "Divine Commands," 266.

[74] Wesley, "Predestination Calmly Considered," 229.

[75] Thomas C. Oden, *John Wesley's Scriptural Christianity* (Grand Rapids: Zondervan, 1994), 258–59.

this divine gift of freedom would be to strip dignity from the individual, a chief characteristic of the child's natural image of God.

McLaren's resonance with relational and organic imagery, along with a resistance to associating God with arbitrary expressions of oppressive power is evident throughout his published works. In *The Secret Message of Jesus*, McLaren argues that in first-century Palestine, the "kingdom of God" was understood as a radical counter voice to "the oppressive empire of Caesar and the oppressed kingdom of Israel."[76] In our contemporary postcolonial world, however, McLaren asserts, "kingdom language . . . is outdated and distant." Additionally, this language "evokes patriarchy, chauvinism, imperialism, domination, and a regime without freedom." McLaren boldly asserts that if Jesus were on earth today, he would not use the phrase "kingdom of God."[77]

Consequently, McLaren offers the following dynamically equivalent phrases: the dream of God, the revolution of God, the mission of God, the party of God, the network of God, and the dance of God.[78] Elsewhere, he proposes global commonwealth of God,[79] God's beloved community,[80] and peaceable kingdom.[81] Each of these phrases is an attempt to capture the essence of the original relational, loving, peace-seeking community associated with Jesus's first-century vision of the kingdom of God.

McLaren is especially concerned by an overemphasis on forensic language, which evokes imagery of a divine courtroom. Instead of the *penal* substitutionary view of the atonement and discussion of *justification* by faith, McLaren understands the cross in the relational, communal imagery of table fellowship.[82] Instead of viewing Jesus as the ultimate fighting champion of the world, who is "committed to making someone bleed,"[83] McLaren believes Jesus is willing to serve as the ultimate shock absorber. Instead of viewing God as a "machine-operator" and "chief engineer," McLaren

---

[76] McLaren, *SMJ*, 14.
[77] Ibid., 139.
[78] Ibid., 147–48.
[79] McLaren, *WMRBW*, 104.
[80] Ibid.
[81] McLaren, *SMJ*, 149–62.
[82] McLaren, *JMBM*, 208–19.
[83] McLaren, *NKOCY*, 119–20.

emphasizes the Trinitarian community as the basis for reality.[84] In sum, while "our best imagery can only point toward God like a finger,"[85] McLaren is clearly pointing to an Arminian vision of God as relational, organic, and communal, as is clear from the following passage:

> For many zealous Reformed folk, the metaphor of God as judge seems to predominate over all other metaphors, and the divine attribute of sovereign will is favored over all other attributes so that God's relation to creation is seen primarily in terms of legal prosecution (as judge) and absolute control (as naked will). If, however, we allow a different metaphor—of community—to become more prominent in our thinking (speaking of the Divine Community of Father, Son, and Spirit), then the attribute of love emerges as a more primal essence of God's being. (After all, before creation God had no evil to judge and nothing to control, yet God existed without boredom, according to our creeds, in an eternal, dynamic, glorious and holy fellowship of love.)[86]

Generous Orthodoxy

According to Henry Knight, "One cannot hear the phrase 'generous orthodoxy' without thinking of Wesley's 'catholic spirit.' Wesley distinguished essential doctrines from opinions, and said that it is in the essentials that Christians of all varieties find their unity."[87] Thomas Oden explains that Wesley's idea of catholic spirit is "not a spirit that seeks first to identify right doctrine, though assuming it, but that seeks to reach out in dialogue, good conscience, faith and fervent intercession for the partner in dialogue."[88]

Like Wesley, McLaren offered *A Generous Orthodoxy* as part of "a needed and ongoing conversation" and with "a sincere request for . . . prayers."[89] In so doing, he sought to "embrace the good in many traditions and historic streams of Christian faith, and to integrate them, yielding a

---

[84] McLaren, *GO*, 187.

[85] McLaren, *WMRBW*, 29.

[86] Ibid., 195.

[87] Knight, "John Wesley and the Emerging Church," 5. See also Franklin, "John Wesley in Conversation," 81.

[88] Oden, *John Wesley's Scriptural Christianity*, 95.

[89] Ibid., 24.

new, generous, emergent approach that is greater than the sum of its parts."[90] In other words, McLaren pursued a third way in the spirit of Wesley's Anglican via media. Whereas Anglicanism originally charted a course between Protestantism and Catholicism, McLaren's third-way generous orthodoxy seeks to transcend the evangelical/liberal divide of the modern era and reframe the conversation on an entirely different plane. In so doing, McLaren acknowledges his debt to one of his chief mentors, Stanley Grenz. In the foreword to the second edition of *Renewing the Center*, McLaren describes Grenz's project in similar terms: "Stan recommended a new center that was on a different plane entirely, a new center that would strive to grapple with the bracing new challenges of postmodernity rather than old paralyzing polarities of modernity."[91]

McLaren and Wesley both embrace an ecumenical faith that pushes doctrinal "opinions" to the margins. According to Knight, Wesley sought to rally warm-hearted believers around the "historic creeds of the ecumenical church."[92] Likewise, McLaren explains his project in similar terms: "The generous orthodoxy of this book never seeks to dispute with lists, but rather, it consistently, unequivocally, and unapologetically upholds and affirms the Apostles' and Nicene Creeds."[93] He goes on to question "the long-term value of highly emphasizing doctrinal distinctives."[94] Instead, McLaren encourages believers to "celebrate orthodox doctrine-in-practice" and "not to bury doctrinal distinctives but rather put them in their marginal place."[95]

Consequently, the priority for both Wesley and McLaren is not to arrive at complete doctrinal agreement, but rather to find a resonance of the heart. In commenting on Wesley's sermon entitled "The Catholic Spirit," which took its text from 2 Kings 10:15, Oden explains, "Wesley was not concerned here with the mixed motives of Jehu, but the form of reconciliation of human estrangement that is due not to intellectual agreement, but goodwill,

---

[90] McLaren, *GO*, 18.

[91] Brian McLaren, "Foreword," in Stanley J. Grenz, *Renewing the Center*, 2nd ed. (Grand Rapids: Baker Academic, 2006), 11.

[92] Knight, "John Wesley and the Emerging Church," 5.

[93] McLaren, *GO*, 28.

[94] Ibid., 32.

[95] Ibid.

a 'right heart.' The major thesis is that we may be of one heart, even though not of one opinion."[96]

Holism

In *A New Kind of Christianity*, McLaren insists that faith is indulgent if it does not seek to bless others.[97] This kind of blessing does not happen by chance, but rather is the result of holistic formation. McLaren explains, "Good thinking (orthodoxy), good being (orthopathy), and good relating (ortho-affinity) must interact with and express themselves through good work and practice (orthopraxy) in the world."[98] According to Franklin, Wesley believed "true religion . . . 'enlightens' heart and hands, affection and behavior. He wanted to cultivate not only Christian thinking but Christian life in its wholeness. Wesley believed that Christianity is, at its essence, a social religion of love."[99]

Henry Knight is convinced that this is an area in which Wesleyan-Arminian theology and ECM sensibilities are especially in tune. Knight observes,

> In theological language, they [ECM] were saying orthodoxy
> was not enough; orthopraxy is needed as well. They are, of
> course, correct. But there is a third term that Wesleyans and
> Pentecostals have been adding to the other two that is like-
> wise essential: orthopathy. It means having a right heart, or in
> Wesley's terms, holy tempers. We need not only right beliefs
> and practices, we need a right heart; we need not only to think
> and do what is faithful, we need to be faithful persons. To put it
> differently, orthopathy does not primarily refer to a warm heart,
> but to a heart formed, governed, and motivated by love.[100]

Actually, there is a fourth term that Knight leaves out: ortho-affinity. This kind of "holistic spirituality"[101] does not develop in isolation as independent

---

[96] Oden, *John Wesley's Scriptural Christianity*, 91.

[97] As noted previously, McLaren credits Newbigin for this key insight. See *GO*, 195–96; *LWWAT*, 169; and *WMRBW*, 24–27.

[98] McLaren, *NKOCY*, 29.

[99] Franklin, "John Wesley in Conversation," 77.

[100] Knight, "John Wesley and the Emerging Church," 6.

[101] Ibid.

monads engage in personal spiritual disciplines. Rather, it is formed in communities. As McLaren writes in *Finding Our Way Again*, "The way of community is about the inward journey, not the journey into *me*, but the journey into *we*."[102] McLaren recognizes the critical role that the Methodist renewal movement played in developing a communal spiritual formation plan following the Reformation.

> Luther and Calvin created Protestant intellectual systems (a kind of conceptual hierarchy) that replaced the Catholic organizational hierarchy. But nobody created a new system of spiritual formation and nurture to replace the richly developed Catholic system of spirituality that had developed during the Middle Ages. . . . Not until the Wesleys did anyone do for spiritual formation what Luther and Calvin had done for doctrine: create a system to replace what had been rejected from Catholicism.[103]

This holistic approach to spiritual formation leads to a balance of personal and social holiness. McLaren points out that Wesley "rediscovered the original power of catechesis as a movement school. He encouraged people to self-organize into small learning cohorts called classes and bands that gathered for spiritual formation, reorientation, and activation."[104] In these meetings, believers held each other accountable in their quest for spiritual growth. For Wesley, a changed heart and internal transformation manifested itself in external social concern.[105] Consequently, the Methodist movement led the way in fighting slavery and advocating for women's rights both inside and outside the church.

Similarly, McLaren's ministry has been characterized by a commitment to both spiritual formation and justice on all fronts. In other words, Wesley and McLaren affirmed both personal and social holiness; however, they placed the accent in different places. Wesley's priority was on personal transformation. Social change then would come as individuals were saved and sanctified. McLaren, however, places greater emphasis on the need for

---

[102] McLaren, *FOWA*, 99–100.
[103] McLaren, *GO*, 219.
[104] McLaren, *WMRBW*, xxi.
[105] Kenneth J. Collins, *A Faithful Witness: John Wesley's Homiletical Theology* (Wilmore, KY: Wesley Heritage, 1993), 163–88.

social holiness, or social justice, without necessarily linking it directly to logically prior personal spiritual transformation.[106]

Pragmatism

Wesley's concern for personal and social holiness was highly practical. He believed one's theology should lead to correct living.[107] According to Coppedge, "Wesley's belief in the importance of a walk of obedient faith was closely connected to his commitment to Christian holiness and was strongly reinforced by his fear of antinomianism."[108] This aversion to antinomianism animated his engagement with Calvinism, which he believed licensed its followers to "avoid any effort to walk in the way of holiness."[109] Wesley was especially concerned with the phrase "imputed righteousness," which he did not find in the Bible. He defended justification by faith and the claim that salvation is the result of Christ's righteousness being imputed to our account; however, the purpose of salvation is sanctification, to make believers actually holy—not just consider them so.[110]

According to Wesley, the logic of unconditional election could lead to dire practical consequences. If God has unconditionally determined the elect for salvation, then they cannot resist. Likewise, if God passes over the reprobate, withholding the necessary resources for salvation, then there is nothing they can do to change that fact, either. Wesley argued that in practice this sort of thinking led to passive resignation. This is the antithesis of the biblical message—that enough grace is offered for anyone to accept the gift of eternal life through faith. Therefore, a wrong view of election could lead to a false sense of security.[111]

Many saw no need to live a life of holiness and obedience since their eternal destiny was secured through a prior confession of faith. Wesley could find no biblical evidence for claiming salvation apart from an active faith expressed in loving obedience to God's Word. It is also important to

---

[106] See Brower-Latz, "A Contextual Reading of John Wesley's Theology," 179–80. To clarify, McLaren cares about personal spiritual formation, but social holiness is the priority.

[107] Ibid., 175.

[108] Coppedge, *Theological Debate*, 140. See also Thomas C. Oden, *The Transforming Power of Grace* (Nashville: Abingdon, 1993), 113.

[109] Oden, *John Wesley's Scriptural Christianity*, 210.

[110] Ibid.

[111] Coppedge, *Theological Debate*, 236–38.

note that Wesley saw willful sin as a lack of faith or trust in God. Therefore, he was intolerant of Christians who claimed salvation despite evident willful sin in their lives.[112] True faith is more than intellectual assent; it is trust evidenced by obedience.[113]

While Wesley's primary focus was on how Calvinism undermines personal holiness, McLaren is fundamentally concerned with the social implications of the doctrine of unconditional election. As this study has shown, McLaren's chief missional impulse is claiming that Christ-followers are blessed to be a blessing rather than elect for privilege.[114] McLaren believes Calvinism has "a legacy of horrible mistakes, misjudgments, and even atrocities." This excessive confidence, sense of superiority, or "manifest destiny," McLaren claims, led to Calvin overseeing the execution of Servetus, the endorsement of slavery in America, the theft of native lands, and the creation and defense of apartheid in South Africa. McLaren does not deny the complexities associated with each of these historical events, but he does believe the common thread is a sense of entitlement fueled by the Calvinist notion of elect for privilege rather than service.[115]

Summary

This chapter has demonstrated that McLaren's project resonates with orthodox Arminian theology and praxis in several domains. While McLaren is a consistent advocate for libertarian freedom, his fundamental concern is protecting the goodness of God, something he believes five-point Calvinism fails to do. This is a key Arminian concern as well.

McLaren's sensibilities reveal a strong resonance with trusting one's most basic and certain moral intuitions when interpreting the Bible. This is most clearly seen in the repudiation of the key Calvinistic doctrine of unconditional election. McLaren recognizes that human intuition is flawed and in need of scriptural correction; however, it is not at odds with divine revelation. Therefore, God's moral categories and human moral intuition must mesh rather than clash at a fundamental level.

---

[112] Oden, *John Wesley's Scriptural Christianity*, 209–11.
[113] Collins, *Faithful Witness*, 165–67. See also Franklin, "John Wesley in Conversation," 79–80.
[114] McLaren, *GO*, 110–11.
[115] Ibid., 194.

McLaren's critique of Calvinistic sovereignty requires an informed engagement with compatibilism. This chapter suggested four arguments against compatibilism that could strengthen McLaren's deconstructive project. McLaren also resonates with Wesleyan-Arminian sensibilities by rejecting forensic metaphors for God and adopting relational, familial, and communal imagery instead. Like Wesley, McLaren also favors generous orthodoxy; a holistic approach to spiritual practice, which includes orthodoxy, orthopathy, ortho-affinity, and orthopraxy; and a practical orientation toward living out the message of holiness both personally and corporately. While this chapter has identified significant common ground between McLaren's project and orthodox Arminian theology, there are areas of tension as well. It is to these points of tension that we must now turn.

Chapter Eight

MCLAREN AND ARMINIAN DISSONANCE

> There are a host of folks troubled by the double predestinarian portrayal of hell that McLaren rightly debunks, but who are attempting to provide cogent, biblical, and helpful ways of speaking about eternal estrangement from God. The stylized approach taken in this book works against allowing those voices to be heard.[1]
>
> —Stanley J. Grenz, Review of *The Last Word and the Word After That*

THIS STUDY HAS DETAILED THE PROFOUND INFLUENCE STANLEY Grenz had upon Brian McLaren. Grenz was so impressed with McLaren's work that he became the driving force behind McLaren receiving an honorary doctorate from Carey Theological College in 2004. Their friendship, however, was not without occasional sharp disagreement. McLaren acknowledges, "Stan and I disagreed on a few issues, including the issue of hell. I was quite shocked that Stan spoke of God having a 'dark side'— sounding a bit like Martin Luther, and Stan felt I was on thin ice in my deconstruction of the traditional view of hell . . . but whatever our disagreements, they didn't weaken our relationship one iota."[2]

Just before his untimely death, Grenz wrote a mixed review of *The Last Word and the Word After That*. While his "overall response to this work [was] very positive," Grenz found plenty to critique. His "biggest hesitation"

---

[1] Stanley J. Grenz, "Review of *The Last Word and the Word After That*," *Journal of the Evangelical Theological Society* 52, no. 3 (September 2009): 663–65, citing 665.

[2] Brian McLaren, email message to author, August 3, 2014.

with the book revolved around McLaren's superficial engagement with the complexities of the subject matter: "There are a host of folks troubled by the double predestinarian portrayal of hell that McLaren rightly debunks, but who are attempting to provide cogent, biblical, and helpful ways of speaking about eternal estrangement from God. The stylized approach taken in this book works against allowing those voices to be heard."[3]

This chapter will consider a few of the leading Arminian voices who have offered a nuanced attempt to balance belief in divine goodness with eternal estrangement. Additionally, we will explore McLaren's biblical hermeneutic in light of the Wesleyan Quadrilateral, as well as offer an analysis of his six-line Greco-Roman hypothesis. This chapter will conclude by considering three of the six lines from this hypothesis: the Fall (the human condition), salvation (the person and work of Christ), and hell/damnation (eschatology).

The Wesleyan Quadrilateral

In *A New Kind of Christian*, Neo and Dan Poole stumble upon a spider web. Neo uses the discovery as an epistemological object lesson. Neo believes that a web is a better model than the image of a static building employed by modern evangelical and liberal foundationalism. Neo says, "What if faith isn't best compared to a building, but rather to a spiderweb? Instead of one foundation, it has several anchor points."[4]

Dan is not fully satisfied, however, so Neo offers a series of metaphors that illustrate the need for multiple forces faithfully interacting in order to create a sense of balance. He then cites the Wesleyan Quadrilateral:

> Stability comes through an interplay of those factors. Stability is not always as simple as a static building sitting on a solid foundation. John Wesley—he was an Anglican, you know—understood this very well: he talked about the church deriving its stability from a dynamic interplay of four forces—what were they? Scripture, tradition, reason, and . . . what was the fourth? Oh yes, spiritual experience.[5]

[3] Grenz, "Review of *LWWAT*," 665.
[4] McLaren, *NKOC*, 54.
[5] Ibid.

McLaren is here favorably citing the Wesleyan Quadrilateral within the context of repudiating modern foundationalism. As this study has shown, McLaren instead opts for a coherentist epistemology, using the metaphor of a web introduced by W. V. O. Quine.[6]

That said, McLaren's appreciation for and employment of the quadrilateral is not fully faithful to Wesley's theological method. The quadrilateral does not function as "a dynamic interplay of four forces" in a symmetrical manner, but rather the Bible is the fundamental authority, while the other three play a supportive role. Therefore, whatever model is chosen to illustrate these forces, it must take into account the undisputed primacy of Scripture if it is to be faithful to the intent of the Wesleyan Quadrilateral.[7] Now, Wesley's approach to a proper handling of Scripture included three primary principles.

The Bible should be read according to its "plain or literal sense unless irrational or unworthy of God's moral character."[8] This does not mean Wesley read every text "literally." He recognized the existence of poetry, parables, and other forms of literature in the Bible. Nevertheless, Wesley opted for the most straightforward, natural reading of the text unless such a reading led to an untenable interpretation in light of reason, moral intuition, or experience.

The straightforward or "clear texts" should help "illuminate obscure texts."[9] Wesley believed that Scripture should interpret Scripture. For the diligent student of the Bible, there is a wholeness that emerges as one passage of Scripture clarifies the teaching of another.[10] Ultimately, as Wesley scholar Thomas Oden puts it, biblical "wisdom comes out of a broadly based dialogue with the general sense of the whole of Scripture, not a single set of selected texts." This has implications for how the testaments should interrelate. While Wesley affirmed the faithfulness of the totality of the

---

[6] Nancey Murphy, *Beyond Liberalism and Fundamentalism* (Valley Forge: Trinity Press International, 1996) 85–109.

[7] See Don Thorsen, "Wesleyan Quadrilateral," in *Global Wesleyan Dictionary of Theology*, ed. Al Truesdale (Kansas City, MO: Beacon Hill, 2013), 443–44. See also Oden, *John Wesley's Scriptural Christianity*, 55.

[8] Oden, *John Wesley's Scriptural Christianity*, 57. See also Robert W. Wall, "Wesley as Biblical Interpreter," in *The Cambridge Companion to John Wesley*, ed. Randy L. Maddox and Jason E. Vickers (Cambridge: Cambridge University Press, 2010), 123.

[9] Oden, *John Wesley's Scriptural Christianity*, 57. See also Wall, "Wesley as Biblical Interpreter," 118.

[10] Oden, *John Wesley's Scriptural Christianity*, 57.

biblical canon, Oden points out, "The Hebrew Bible is earnestly studied by Christians in relation to its having been fulfilled in Jesus Christ."[11]

Wesley revered the consensus of the historic church and consistently sided with the early church fathers in matters of textual dispute. According to Oden, "The historical experience of the church, though fallible, is the better judge overall of Scripture's meanings than later interpreters."[12] Wesley's father instilled in his son a healthy respect for the ancient church; consequently, the younger Wesley believed the views of the early church fathers were essential "for the practice of ministry."[13] Wesley's paleo-orthodox sensibilities are especially evident at this juncture.

So how does McLaren's new kind of hermeneutic stack up to Wesley's methodology? McLaren is remarkably in step with Wesley's first principle. As a former English instructor, McLaren employs the same principles in reading the Bible that he does when engaging other works of literature. This includes discerning the most natural reading of the biblical text in light of literary, cultural, and historical factors and context.[14] It also includes reading a passage in light of its narrative context, including the immediate pericope or "wiki story," as Scot McKnight calls it.[15] Likewise, each story should be read in view of its connection to the larger overarching biblical story.[16]

As seen, Wesley accepted the most natural reading unless such a reading led to rational incoherence or an interpretation that was inconsistent with one's understanding of the character of God. McLaren's approach resonates well with Wesley's thinking at this point. McLaren admits that certain Old Testament passages are troubling; therefore, he cannot accept violent passages at face value because they violate the first principle that Wesley has articulated—namely, they undermine the character of God. Consequently, McLaren seeks an alternative reading that is faithful to the picture of divine goodness that emerges in the dynamic interplay between

---

[11] Ibid., 57–58.

[12] Oden, *John Wesley's Scriptural Christianity*, 59.

[13] Ibid., 65.

[14] McLaren, *GO*, 157. Brian McLaren, "A New Kind of Bible Reading," *brian d. mclaren* (website), unpublished paper, 4–5, n. d., accessed May 25, 2014, http://www.brianmclaren.net /A%20New%20Kind%20of%20Bible%20Reading.pdf.

[15] Scot McKnight, *The Blue Parakeet* (Grand Rapids: Zondervan, 2008), 63–65.

[16] McLaren, "New Kind of Bible Reading," 1–2.

his most certain moral intuitions and a faithful reading of the life and teaching of Jesus in the Gospels.

McLaren is equally in tune with Wesley's second principle of interpreting the unclear passages of Scripture in light of the clear. Scripture should be interpreted in light of Scripture. No passages of Scripture are clearer to McLaren than the Gospel accounts of Jesus. The sections of the Bible that portray God as vengeful, violent, petty, and jealous, on the other hand, are confounding, deeply disturbing, and unclear in light of our best and most certain moral intuitions. These passages cloak the true character of God. The Gospel accounts, on the other hand, portray a picture of God that resonates with our most certain intuitions regarding love, justice, and goodness. These passages most clearly disclose the true character of God. Consequently, McLaren appears to be on firm Wesleyan soil when he interprets violent and exclusionary passages through a peaceful, inclusive, Christocentric lens. This kind of ethical reading of the Bible is central to McLaren's new kind of hermeneutic. While McLaren might be employing this second principle of interpretation in ways that Wesley himself did not, it appears that he is operating according to its general intent.

This leads to Wesley's third principle of interpretation: a reverence for the historic voice of the "primitive church."[17] This third hermeneutical principle, however, is where the tension begins to surface. As discussed in Chapter Six, conservative and postconservative evangelicals disagree over the purpose of theology. According to Olson, paleo-orthodox advocates believe "modern Christians should respect the church fathers and early Christian councils . . . and should even regard these sources as authoritative for biblical interpretation."[18] Oden has gone so far as to say, "Interpreters who pretend to improve upon apostolic testimony are tampering with the evidence."[19]

On the other hand, postconservatives believe "the constructive task of theology is never finished because God always has new light to break forth from his Word."[20] That does not mean postconservatives do not respect

---

[17] Oden, *John Wesley's Scriptural Christianity*, 65.

[18] Ibid., 22.

[19] Thomas C. Oden, *Rebirth of Orthodoxy* (New York: HarperCollins, 2003), 123. Oden believes progress can be made in our "attempts to grasp and articulate ancient ecumenical teaching," but authentic "progress advances in understanding that which has been already once for all given fully and adequately in the deposit of faith."

[20] Roger E. Olson, *Reformed and Always Reforming* (Grand Rapids: Baker, 2007), 29.

tradition, however. Postconservatives respect tradition, but they hold open the possibility of discovering new insights from Scripture. This is why creative theology is encouraged by and supported among postconservatives, even though not all postconservatives endorse every constructive project.[21]

Now, McLaren cites tradition often, but it is frequently the minority report. Wesley, as a paleo-orthodox Arminian, placed stock in the role of the Holy Spirit to guide the early church to a consensus of belief concerning doctrinal issues. Dissenting voices, therefore, were viewed as suspect. Wesley was especially reverent toward the Nicene, Athanasian, and Apostles' creeds.[22] Consequently, McLaren's alignment with open theism, for instance, places him at odds with Wesley, Oden, and other conservative Arminians.[23]

Here is an area in which McLaren's project potentially could benefit from traditional orthodox Arminian resources. According to Laurence Wood, the Arminian position related to divine providence, foreknowledge, and human freedom that enjoys the historic place of honor is Boethius's Eternal Now, the essence of which resonates with the thinking of the early Greek fathers as well as Wesley.[24] In light of recent interest in open theism, Wood wonders, "Why has the church not embraced [open theism] previously in her 2000 years—except for a few individuals?"[25] Wood claims that a move among Arminians toward open theism is unwarranted since the Eternal Now perspective provides all that is necessary—namely, the support of tradition and a coherent articulation of libertarian freedom,

---

[21] Consider, for instance, open theism. Not all postconservatives are open theists, but postconservatives tend to recognize this project as a legitimate exercise in constructive theology. While not personally an open theist, Olson defends the right of open theists to be called Arminian: "Arminianism is a big tent and centered set. Open theism is under it and in it. It's time all Arminians simply acknowledged that and quite [sic] trying to exclude open theists." Roger E. Olson, "Is Open Theism a Type of Arminianism?" *Roger E. Olson* (*Patheos* blog), November 10, 2012, http://www.patheos.com/blogs/rogereolson/2012/11/is-open-theism-a-type-of-arminianism/.

[22] Wesley also was partial to the fathers who lived prior to the Council of Nicea in AD 325. See Oden, *John Wesley's Scriptural Christianity*, 65–71.

[23] As someone with sympathies toward open theism, McLaren is under the tent of postconservative Arminianism, which Olson argues (and this study concurs) is an acceptable stream of orthodox Arminianism. To declare McLaren out of step with orthodox Arminianism on this point, therefore, would be misleading given the stated criteria this study is using. Rather, it is more accurate to characterize McLaren as out of sync with *conservative* Arminianism, which should be distinguished from *orthodox* Arminianism.

[24] Laurence W. Wood, "Divine Omniscience: Boethius or Open Theism?" in *Wesleyan Theological Journal* 45, no. 2 (Fall 2010): 42–48. See also John Wesley, "On Predestination," *The Works of John Wesley*, vol. 6, 3rd ed. (Grand Rapids: Baker, 1978), 225–30, citing 230.

[25] Wood, "Divine Omniscience," 42.

which is one of the motivating factors for adopting this new view.[26] In other words, Wood is honoring the conservative Wesleyan-Arminian principle of revering consensual church tradition when a time-tested position successfully weathers the storms of critical scrutiny.[27] Supporters of the Boethian view argue that God's eternal perspective resolves the problem of human freedom. Since God does not observe one's choice prior to one's deliberating and choosing, but rather views the choice from an eternally timeless perspective, then the choice in question is not determined and human liberty, dignity, and significance are secure.[28]

It is worth noting that Wood believes the Eternal Now view also has the great advantage of aligning with the contemporary scientific consensus.[29] Einstein's space-time relativity theory, which replaced the dominant Newtonian paradigm, affirms that space and time "are inseparably woven together like a single piece of fabric" rather than "two separate entities."[30] One relevant implication for the topic at hand relates to the now well-established belief that a universal clock does not exist. It is true that time is uniform for those who occupy the same space-time inertial frame of reference on earth, but it would slow down considerably for someone traveling through space at nearly the speed of light since the space traveler would be experiencing a different inertial frame of reference. Wood argues that this scientific insight enhances the plausibility of the Eternal Now model: "God has simultaneous knowledge of all time. This does not negate the real, unfolding developments that take place in our Earth time, however. God transcends all inertial frames of reference because God transcends the world as its Creator."[31]

Consequently, defenders of Boethius argue that the Eternal Now position possesses considerable capital: it has the support of tradition, while safeguarding both a robust model of divine omniscience and a libertarian form of human freedom. It has the additional advantage of meshing with

---

[26] Ibid.
[27] Whether or not the Eternal Now view adequately protects libertarian freedom is a matter of ongoing debate.
[28] Linda Zagzebski, *Philosophy of Religion: An Historical Introduction* (Oxford: Blackwell, 2007), 111.
[29] Wood, "Divine Omniscience," 48–66.
[30] Ibid., 50.
[31] Ibid., 50–52.

Einstein's space-time relativity theory. While the debate among Boethians and open theists will undoubtedly continue in Arminian circles, the relevant point here is that by opting for open theism *before* carefully exploring the Boethian position, McLaren is not only at odds with the majority report Arminian position, but arguably with contemporary science as well.[32]

The Six-Line Greco-Roman Hypothesis

McLaren's penchant for constructive theology, however, extends well beyond his endorsement of open theism. In *A New Kind of Christianity*, McLaren argues that the conventional Western Christian storyline of (1) Eden, (2) Fall, (3) Condemnation, (4) Salvation, (5) Heaven, and (6) Hell/Damnation owes more to Greek philosophy and Roman Imperialism than it does to the sacred biblical text.[33] McLaren rejects the Greco-Roman god (Theos) and embraces the Jewish God (Elohim), whom he claims is best understood through the lens of the three-dimensional narrative of creation, liberation, and peaceable kingdom.[34] *A New Kind of Christianity* not only severed McLaren's remaining ties to conservative Evangelicalism, but it also drove a permanent wedge between the emergent and emerging wings of the ECM.[35] The content of McLaren's *magnum opus* also raised serious questions as to whether he could still be properly considered a postconservative evangelical in light of Olson's criteria.

McLaren's deconstructive/reconstructive project is considerably more radical than the openness of God project, although open theism turns out to be a central component in his three-dimensional narrative as well. In this project, McLaren not only goes against consensual church tradition, but he also questions several key conventional doctrines that have been embraced by orthodox Calvinists and Arminians alike.

Scot McKnight, in his review of *A New Kind of Christianity* writes, "Brian is not only poking evangelicals, he is also calling everything about Christian

---

[32] The Boethian position is especially worthy of McLaren's careful consideration since he claims one of the major components of "a new approach to the Bible" must include a proper respect for the best and most current scientific theories. See McLaren, *NKOCY*, 68. For a different perspective on whether contemporary physics supports the Boethian view, see Alan G. Padgett, "Is God Timeless? A Reply to Laurence Wood," *The Asbury Theological Journal* 60, no. 1 (Spring 2005): 5–8.

[33] McLaren, *NKOCY*, 34–45.

[34] Ibid., 46–66.

[35] Phyllis Tickle, *Emergence Christianity* (Grand Rapids: Baker, 2012), 143.

orthodoxy—from the ecumenical creeds through the Reformation and up to present-day evangelicalism—into question."[36] While this statement surely is hyperbolic, McKnight accurately underscores the extreme nature of McLaren's *A New Kind of Christianity* proposal. McLaren calls for a deep, wholesale paradigm shift, rather than the kind of incremental tweaks that he and others have attempted in the past without leaving the confines of the Greco-Roman six-line narrative. McLaren explains,

> In recent years, hundreds of writers, pastors, and thinkers—
> probably thousands—have dared to tweak various elements or
> lines in this story, I among them. We might question conven-
> tional theories of atonement or the nature and population of hell
> or whether concepts like original sin or total depravity need to
> be modified. In other words, we suggest that this line should be
> a little longer, that one a little shorter. But seldom do we ques-
> tion whether this shape as a whole is morally believable and
> whether it can be found in the Bible itself.[37]

McLaren finally came to the point where he had to admit that his "theological lens" was scratched. Consequently, he opted for a new pair of glasses altogether. The pair of glasses that he chose, however, is what put McLaren at loggerheads with both conservative *and* postconservative Arminianism.

In fairness to McLaren, it should be emphasized that he is not proposing an entirely new storyline, but rather an "ancient/future" narrative that he believes is faithful to "the first three centuries of Christian history."[38] Nevertheless, there is a recurring tension that surfaces in McLaren's writings. On the one hand, McLaren affirms and never denies the ecumenical creeds, particularly the Apostles' and Nicene.[39] On the other hand, he is critical of the very church fathers who constructed the creeds, as well as

---

[36] Scot McKnight, "Rebuilding the Faith from Scratch: Brian McLaren's 'New' Christianity Is Not So Much Revolutionary as Evolutionary," *CT* 53, no. 3 (March 2010): 59.

[37] McLaren, *NKOCY*, 35. One example of McLaren doing this can be found in "The Cross as Prophetic Action," in *Proclaiming the Scandal of the Cross*, ed. Mark D. Baker (Grand Rapids: Baker, 2006), 110–21.

[38] Ibid.

[39] Brian McLaren and Scot McKnight, "Brian McLaren: 'Conversations on Being a Heretic,'" *Q Ideas* (website), n. d., accessed June 21, 2014, http://qideas.org/articles/brian-mclaren-conversations -on-being-a-heretic/.

those who subsequently misused the creeds as a "club" of enforcement.[40] He correctly argues that winners write history, and winning a religious debate does not necessarily guarantee Holy Spirit support.[41]

He claims to be standing in the stream of a minority tradition that includes "the desert fathers and mothers, the Celts, the Franciscans, the Anabaptists, the Catholic and Protestant mystics, not to mention the other main wing of the faith known as Eastern Orthodoxy."[42] This support for minority perspectives in church history mirrors his postcolonial sensitivity to contemporary marginalized voices due to oppressive Western colonization and imperialism. In short, McLaren is not dispensing with tradition entirely, and he seeks to honor the ancient ecumenical creeds, yet in good postmodern fashion he is suspicious of those in power and is acutely aware of the church's persistent failure to follow the leading of the Holy Spirit. This creative tension is a hallmark of McLaren's later writings especially.

That said, McKnight is largely unsympathetic to McLaren's *A New Kind of Christianity* project. He accuses McLaren of relying heavily upon the work of modern liberal theologians who blame the downfall of the Christian movement on an unholy alliance with Constantine and subsequent political power brokers.[43] McKnight concludes, "For me, Brian's new kind of Christianity is quite old. And the problem is that it's not old enough."[44] In light of McKnight's critique, Wood's query to open theists is equally apropos at this juncture. We could just as easily reframe the question to McLaren in this manner: "Why has not the church embraced the three-dimensional narrative instead of the six-line narrative in her 2000 years—except for a few individuals?"

This question has force. It is a strong claim to have only now rediscovered the true shape of the biblical narrative. Such a claim is not impossible. After all, the ancient Israelites often lost their way—sometimes in a remarkable fashion. The original disciples frequently appear slow to comprehend what to us now seems obvious. The Crusades, conquistadors,

---

[40] McLaren, *GO*, 28.
[41] Ibid., 29–30.
[42] McLaren, *NKOCY*, 263, ch. 4n1. See also McLaren, *GSM*, 43. In this book, McLaren follows Richard Rohr in calling the minority report tradition "alternative orthodoxy."
[43] McKnight, "Rebuilding the Faith," 60.
[44] Ibid., 66.

slavery, apartheid, and colonialism all testify to the propensity of large swaths of Christians through the centuries to wander off the path as well. Nevertheless, by jettisoning conventional doctrines such as total depravity, the atonement, and eternal damnation, one could argue that McLaren does not lighten the load for his reader as he admirably intends, but rather simply ties different millstones around their necks.[45] In other words, he seems to exchange one set of problems for another.

To accept McLaren's hypothesis—that the majority of the Christian church for the past seventeen hundred years has believed a "barbarous" and "hideous" false gospel narrative—raises several new vexing questions.[46] For instance, what are the implications for divine providence, Holy Spirit guidance, and Christ's concern for the church?[47] If the six-line Greco-Roman hypothesis is true, one wonders if it is "believable" to view the Christian movement as a joint divine-human endeavor (as McLaren claims), with humans serving as junior partners and God as the active senior partner.[48] Would it not seem more accurate to envision the Christian church as a privately owned and operated human religious franchise in which God divested interest centuries ago? McLaren's proposal, at this juncture, seems to be vulnerable to the charge of promoting a kind of deistic indifference.

Additionally, if the vast majority of humans have misunderstood the central message of the Bible, what does this suggest about God's ability to function as a good and faithful communicator?[49] McLaren might answer this final question by saying, "We, like the Pharisees in the Gospels, can never underestimate our power to be wrong about God and God's view of things."[50] Such a response, however, ironically brings us full circle and right back into the neighborhood of one of the doctrines McLaren rejects— namely, total depravity. In light of these questions, it is not altogether unfair to wonder if McLaren's six-line Greco-Roman hypothesis creates more problems than it actually solves.

---

[45] McLaren, *NKOCY*, 35.

[46] Ibid., 44.

[47] H. Orton Wiley and Paul T. Culbertson, *Introduction to Christian Theology*, vol. 1 (Kansas City, MO: Beacon Hill, 1947), 17.

[48] McLaren, *NKOCY*, 47.

[49] Wiley and Culbertson, *Introduction to Christian Theology*, 49.

[50] McLaren, "What Is Justice?" in *JP*, 22.

But McLaren's six-line hypothesis faces additional hurdles. Concerns over syncretism with Greek philosophy and an unholy alliance with Roman political power do not originate with McLaren, as McKnight points out. McLaren actually does take credit, however, for the epiphany of linking the six-line Christian narrative with six Greek themes: (1) Platonic Ideal/Being, (2) Fall into the Cave of Illusion, (3) Aristotelian Real/Becoming, (4) Salvation, (5) Platonic Ideal, and (6) Greek Hades.[51] According to McLaren, this theory originates with him, as far as he can tell.

The steps leading to this realization were described in Chapter Three, but it culminated for McLaren as he was diagraming on a napkin during a meal. McLaren claims many readers have resonated with the six-line Greco-Roman hypothesis; however, he is unaware of any academicians who agree with his theory.[52] While McLaren cites several sources to buttress his criticism of the general hellenization of the Christian faith, his six-line hypothesis, in particular, is out on a tenuous branch by itself without academic support.[53] This should be reason enough to question giving the six-line Greco-Roman narrative hypothesis the central place in his overall apologetic deconstructive strategy.

Additionally, the charge of syncretism with Greek philosophy is itself controversial.[54] It is noteworthy that postconservative Arminian theologian John Sanders, one of the leading advocates for open theism, reversed his position on this issue in the second edition of *The God Who Risks*. Sanders explained, "I have changed my mind concerning the degree to which the early church fathers were negatively influenced by Hellenistic philosophy."[55] He goes on to credit Paul Gavrilyuk's *The Suffering of the Impassible God*, as the key book that changed his mind.[56] Sanders explains,

> One of the main obstacles for me had been the affirmation of divine impassibility by the fathers. From the middle ages until

---

[51] McLaren, *NKOCY*, 41.

[52] Brian McLaren, in discussion with the author, March 20, 2014.

[53] This is an important point to make since the ECM has been committed to the checks and balances that flow from a communal engagement with ideas rather than a lone-ranger approach.

[54] For a helpful discussion of the hellenization of the early Christian church, see Frances M. Young, *The Making of the Creeds* (London: SCM, 1991).

[55] John Sanders, *The God Who Risks*, 2nd ed. (Downers Grove: InterVarsity Press, 2007), 140–41.

[56] Ibid. See Paul Gavrilyuk, *The Suffering of the Impassible God* (Oxford: Oxford University Press, 2004).

today, impassibility has generally meant that God is not affected by creatures. This baffled me because these same fathers also said that God responded to our prayers, was compassionate and even experienced changing emotions. It seemed to me that they contradicted themselves. However, it seems that most of the early church fathers had a different meaning in mind. Though there is no single definition of impassibility in the fathers, generally speaking they meant only that God could not suffer physically since God was not embodied or that God could not be forced to suffer or that God is not overcome by emotions as we are apt to do.[57]

In summary, McLaren hangs much of his emergent apologetic project on the questionable six-line Greco-Roman hypothesis. This decision, however, is an ill-advised apologetic maneuver given the theory's novelty and lack of discernable academic support. That said, McLaren still possesses the necessary resources to advance his hypothesis by appealing to his reconstructed hermeneutic. McLaren believes competing voices exist within Scripture. This is not a problem, McLaren reasons, because the Bible is an inspired portable library in which a plurality of opinions and perspectives are expected. Consequently, it would be perfectly acceptable to suggest that the Bible contains some passages that support the three-dimensional narrative while also containing passages that support the six-line narrative. Ongoing vigorous debate concerning which narrative ultimately best represents the most mature and "morally believable" message of the Bible should be seen as a healthy and productive pursuit both within the canon and among interpreters down through history.[58]

Another advantage of this approach is that this aspect of McLaren's hermeneutic aligns with Wesley's second principle—namely, that Scripture should interpret Scripture. As noted, Wesley believed biblical "wisdom comes out of a broadly based dialogue with a general sense of the whole of Scripture, not a single set of selected verses."[59] While Wesley held to

---

[57] Ibid.
[58] McLaren, *NKOCY*, 81–86.
[59] Oden, *John Wesley's Scriptural Christianity*, 57–58.

the internal coherence of the canon,[60] McLaren points to a deeper form of coherence that emerges when a culture fosters and preserves a plurality of voices around a subject of pressing importance.[61]

It also should be noted that McLaren need not discard his six-line Greco-Roman theory to adopt this strategy. In tandem with this alternative approach, McLaren could still propose the six-line Greco-Roman hypothesis, but simply as an optional theory worthy of ongoing investigation and dialogue, rather than as the nonnegotiable centerpiece of his apologetic. This more modest approach is not only in sync with McLaren's hermeneutic, it also aligns nicely with the "epistemic humility" found in the theological methodology proposed by Arminius.[62] Additionally, it meshes with McLaren's dialogical demeanor, as well as his commitment to a proper confidence and chastened epistemology that characterizes so much of his overall post-critical project.

The Human Condition

According to McLaren, the second line in the Christianized version of the Greco-Roman narrative is "the Fall," which is closely related to total depravity. McLaren asserts, "Nobody in the Hebrew Scriptures ever talked about original sin, total depravity, 'the Fall,' or eternal conscious torment in hell."[63] McLaren argues that the traditional Christian interpretation of "the Fall" and the subsequent alienation between God and humanity expressed through the doctrine of total depravity has more in common with the Greek notion of the perfect realm of forms and "the Fall" into Plato's cave of illusion than it does with the biblical account. According to this narrative, God is repulsed by the depravity of humanity, who now resides in the unsavory world of stories and Aristotelian becoming. McLaren believes this distorted reading of the biblical account makes God look less like Elohim and more like Theos or Zeus.[64] McLaren finds this picture of God unsavory and the

---

[60] Ibid. See also Albert C. Outler, "The Wesleyan Quadrilateral—in John Wesley," *Wesleyan Theological Journal* 20, no. 1 (Spring 1985): 24.

[61] McLaren, *WMRBW*, 59.

[62] Stanglin and McCall point out, "Arminius declared that Christians must acknowledge the difficulty of discovering the truth on all subjects of theology." See Keith D. Stanglin and Thomas H. McCall, *Jacob Arminius: Theologian of Grace* (New York: Oxford University Press, 2012), 206.

[63] McLaren, *NKOCY*, 37.

[64] Ibid., 42–43.

claim of an ontological shift in human nature, as the result of a single act of disobedience, to be rationally and morally untenable.

How does McLaren's rejection of total depravity compare to the traditional orthodox Arminian position? The doctrine of total depravity, while the first point in the Calvinist TULIP, was fully embraced by Wesley.[65] Olson explains how total depravity fits into the Arminian theological system:

> Classical Arminian theology, such as that of John Wesley (1703–1791), affirms the total depravity of human beings and their utter helplessness even to exercise a good will toward God apart from God's supernatural, assisting grace. It attributes the sinner's ability to respond to the gospel with repentance and faith to prevenient grace—the illuminating, convicting, calling, and enabling power of the Holy Spirit working on the sinner's soul and making them free to choose saving grace (or reject it).[66]

Wesley challenged the "optimistic anthropology" of the Enlightenment.[67] If the doctrine of original sin was discarded, he believed the whole basis for Christianity would be stripped away. According to Wesley, original sin is a characteristic of true religion.[68] Only Christianity can explain the ambiguity of humanity, which is capable of goodness because the race was created in the image of God, yet capable of evil due to original sin.[69]

Wesley believed humans, as originally created, possessed the image of God in three distinct ways: the natural image, the political image, and the moral image of God.[70] The *natural image* primarily separated humankind ontologically from the rest of creation. H. Orton Wiley and Paul Culbertson explain, "By virtue of his personality man possesses certain powers, faculties, and characteristics. Among these are three of special significance:

---

[65] Allan Coppedge, *John Wesley in Theological Debate* (Wilmore, KY: Wesley Heritage Press, 1987), 135.

[66] Roger E. Olson, *Against Calvinism* (Grand Rapids: Zondervan, 2011), 67. See also Roger E. Olson, *Arminian Theology* (Downers Grove: InterVarsity Press, 2006), 33.

[67] Stanley J. Grenz and Roger E. Olson, *20th-Century Theology* (Downers Grove: InterVarsity Press, 1992), 17.

[68] Coppedge, *Theological Debate*, 135.

[69] Oden, *John Wesley's Scriptural Christianity*, 155–76.

[70] Wiley and Culbertson, *Introduction to Christian Theology*, 156–57. The authors limit their discussion to the natural and moral image.

spirituality, knowledge, and immortality."[71] The *political image* was the authority entrusted to humanity to govern and exercise dominion over creation. The *moral image* was holiness: the ability to live a righteous life, flowing out of a heart of loving obedience to the divine father.[72] The Fall was a cataclysmic event that fractured the image of God and all of creation. As a result, "man no longer possessed the glory of his moral likeness to God."[73] Adam's sin was imputed to the whole race. Wesley is not clear how this happens, only that it does.[74] Humankind is totally depraved.[75] For Wesley, this understanding of original sin is the basis for justification. Without this belief, there is no reason for the cross. As Oden puts it, "A high doctrine of original sin is the premise and companion of a high doctrine of grace."[76]

While Wesley shared much in common with the reformers, his doctrine of prevenient grace was distinctive. Through prevenient grace, which is offered to all humanity, some measure of libertarian freedom is restored. This makes each person a responsible agent in the process of salvation, yet God receives all the credit since humans are impotent apart from divine grace. Prevenient grace covers the guilt of original sin, makes possible general revelation through creation and conscience, and becomes saving grace for those who are not morally responsible. For Wesley, prevenient grace holds together two key Christian concepts: total depravity and freedom of the will. All humanity is fallen yet still responsible.[77]

Wesley's notion of prevenient grace is what keeps the charges of Pelagianism or semi-Pelagianism at bay. In fact, Chris Bounds argues that the affirmation of prevenient grace places Wesley squarely in the semi-Augustinian camp.[78] For Wesley, grace is what makes possible a free

---

[71] Ibid.

[72] Ibid., 158.

[73] Ibid., 164–65.

[74] Oden, *John Wesley's Scriptural Christianity*, 158.

[75] Wiley and Culbertson, *Introduction to Christian Theology*, 177.

[76] Oden, *John Wesley's Scriptural Christianity*, 169.

[77] See Wiley and Culbertson, *Introduction to Christian Theology*, 261–63, and Oden, *John Wesley's Scriptural Christianity*, 243–52.

[78] Bounds argues that semi-Augustinianism is an expression of divine-human synergism, while semi-Pelagianism does not represent historic Wesleyan-Arminianism because it is an expression of human-divine synergism. See Christopher T. Bounds, "How Are People Saved? The Major Views of Salvation with a Focus on Wesleyan Perspectives and Their Implications," *Wesley and Methodist Studies*, vol. 3 (Spring 2011): 31–54, citing 52–53.

libertarian response to God. Allan Coppedge explains the central importance of this doctrine in Wesley's theology:

> First, it made it possible for him to say that man in no way
> merits his own salvation; he is completely dependent on God
> for his redemption. Secondly, the concept of prevenient grace
> provided a basis for human responsibility. . . . Thus, Wesley
> provided a balance between Calvinism on the one side, which
> emphasized that salvation was completely God's work, and the
> Pelagians on the other, who stressed the freedom of man and
> his attendant responsibility. By means of a prevenient grace that
> is universally provided for all mankind, God receives all the
> glory for man's redemption, even his ability to exercise faith and
> receive salvation.[79]

While Wesley avoided Pelagianism in its various permutations, the same cannot be said for McLaren.[80] By rejecting the traditional doctrine of total depravity, McLaren is vulnerable to the charge of Pelagianism, or at least semi-Pelagianism, and consequently out of step with orthodox Arminianism.[81]

McLaren's position is similar to that of Philip Limborch (1633–1712), who was a later Remonstrant leader. Unlike Arminius, Limborch denied total depravity. According to Olson, Limborch believed "humans after Adam are born without guilt or such corruption as would make actual, presumptuous sinning inevitable."[82] Limborch believed "a network of sin within the human race seduces people to commit actual sins."[83] This is

---

[79] Coppedge, *Theological Debate*, 137.

[80] This charge of Pelagianism does not concern McLaren, however. In an email exchange with the author, McLaren admitted that he "never studied Arminius, nor did I study Pelagius. If I were to do so today, I would keep my eyes open for ways their views were trying to open up political space against the domination of Calvin's Dutch successors and Augustine's imperial affinities." In other words, McLaren would be more concerned with the broader sociological and political context of the day than the actual theological and philosophical content that was debated within the Christianized version of the six-line Greco-Roman narrative. Brian McLaren, email message to author, March 25, 2014.

[81] Olson, *Arminian Theology*, 137–57. Olson points out that while Limborch was inconsistent at times in his published writings, the overall tenor of his work points to liberal Arminianism. See also Thomas C. Oden, *The Transforming Power of Grace* (Nashville: Abingdon, 1993), 108–24.

[82] Olson, *Arminian Theology*, 147.

[83] Ibid.

comparable to Girard's mimetic theory in that original sin is grounded in social dynamics rather than in genetic transmission. Limborch's form of Arminianism differs from the orthodox Arminianism that can be traced back to Arminius. Olson emphasizes, "It is important to mark a clear line between true, classical Arminianism and Remonstrantism that follows Limborch and later Arminians of the head, most of whom became deists, Unitarians and free thinkers."[84]

The Person and Work of Christ

While McLaren personally affirms the divinity, death, and bodily resurrection of Christ, he consistently emphasizes the kingdom of God teachings and example of Jesus in his writings. In this section, this study will compare McLaren's views with orthodox Arminianism in three areas: the divinity of Christ, the atonement, and the resurrection of Christ.

The Divinity of Christ

Not surprisingly, Wesley never tired of using creedal language in his discussion of Christ's nature.[85] According to Oden, "Wesley at no point hinted that there is a needed purification, progression or remodeling of ancient ecumenical Christological definitions."[86] He honored the classic roles of Christ "as prophet, priest, and king."[87] McLaren affirms the deity of Christ; however, due to his temporal kingdom of God lens, he tends to focus more on the humanity of Jesus and his role as prophet of social justice and initiator of a countercultural kingdom. This is particularly evident in his approach to interfaith dialogue. Instead of challenging adherents of other religions to embrace the divinity of Christ, he encourages them to focus on the facets of the life and teachings of Jesus that their respective religions honor. In so doing, McLaren hopes a common ground surrounding the ethical teachings of Jesus will provide a much-needed starting point in cultivating empathy, trust, and a more peaceful shared local and global existence.[88]

---

[84] Ibid., 148. For Olson, "Arminians of the head" is another way of referring to Arminians who embraced Liberalism. See also Coppedge, *Theological Debate*, 36.

[85] Oden, *John Wesley's Scriptural Christianity*, 177.

[86] Ibid.

[87] Ibid., 187. See also Kenneth J. Collins, *A Faithful Witness: John Wesley's Homiletical Theology* (Wilmore, KY: Wesley Heritage, 1993), 44–56.

[88] McLaren, *SMJ*, 7–8 .

McLaren is not alone when it comes to bridge-building strategies in the realm of interfaith dialogue and apologetics. C. S. Lewis believed Christianity is not the only religion that possesses legitimate revelation but is rather the pinnacle of divine disclosure.[89] Christians should acknowledge and honor truth, beauty, and goodness wherever it is found—in other religions and even in pagan philosophy and mythology.[90] This generous view of revelation is evidence of God's goodness and care for people in all cultures, at all times.[91] Nevertheless, Lewis was convinced that the fullest expression of God's revelation could be found in the person of Jesus Christ, God incarnate.

This conviction that Jesus of Nazareth stands as a unique historical figure informs Lewis's arguably best-known apologetic argument, the trilemma (i.e., lord, liar, or lunatic).[92] In this argument, Lewis seeks to logically demonstrate that Jesus could not have been what most non-Christians (and most proponents of liberal theology in Lewis's day) claim him to be—a great human moral teacher, but not divine. The force of the argument attempts to prove that given Jesus's extraordinary claim to divinity, either he was who he claimed to be—God in the flesh—or he was morally or mentally unsound (i.e., liar or lunatic). The one thing he logically could not have been in light of his lofty claims to monotheistic divinity was a merely great human moral teacher.[93]

Exploring the soundness of Lewis's argument is beyond the scope of this study. Instead, what is germane to this discussion is noticing how both McLaren and Lewis view people of other faiths with a generous inclusivity. Lewis's generous inclusivity, however, inevitably leads to a stark, unavoidable, exclusive either-or proposition. Either Jesus is God or he was a morally or mentally bankrupt human being, unworthy of reverence. In

---

[89] C. S. Lewis, *The Problem of Pain* (New York: Macmillan, 1962), 23–24.

[90] C. S. Lewis, *Reflections on the Psalms* (New York: Harcourt Brace, 1958), 85–89.

[91] C. S. Lewis, "Christian Apologetics" in *God in the Dock* (Grand Rapids: Eerdmans, 1970), 91–101.

[92] C. S. Lewis, *Mere Christianity*, 3rd ed. (New York: Macmillan, 1952), 54–56.

[93] The trilemma can be challenged from many angles, including the common liberal perspective that Jesus never claimed divinity. According to this view, the apparent claims to divinity found in the gospel accounts were the work of early followers who sought to elevate Jesus to the status of divinity. For a discussion of these challenges to the trilemma, see Peter Kreeft and Ronald K. Tacelli, *Handbook of Christian Apologetics* (Downers Grove: InterVarsity Press, 1994), 150–74. Kreeft and Tacelli expand the trilemma to a quintilemma: lord, liar, lunatic, myth, or guru, and they then proceed to offer a response to each of these challenges.

contrast, McLaren's generous inclusivity stops well short of such an exclusive proclamation. McLaren heartily agrees that Jesus is universally respected among world religions as a "great prophet," "a legitimate manifestation of the divine," and "one of humanity's most enlightened people."[94] McLaren concurs with Lewis that this universal admiration for the founder and centerpiece of the Christian religion raises Jesus to a place of unique honor. This, however, is where Lewis and McLaren part ways.

Lewis uses this shared reverence for Jesus across faith systems as an opportunity to confront people with a difficult choice—either Jesus was God or a bad person. This approach humbles, perhaps even embarrasses, the conversation partner by logically exposing the folly of honoring Jesus as a great moral teacher without bowing the knee to his divinity. McLaren, on the other hand, is not looking to conquer, divide, debate, exclude, or call sinners to salvation within the old six-line Greco-Roman narrative. Since eternal damnation is not a serious concern, McLaren seeks to unite people of all faiths to address pressing global problems of creation care, social justice, and economic equity.[95]

McLaren's focus is practical and pragmatic, but no less significant in his mind given his temporal rather than eternal soteriological grid. To press the implications of Lewis's trilemma would undermine McLaren's kingdom of God apologetic project of peace, justice, and equity. These competing approaches to interfaith dialogue illustrate not only a difference between Lewis and McLaren, but also important distinctions between hard apologetic modern and soft apologetic postmodern sensibilities.

The Atonement

McLaren defines salvation as personal and social "liberation," as his three-dimensional narrative makes clear.[96] Consequently, he rejects the claim that "Jesus came to solve the problem of 'original sin.'"[97] For McLaren, the cross is fundamentally about reconciliation rather than atoning for

---

94 McLaren, *SMJ*, 7.
95 McLaren, *EMC*, 269–301.
96 McLaren, *NKOCY*, 65.
97 McLaren, *EMC*, 79. See also McLaren, *JMBM*, 106.

humanity's sin. It is where Christ most clearly models the absorption of pain, mistreatment, and betrayal in lieu of revenge.[98]

McLaren offers helpful insights into the nature of the cross that are consistent with the orthodox Arminian vision of reality, such as divine solidarity with human suffering and the powerful example of nonviolent resistance. His outright rejection of not only the forensic penal substitutionary theory, but of the concept of atonement in general as a valid contemporary Christian doctrinal category, however, is a clear departure.

McLaren once again finds himself in the minority stream of Christian tradition, as Oden makes clear: "Few points of ecumenical teaching have received such wide consensus as the premise that Christ's death was a sacrifice for the sin of others."[99] McKnight puts this point in stark terms: "The atonement, in other words, is the good news of Christianity—it is our gospel. It explains how that gospel works."[100] Elsewhere, McKnight writes as if he is describing McLaren: "Others focus exclusively on the kingdom vision of Jesus, with the result that atonement becomes little more than liberation; few would want to deny the importance of freedom, but atonement is more than that."[101]

Instead of focusing on just one particular facet of the atonement, McKnight believes the correct approach is similar to a round of golf that requires the skillful utilization of a range of clubs as the lie of the ball and shape of the course demand. In other words, one must be missiologically savvy when discussing the atonement. Every theory has its time and place, depending upon the missiological context. This approach dovetails nicely with the kind of ad hoc apologetics discussed in Chapter Six. McKnight elaborates, "The game of atonement requires that players understand the value of each club as well as the effort needed to carry a bag big enough and defined enough so that one knows where each club fits in that bag."[102]

Oden also underscores the diversity of metaphors used in Scripture to describe the atonement. Oden claims that there are "four spheres from

---

[98] McLaren, *WMRBW*, 160. See also McLaren, *GO*, 97.
[99] Thomas C. Oden, *The Word of Life: Systematic Theology Volume Two* (New York: HarperCollins, 1992), 385.
[100] Scot McKnight, *A Community Called Atonement* (Nashville: Abingdon, 2007), 1.
[101] Ibid., 15–16.
[102] Ibid., xiii.

which metaphors for understanding salvation were largely taken . . . liberation of slaves, the fair procedures of a courtroom, the loss of a family member, and the sacrifice offered at the Temple."[103] In light of the diversity of biblical metaphors, Olson argues that there is no standard Arminian theory of the atonement, although all orthodox Arminians affirm the fact of Christ's atoning sacrifice for humanity's sin.[104]

Wiley and Culbertson explain why Christ's atoning death was necessary: "God could not in His wisdom and holiness and goodness affix a penalty to a law, and then permit disobedience to pass with impunity. Without some external intervention, the whole human race would have been hopelessly and eternally lost."[105] Oden underscores the climactic nature of the cross: "The work of [Jesus's] life is consummated in the atoning deed of his death, to be a sacrifice not only covering and redeeming our primordial guilt inherited from the history of sin, but also the actual sin resulting from our free decisions and collusions."[106] McKnight argues that believers are free to choose from a range of metaphors when discussing the nature of the atonement; however, denying the necessity of Christ's sacrifice is not an option.

McLaren's view of the cross, consequently, has more in common with Socinianism than orthodox Arminianism.[107] According to Wiley and Culbertson, Laelius and Faustus Socinus first proposed this particular expression of the moral influence theory in the seventeenth century as an alternative to the penal substitutionary theory, which is also McLaren's primary target. These authors contend that Socinianism "denies any idea of propitiation or satisfaction. It holds that Christ's death was merely that of a noble martyr, whose loyalty to truth and faithfulness to duty, furnish us with a noble incentive to moral improvement."[108] The theory insists that "God is free to forgive sin without any satisfaction to divine justice."

---

[103] Oden, *Word of Life*, 357.

[104] Olson, *Arminian Theology*, 238. For a survey of the diversity of thinking regarding atonement theories among Arminians, see 221–41.

[105] Wiley and Culbertson, *Introduction to Christian Theology*, 219.

[106] Oden, *John Wesley's Scriptural Christianity*, 181.

[107] Many Socinians were Unitarians. While McLaren is friendly toward Unitarians, his writing exhibits a consistent commitment to Trinitarianism. For instance, see McLaren, *JMBM*, 125–32.

[108] Wiley and Culbertson, *Introduction to Christian Theology*, 231.

Wiley and Culbertson conclude, "It is evident that this theory, instead of explaining, merely denies the necessity of the atonement."[109]

The Resurrection of Christ

This study has confirmed McLaren's belief in the bodily resurrection of Christ. It also points out that he has rarely discussed this central doctrine in his books. Additionally, this study identifies similarities between McLaren's use of narrative and the postliberal employment of realistic narrative. As Wood explains, "Realistic narrative is not concerned with what history is real and what is not. Stated simply, 'realistic narrative' is retelling the story as literally presented in the text itself without subjecting it to critical examination based on modern historical methods."[110] Based on this definition, however, it is clear that McLaren is not completely in step with the postliberal view on this point since he self-identifies his engagement with Scripture as "a personal/critical/literary approach."[111] In so doing, McLaren has "complete freedom to ask questions about the Bible's sources, development, internal tensions, biases, accuracy, cultural context, and genre."[112]

That said, McLaren does seem to approach the New Testament miracle accounts, including the resurrection of Jesus, in a postliberal manner in *We Make the Road by Walking*. He does not assume that all of his readers believe in miracles.[113] For McLaren, this does not pose a problem. Rather than insisting on the historical texture of the miracle accounts, he simply poses the following question: "What happens to us when we imagine miracles happening?"[114] In other words, McLaren's focus seems to be on the transformative power of an engaged imagination rather than the transformative power of a literal risen Christ.

Wiley and Culbertson represent the orthodox Arminian position when they write, "The historical fact of the resurrection is intensely significant."[115]

---

[109] Ibid.

[110] Laurence W. Wood, *Theology as History and Hermeneutics* (Lexington: Emeth Press, 2005), 153.

[111] Brian McLaren, "The Problem Isn't the Bible," *Patheos* (website), June 18, 2014, http://www.patheos.com/Topics/2014-Religious-Trends/Progressive-Christian/The-Problem-Isnt-the-Bible-Brian-McLaren-06182014.html.

[112] Ibid.

[113] McLaren, *WMRBW*, 97.

[114] Ibid.

[115] Wiley and Culbertson, *Introduction to Christian Theology*, 211. McLaren influence Lesslie Newbigin also discusses the importance of a historical bodily resurrection: "If, in fact, the tomb

The authors explain that Christ's resurrection "was not merely a return from the grave to the same natural status, it was a transcendent event."[116] Therefore, among other things, the historical resurrection of Christ "furnishes the ground for our justification," confirms "Christ's prophetic ministry," explains "the complete and instantaneous change which took place in the minds of the disciples," and becomes "the guaranty of our future resurrection."[117] Wesleyan-Arminian apologist William Lane Craig agrees: "The earliest Christians saw Jesus' resurrection as both the vindication of his personal claims and as the harbinger of our own resurrection to eternal life. If Jesus rose from the dead, then his claims are vindicated and our Christian hope is sure; if Jesus did not rise, our faith is futile and we fall back into despair."[118]

According to Wood, the attempt of Hans Frei and George Lindbeck (and, it would appear, McLaren as well), to separate the historicity of the text from the story itself creates an unstable "dualism of hermeneutics and history."[119] Wood calls this dualism "the *textuality of Jesus* and the *historicity of Jesus*."[120] Wood appreciates how "'realistic narrative' has focused the need to listen to the Bible on its own terms, and this is an important advance over modernist theology."[121] Nevertheless, there is reason for legitimate concern. Wood has issued an appropriate word of caution at this juncture.

Christianity is a historical space-time religion, which cannot be reduced to a set of moral precepts, an engaging story, or philosophical propositions. Arminian orthodoxy honors the Bible as a record of God's historical interaction with the nation of Israel and subsequently the early Christian church.

---

was not empty on that Sunday morning, then the crucifixion of Jesus has to be understood quite differently from the way it is to be understood if the tomb was empty." Lesslie Newbigin, *Proper Confidence* (Grand Rapids: Eerdmans, 1995), 77.

[116] Wiley and Culbertson, *Introduction to Christian Theology*, 212.

[117] Ibid., 211–12.

[118] William Lane Craig, *Reasonable Faith* (Wheaton: Crossway, 1984), 255. Craig also presents multiple arguments for the historical resurrection of Jesus, 255–98.

[119] Wood, *Theology as History and Hermeneutics*, 157. Robert Greer argues that Lindbeck fully affirms the reality of Christ's resurrection. He explains, "Lindbeck did not intend the term 'history-like' to take the side of theological Liberalism and argue for the possible fiction of Jesus, the Christ-event, etc. That would have put Lindbeck in the middle of the very debate he was attempting to avoid. Rather, the term was intended to keep the theologian off balance, rendering irrelevant the modernist agendas of the two camps." See Robert C. Greer, *Mapping Postmodernism* (Downers Grove: InterVarsity Press, 2003), 149.

[120] Wood, *Theology as History and Hermeneutics*, 157.

[121] Ibid., 155.

If the space-time character of the central creedal doctrines of incarnation, atonement, and resurrection is discarded, then the entire Christian narrative takes on an alien shape.

Eschatology

In this final section, McLaren's rejection of the doctrine of eternal damnation will be considered in light of orthodox Arminian teaching. In conjunction with this issue, the fate of the unevangelized also will be explored.

Hell and Rethinking Eternal Damnation

McLaren attempts to deconstruct the conventional doctrine of hell in the *The Last Word and the Word After That*. In the introduction, he explains his fundamental motivation for writing the book:

> As I see it, more significant than any doctrine of hell itself is the view of God to which one's doctrine of hell contributes. William Temple once said that if your concept of God is radically false, the more devoted you are, the worse off you will be. So this book is in the end more about our view of God than it is about our understandings of hell. What kind of God do we believe exists? What kind of life would we live in response? How does our view of God affect the way we see and treat other people? And how does the way we see and treat other people affect our view of God?[122]

McLaren believes that the concept of eternal conscious torment was introduced into Jewish consciousness during the intertestamental period through Mesopotamian, Egyptian, Zoroastrian, and Greek sources.[123] McLaren argues through the characters in *The Last Word and the Word After That* that Jesus did not believe in a literal hell, but rather used this language as a rhetorical device to challenge the religious leaders of the day.[124]

---

[122] McLaren, *LWWAT*, xii.
[123] Ibid., 49–73.
[124] Ibid., 74–81.

In *A New Kind of Christianity*, he extends this argument and places hell and eternal damnation within the broader six-line Greco-Roman narrative.[125]

The beginning of this chapter discusses Grenz's review of *The Last Word and the Word After That*. While Grenz had several positive things to say about the final installment in the *New Kind of Christian* series, he fears McLaren's "stylized approach" to the doctrine of hell could mute the work of those "who are attempting to provide cogent, biblical, and helpful ways of speaking about eternal estrangement from God."[126]

While Grenz does not list particular scholars who are engaging this eschatological subject matter in a responsible, creative, and nuanced manner, one contemporary example is Jerry Walls, the author of *Hell: The Logic of Damnation*. Walls joins McLaren in rejecting unconditional election and reprobation on moral grounds, but rather than jettisoning belief in eternal damnation, he presents a carefully reasoned construal of eternal separation that seeks to safeguard both divine goodness and human freedom.[127] It is noteworthy that while McLaren cites Walls in *The Last Word and the Word After That*,[128] *Hell: The Logic of Damnation* is absent from his survey of historical and contemporary academic literature on this subject matter.

While McLaren consistently equates hell with eternal conscious torment, he does not carefully consider other articulations of eternal separation from God. In so doing, he succumbs to the same type of false dichotomy that he so frequently and forcefully critiques throughout his corpus.[129] Walls, on the other hand, offers a rigorous argument that is a fitting left-brain complement to Lewis's imaginative eschatological fantasy, *The Great Divorce*.[130]

---

[125] McLaren, *NKOCY*, 34–45.

[126] Grenz, "Review of *LWWAT*," 665.

[127] Walls also joined McLaren as two of the experts interviewed in the documentary *Hellbound?* See *Hellbound?*, dir. Kevin Miller (Abbotsford, BC, Canada: Kevin Miller XI Productions, 2012), DVD.

[128] McLaren, *LWWAT*, 97. McLaren quotes Walls without a reference as saying, "If there is no God, no heaven, no hell, there simply is no persuasive reason to be moral." In correspondence with this author, McLaren confirms his respect for Walls and regret for overlooking his influential treatment entitled *Hell: The Logic of Damnation* (Notre Dame, IN: University of Notre Dame Press, 1992). Brian McLaren, email message to author, January 6, 2006.

[129] D. A. Carson points out McLaren's tendency to set up false antitheses in *Becoming Conversant with the Emerging Church* (Grand Rapids: Zondervan, 2004), 129.

[130] C. S. Lewis, *The Great Divorce* (New York: Macmillan, 1946). McLaren briefly discusses *The Great Divorce* in his commentary in the back of *LWWAT*. He mentions the "'locked from the inside'

In this defense of eternal estrangement, Walls understands the biblical imagery of fire and darkness as metaphorical rather than a literal, physical description of hell.[131] He notes that "John Wesley also took the worm to be a reference to the guilty conscience the damned will suffer, but he further elaborated on the idea, suggesting that it likewise represents several other distressing feelings and passions."[132] Instead of a literal "lake of fire," in which the damned experience physical torture without end for all of eternity, Walls follows Lewis in viewing eternal separation as disintegration and isolation.[133] The damned choose not to cooperate with the grace that God has extended to them. Consequently, they drift further away from the only source of hope, joy, love, peace, goodness, relationality, and wholeness. In so doing, their entire being unravels. Lacking the unifying and transformative dynamic of divine grace, such creatures eventually must endure the implications of their temporal choices and live an eternally wispy, unsubstantial existence that is a reflection of the character they have developed. God works with every person as long as there remains a spark to fan into flame.[134]

God respects the libertarian freedom and dignity of human creatures. Consequently, "each makes up his own individual world of self-inflicted suffering."[135] Grace is extended to all, but God will not override the choices of those who prefer their own selfish desires. In this vision of the afterlife, God does not unconditionally elect the reprobate for damnation. Walls and McLaren both reject the Calvinistic underbelly of unconditional election. Walls and McLaren are also united in rejecting the cruel picture of the damned simmering in a literal, eternal lake of fire. Additionally, Walls and McLaren are equally committed to finding a vision of the afterlife that does justice to the character of God and the dignity of humanity.

---

view of Dallas Willard and C. S. Lewis," but ultimately sides with Newbigin, who believes these are attempts at "trying to answer questions that aren't the best questions to ask." McLaren, *LWWAT*, 188.

[131] Walls, *Hell*, 139–55. For further consensual support of interpreting this imagery as metaphorical, see Thomas C. Oden, *Life in the Spirit* (New York: HarperCollins, 1992), 452.

[132] Walls, *Hell*, 141. Walls also discusses the views of Augustine, Aquinas, and Calvin, noting that "Augustine is concerned to establish the case that the fire of hell is real material fire and is used by God as a means to punish the wicked in their bodies," while "later theologians . . . further developed and emphasized the spiritual dimension of the torment of hell."

[133] Ibid., 145.

[134] Lewis, *Great Divorce*, 96.

[135] Walls, *Hell*, 145.

The difference, however, is that Walls remains convinced that hell is an integral and nonnegotiable part of the Christian story because Jesus himself seemed to embrace it[136] and libertarian freedom seems to demand it. Walls explains,

> A little reflection reveals, however, that the doctrine of hell is closer to the heart of the traditional Christian belief than we may initially think. This is most evident when we recall that Christianity is primarily a scheme of salvation. Its main thrust is a message of how we can be saved from our sins and receive eternal life. Salvation, however, is not inevitable. One may choose to remain in sin and resist God's offer of salvation. Here is where hell comes in: it is the alternative to salvation.[137]

Because God honors libertarian freedom, there must be an alternative when one rejects the divine offer of salvation. McLaren's proposal, however, calls into question one of the key themes woven throughout his own corpus—namely, libertarian freedom. McLaren does not address how libertarian freedom and human integrity are safeguarded in a narrative that does not provide an alternative to eternal salvation.

Additionally, Walls believes that the traditional notion of salvation is accompanied by a "sense of urgency and moral seriousness," and it offers a vision of "the majesty and glory of God's work to save his fallen children."[138] Removing eternal damnation from the narrative completely alters the shape of the Christian storyline, as McLaren also is keenly aware. Walls draws out the implication: "If Christianity is indeed about salvation, and if salvation comes to mean something very different when hell drops out of sight, then the doctrine of hell is an important part of Christianity. Indeed, it may be essential, at least in some form, if Christianity is to avoid trivialization."[139]

---

[136] Jerry L. Walls, "Will God Change His Mind? Eternal Hell and the Ninevites," in *Through No Fault of Their Own*, ed. William V. Crockett and James G. Sigountos (Grand Rapids: Baker, 1991), 61.

[137] Walls, *Hell*, 7.

[138] Ibid.

[139] Ibid. "Trivialization" seems like an overstatement here. McLaren would surely argue that his project of promoting a temporal kingdom of God vision is hardly trivial in light of the world crises and injustices that need to be addressed.

It is beyond the scope of this study to explore Walls's provocative and penetrating vision of the afterlife in detail.[140] His argument is introduced at this juncture for the purpose of simply suggesting another viable Arminian resource that McLaren could have accessed in his quest to cogently challenge the Calvinist doctrine of unconditional election. In so doing, McLaren could have adopted a view of eternal estrangement that is consistent with the goodness of God, human libertarian freedom, and his deepest, most certain moral intuitions without jettisoning a commitment to consensual Christian tradition. Walls's responsible engagement with this difficult subject matter is the kind of "cogent, biblical, and helpful" resource that might help not only McLaren, but also those who have been hindered by the "stylized approach" that Grenz cautioned against.[141]

Fate of the Unevangelized

Regarding the fate of the unevangelized, a central assertion of both orthodox Arminianism and Calvinism is that Jesus is the only way to God. If this is so, then the question of what happens to those who die without hearing the gospel is both poignant and puzzling. Throughout his writings, however, McLaren echoes the sentiments of Lesslie Newbigin by discouraging such ponderings as pointless.[142] The clear message is that believers should focus on their own salvation rather than wonder about the eternal status of someone else's soul. Newbigin cites Jesus's chastisement of the disciples' improper curiosity as a precedent.[143]

In *A Generous Orthodoxy*, McLaren uses the following vignette to illustrate his discomfort with engaging this question: "Imagine you are driving down a country road, on a journey west from New York to Los Angeles. You find yourself at a flashing red light somewhere in South Florida. You can turn left, turn right, or go straight. . . . None of the roads leads in the

---

[140] For a popular treatment, see Jerry L. Walls, *Heaven, Hell, and Purgatory* (Grand Rapids: Brazos, 2015). In the endorsements that appear on the back cover and opening pages of this book, John Stackhouse writes, "No one in our time has worked more diligently to understand heaven, hell, purgatory and the related cluster of issues than has Jerry Walls." Francis Beckwith adds, "Jerry Walls shows once again that on the four last things—death, judgment, hell, and heaven—he is by far the most thoughtful evangelical philosopher."

[141] Grenz, "Review of *LWWAT*," 665.

[142] See McLaren, *NKOC*, 85, and *GO*, 113.

[143] McLaren, *LWWAT*, 103.

general direction of Los Angeles. What do you do? Which road do you take? *What are you doing in Florida anyway?*"[144] McLaren claims that this is how he "feels when I'm offered a choice between the roads of exclusivism (only confessing Christians go to heaven), universalism (everyone goes to heaven), and inclusivism (Christians go to heaven, plus at least some others)."

He acknowledges that each option has strengths and weaknesses; however, "none of them is the road of my missional calling: blessed in this life to be a blessing to everyone on earth."[145] In *The Last Word and the Word After That*, McLaren, through a character named Casey, also ties Newbigin's notion of "elect for privilege" to this kind of "improper and disobedient" speculation. She writes, "Our approach . . . should be predicamental: we should focus on ourselves—believing, following, doing the will of God, joining God in his mission, coming to the light, etc."[146] One can appreciate McLaren's sense of missional calling to focus on the temporal needs and crises of this world. Indeed, a robust Arminian theology heartily endorses his emphasis on election for service rather than for privilege. Nevertheless, McLaren's perspective on this subject is vulnerable to critique in three areas.

First, inclusivism is improperly defined. The definitions that McLaren offers are excessively terse and, additionally, the inclusivist definition is inaccurate. Inclusivism does not offer an estimate regarding how many unevangelized people might end up in heaven. To define inclusivism as "Christians go to heaven, plus at least some others" is misleading. According to inclusivism, every unevangelized person could respond favorably to the gospel and go to heaven. Certainly, that would be consistent with this "wider hope" position.[147]

Inclusivists believe salvation only comes through Jesus; however, this does not necessarily mean a person must consciously and explicitly embrace the gospel in this life to be saved. Since some die without a legitimate chance to receive the gospel, God either will provide such an opportunity to respond to the gospel after this earthly existence or will judge people

[144] McLaren, *GO*, 113.
[145] Ibid.
[146] McLaren, *LWWAT*, 103.
[147] John Sanders, *No Other Name* (Grand Rapids: Eerdmans, 1992), 131.

according to the light they have received during this life.[148] According to the standard inclusivist position, no one will be excluded due to a lack of information. Therefore, it is theoretically possible that all people will eventually exercise their libertarian freedom in a responsible way and end up in heaven.

Second, McLaren exhibits categorical confusion on this issue. McLaren (and perhaps Newbigin as well) has seemingly missed the primary point regarding the "fate of the unevangelized" discussion.[149] Jesus reprimanded the disciples for asking about the future destiny of a particular person. The "fate of the unevangelized" debate, however, is a categorically different matter altogether. Instead of idle conjecture regarding the status of a particular person's eternal soul, this discussion is a corollary to a much larger theoretical issue: the problem of evil.[150]

The real issue at stake is the nature of God's character. If God is all-powerful and perfectly good, then why should anyone pass into eternity without an opportunity to hear and respond to the gospel? If God is all-powerful (which includes infinite wisdom, creativity, and ingenuity), then God possesses the ability to make sure every person hears the gospel through some means. And if God is perfectly good, then he would be motivated to implement such a plan. Yet billions of people have lived and died without hearing the gospel and passed into eternity without knowledge of the only means by which they could have been saved. In other words, it would appear that either God is incapable of providing a way of salvation that is accessible to all people in this life, or God is not motivated to do so. Either way, one is left with a sub-biblical view of God. A thoughtful response to this dilemma is an especially worthwhile pursuit for those who, like McLaren, have a burden for defending the goodness of God.

---

[148] For a discussion of various theories suggested by the wider hope or inclusivist position, see John Sanders, "Inclusivism," in *What About Those Who Have Never Heard?*, ed. John Sanders (Downers Grove: InterVarsity Press, 1995), 21–55. See also Sanders, *No Other Name*, 131–286, and Clark H. Pinnock, *A Wideness in God's Mercy* (Grand Rapids: Zondervan, 1992), 157–75.

[149] McLaren's interpretation of Newbigin in this context is especially germane. Whether McLaren's interpretation is entirely faithful to Newbigin's intent is beyond the scope of this study. For one of Newbigin's discussions of this subject, see Lesslie Newbigin, *The Gospel in a Pluralist Society* (Grand Rapids: Eerdmans, 1989), 177–83.

[150] John Sanders, "Introduction," in *What About Those Who Have Never Heard?*, 8.

Third, McLaren offers a false dichotomy. It is ironic that McLaren, who is characterized by openness to inquiry on almost any subject, proposes a "don't ask, don't tell" policy on this issue.[151] Neo becomes impatient with Dan Poole when Dan is not satisfied with the answers his mentor provides on this subject. Neo chastises Dan like Jesus corrected his disciples. But why should this particular question related to the fate of the unevangelized elicit such a response when every other question is fair game for McLaren and those who have benefitted from the open, conversational nature of emergence Christianity? This seems like a fair question. The problem appears to be associating this subject matter with an "elect for privilege" attitude rather than using our energy and election for service. This categorical confusion, in turn, leads to a false dichotomy.

There is no logical or existential tension between rigorously engaging the problem of evil on the one hand and serving missionally on the other. Once one sees that this question is not idle conjecture regarding a particular person's eternal destiny, but rather a legitimate inquiry regarding the character of God, it becomes clear that this topic actually dovetails into a missional mindset. This is especially so when one realizes that the fate of the unevangelized is, according to John Sanders, "Far and away . . . the most-asked apologetic question on U.S. college campuses."[152] If this is the most asked apologetic question, then it is our missional responsibility to offer a compelling and satisfying response. For McLaren, who self-identifies as an evangelist at heart, this is a missed opportunity to correct a common misconception of divine exclusivity and offer an alternative vision of God's compelling inclusive character.[153]

---

[151] It is especially surprising that McLaren, who possesses postconservative constructivist sensitivities, would not only reject inclusivism but the also the right of fellow believers to probe the "fate of the unevangelized" question with fresh perspective and moral sensitivity.

[152] Sanders, "Introduction," in *What About Those Who Have Never Heard?*, 7.

[153] Brian McLaren, email message to author, July 20, 2009. Wesley and McLaren both can be construed as "evangelists at heart." Wesley, however, never wavered from the priority of saving souls, while McLaren focuses on the temporal soteriological implications of the gospel. See Patrick S. Franklin, "John Wesley in Conversation with the Emerging Church," *The Asbury Journal* 63, no. 1 (2008): 77–79.

The inclusivist position is the option chosen by most Arminians, including Wesley,[154] C. S. Lewis, Clark Pinnock, Walls, and Sanders.[155] It is also the position adopted by many postconservative evangelicals.[156] This view makes room for a universal call, but insists upon an individual libertarian response to secure salvation. Advocates of this view argue that it safeguards the goodness of God, as well as the freedom and dignity of humanity. Additionally, it does not insist that anyone will ultimately experience eternal estrangement since such a choice is left up to each libertarian creature. In short, the Arminian position again provides the necessary resources to address McLaren's concerns.

---

[154] For a discussion of Wesley's inclusivist position, see Randy L. Maddox, "Wesley and the Question of Truth or Salvation through Other Religions," *Wesleyan Theological Journal* 27 (1992): 7–29, and Philip R. Meadows, "Candidates for Heaven: Wesleyan Resources for a Theology of Religions," *Wesleyan Theological Journal* 35, no. 1 (2000): 99–129.

[155] Sanders, *No Other Name*, 249–57. For another discussion of this topic, see Oden, *Life in the Spirit*, 327–28.

[156] See Millard J. Erickson, *The Evangelical Left* (Grand Rapids: Baker, 1997), 29–31.

Chapter Nine

WHAT CAN EVANGELICALS LEARN FROM BRIAN MCLAREN?

One of the lessons that I think evangelicals can and should learn from Brian McLaren is the value of a generous and charitable spirit. Brian has won a lot of supporters because of his demeanor. In my opinion, evangelicals lose support where they might not have because of their lack of graciousness and generosity. Even Hannibal Lector despised rudeness![1]

—John R. Franke

AS THIS STUDY DRAWS TO A CLOSE, WE TURN TO ONE FINAL question: "What can evangelicals learn from Brian McLaren?" (Note that this is different from asking "Is Brian McLaren still an evangelical?") As this book has demonstrated, many conservative Calvinist gatekeepers have unofficially ostracized McLaren from the evangelical fold. During the early years of the "Emergent McLaren" era, several Calvinist critics were eagerly engaging each new McLaren book before the ink could dry. But since the publishing of *A New Kind of Christianity* in 2010, McLaren's books have received little attention among conservative Christians, which is remarkable since just five years prior he was selected by *Time* magazine as one of the most influential voices in the evangelical world. As McLaren points out, however, by the time he participated in his son's gay commitment ceremony

---

[1] John Franke, email message to author, June 8, 2015.

in 2012, there wasn't much blowback because the gatekeepers had already "excommunicated" him from the evangelical community.[2]

So, for conservative evangelical gatekeepers, the war on the ECM, in general, and Brian McLaren, in particular, is over and has been for some time.[3] The only reason for a conservative evangelical to mention McLaren in the wake of this "victory" would seem to be for the purpose of recounting a cautionary tale. (Think back to the article entitled "Wings of Wax? The Strange Yet Familiar Tale of Brian, Rob, and Don" that was discussed in the first chapter of this book.) But is McLaren's contribution to Evangelicalism nothing more than to serve as a bad example?

I was curious to find out what a diverse cross-section of current and former evangelical leaders have to say about McLaren's legacy. I was especially interested to hear how several key conservative Calvinist leaders would respond to the following question: "What does Brian McLaren have to offer Evangelicalism a decade following his selection by *Time* magazine as one of the most influential evangelicals in America?" I posed this question to John Piper, John MacArthur, Albert Mohler, D. A. Carson, Mark Driscoll, and Kevin DeYoung, since each of these Calvinist leaders has critically engaged McLaren during the past decade. Unfortunately, none of them chose to respond to my question. It is always risky to build an argument from silence, so I cannot say with certainty why they declined to respond. Perhaps it is because they believe McLaren has nothing to offer Evangelicalism beyond a cautionary tale. Perhaps they believe McLaren is no longer worthy of discussion. Perhaps they were simply too busy.

To his credit, however, prominent Calvinist author David Wells did reply to my query. Wells minced no words in offering a clear riposte: "If [conservative Calvinists] know McLaren at all, they *revile* him. As he has increasingly moved toward the old Protestant liberalism he has increasingly alienated himself from many evangelicals. My view is that McLaren was a flash in the pan."[4] Wells's response is forthright and revealing. He claims conservative Calvinists either are unaware of McLaren, which

---

[2] See Krista Tippett, "Transcript for Brian McLaren—The Equation of Change," *On Being* (website), March 13, 2014, http://www.onbeing.org/program/transcript/6174.

[3] For instance, see Anthony Bradley, "Farewell Emerging Church, 1989–2010," *World Magazine*, April 14, 2010, http://www.worldmag.com/2010/04/farewell_emerging_church_1989_2010.

[4] David Wells, email message to author, July 2, 2015; emphasis mine.

demonstrates how thoroughly he has been expunged from their collective tribal memory, or they *revile* the emergent leader due to a regrettable drift into liberal apostasy.

It is worth underscoring precisely what Wells says. Wells does not say that conservative Calvinists revile McLaren's theology. No, he says "they revile *him*"—that is, McLaren the person. This is telling. According to the *Oxford Dictionary*, to revile someone is to "criticize in an abusive or angrily insulting manner."[5] Unfortunately, as this study has revealed, Wells is hardly the first and only conservative Calvinist evangelical to engage in this kind of "abusive and angrily insulting" personal, ad hominem attack on McLaren. (Think back to Chapter Six in which several Southern Baptist Theological Seminary faculty were cited for calling McLaren self-serving, a wolf in sheep's clothing, and the craftiest of the serpents of the field . . . following in the train of his father, the devil.)

Fortunately, not all Calvinist leaders engage in strident and abusive personal attacks. Richard Mouw, whom McLaren cited favorably in *A Generous Orthodoxy*, is one Calvinist scholar who has lobbied for a "kinder, gentler Calvinism."[6] Mouw admonishes his brethren with the following advice:

> One area, for example, where I believe Calvinism has been embarrassingly weak is in ethics. . . . Calvinists have certainly not stood out in the Christian community as especially pure people when it comes to the way they behave. They have frequently been intolerant, sometimes to the point of taking abusive and violent action toward people with whom they have disagreed. They have often promoted racist policies. And the fact that they have often defended these things by appealing directly to Calvinist teachings suggests that at least something in these patterns may be due to some weaknesses in the Calvinist perspective itself. On such matters, it seems clear to me that Calvinists ought to repent and admit to the larger Christian community that we have much to learn from others—from

---

[5] See http://www.oxforddictionaries.com/us/definition/american_english/revile.
[6] McLaren, *GO*, 195n92.

Mennonites, from black members of South African Pentecostal churches, from the followers of Saint Francis, and many others.[7]

Also speaking from within the Reformed tradition, John Franke agrees that conservative Calvinist evangelicals have much to learn from non-Calvinists and former Calvinists like McLaren. Franke writes, "One of the lessons evangelicals could and should learn from Brian McLaren is the value of a generous and charitable spirit. Brian has won a lot of supporters because of his demeanor. In my opinion, evangelicals lose support where they might not have because of their lack of graciousness and generosity. Even Hannibal Lector despised rudeness!"[8]

Calvin College Professor of Philosophy James K. A. Smith also notes the ironic hubris that can sometimes accompany a conversion to Calvinism: "How strange that discovering the doctrines of grace should translate into haughty self-confidence and a notable lack of charity."[9] Greg Dutcher, author of *Killing Calvinism*, likewise laments the arrogance displayed by many Calvinists: "What if we stopped mocking other believers who disagree with Calvinism? . . . Imagine if the first words that came to mind when people thought of Calvinists were 'gentle' and 'empathetic' instead of 'scholarly,' 'argumentative,' and 'arrogant.'"[10] It is worth recalling at this juncture that McLaren was not driven away from Reformed theology because of "arguments against Calvinism," but rather "the behavior and manner of Calvinists themselves."[11]

While most conservative Calvinists I contacted chose not to respond to my question about McLaren's evangelical legacy, several authors and speakers from the postconservative and progressive camps were happy to comment. Former Emergent Village National Coordinator Tony Jones said McLaren's "best gift is faithful yet surprising readings of Scripture. He

---

[7] Richard J. Mouw, *Finding Calvinism in the Las Vegas Airport* (Grand Rapids: Zondervan, 2004), 114–15; emphasis mine. See also James K. A. Smith, *Letters to a Young Calvinist* (Grand Rapids: Brazos, 2010), 69–70.

[8] John Franke, email message to author, June 8, 2015.

[9] Smith, *Letters to a Young Calvinist*, xi–xii. In this citation, Smith is talking about his own conversion, but he admits that he also has noticed this pattern in some New Calvinism converts as well.

[10] Greg Dutcher, *Killing Calvinism* (Adelphi, MD: Cruciform Press, 2012), 99.

[11] Brian McLaren, email message to author, July 20, 2009.

is truly a genius at that."[12] Frank Schaeffer, who helped his father, Francis, create the Religious Right in the early 1980s, thinks McLaren "offers evangelicals a great gift that they ignore to their loss, namely a viable vibrant faith based on how one lives and who one is rather than on a checklist of theological teachings."[13]

Tony Campolo, who co-authored with McLaren *Adventures in Missing the Point*, believes "Brian's emphasis on a holistic, inclusive gospel is an important ongoing message for all of Evangelicalism."[14] Steve Harper, a retired Asbury Seminary professor and administrator, believes McLaren "offers the future evangelical world a faithful witness to the gospel and to orthodoxy that is love-based, grace-filled, and Spirit-responsive."[15] Mark Scandrette, an early emergent trailblazer and author of *Soul-Graffiti*, predicts that "in twenty or thirty years, McLaren will be regarded as a faithful voice for historic Christian faith, and his simple, straightforward writing may find an enduring audience among evangelicals."[16] Tim Conder, another early emergent leader and author of *The Church in Transition*, believes "the tone of kindness and curiosity that McLaren has always nurtured in preaching, teaching, writing, and spiritual guidance still stands as a powerful example to the conservative Christian community as it struggles with this present landscape that they fear marginalizes their own voice, despite their authorship of and extreme privilege in this context."[17]

While each of these comments is worthy of amplification, as the author of this study, I believe the most important lesson that evangelicals can learn from McLaren is his "tone of kindness" (as Conder states) and "generous and charitable spirit" (as Franke puts it). McLaren's kindness and generosity ultimately flow from a deep and abiding belief in the goodness of God. As this study has shown, McLaren believes God loves all people without reservation, despite gender, sexual orientation, ethnicity, or religious expression. He believes the core teaching of the gospel is to break down the walls of division that create a sense of exclusive superiority, discrimination, and

---

[12] Tony Jones, email message to author, June 8, 2015.
[13] Frank Schaeffer, email message to author, June 10, 2015.
[14] Tony Campolo, email message to author, July 2, 2015.
[15] Steve Harper, email message to author, June 29, 2015.
[16] Mark Scandrette, email message to author, June 12, 2015.
[17] Tim Conder, email message to author, July 8, 2015.

imperialistic oppression and increase the distance between "us" and "them." Consequently, Christ-followers are elect for service, rather than privilege.

Additionally, McLaren's generous and charitable spirit as a reflection of the goodness of God is also a faithful response to the classic apologetic text found in 1 Peter 3:15–16 (NIV), which reads:

> But in your hearts set apart Christ as Lord. Always be pre-
> pared to give an answer to everyone who asks you to give the
> reason for the hope that you have. But do this with gentleness
> and respect, keeping a clear conscience, so that those who
> speak maliciously against your good behavior in Christ may be
> ashamed of their slander.

Evangelical leaders have done a commendable job with the first part of this apologetic mandate—namely, to give the reason for the hope that they have. There is no shortage of rational apologetic resources that lay out a range of cogent arguments for the Christian faith.

That said, the evangelical community has struggled with the second half of this mandate, to offer an apologetic with "gentleness and respect." In other words, evangelicals have focused so much on rational intelligence in the realm of apologetics that the appropriate emotional, ethical, and social intelligence is often lacking. As it turns out, the very area in which contemporary Evangelicalism has been under-resourced is the very area in which McLaren excels—as an apologetic model for emotional, ethical, and social intelligence.

McLaren discusses the need in contemporary apologetics for both credibility and plausibility, which includes engaging "social and emotional questions."[18] He explicates his commitment to holism with an accent on plausibility as follows:

> That's why I believe that we should test a [biblical] interpretation
> by reason and scholarship, using our rational intelligence—as
> we have traditionally done. But we must go farther, and also test
> our interpretations by conscience, using our emotional, ethical,
> and social intelligence—which we have seldom done. . . . Put

---

[18] McLaren, COOS, 83.

differently, interpreting texts with mathematical intelligence apart from social, emotional, and ethical intelligence is unintelligent, antisocial, and unethical.[19]

While McLaren is discussing emotional, ethical, and social intelligence in the realm of biblical hermeneutics in this passage, the insight can be extended to contemporary apologetics in all its dimensions. There is an important takeaway in this passage; namely, apologetics must be holistic.[20]

It is not enough to provide rational answers for the hope that we have. These answers also must be presented with moral, emotional, and social sensitivity. As Franke said, "Evangelicals lose support where they might not have because of their lack of graciousness and generosity." In other words, even if evangelicals reject McLaren's theological proposals, there is still much to learn from his apologetic methodology, which emphasizes "gentleness and respect." And this is an important resource at a time when evangelicals are mired in a no-win culture war that all too often focuses on protecting the rights, privileges, and boundaries of our own in-group rather than loving and extending grace to those living outside the evangelical enclave.

In conclusion, if McLaren's project generates a greater interest in defending the faith with emotional, ethical, and social intelligence, then his new kind of Christian apologetic will have made a significant contribution indeed. It is my hope that the modest constructive suggestions offered in this study also will contribute to the cause of communicating the goodness of God to a world in desperate need of an accurate and compelling portrayal of the Prince of Peace.

To that end, it is also my hope that those who continue to use the term evangelical (myself included) will strive to develop a kinder, gentler form of Christianity, not as a capitulation to culture but as a faithful response to the biblical apologetic mandate. For some of us, this might require retraining our collective moral palate in order to discover anew the scintillating flavors of gentleness, kindness, respect, and goodness. This might also require a

---

[19] McLaren, "New Kind of Bible Reading," 8. See also McLaren, *LWWAT*, 193.

[20] For a full-scale treatment of this kind of comprehensive approach to defending the faith, see Scott R. Burson and Jerry L. Walls, *Holistic Apologetics: Advancing the Gospel with Moral, Emotional, Rational, and Social Intelligence* (Grand Rapids: Baker Academic, forthcoming).

willingness to starve our obsessive need to be right and to refrain from the all too common side dish of rudeness. It is this author's contention that we would be well advised to follow some of McLaren's helpful apologetic recipes, even if aspects of his theology are unpalatable. But if evangelicals find the thought of learning something from Brian McLaren simply too nauseating, perhaps we could at least agree to learn a thing or two about civility from Hannibal Lector.

THE US EMERGING CHURCH MOVEMENT

The Development of the ECM in the US

ACCORDING TO TONY JONES, ONE OF THE FOUNDERS OF THE US ECM, "the emergent phenomenon began in the late 1990s when a group of Christian leaders began a conversation about how postmodernism was affecting the faith."[1] The ECM can be traced back to a group of young evangelical leaders who had gathered together under the auspices of Leadership Network (LN).[2] Doug Pagitt[3] was charged with the task of locating "the next Bill Hybels" or "the next Rick Warren."[4]

This new group, known as the Young Leaders Network (YLN), gathered in 1997 for a brainstorming session in Colorado Springs. The original intent was to discuss ways to improve Generation X ministry; however, one of the attendees, Brad Cecil, steered the group in a different direction.[5] Cecil

---

[1] Tony Jones, *The New Christians* (San Francisco: Jossey-Bass, 2008), 41. See also Eddie Gibbs and Ryan Bolger, *Emerging Churches* (Grand Rapids: Baker, 2012), 32.

[2] The Dallas, Texas-based LN was founded in 1984 for the purpose of "foster[ing] church innovation and growth by diligently pursuing its far-reaching mission statement: to identify, connect, and help high-capacity Christian leaders multiply their impact." See McLaren, *NKOC*, viii. For another recounting of the key early milestones of the ECM, see Ed Stetzer, "The Emergent/ Emerging Church: A Missiological Perspective," in *Evangelicals Engaging Emergent*, ed. William D. Henard and Adam W. Greenway (Nashville: B&H Publishing, 2009), 52–69.

[3] Jones and Pagitt had met while serving as youth pastors in Minneapolis, before Pagitt was hired by LN. Pagitt was told to search the country for the next generation of up-and-coming evangelical leaders.

[4] Jones, *New Christians*, 42.

[5] Cecil, the pastor of Axxess Fellowship in Arlington, Texas, had been reading postmodern philosophy and had attended a conference featuring John Caputo and Jacques Derrida at Villanova University a few years earlier. See Jones, *New Christians*, 41. For Cecil's comments concerning generational ministry, see Gibbs and Bolger, *Emerging Churches*, 33.

argued that the problem was not fundamentally generational but cultural. He reasoned that a major cultural shift was underway, and Christian ministry needed to recalibrate accordingly. Cecil sketched his historical understanding of the modern-to-postmodern transition on a whiteboard. Jones recalls, "By the time Brad was done, the board was covered with a timeline stretching from Jesus to the present, littered with names like Foucault and Descartes and Rorty and Kant."[6] Cecil would later develop this impromptu history lesson into a PowerPoint presentation that "has attained legendary status among emergents."[7] The YLN brain trust, which included Pagitt, Chris Seay, and Mark Driscoll,[8] agreed that Cecil was essentially correct in his analysis.

The following year, the group sponsored a conference in Glorieta, New Mexico, which attracted a few hundred evangelical pastors, including around fifty youth ministers, to hear speakers such as Stanley Grenz, Jimmy Long, Sally Morgenthaler, Leonard Sweet, and Driscoll.[9] The term "postmodern" was central to the conversation.[10]

Following this conference, regional gatherings sprung up across the country. This is when the "emerging church" term started to surface.[11] Over the next few years, the YLN went through a variety of name changes, including the Theological Working Group and the Terranova Project, before settling on the term "emergent" or, officially, Emergent Village (EV) in 2001.[12] Jones served as the national coordinator for EV from 2005 to 2008,[13] at which time the position was eliminated "to streamline, decentralize, and reduce expenses."[14] For several years, EV, which described itself as "a

[6] Jones, New Christians, 42–43.

[7] Matt Rawlings, "Brad Cecil's Legendary Powerpoint," Pastor Matt (blog), June 13, 2009, http://pastormattblog.com/2009/06/13/867/.

[8] Seay is the pastor of University Baptist Church in Waco, Texas, while Driscoll was the founding pastor of Mars Hill Church in Seattle, Washington, which closed all of its campuses in 2014.

[9] Tony Jones, The Church Is Flat (Minneapolis: JoPa Group, 2011), i.

[10] Ibid.

[11] Ibid., ii. Karen Ward popularized the term "emerging churches" by launching the website www.EmergingChurches.org in 1999. See Gibbs and Bolger, Emerging Churches, 30.

[12] Jones, New Christians, XVII. See also Gibbs and Bolger, Emerging Churches, 32; Stetzer, "The Emergent/Emerging Church," 59, and Jim Belcher, Deep Church (Downers Grove: InterVarsity Press, 2009), 47.

[13] Jones was paid for this role from 2006–2008. Tony Jones, email message to author, August 4, 2014.

[14] Shayne Lee and Phillip Sinitiere, Holy Mavericks (New York: New York University Press, 2009), 88.

growing, generative friendship of missional Christian leaders,"[15] hosted national and regional conferences, and the group served as a catalyst to facilitate conversation on a wide range of topics, mostly under the banner of postmodern and postcolonial concerns. Jones wrote in 2008, "If the emergent church has anything rare, or even unique, it's the nexus of theory and praxis, of innovative theology and innovative practice. These twin impulses of rethinking theology and rethinking church are driving the nascent growth of emergent Christianity."[16]

By 2009, many were proclaiming the demise of the ECM.[17] Even prolific ECM blogger Andrew Jones raised the possibility that the ECM had run its course. In early 2010, *World Magazine*, a conservative Calvinistic periodical, published an article entitled "Farewell, Emerging Church."[18] In response to such premature obituaries, Jonathan Brink posted on the EV website in early 2011 "The State of Emergence 2010," summarizing the previous two years as follows:

> In many ways this public declaration of death was needed. What arguably died was a perception of the slick marketing model aimed at middle class, white hipsters saddled in the corner of Starbucks with their Macs. This stereotype has run its course and run out of favor. It had to die. What didn't die were the underlying questions that fueled the movement in the first place. People were still gathering together in pubs, coffee houses, and homes, wrestling with questions of faith, reformation, atonement, the goodness of God, what it means to follow Jesus, and how to live in a post-Christian culture.[19]

Phyllis Tickle concurred with Brink, that the movement did not die, but rather a "deceptive and destructive public persona" had passed away.[20]

---

[15] See Jones, "Foreword" in Doug Pagitt, *A Christianity Worth Believing* (San Francisco: Jossey-Bass, 2008), viii.

[16] Jones, *New Christians*, XIX.

[17] For instance, see John Piper, "John Piper—The Emergent Church," *YouTube*, March 24, 2010, https://www.youtube.com/watch?v=MkGq5A4QEjg.

[18] Phyllis Tickle, *Emergence Christianity* (Grand Rapids: Baker, 2012), 112. Tickle misidentifies Andrew Jones as "Anthony" Jones.

[19] Ibid., 112–13.

[20] Ibid., 113.

Even if some element of the ECM has expired, it would be a misstep to consider the movement homogenous.[21] John MacArthur is one critic who succumbed to painting the whole movement with the same unflattering brush:

> The recent wave of popular books written by leading figures in the Emerging Church movement has unleashed an unprecedented flood of vulgarity and worldliness onto Christian booksellers' shelves. Obscenity is one of the main trademarks of the Emerging style. Most authors in the movement make extravagant use of filthy language, sexual innuendo, and uncritical references to the most lowbrow elements of postmodern culture, often indicating inappropriate approval for ungodly aspects of secular culture.[22]

Not all who have participated in the ECM have grown in the same direction and not all remained affiliated with the movement. Mark Driscoll is a case in point. Following the initial conference in New Mexico and after a few years of ongoing dialogue and speaking around the country, Driscoll eventually distanced himself from the group "because of theological differences."[23] During the mid-to-late 1990s, Driscoll studied postmodern philosophy and spoke frequently on shifting "the conversation from reaching Generation X to reaching postmodern culture."[24] As the YLN was forming, Driscoll recalls "another pastor . . . who was a few years younger than [his] dad" joining the group. "His name was Brian McLaren."[25] The elder McLaren quickly emerged as the "team leader."[26] Before long, however, it became clear that Driscoll and McLaren were moving in starkly different theological directions. Driscoll recounts the fundamental divide as follows:

---

[21] See Tim Conder, *The Church in Transition* (Grand Rapids: Zondervan, 2006), 22–26, and Lee and Sinitiere, *Holy Mavericks*, 79.

[22] John MacArthur, *The Truth War* (Nashville: Thomas Nelson, 2007), 139.

[23] Mark Driscoll, *Confessions of a Reformission Rev.* (Grand Rapids: Zondervan, 2006), 20.

[24] Ibid., 98. See also Mark Driscoll, *The Radical Reformission* (Grand Rapids: Zondervan, 2004), 16–17. For a firsthand description of Driscoll's talk on the modern-to-postmodern shift at Gen X 2.0, see Belcher, *Deep Church*, 25.

[25] Driscoll, *Reformission Rev.*, 98. See also McLaren, "Introduction," in *JP*, 15.

[26] Mark Driscoll, "A Pastoral Perspective on the Emergent Church," *Criswell Theological Review* 3, no. 2 (Spring 2006): 89.

Because he comes from a pacifistic Brethren background, such things as power and violence greatly trouble him. His pacifism seems to underlie many of our theological disagreements since he has a hard time accepting such things as the violence of the penal substitutionary atonement, parts of the Old Testament where God killed people, and the concept of conscious eternal torment in hell.[27]

Driscoll did not leave the broader ECM conversation, but he did discontinue fellowship with EV members, including McLaren, Pagitt, Tony Jones, and Andrew Jones.[28]

Classifying the ECM

Several noteworthy attempts have surfaced from both inside and outside the movement to explain and clarify ECM diversity. Since Driscoll was an early member of the YLN, it is appropriate to begin with his classification.

After several years, the movement would eventually crystallize to the point where Driscoll could discern what he calls "four lanes" on the ECM highway: emerging evangelicals, house church evangelicals, emerging reformers, and emergent liberals. According to Driscoll, *emerging evangelicals* maintain the same message but seek to update their methodology. *House church evangelicals* focus on ecclesiology, believing church is best done in small groups in homes. *Emerging reformers*, the lane with which Driscoll identifies, are trying to find the best way to maintain a traditional Reformed faith in a postmodern context. The final lane, *emergent liberals*—as Driscoll calls them—are questioning many of the core doctrines of the historic, orthodox Christian faith. Driscoll places McLaren and those associated with EV in this last lane. Driscoll does not have any "grave concerns" with those in the first three lanes, but he believes those in this fourth lane have "gotten off the highway and are totally lost out in the woods."[29] While Driscoll's distinctions provide some helpful categories, his treatment

---

[27] Driscoll, *Reformission Rev.*, 99.
[28] Ibid.
[29] Mark Driscoll, "Navigating the Emerging Church Highway," *Christian Research Journal* 31, no. 4 (2008), posted online June 10, 2009, http://www.equip.org/articles/navigating-the-emerging-church-highway/#christian-books-2.

of EV lacks the necessary nuance, especially since participants in this stream generally consider themselves either postconservative or postliberal.

Like Driscoll, Ed Stetzer developed a taxonomy to explicate the diversity within the ECM. He divides the movement into three categories: relevants, reconstructionists, and revisionists.[30] Stetzer claims that *relevants* focus on understanding contemporary culture and communicating the unchanging gospel message with cultural awareness and sensitivity. This grouping is similar to Driscoll's emerging evangelical lane.

Reconstructionists focus on ecclesiastical structures and often gravitate to the house church model, comparable to Driscoll's house church evangelicals. Stetzer's final classification, the *revisionists*, receives most of the harsh critique and is interested in revising both "methodology and theology."[31] This final group is consistent with Driscoll's emergent liberals classification.

Stetzer's taxonomy on the whole is preferable to Driscoll's distinctions. The term "revisionists" is more accurate than "emergent liberals." Still, those associated with EV do not see their project as purely revisionary in nature. They are proposing an "ancient-future" faith that is "kicking-back/ leaning-forward," reclaiming and integrating elements of tradition with progressive innovation appropriate to the contemporary cultural milieu.[32] In fact, McLaren understands his project as largely recovering key aspects of the ancient gospel message that have been lost due to various cultural and political accommodations throughout history.

Nevertheless, Stetzer's taxonomy has struck a chord with several in the Reformed tradition. Gary Gilley favorably cites Stetzer's classification in *Reforming or Conforming*,[33] as do William Henard and John Hammett in *Evangelicals Engaging Emergent* and Jim Belcher in *Deep Church*.[34] Andrew Jones also affirms Stetzer's delineation.[35]

---

[30] Ed Stetzer, "The Emergent/Emerging Church," 72. Stetzer claims that his taxonomy informed Driscoll's categories.

[31] Ibid.

[32] McLaren, *GO*, 18. See also Robert Webber, *Ancient-Future Faith* (Grand Rapids: Baker, 1999).

[33] Gary Gilley, "The Emergent Church," in *Reforming or Conforming?*, ed. Gary L. W. Johnson and Ronald N. Gleason (Wheaton: Crossway, 2008), 274–75.

[34] William D. Henard, "Introduction," 2, and John Hammett, "The Church According to Emergent/Emerging Church," in *Evangelicals Engaging Emergent*, 222. See also Belcher, *Deep Church*, 45–46.

[35] See Andrew Jones, "Ed Stetzer Gets It," *Tall Skinny Kiwi* (blog), January 8, 2006, http:// tallskinnykiwi.typepad.com/tallskinnykiwi/2006/01/ed_stetzer_gets.html.

Mark Devine attempts to simplify the distinctions within the movement by dividing the ECM into two camps: doctrine friendly and doctrine wary/averse. In the *doctrine-friendly* grouping, he includes such representatives as Driscoll and Tim Keller. In the *doctrine-wary/averse* clan, he includes McLaren and other members of EV.[36] While the attempt to simplify is commendable, it misses the mark. Most EV participants, including McLaren, are not resistant to doctrine in general but to certain doctrines in particular. For instance, many members of EV value the importance of the cross, but they reject requiring adherence to the penal substitutionary theory as the litmus test for orthodoxy. This is not a new distinction. C. S. Lewis made this same point in *Mere Christianity* when he discussed the danger of confusing theories of the atonement with the actual efficacy of the atonement itself.[37] McLaren and others in EV are also concerned about how doctrine is used in the church, often for the purposes of drawing lines of exclusion. Therefore, those associated with EV typically gravitate to a "centered" rather than "bounded" understanding of doctrine. This preference for a centered understanding of doctrine, however, is not the same as rejecting doctrine altogether.[38]

In *Emerging Churches*, Gibbs and Bolger define churches in the ECM as "missional communities arising from within Postmodern culture and consisting of followers of Jesus who are seeking to be faithful in their place and time."[39] Instead of dividing the movement into subgroups, their study identifies common salient features. The project is built around personal interviews with ECM leaders from the US and abroad. It is the most comprehensive treatment that allows leaders of the movement, in all forms of ecclesiology, to speak for themselves. Therein lies its significant contribution. The book includes an appendix of fifty first-person testimonial

---

[36] Mark Devine, "The Emerging Church: One Movement—Two Streams," in *Evangelicals Engaging Emergent*, 7–8.

[37] C.S. Lewis, *Mere Christianity* (New York: Macmillan, 1960), 57.

[38] For a discussion of "bounded" and "centered" approaches to doctrine, see Stanley J. Grenz and John R. Franke, *Beyond Foundationalism* (Louisville: Westminster John Knox Press, 2001), 8–9, and Belcher, *Deep Church*, 79–87. Belcher adds the third category of "relational-set" and attributes it to Tony Jones's understanding of a guiding "relational hermeneutic" when formulating doctrine.

[39] Gibbs and Bolger, *Emerging Churches*, 28.

accounts.[40] Through empirical research, the authors conclude that the contours of the ECM can be described as congregations that are attempting to:

- Identify with the life of Jesus.
- Transform the secular realm.
- Live highly communal lives.

Because of these three activities, they:

- Welcome the stranger.
- Serve with generosity.
- Participate as producers.
- Create as created beings.
- Lead as a body.
- Take part in spiritual activities.[41]

In his follow-up book, *Churchmorph*, Gibbs underscores that the ECM is not "a single movement," but rather is best understood as multiple "streams that diverge and converge and then create new tributaries. True to its label, it continues to be an 'emerging' movement that cannot be encapsulated in precise definitions."[42]

Ray Anderson, a former colleague of Gibbs and Bolger at Fuller Seminary, offered his own assessment in *An Emergent Theology for Emerging Churches*.[43] In this book, which includes a foreword by McLaren, Anderson likens elements of today's ECM to the "first-century emerging church in Antioch."[44] While Anderson draws interesting parallels between the contemporary context and the tensions that existed between the ancient churches in Jerusalem and Antioch, this book fails to offer concrete critique or clarification to be of much value in better understanding the current state of the ECM.[45]

---

[40] Ibid., 239–328.

[41] Ibid., 45.

[42] Eddie Gibbs, *Churchmorph* (Grand Rapids: Baker, 2009), 37. Gibbs provides a good summary of ECM taxonomies in the appendix to this book, 201–206.

[43] Ray Anderson, *An Emergent Theology for Emerging Churches* (Downers Grove: InterVarsity Press, 2006).

[44] Ibid., 10.

[45] Ibid., 54n9. Within the context of interacting with the concepts of modernity and postmodernity, Anderson defers to McLaren's "clear and compelling discussion of what is meant by these terms."

Tony Jones is resistant to providing overly restrictive delineation, stating that the "ECM is notoriously difficult to define, both because it is a young movement that is still rapidly evolving and because its adherents regularly defy the definitions put upon them by observers and scholars."[46] Nevertheless, he tentatively offers three common characteristics of emergent Christians: they are typically disillusioned with "modern American Christianity," they long for "inclusion," and they are hopeful about the future.[47] He is especially partial to a definition of the ECM offered by Warren Bird in the *Encyclopedia of Religion in America*: "The emerging church movement is a loosely aligned conversation among Christians who seek to re-imagine the priorities, values and theology expressed by the local church as it seeks to live out its faith in postmodern society. It is an attempt to replot Christian faith on a new cultural and intellectual terrain."[48]

Phyllis Tickle offers her own binary classification: emergent and emerging.[49] She argues that the dividing line between these two groups is orthonomy versus theonomy.[50] Tickle places McLaren, Pagitt, and Jones in the *emergent* camp. She defines "orthonomy" as "the employment of aesthetic or harmonic purity as a tool for discerning the truth—and therefore the intent and authority—of anything, be that thing either doctrine or practice."[51] On the other side of the ledger, Tickle identifies pastors Dan Kimball and Erwin McManus as examples of those who embrace "theonomy," which she defines as "the principle that only God can be the source of perfection in action and thought."[52] According to Tickle, this *emerging* camp grounds its view in *sola scriptura*, while *emergent* "orthonomy" emphasizes "tradition, reason, and inspiration as conduits for safely receiving the holy."[53]

In her 2012 follow-up book, *Emergence Christianity*, Tickle expands upon the practical and theological differences between emergent and

---

[46] Jones, *Church Is Flat*, 3. See also John R. Franke, *Manifold Witness* (Nashville: Abingdon, 2009), 31–41.

[47] Jones, *New Christians*, 70–72.

[48] Warren Bird, "Emerging Church Movement," in *Encyclopedia of Religion in America*, ed. C. H. Lippy and P. W. Williams (Washington, DC: CQ Press, 2010), 682. As quoted in Jones, *Church Is Flat*, 5.

[49] Phyllis Tickle, *The Great Emergence* (Grand Rapids: Baker, 2008), 163.

[50] Ibid.

[51] Ibid., 149.

[52] Ibid., 150.

[53] Ibid.

emerging.[54] In stark contrast to emerging, Tickle finds the emergent camp to be "aggressively all-inclusive and nonpatriarchal," while Scripture is valued for its "actuality" rather than its "historicity or literal inerrancy." Emergents reject modern approaches to the Bible, such as the reduction of God to "outlines and bullet points of our logic."[55] Nevertheless, both camps, despite their many differences, are nested under the broader umbrella that Tickle calls "Emergence," which includes not only the emerging and emergent camps, but also the "neo-Monastics," the "House Church," the "Missionals," the "Hyphenated," and the "Cyber Church."[56]

Tom Sine in *The New Conspirators* also discusses the new expressions of Christian spirituality in broader terms and, in so doing, expands the conversation beyond the ECM. Sine separates the broader movement of young evangelicals into: emerging, missional, mosaic, and monastic. Sine claims that the emerging stream, in particular, is committed to narrative theology, culturally sensitive models of ministry, experiential worship, a willingness to innovate, communal forms of ecclesiology, and a commitment to social justice.[57]

While recognizing the diversity of the movement, sociologists Shayne Lee and Phillip Luke Sinitiere, authors of *Holy Mavericks*, offer a well-crafted summary of the broader ECM phenomenon as "a nurturing friendship and generative conversation devoted to deconstructing Christian history, doctrine, attitudes, rituals, practices, and politics from the negative effects of modernity in order to construct a faith that addresses the existential needs of the emerging culture."[58]

Scot McKnight, who is a leading interpreter of the ECM, has "studied the movement and interacted with its key leaders for years—even more, I happily consider myself part of this movement or 'conversation.'"[59] In a 2007

---

[54] Tickle, *Emergence Christianity*, 142.

[55] Ibid.

[56] Ibid., 139–57.

[57] Tom Sine, *The New Conspirators* (Downers Grove: InterVarsity Press, 2008), 31–55.

[58] Lee and Sinitiere, *Holy Mavericks*, 79–80.

[59] Scot McKnight, "Five Streams of the Emerging Church," *CT* 51, no. 2 (February 2007): 34–39, citing 35. McKnight became increasingly concerned with Emergent's lack of emphasis on evangelism. Consequently, he and other ECM participants, including Dan Kimball, chose to distance themselves from EV and develop "partnerships with other leaders who want to support one another in this missional-and-evangelism direction." See Scot McKnight, "Emerging and Emergent: Our New Network," *Jesus Creed* (blog), September 24, 2008, http://blog.beliefnet.com/jesuscreed /2008/09/emerging-and-emergent-our-new.html.

CT article entitled "The Five Streams of the Emerging Church," McKnight references the nine descriptors of Gibbs and Bolger, and distinguishes "emerging" from "Emergent."[60] McKnight offers an incisive aerial observation: "emerging is the wider, informal, global, ecclesial (church-centered) focus of the movement, while Emergent is an official organization in the U.S. and the U.K. Emergent Village. . . . While Emergent is the intellectual and philosophical network of the emerging movement, it is a mistake to narrow all of emerging to Emergent Village." McKnight goes on to identify "five streams flowing into the emerging lake": prophetic (or at least provocative), postmodern, praxis-oriented, post-evangelical, and political.[61]

In *Emerging Evangelicals*, anthropologist James Bielo characterizes the ECM as a "cultural critique" of and "severe disenchantment with America's conservative Christian subculture."[62] Bielo identifies this conversation swirling around the following "intersecting points of dialogue": theology, missiology, ecclesiology, liturgy, and politics.[63] According to social scientists Gerardo Marti and Gladys Ganiel, authors of *The Deconstructed Church*, "the ECM is one of the most important reframings of religion within Western Christianity in the last two decades."[64] The authors claim the ECM values "autonomy, diversity, and dissent"[65] and targets both self-identifying Christians and nonbelievers as it challenges primarily "conservative/evangelical/fundamentalist Protestantism."[66]

---

[60] McKnight, "Five Streams," 36–39.

[61] Ibid., 34–39. See also Scot McKnight, "The Ironic Faith of Emergents," *CT* 52, no. 9 (September 2008): 62–63 .

[62] James S. Bielo, *Emerging Evangelicals* (New York: New York University Press, 2011), 5–6.

[63] Ibid., 10.

[64] Gerardo Marti and Gladys Ganiel, *The Deconstructed Church* (Oxford: Oxford University Press, 2014), 5.

[65] Ibid., 6.

[66] Ibid., 26.

STANLEY GRENZ AND THE POSTMODERN TURN

An especially significant influence in shaping McLaren's (and the ECM's) understanding of the postmodern turn was Stanley Grenz, who was the Pioneer McDonald Professor of Baptist Heritage, Theology, and Ethics at Carey Theological College in Vancouver, British Columbia, until his premature death in 2005.

Grenz focused on the contributions of three central modern historical figures. First, the seeds of modernity can be traced back to English philosopher and scientist Francis Bacon (1561–1626), whose concern for harnessing "power over nature" through the scientific method initiated the modern project.[1] Second, following the anthropocentric spirit of the Renaissance, French philosopher René Descartes (1596–1650) was responsible for laying "the philosophical foundation for the modern edifice" when his methodology of doubting led to his famous declaration, *Cogito ergo sum*.[2] With this newfound, certain confidence in autonomous human reason, Descartes was defining "human nature as a thinking substance and the human person as an autonomous rational subject."[3] Third, British scientist Isaac Newton (1642–1727) shortly thereafter introduced a scientific vision of the natural world as an overarching macro machine, operating according to infallible mechanistic laws that could be discovered by the autonomous human

---

[1] Stanley J. Grenz, *A Primer on Postmodernism* (Grand Rapids: Eerdmans, 1996), 2.
[2] Stanley J. Grenz, "Star Trek and the Next Generation," in *The Challenge of Postmodernism*, ed. David S. Dockery (Wheaton: BridgePoint, 1995), 89–103, citing 90.
[3] Grenz, *Primer on Postmodernism*, 3.

mind.[4] According to Grenz, "The modern human can appropriately be characterized as Descartes's autonomous, rational substance encountering Newton's mechanistic world."[5]

These men set the stage for the following epistemological assump-. tions.[6] First, modernity sought to bring the full range of knowledge under the jurisdiction of objective, neutral human reason. The external objective world was thought to correspond to the internal structure of the human mind. Second, the modern era was committed to the idealism of "inevitable progress."[7] Knowledge, in all its respective disciplines, was considered "certain, objective, and good."[8] Consequently, the modern project aspired to use science and education to "free us from our vulnerability to nature, as well as from all social bondage."[9] Third, modernity gave birth to a "radical individualism," which disconnects the "autonomous self" from tradition and community.[10]

Grenz argues, "Postmodernity is the questioning of these theses."[11] Consequently, postmodernism is a protest and, as such, is fundamentally "anti-modern."[12] The term "postmodernity," on the other hand, describes the era and milieu following modernity.[13] Grenz argues that the postmodern intellectual critique gained traction when deconstruction emerged in the 1970s as a tenet of a popular literary theory known as structuralism.[14]

Structuralists claim that "language is a social construct," and, as such, it serves as a vehicle for individuals and communities to organize experiences into a meaningful narrative. Grenz claims that structuralists believe in the universality of a "common invariant structure" within the stories

---

[4] Grenz, "Star Trek," 90.

[5] Ibid., 90–91.

[6] Stanley J. Grenz, *Revisioning Evangelical Theology* (Downers Grove: InterVarsity Press, 1993), 15–17.

[7] Ibid., 15.

[8] Grenz, *Primer on Postmodernism*, 4.

[9] Ibid.

[10] Ibid. Grenz claims that the Enlightenment conception of freedom was focused on individual rather than collective liberty.

[11] Grenz, *Revisioning Evangelical Theology*, 15.

[12] Grenz, *Primer on Postmodernism*, 42. Elsewhere, Grenz nuances this statement to suggest that postmodernism also "retains the modern . . . especially its elevation of skeptical rationality." See Stanley J. Grenz, *Renewing the Center*, 2nd ed. (Grand Rapids: Baker Academic, 2006), 176–77.

[13] Grenz, *Primer on Postmodernism*, 12.

[14] Ibid., 5.

that are told in "all societies and cultures."[15] Deconstructuralists accepted much of the structuralist project; however, they rejected the belief in a common, stable, cross-cultural universal structure. Rather, the deconstructuralists claim that each text is relative and specific to its cultural context and relies upon the subjective engagement of the interpreter with the text.[16] Postmodern philosophers appropriated the tenets of this literary theory for their work.[17]

In light of this shift in how the nature of reality should be understood, French philosopher Jacques Derrida (1930–2004) wrote vigorously against "onto-theology" and the "metaphysics of presence."[18] Derrida argued that it was futile to formulate ontological depictions of reality as if an independent, objective world actually exists. Likewise, he critiqued the claim that "something transcendent is present in reality."[19] Consequently, he concluded that all we are left with are individual interpretations.[20]

French historian and philosopher Michel Foucault (1926–1984) shifted the conversation to the issue of power. He claimed that every attempt to acquire knowledge is a maneuver to gain control over that domain of reality. Foucault was especially concerned with how social institutions wield power and "engage in violence" by imposing a subjective perspective on collective society.[21] American philosopher Richard Rorty (1931–2007) focused on the subject matter of truth, rejecting the notion of correspondence between the external world and the internal mind of the knowing subject, as well as the "internal coherence of the assertions themselves."[22] He said the human community should forgo the quest for universal, objective truth and settle for interpretation.[23]

The features of the postmodern protest stand in direct opposition to the modern project. First, rather than bedrock confidence in human progress,

---

[15] Ibid.

[16] Grenz, "Star Trek," 92–93.

[17] Ibid., 93.

[18] Ibid.

[19] Grenz, Primer on Postmodernism, 6.

[20] Ibid.

[21] Grenz, Primer on Postmodernism, 6. For more on Foucault, see James K. A. Smith, Who's Afraid of Postmodernism? (Grand Rapids: Baker, 2006), 81–107.

[22] Grenz, "Star Trek," 93.

[23] Ibid.

the postmodern spirit is characterized by a "gnawing pessimism."[24] In the wake of a war-torn twentieth century, postmodern people see "life on earth as fragile and believe that the continued existence of humankind is dependent on a new attitude of cooperation rather than conquest."[25] Second, postmodernism rejects the claim that "truth is certain" and rationality is the only route to knowledge. Accordingly, postmodern epistemology accommodates not only reason, but the full range of human faculties, including "the emotions and the intuition" as well.[26] Third, the postmodern perspective rejects the quest for a universal shared essence in favor of communal particularity.[27] Consequently, universalizing metanarratives are rejected and localized stories are celebrated.

---

[24] Ibid.

[25] Grenz, *Primer on Postmodernism*, 7.

[26] Ibid.

[27] Ibid., 8.

MCLAREN'S MARKS OF MODERNITY

IN *A NEW KIND OF CHRISTIAN*, NEO EXPLAINS TO DAN POOLE ten features of the modern era. The following is a summary.

Conquest and control. Neo explains the Enlightenment project as Western European culture, in diverse expressions, gaining dominance over everything within its purview, including nature, humanity, and technology. This led to a multitude of positive discoveries; however, despite these benefits and the accompanying hope of continual social and scientific progress, a positive moral rudder was frequently lacking. Consequently, modern humanity too often used its power to create systems and vessels to shrink the world and overtake the land, customs, and finances of other people groups. Overcoming obstacles of all kinds, including indigenous people, was just the first step; managing this subjugation became the ongoing project.

Mechanization. In order to conquer and control, one must have the appropriate technology. Consequently, the second characteristic of modernity is a core commitment to the machine. For modern humanity, quality is associated with the latest, most technologically advanced unit in the product line. In a world where mechanization is king, the king of the universe is someone who can control the whole machine: a great, powerful, "engineer-God."[1] Against this backdrop, Calvinistic theology emerged. Whereas the secular segment of the modern world viewed naturalistic determinism as the ultimate context of life, Calvinistic theology and its

---

[1] McLaren, *NKOC*, 16.

commitment to total theological determinism became the guiding lens for many Christians, especially American evangelicals, in the modern era.

Analytical reason. Neo continues his argument: "If the world is an intelligible machine—and science is the master screwdriver to take it apart—then analysis is the ultimate form of thought, the universal screwdriver."[2] The modern world has broken down the universe into increasingly manageable parts. After deconstructing the constituent elements and observing them from every angle, each system can be reassembled, but with much greater insight, knowledge, and control over the subject in question. The degree to which "*thinking* and *analyzing* seem to be synonymous suggests how successful modernity has been" in elevating rationality to a privileged status.[3]

Secular science. If reality is mechanistic and analysis is the means by which the machine can be understood and controlled, then it is not difficult to see how science became the queen discipline of the modern era. This was not just a commitment to science, but rather a commitment to *naturalistic*, secular science—the belief that everything in reality, including human beings, can be explained in purely naturalistic terms.[4] In this kind of world, "religion was scurrying in retreat . . . fleeing the exterminating gas of modern science and secularism, like cockroaches from an apartment building."[5]

Absolute objectivity. Modern naturalistic scientists believed that every apparent mystery in the world was in principle knowable and, therefore, open to human investigation and comprehension. Neo asserts that clearheaded, rational objectivity became the mantra for modern humanity. What developed during the Enlightenment was an extreme confidence that human beings could climb to the appropriate altitude, where a detached Archimedean perspective would answer all of humanity's questions.

Criticism. If the overriding belief is in objective, absolute truth that has been obtained through proper execution of the scientific method, then all dissenting viewpoints should be subjected to scrutiny. Differences of

---

[2] Ibid.
[3] Ibid., 17.
[4] Ibid.
[5] Ibid.

opinion were adjudicated through "debate, dialectic, argument, and discussion."[6] The modern era framed disagreement as a win-lose affair, with all of the attending in-grouping and out-grouping.

Modern nation-state and organization. With the collapse of the medieval feudal system, modernity ushered in new ways of organizing society, "from the assembly line to the picket line to the party line."[7] Organization came alongside the development of urban centers. As more people flocked to centralized cultural pockets, there was a growing need to systematically organize the masses into manageable units.

Individual human autonomy. In the modern era, the individual became the centerpiece, and communal traditions were rejected. Neo explains, "As mechanistic organizations pursued conquest and control, communities were disintegrated, leaving their smallest constituent parts—individuals—disconnected and hanging in midair."[8] This commitment to the individual is manifested in various ways in modern Evangelicalism, including an overemphasis upon the eternal dimensions of individual salvation at the expense of the temporal communal implications of the gospel.

Protestantism and institutional religion. While naturalistic, secular science became the dominant worldview of the modern age, pushing religion to the margins, the spiritual dimension of life could not be extinguished. Christianity most thrived in its "institutional . . . and Protestant forms (protesting not just Catholicism but medievalism and premodernism in general)."[9]

Consumerism. As modern people broke away from the feudal system and adopted capitalistic economies, people were free to purchase whatever they wanted. The steady advancement of technology has fueled the human desire for more and supported the *newer is better* mentality. This consumerism has fed a collective greed that contributes to the erosion of altruistic impulses.

---

[6] Ibid.
[7] Ibid., 18.
[8] Ibid.
[9] Ibid.

BRIAN MCLAREN EMAIL CORRESPONDENCE

The date provided for each email exchange is the date that McLaren responded to the author's query.

JANUARY 6, 2006

Burson: Have you been particularly influenced by any contemporary open theists?

McLaren: I spent several years as a Calvinist, under the influence of one of my early mentors. I gradually moved to a more or less open theism position (before I really heard of the term) simply out of fatigue with the intellectual gymnastics (and ethical ugliness) of keeping the Calvinist boat afloat in my mind. I haven't gotten involved with that debate because I'm not a big fan of the warfare language that some are using. I prefer to frame the matter in terms of "the openness of God's universe," suggesting that a good and creative God would want to create an open universe, not a deterministic one. The most helpful writer for me on this has been John Haught, *God After Darwin*. Since I've been so influenced by Lesslie Newbigin and N. T. Wright, I probably define salvation differently from most Evangelicals. When you define salvation differently (not primarily as getting one's soul into heaven after death, but having to do with God's continuing healing and rescue of all creation), you define election differently, the whole Bible looks different, and the old Calvinism debates make so much less sense.

Burson: Have you read Jerry Walls's book, *Hell: The Logic of Damnation?* In my opinion, it does a plausible job of holding together the goodness of God with libertarian human freedom against the backdrop of a *Great Divorce* vision of the afterlife.

McLaren: I haven't read it. For some reason, I didn't come across it when doing my research for the *Last Word* [*LWWAT*]. I wish I had been able to read it before completing the book, as there really is relatively little creative and thoughtful work being done on the subject, and I have a lot of respect for Jerry's work at Asbury.

JULY 20, 2009

Burson: From my study, five-point Calvinism, in its purest form, seems to be the closet thing to bad monotheism that you have in mind. I know [for you] Calvinism isn't entirely to blame, but it leads to a distorted view of God as mechanistic, deterministic, and one who creates definite in-groupings and out-groupings. Believing that God operates in this manner, it stands to reason that adherents to such a system would also operate in this fashion, creating their own in- and out-groups with all kinds of attending baggage. In other words, in this case "bad" theology (orthodoxy) leads to "bad" actions (orthopraxy). Is this an accurate representation?

McLaren: You've summarized my thinking very well! You'll see a lot of this spelled out in the manuscript [*NKOCY*].

Burson: You've mentioned to me in the past that you embraced Calvinistic theology during one formative stretch during your early years. Would you be able to pinpoint those years for me?

McLaren: One of the people who discipled me in my early years was David Miller. He was a Young Life leader. I believe I first attended a Bible study with him when I was about fifteen, which would have been 1971. A few years after that, he went to seminary (Gordon Conwell) and came back a stronger Calvinist. It was probably around 1974 (I would have been a senior in high school—or maybe it was '75 or '76). I remember him telling me about double predestination, and I thought (and maybe said), "If that's what the Bible teaches, I don't believe the Bible." But Dave also got me listening to

R. C. Sproul tapes (then via the Ligonier Valley Study Center), and gradually, I acquiesced to what I sensed was the strongest biblical teaching from Romans and Ephesians especially.

Burson: Would you mind telling me who your primary Calvinistic theological influences were during the years that you identified as a Calvinist? I know Francis Schaeffer was one (though Schaeffer spent most of his time preaching and teaching strong Arminian themes and was an inconsistent Calvinist on the free will-determinism issue).

McLaren: It would have been R. C. Sproul. Somehow I ended up being given several boxes of tapes by a Reformed Baptist guy from New Jersey, Albert Martin . . . I listened to hundreds of hours of tapes by these two fellows. I also avidly read Schaeffer, but as you say, his Calvinism didn't come through so much.

Burson: What ultimately led to your shift from Calvinism to another branch of Christianity?

McLaren: When I saw Calvinism allying itself with Theonomy and the hard-core Religious Right, I know I began to lose confidence. As well, I remember getting a journal called *Credenda*. Every time I read it, I was pushed not only away from Calvinism, but toward atheism. That anybody could be so arrogant, critical, pompous, derisive, dismissive, and utterly sure of themselves struck me as dangerous. . . . So it wasn't arguments against Calvinism, it was the behavior and manner of Calvinists themselves.

I had drifted from Calvinism without disavowing it, I suppose, through the 90s. But in the late 90s, I started reading Lesslie Newbigin. His simple line—that the greatest heresy in the history of monotheism is a misunderstanding of election—gave me permission to leave that whole system behind. It was an important breakthrough in my life. I see Newbigin as my primary liberator from Calvinism. Meanwhile, of course, I had been exposed to so many good and solid Christians of other traditions . . . from C. S. Lewis to Anthony Bloom to Walker Percy and Gabriel Marcel, etc.

Burson: Have you ever studied free will and determinism in detail? I know you are writing mostly general and popular books. I also know you entered the University of Maryland as a philosophy major before switching to English, so I am curious if you were ever introduced to the categories of hard determinism, libertarianism, and soft determinism (aka compatibilism)?

McLaren: I was exposed to various forms of determinism in literature, secular philosophy and psychology, and in Christian theology. My struggles with Calvinism in my Christian life sensitized me to the issue in my studies. In literature, for example, I read a lot of Milton—plus an early American Puritan pastor/poet, Edward Taylor. I saw both the devotional beauty within Calvinism . . . and the psychological weirdness too. I read a lot of B. F. Skinner along the way . . . and the polar opposite in Sartre. Really . . . the theme runs through Western culture from the ancient Greeks, so I couldn't help but bump into it left and right.

I may have bumped into the three categories you mention, but I eventually lost interest in "solving" the issue. I think the main breakthrough for me in this regard went hand in hand with a conclusion I reached in the late 90s as I was rethinking modernity, etc. I realized that one either begins with a system or a narrative. (Quine helped me see this, although I found his writing to be almost impenetrable. What he called a web of belief I began to see as a narrative . . . not just facts and beliefs, but facts and beliefs arranged as a storyline.) I became convinced (and still am) that narratives form us before systems do, and that systems are often apologetics for a covert narrative—and in particular, a Greco-Roman neo-platonic imperial/colonial narrative that claims objectivity in the interest of conquest. As a Christian, I want to operate in a different narrative—one that begins with a good and loving God creating a real world. In that kind of world, determinism makes no sense. (I realize this might sound a bit fideist, but it's not that simple. Obviously, all this could be finely nuanced and argued, but this is the general shape of things for me.)

Burson: Was there a moment when you just knew intuitively that this story was not "good" and for that reason could no longer follow with integrity?

McLaren: In addition to what I've said above, I would add that the Religious Right in the 90s, culminating in the presidency of George W. Bush, played a huge role in my rejection of the Calvinist framing story, which now I take to be essentially the Greco-Roman/imperial storyline painted over with Bible verses.

Here's how I think it worked. As an evangelist at heart, I love helping people get connected with God. But that got harder and harder through the 90s, as "God" became the product and property of the Religious Right. I started to see that the slaughter/land theft/apartheid of the Native Americans, the enslavement of Africans, segregation in the Deep South, Apartheid in South Africa, and now the anti-gay, anti-Muslim, we're-gun-ning-for-world-war-three, culture-war mentality of American Evangelicals all had something in common . . . and it was the hyper-confidence of Calvinism (or Greco-Romanism, or Imperial thinking).

Burson: Finally, which thinkers and writers have influenced your "Openness of God's Universe" perspective, as you called it in a previous email? I know you have intentionally resisted entering into this public debate concerning free will theism and the openness of God, but it does appear that your approach resonates nicely with John Sanders's *The God Who Risks*. Have you read Sanders much, this book in particular? How do you keep from slipping from Open Theism to Process Theology? What role might Trinitarian thought play in this regard? Or maybe you don't care if some people see your openness theory influenced by Process Theology?

McLaren: This is a huge subject. I don't think I read *The God Who Risks*. I read several of Greg Boyd's books, and several of Clark Pinnock's. I felt that Greg Boyd (at that point . . . who I know has continued to grow and whom I respect greatly) was still reading the Bible like a fundamentalist (maybe simply because that's the way his audience reads it), and that Clark Pinnock was a bit more free from fundamentalist assumptions. Something told me that this argument was important and worthwhile for Evangelicals to have, but that it wasn't my argument . . . I was excavating a couple layers deeper.

On process theology, I read one of John Cobb's books years ago and actually found it very inspiring . . . not to say I "bought" process theology, but that I saw he was trying to solve some problems that needed to be solved. Later I read John Haught's book *God After Darwin*, which I thought made a wonderful use of a) process theology, b) social trinitarianism, c) kenosis theory, and d) eschatological realism (like Pannenberg, Grenz). Somehow, in that cocktail, process theology has something better to offer than just process theology alone. . . . All of these approaches, I think, try to think of God outside of neo-Platonic categories, which is part of what we're all grappling with. The danger—and this might be the downside of process theology that your question (slipping into) implies—is that we can escape from transcendent Platonism into immanent pantheism, trading one set of problems for another. I think it's inherent in the idea of a Creator, and in everything science tells us about creation, that God does not equal the universe. Yes, the two can be deeply interrelated, but as soon as we have God becoming less and less distinguishable from the universe, alarm bells go off for me. So . . . I am comfortable with saying that God wanted to create a real universe . . . not a puppet universe. The way I think I say it in the new book [*NKOCY*] is that the universe is not under control, nor is it out of control, but it is in relationship.

JANUARY 9, 2014

Burson: A few years ago we corresponded about your relationship to the Openness of God camp. You told me you preferred using the phrase, "Openness of God's universe." You also mentioned that you weren't attracted to parts of the Openness of God movement, namely, its emphasis on spiritual warfare. Would you mind elaborating on this for me? I have not seen an emphasis on spiritual warfare in my research of the Openness movement, at large. However, I have noticed that Greg Boyd has written on spiritual warfare. Would you mind clarifying this for me?

McLaren: Yes, several years ago, Greg was seen as one of the main spokespeople for Openness of God, and it's his emphasis on a literal Satan and cosmic warfare that I find highly problematic, although I like Greg very much and appreciate his larger project. These days, other figures seem more ascendant—especially Thomas Oord—and the warfare theme is less central, if present at all for them.

My other problem with some Openness people some years ago was that they tended to proof-text for their position in the same ways that their counterparts did, just using different texts. Again, this is less true now. I think Thomas Oord has been very wise to emphasize that "relationality" implies openness. Rather than presenting a non-determined future as an aspect of God's weakness or a limitation on God's power, this emphasis allows the Openness community to present a non-determinative relationship with the universe as a reflection of God's relational (and Trinitarian) way. It's not less power—but a higher kind of power: relational rather than determinative power.

JANUARY 21, 2014

Burson: I understand your resistance to Calvinism, but why did you not consider some of the more traditional Arminian models, such as Simple Foreknowledge, Molinism, and the Eternal Now, before embracing the more novel Openness view? In other words, what was it about the traditional Arminian options that did not fully satisfy your concerns with Calvinism?

McLaren: Scott—great question. I'll offer a short reply here—and would welcome follow-up if this isn't clear.

It seems to me that both traditional Arminianism and Calvinism are (currently) framed as answers to the question, "Why do some people end up in heaven and some people in hell?" They end up talking about Divine Agency and larger issues, but they do so to answer a question about who is "saved," with saved being defined as being saved from the eternal consequences of original sin.

I think my starting point as a young Plymouth Brethren boy was more or less Arminian. When I was "evangelized" for Calvinism, I resisted. Calvinism sounded cruel and made God seem capricious. But eventually, I decided I'd rather lodge the "benefit of the doubt" in the sovereign choice of a good God than in the contingencies of frail human choice. It's hard for me to believe now that doing so satisfied me, but for some years, it more or less did.

What happened to me in the 1990s was that I began to grow dissatisfied with the whole narrative in which Calvinism and Arminianism took shape and functioned. I couldn't have articulated it like that in the beginning, but looking back, I think that's what happened. In other words, I stopped wondering whether Calvinism or Arminianism was the right answer to the question; I started wondering whether they were answering the right question in the first place.

Since most if not all our ideas are, in one way or another, interconnected, I think I was experiencing a paradigm shift, where my whole narrative and conceptual framework were shifting. Calvinism and Arminianism seemed like two variants within the old framework. Does that make sense?

Once out of the old narrative (what I often call the six-line narrative), the question of God's agency and relation with the universe certainly doesn't go away. That's where I think the open theist and process folks, plus Jürgen Moltmann and others have a lot to offer. The question stops being something I would expect to find a single, definitive, timeless "Christian" answer to in the Bible, since Biblical writers were working within their own conceptual frameworks, and however we understand divine inspiration, it apparently doesn't infuse an eternal or absolute transcendent paradigm (in which, for example, quantum theory has a place, or neurobiology, etc., etc.). I think we see a wide range of understandings of God's agency in the Bible—from very "soft touch" in Ecclesiastes or Esther, to "contested touch" in Job, to high control in Matthew, to more inherent in some passages in Pauline writings ("Christ is all, and in all," etc.).

I think this question—the agency of God and God's relationship to the universe—is one of the most important and problematic questions in all Christian (and Jewish and Muslim) theology today. From cosmology to neurobiology to quantum theory, we know a lot more about the universe than we used to (and we know more about how little we know too), which causes us to rethink a lot of what we thought about God. Kings, slavemasters, chess games, and giant clocks aren't sufficient metaphors anymore, I think, which is why we need theologians like you engaging with these areas!

Burson: Thanks, Brian. That response is helpful. I understand your shift on original sin and how that changes the paradigm from being saved from original sin and the consequences of it (hell) to being saved or liberated from personal and systemic evil in this world in a variety of manifestations. So you were asking questions that the traditional Calvinism-Arminianism debate was not answering for you.

One follow-up, however: For me, and I believe for Wesley, as well, the fundamental issue between Calvinists and Arminians isn't soteriology (once saved, always saved vs. you can lose your salvation), but rather the nature of God's character. Is God really loving and good toward all people or does God play favorites (elect and non-elect)? So it seems to me that the really critical issue between Calvinists and Arminians is whether or not God loves all people in any meaningful sense of the word.

McLaren: Yes. I think this is very well said, and I agree.

Burson: This issue has both temporal and eternal implications, as well as theoretical and practical import, because it would be very difficult if not impossible for me to fully commit myself to a God who isn't on the side of each and every creature. Five-point Calvinism, properly understood, cannot say that God is on the side of every person. He is playing favorites.

McLaren: Yes, I agree, although I can imagine my Calvinist friends bristling at this and saying that it's not God's fault that Adam and Eve plunged everyone into a state of damnation, etc., etc.

Burson: The Arminian conception of God, however, is very different. The Arminian God wants the ultimate flourishing of each and every one of His creatures and works with us individually and collectively in a non-determining, cooperative sense to bring that about. When framed in this manner, apart from the soteriological issues of original sin and eternal destiny, it seems to me that you strongly resonate with the Arminian view of God's character, whether or not you use the term "Arminian." Is that fair to say?

McLaren: More than fair. It's spot on.

MARCH 25, 2014

Burson: My view is that you endorse an essentially open theist position (preferring the openness of God's universe phraseology), but have not wrestled with the minutiae of the relevant scientific issues. Rather, you are more concerned with endorsing a view that is non-deterministic, non-mechanistic and makes room for true becoming in a co-creational, evolutionary framework. I believe, if I am reading you correctly, that you do not believe the actual future is known to God, but rather the future is evolving as part of a co-creational project that includes input from God, humanity and the rest of creation. God is cooperatively calling to us from the future, not deterministically driving history along from behind. Is that a fair reading?

McLaren: Yes, a spot-on reading.

McLaren: [In response to the on-going Calvinism-Arminianism thread] I never studied Arminius, nor did I study Pelagius. If I were to do so today, I would keep my eyes open for ways their views were trying to open up political space against the domination of Calvin's Dutch successors and Augustine's imperial affinities. In other words, I wouldn't expect them to be telling me a great deal about the nature of the universe—but I would expect them to be fighting a good fight against the political usefulness of deterministic dogma, which tends to tell people to stay in their places, comply, and be afraid. When one is in power and wants to stay in power, one naturally presents God as a powerful being who defends the status quo and orders things to be as they are. When one is oppressed and seeks freedom, one naturally presents God as a free being who bestows freedom on God's creatures. My sense is that the latter is more in tune with the gospel (not to mention the Exodus).

JUNE 25, 2014

Burson: I know your crisis in the 1990s shifted you out of what Roger Olson would call conservative evangelicalism. I am guessing your interaction with the Young Leaders Network and during the early stages of the development of Emergent, you would have been exposed to post liberal thinkers and thought. Would you mind giving me the main post liberal influences on your thought?

McLaren: I read some George Lindbeck and Hans Frei in the late 90s and sensed that the "Yale School" was engaging issues of postmodernity more intelligently than either traditional liberals or conservatives. I had mixed feelings about Stanley Hauerwas but appreciated a lot of what he was doing. Newbigin was a big influence, and I discovered him through Chris Seay in the early "Young Leader Networks" days. The same was true of David Bosch. I read about Wittgenstein but didn't read him.

Burson: You were also simultaneously (correct me if I am wrong) reading and interacting with what Olson calls post conservatives (Pinnock, Grenz, Franke, Murphy).

McLaren: Very much so. Stan Grenz became something of a mentor and gave me a lot of encouragement. I never met Pinnock, but read him. I always felt that he used a more fundamentalist hermeneutic to make non-fundamentalist points. I appreciated some of his points, but not that hermeneutic. Dave Tomlinson's *Post-Evangelical* resonated deeply with me.

Burson: Would you say one of these two groups (Postliberal or Postconservative) was more dominate in the development of your thinking at a given time on your journey or did both have a complementary and relatively equal influence?

McLaren: I had relationships with post conservatives, but found the post liberals more expansive because they had a broader canvas, so to speak, to paint on.

Burson: Thanks, Brian, for your careful and helpful responses. Quick follow-up on a few items: (1) Would you mind amplifying your ambivalence concerning Hauerwas? I am assuming his model of Christ and culture might be a problem for you?

McLaren: I think Stanley had the right prescription for mainline protestantism of the 50s–90s. His call to "sectarianism" and to be the alternative community that doesn't concentrate much on "the world" was probably what the mainline church needed during that era. But then the Religious Right took up that mantle—trying to in a sense own and run society. If mainline protestants continue to withdraw/isolate/etc., they abandon the field, so to speak, to the religious right. I think that's a mistake. Friends of mine who know John Howard Yoder's work better than I do tell me that they think SH doesn't understand JHY's full agenda. Yoder spoke somewhere of concentrating on one challenge, and then, when it is achieved, moving on to the next one. His vision wasn't of creating an alternative society, but of working from a countercultural community to be salt and light in a constructive way in society.

Burson: (2) In reading *We Make the Road by Walking*, I was intrigued by your handling of miracles in chapter 21, "Significant and Wonderful." It seems to me you are doing something similar to Hans Frei here. His "realistic narrative" methodology sought a via media between the conservative and liberal modern approaches of using the text for either facts/proofs or ethical principles. In both cases the story was missed. By subordinating the historical question, he invited the reader to enter into the story and read it as a realistic narrative without tripping over the historical questions, such as the factuality of miracle accounts. It seems to me you are doing something similar here. The story itself has a certain innate power to transform if the imagination is engaged. Would you agree?

McLaren: Yes. Practically speaking, I don't want literalists to miss the meaning of the sign, as if ancient people lived with a natural-supernatural dichotomy, in which miracles proved things. Since we can neither prove nor disprove today that miracles happened back then, I don't see any value in that kind of miracles-as-proof argument. Nor do I want non-literalists to get so focused on "demythologizing" that they also miss the meaning of the story. I think Jack Caputo once said that the Enlightenment drove away one ghost too many—the Holy Ghost. In other words, in their attempt to eliminate superstition, they unintentionally reduced the world of meaning. I remember an African American Pentecostal preacher once said to me, "Don't take away the magic." I think there is a magic to meaning that can be real whether or not supernatural miracles happened or happen.

I just was leading a workshop on the new book and when we did the chapter on miracles, a lot of people shared miracle experiences. Several of them said, "I don't believe in miracles, but I experienced this . . ." In each case, the point wasn't that they had to prove the miracle happened—or not, but that they received some powerful meaning through the experience.

July 24, 2014

Burson: In a few places, you write that a religion is judged by the benefits it provides non-adherents. You attribute this statement to one of your former mentors. Would it be possible for you to identify the name of this mentor? I am guessing Dallas Willard, but if you could confirm that would be helpful.

McLaren: It was DW.

AUGUST 3, 2014

Burson: In your response to the Kevin Miller article this past spring that appeared on the *Leadership* website (Miller critiqued you, Bell and Donald Miller for flying too close to the sun), you wrote on your blog that an older evangelical mentor once advised you to follow your conscience and not trim your sails. He wished he had been less concerned with evangelical gatekeepers when he was younger. Would you mind sharing with me the name of this evangelical mentor?

McLaren: It was Stan Grenz. The conversation was very poignant. I forget the exact timing, but it was something like this: Stan called me for some reason—I can't remember why, but he ended up telling me how disappointed he was in the state of Evangelical scholarship, and that if he could have done it again, he would have been what he called a "postmodern pietist" in Mainline scholarly circles where there would have been more academic freedom, etc. He encouraged me not to trim my sails or be afraid. (He had been a deeply encouraging presence in my life for some years.)

A few days later—or it might have been a week, word came that he had died. I flew up for the funeral, and when I got home, there was a package waiting. It was a set of CDs from a seminar at Regent College where my work had been roundly critiqued—but where Stan had been more or less my defender. I took a drive and listened to the CDs in my car and at one point, pulled over to the side of the road and cried for the loss of such a good friend.

Stan and I disagreed on a few issues, including the issue of hell. I was quite shocked that Stan spoke of God having a "dark side"—sounding a bit like Martin Luther, and Stan felt I was on thin ice in my deconstruction of the traditional view of hell. As I recall, he held to a bit more traditional ecclesiology too, but whatever our disagreements, they didn't weaken our relationship one iota.